Palm Programming

for the absolute beginner

Check the Web for Updates

To check for updates or corrections relevant to this book and/or CD-ROM visit our updates page on the Web at **http://www.prima-tech.com/updates**.

Send Us Your Comments

To comment on this book or any other PRIMA TECH title, visit our reader response page on the Web at **http://www.prima-tech.com/comments**.

How to Order

For information on quantity discounts, contact the publisher: Prima Publishing, P.O. Box 1260BK, Rocklin, CA 95677-1260; (916) 787-7000. On your letterhead, include information concerning the intended use of the books and the number of books you want to purchase.

Palm Programming

for the absolute beginner

ANDY HARRIS

A Division of Prima Publishing

Important: Prima Publishing cannot provide software support. Please contact the appropriate software manufacturer's technical support line or Web site for assistance.

Prima Publishing and the author have attempted throughout this book to distinguish proprietary trademarks from descriptive terms by following the capitalization style used by the manufacturer.

Information contained in this book has been obtained by Prima Publishing from sources believed to be reliable. However, because of the possibility of human or mechanical error by our sources, Prima Publishing, or others, the Publisher does not guarantee the accuracy, adequacy, or completeness of any information and is not responsible for any errors or omissions or the results obtained from use of such information. Readers should be particularly aware of the fact that the Internet is an ever-changing entity. Some facts may have changed since this book went to press.

ISBN: 0-7615-3524-1
Library of Congress Catalog Card Number: 2001-091130
Printed in the United States of America

00 01 02 03 04 DD 10 9 8 7 6 5 4 3 2 1

Publisher:
Stacy L. Hiquet

Associate Marketing Manager:
Heather Buzzingham

Managing Editor:
Sandy Doell

Acquisitions Editor:
Melody Layne

Project Editor:
Estelle Manticas

Technical Reviewer:
D. Stéphane Thibault

Copy Editor:
Hilary Powers

Interior Layout:
Marian Hartsough

Cover Design:
Prima Design Team

Indexer:
Sharon Shock

To the newest one.

I love you already.

Acknowledgments

I begin by thanking God from whom all flows.

Thanks to Heather, Elizabeth, and Matthew. You are everything to me. I appreciate your patience as I work on these things.

The folks at Prima have been wonderful to work with throughout this process. Special thanks to Melody for your ongoing friendship and work on the entire series. Thank you to Kim for your continued guidance and support. Estelle, I really appreciate what you have done for this book; I've enjoyed working with you. Special thanks to Hilary—it must not be fun to be my copy editor, yet you did a phenomenal job taking my mush and turning it into readable text. I'm amazed at and thankful for your skill and your sense of humor. Thank you to Stéphane for your technical editing skills. Your grasp of PocketC and programming in general is very impressive. I appreciate the many times you improved my code or submitted suggestions. Thanks also to the many people that the author never gets to meet in the process of creating a book. Without the efforts of those in production, proofreading, and the many other parts of the publishing industry, this book would never make it to market.

I would also like to thank the PocketC community. First, I need to acknowledge Jeremy Dewey, the developer of PocketC, for a terrific product and wonderful support. I appreciate your answering all my dopey questions.

I'd also like to thank all the PocketC developers that gave me input, advice, and encouragement during this project. Special thanks to Wolfgang, (great tutorial and WinCE advice), Joe Stadolnik (Developer of PtoolboxLib), Mario Schlesinger (Original author of Ccontrols), and Paul Nevai, for the excellent Peditor program and his gracious upgrade of my license.

Many thanks to all the other contributors to the orbworks message board, and those who contributed libraries or software to the CD-ROM.

About the Author

Andy Harris began his teaching career as a high school special education teacher. During that time, he taught himself enough computing to do part time computer programming and consulting work. He began teaching computing at the university level in the late 1980s as a part-time job. Since 1995, he has been a full time lecturer in the Computer Science Department of Indiana University / Purdue University, Indianapolis (IUPUI). He manages the IUPUI Streaming Media Lab for the CS department, and teaches classes in several programming languages, including Java, Visual Basic, Perl, JavaScript/ DHTML, Virtual Reality, programming on Portable Devices, and Streaming Media.

Contents at a Glance

Contents

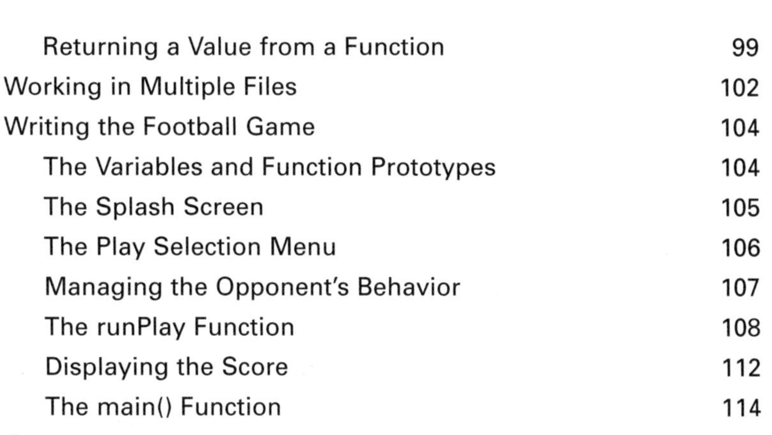

CHAPTER 5

Using the Graphics Mode: The Sketcher 117

CHAPTER 8 Creating a Smart Opponent: The Tic-Tac-Toe Game 223

Memo Access: The Life Game 259

Databases and Pointers: The Password Keeper 287

Introduction

I was lucky enough to learn computer programming in a very different time. Back when I was learning (in the early 1980s), computers were simple. Most did not have disk drives, none had sophisticated (or even color) graphics, and there was little software you could purchase. The only way to get any use out of these machines was to write programs for them. Of course, I started by typing in games that others had written, because I wanted to play them. Soon enough, I learned how to modify the games so I could win, and I then graduated to writing my own games. The limitations of the hardware were not a big impediment, because the creative process was so intense. The programming languages available at the time were cheap (or free) and reasonably simple to learn. Best of all, I was having as much fun writing the programs as I did playing them.

Computing has gotten much more sophisticated. It's easy to find desktop calculators with more processing power than the mightiest machines of my early days. This has also meant that it is much more intimidating to learn how to program than it used to be. Compilers are very sophisticated, there's a huge variety of programming languages out there, and the computers themselves are quite complex, with a phenomenal number of features.

Awhile back, I bought my first PDA (personal digital assistant) using the Palm operating system, and I was instantly in love. This was a machine with a remarkable amount of capability that I really could carry in my pocket. Like many others, I saw parts of my life transformed by this little device. Since I am a programming teacher, I was interested in writing programs for the Palm system. I discovered PocketC, and found the language to be a perfect companion to the Palm itself. PocketC—like the Palm operating system—is powerful without being extravagant, convenient enough to use anywhere you can take your Palm, easy to use, and easily extensible to solve problems unique to you.

When I first moved to programming on the Palm from the PCs I have been using, I was worried about the limitations of the device. After all, the computer has a tiny screen, no disk drives, a relatively small amount of memory, and very limited graphics capabilities. But these seeming disadvantages make the Palm platform an ideal environment to learn programming, just like my earliest experiences.

It turns out that PDAs are a perfect place for beginning programmers to practice their art. There is almost certainly some kind of program you wish you had on your Palm that you cannot find. Perhaps you need to do some type of calculation frequently in your work, or you wish you could keep a certain kind of database with you all the time. You'll be able to do these things by the end of the book.

I'll teach you real programming in this book. You will learn how to write databases, you'll learn how to create graphic interfaces with buttons and input controls, respond to Graffiti input, and many other things that are part of serious modern programming. If I do my job correctly, you will be able to generalize enough to build whatever kinds of programs you want for your PDA.

Real programming does not have to be boring. I'll begin each chapter by showing you some interesting game or diversion you will be able to write by the end of the chapter. Throughout the chapter, I'll show you some concise examples that clearly demonstrate a key idea, and by the end of the chapter, I'll show you how to put the new elements back together to build the game you saw at the start. You should be able to work through each chapter in an evening or two.

Well, that's enough talking! Turn the page, and learn how to make your PDA even *more* fun and productive than it already is!

How to Use this Book

Learning to program a computer is a complex progression of skills. If you have never done any programming at all, you will probably find it easiest to go through the chapters in order. Of course, if you are already an experienced programmer, it might not be necessary for you to do more than skim through the earliest chapters, to see how PocketC differs from languages you might already know. In either case, programming is not a skill you can learn by reading. You'll have to write programs to learn. This book has been designed to make the process reasonably painless.

You'll see a complete program demonstrating some key ideas at the beginning of each chapter. Then you'll look at a series of small programs that illustrate each of the major points of the chapter. Finally, you'll put these concepts together to build the larger program you saw at the beginning. You'll be able to see important ideas in simple, straightforward code, and you'll also see more involved programs that put multiple ideas together. All the programs are short enough that you can type them in yourself (which is a great way to look more closely at code), but they are also available on the CD-ROM.

Throughout the book, I'll throw in a few more tidbits, notably:

These are good ideas that experienced programmers like to pass on.

These will suggest techniques and shortcuts that will make your life as a programmer easier.

There are a few areas where it's easy to make a mistake. I'll point them out as we go.

In the Real World

As you examine the games and diversions in this book, I'll show you how the concepts are used in non-gaming contexts.

CHALLENGES

At the end of each chapter, I'll suggest some programs that you can write with the skills you've learned so far. This should help you start writing your own programs.

Writing and Compiling PocketC Programs: The Bad Joke Program

In this chapter, you'll get your first introduction to the world of programming in general. You'll begin the transition from using programs that others have written to actually writing your own programs. Specifically, this chapter presents the following subjects:

- Downloading and installing the PocketC compiler
- Writing a simple program on the PDA using the memo editor
- Writing programs on the desktop editor
- Using the POSE emulator for desktop testing
- Writing the most basic PocketC applet
- Compiling a program
- Checking and fixing mistakes
- Adding an icon to a program so that it can be run from the application screen

The Waiter Program

As you can see by the program introduced in Figure 1.1, you can harness the awesome computing ability of your PDA to tell one of the world's worst jokes.

When the program starts up, the user sees the series of small screens shown in Figure 1.2. Each contains a line from the classic waiter joke. After the punch line is delivered, the program ends.

This chapter includes everything you need to know to write this program. However, there is a lot to learn, so it's better to start with a simpler program. Toward the end of this chapter, the Waiter program returns—with its innards revealed.

Saying Hello to the World

It is a tradition in computer programming to begin any exploration of a new programming language with a program that exclaims, "Hello, world!" This is a goofy tradition, but it makes a lot of sense. This type of program is usually quite simple, and it allows you to concentrate on the mechanics of your editing and compiling software before worrying about the details of the programming language. Figure 1.3 demonstrates the Hello World program done in PocketC. To get to that point, however, you need to learn a lot of useful things, including how to get set up and start working in PocketC.

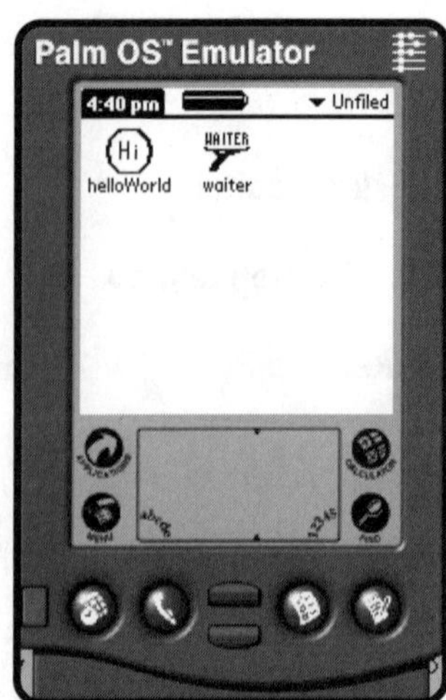

FIGURE 1.1

The Application screen shows a new program called Waiter.

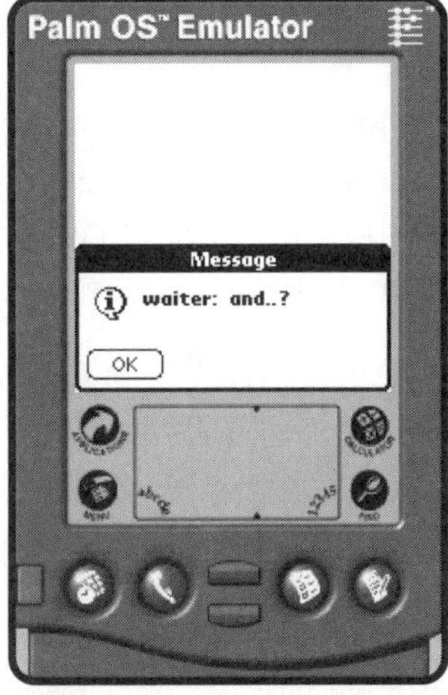

FIGURE 1.2

Technology can't improve a bad joke.

FIGURE 1.3

The classic first program

Installing the PocketC Compiler

Computers have an extremely limited set of instructions built into their hardware. Programming languages such as PocketC allow you to write instructions in an English-like dialect that can be translated into the low-level instructions the computer can actually understand.

You'll need two programs for programming on your PDA. First, you'll write the code in a text editor. (The Memo Pad that comes with the Palm OS works fine, but you may want to investigate another text editor, such as pedit, which is discussed later in this chapter.) In addition to a text editor, you need some sort of program that can translate the English-like code you write into the binary values the computer really understands. This is where the PocketC compiler comes in. This program takes the code and converts it into a form your PDA can run.

> **IN THE REAL WORLD**
>
> **Technically, PocketC does not compile code directly into the PDA's machine language—it uses a special language called *byte code* instead. This means that you will need PocketC to run the programs. There is a special free version of PocketC called the *PocketC runtime* that is designed just for this purpose.**

To get started, install the PocketC application onto your PDA. You can find it on the CD-ROM packaged with this book, or you may want to get a more recent version from the developer's site, at http://www.orbworks.com. The version on the CD-ROM can be used to run PocketC programs indefinitely, but it will only allow you to compile programs for the first 30 days after you install it. This should be plenty of time to learn most of the concepts in this book; and after that, you will probably find that the program is well worth the registration fee because it allows you to do so much with your PDA device. You will need to install both the pocketc.pdb and mathlib.pdb files. You might also want to store the documentation in your PDA by copying the HTML to iSilo or some other document reader. I find it very useful to have the documentation on board the PDA, as I often don't have the written docs with me when I want to write a program.

IN THE REAL WORLD

As you gain more experience programming on your PDA, you will accumulate a suite of tools to help you in your development. Here is how I like to have my machine set up for PocketC programming: I have generated a special group for PocketC, and have placed PocketC itself in this group. My favorite text editor is pedit, by Paul Nevai. It is much more powerful than the default Memo Pad, and it has some features that make it especially appropriate for programming, like the ability to automatically indent, use fixed-width fonts, and directly access the PocketC compiler. I also have the freeware version of iSilo in this directory, loaded up with the documentation for PocketC. Since many Palm programs provide documentation in HTML format, it's very nice to have some of that documentation available on the PDA. I find this to be an easy way to have the appropriate documentation with me on the road.

Finally, I have a number of other utilities in the PocketC group. These utilities are used for generating bitmap images, creating forms, and for some other special programs. I will introduce these specialty programs as they are needed in the book. Of course, you don't have to set up your machine like I did mine, but this is a setup that works for me, and I recommend it as a starting place.

The Hello World Program

The code for the Hello World program is so simple you can make it out even if you've never looked at a line of programming before:

```
//helloWorld
//The classic first program
//Andy Harris, 2/11/01

main(){
  alert("Hello, world!");
} // end main
```

Although the program is not complex, it is very typical. Almost all programs will follow the basic conventions you learn when writing this code.

The best way to learn programing is to do it, so open up Memo Pad or another text editor and type in the code *exactly* as you see it. Compilers are very picky, so even things like capitalization, spelling, and punctuation can have a huge (usually negative) effect. Figure 1.4 demonstrates the Hello World program being edited in the memo application.

FIGURE 1.4

Using Memo Pad to edit the Hello World program

Adding Comments to Your Code

The first thing to note is the very first line:

```
//helloWorld
```

This line signifies the name of the program. While the Palm OS is not as concerned with file names as a traditional operating system would be, the first line of a memo is often used as the memo's name. This is especially true with PocketC, because the first line will be the name of the program you have created. It's important to choose a good name that will make sense to you later. (I tend to stick to one-word names, so I won't have any problems if I try to work with the file on a desktop machine.) The two slashes indicate that this line is a comment. This means that the compiler will not try to interpret anything on the line as a command to execute. Comments are usually used to mark important information about a program, or to explain things that may be unclear later. I usually include a block of comments at the beginning of my programs to remind myself of the name of the program and what it is supposed to do, as well as who wrote it and when.

PocketC, like most versions of C, supports two forms of comments. The compiler will ignore any line that begins with the // characters, as well as the remainder of any line where the // characters appear after the beginning of the line. If you have several lines of text that you wish the compiler to ignore, you can surround them with /* and */. All the code between these markers will also be ignored. The type of comment characters you use can be a matter of personal preference. The most important thing is to use lots of comments to make your code easier to follow. This will also make your code easier to fix when it breaks down.

The main() Function

The PocketC language is based on a unit called the *function*. A function is nothing more than a list of commands with a name. (Okay, it's a little bit more than that—but for now, that's a good definition to go on with.) Every program in PocketC has a `main()` function. When your program runs on the PDA, the code in your `main()` function will immediately run. Functions have a set of parentheses at the end of their names. Sometimes you will place values inside the parentheses, and sometimes you will not. Generally, the `main()` function does not require a value between the parentheses, but the parentheses still have to be there.

If you look closely at the `main()` line, you will also see a curly brace ({) character at the end of the line. This character signifies that some sort of *block* is going to begin. If you have done some word processing in older systems (or in HTML), you are already familiar with this concept. (In modern word processing programs you mark the beginning and end of the text by highlighting it, but you still somehow must mark a range of text.) You might want to copy a chunk of text, so you mark its beginning and end. In programming, blocks of code are often marked with characters such as the braces used in PocketC. The { character tells the compiler to expect one or more lines of code, which should all be interpreted as the function called `main()`. The compiler will expect a closing curly brace to signify the end of the function. If you look at the code, you will see that the } does appear as expected at the end of the program.

Take a careful look at how the program is indented. There is one line of code between the `main(){` statement and the } character. That one line is indented. PocketC is not fussy about how you use spaces (or even carriage returns) in your program code. Programmers take advantage of this indifference to white space as an important programming tool. Most programmers indent between any pair of braces. This is done for a couple of reasons. First, it helps to clarify that the indented code is part of a larger structure (in this case a function, but you'll learn a lot of other structures very soon). Perhaps more importantly, the fact that the

In the Real World

Programmers in the real world refer to topics such as code layout and commenting as *programming style.* People have passionate arguments about what constitutes good style. If you write code professionally as part of a team, you will most likely have to adopt some sort of style guidelines established by the team. However, when you are just starting out, you can be a little more flexible. The exact style you choose is a personal decision, but its effects can be far-reaching. A good programming style should make it easier for you to write your programs, and should assist you in understanding the programs and fixing them. The style guidelines I use in this book will be consistent with these goals, and I recommend that you start with them. Specifically, I indent two characters for each block I'm creating, I keep the left brace ({) on the same line as the command before it, and I always add a comment after the right brace (}) to indicate what is being ended. I describe common programming style guidelines as they apply to techniques throughout the book.

code is not all the way at the left margin helps the programmer remember that there is a structure still open, and that the code cannot be run until the function is finished.

You might also notice that I added a comment to remind myself what the } means. That may seem silly and unnecessary, but it's a very good habit to get into. Down the road, you may find yourself with several different structures all nested inside one another, each ending with a right curly brace. It might be a very good idea to remind yourself exactly what structure you are ending with a given } character.

The alert() Function

Most of the program's action happens in this line:

```
alert("Hello, world!");
```

This line causes a little box to appear on the screen. The box contains the "Hello, world!" text. The line can be changed to output any text value you wish. The `alert` term is the name of a function that is already built in to PocketC. Almost everything interesting you will do with PocketC involves either building or using functions. The `alert()` function is already built in, so you can use it as a command. It expects some text in quotes ("") between the parentheses. Any text you send to the function will be sent to the screen in a little box. The program waits for the user to press the OK button on the box before continuing on. The little box that is generated is an example of a *dialog box*. You have probably encountered dialog boxes as a user, so they aren't really new to you. As a programmer, you just need to remember that you can use the `alert()` function to send some sort of message to the user.

The `alert()` technique is very easy to use, but it can be a little annoying. Later on you'll learn how to use some other techniques for output, but the alert statement is terrific for when you're just starting out.

At the end of the alert line, you might notice a semicolon (;) character. This character is used to signal to PocketC that this is the end of a line of code. PocketC requires code to be broken into small parts, each dealing with a specific logical thought. Those smaller pieces are called *lines* because they usually each take a line on the editor screen. However, the size of a program line can be longer than the size of an editor line. That is a really good thing in PocketC, because Memo Pad has a much narrower screen than text editors on typical computers. Sometimes you will need to split a *logical line*—a statement representing a complete expression of PocketC syntax—into several lines of the text editor. The semicolon indicates that the logical line is really over. It sounds very complicated, but it really isn't. Essentially, you should end every line of code with a semicolon, except those lines that already end with a { or a } character.

Ending the main() Function

The last line of the program consists only of a right curly brace (}) and a comment. The brace character indicates the end of the function, and it is aligned with the function name to indicate this. I also added a comment to help clarify the meaning of the brace.

Compiling Your Program on the PDA

You can write programs with a text editor, but the code you generate cannot be executed in that format. Remember, all computers—not just PDAs—have very limited sets of instructions built into the hardware of the device. Ultimately, any program must be translated into those specific instructions before the computer can follow the commands. This step is called *compiling*, and the program that does this step is called a *compiler*. To run your PocketC programs, you must enter the PocketC compiler and use it to compile the program.

As I said earlier, to be absolutely correct, I must mention that PocketC technically does not compile code to the Palm OS hardware commands; it uses a special format called *byte code.* This format can be run in the PocketC environment. This is why you must have a form of PocketC to run programs written with that language. Sometimes, PocketC programs are referred to as *applets* because the Java language uses a very similar technique, and the word for a "miniature application" is irresistibly useful.

Compiling a Program

Figure 1.5 shows the main screen of PocketC. Your program will not be listed here yet, because it has not yet been compiled. Click on the Compile button, and you will see a list of PocketC programs that are available as memo notepads on your PDA, as shown in Figure 1.6.

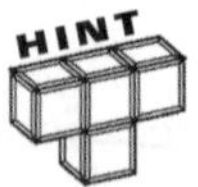

From here on out, only the emulator screen will be shown in the Figures.

You will see a list of memos that start with the // characters. PocketC regards any memo that starts with these characters as a C program, and lists it here as a file that can be compiled. This is why you must start all PocketC programs with a comment. That comment will become the name of the program. If you have written a program and you cannot find it on the compile menu, open the file and add the comment characters to the beginning.

The text form of the program is usually referred to as *source code,* and the compiled version is sometimes called *object code.*

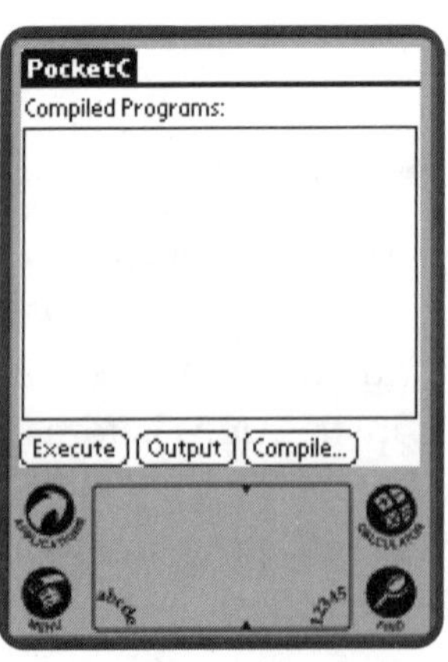

FIGURE 1.5

The main screen shows programs that have already been compiled (or it would if there were any).

FIGURE 1.6

All the files on the PDA that are marked as PocketC programs are listed here.

Once you have located the Hello World program in the compile list, highlight it and click the Compile button again.

If all went well, you will see the main screen of PocketC again (as shown in Figure 1.7) with "helloWorld" listed as one of the compiled programs.

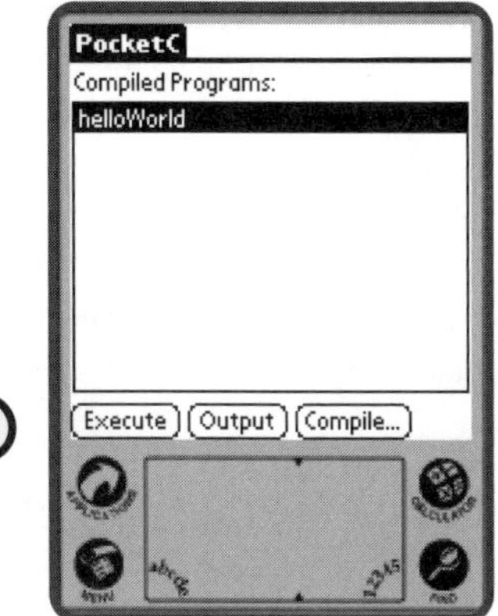

FIGURE 1.7

Now the Hello World program is compiled.

Dealing with Errors in the Code

Don't be too upset if the program reports an error. Even professional programmers tend to have many errors in their code. Fortunately, the error messages in PocketC are reasonably clear, and you can often find the mistakes without too much effort. For example, if you forget to put the semicolon at the end of the `alert("Hello, world!")` line, you will see the error message shown in Figure 1.8 when you try to compile.

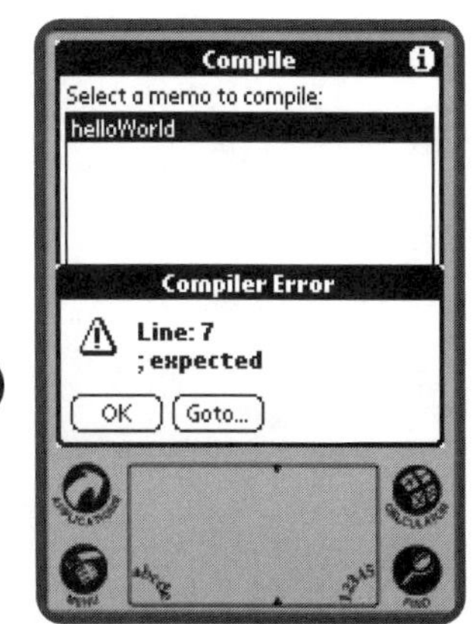

FIGURE 1.8

PocketC wants to know for sure when you're ending a line.

Read the error message carefully, and then click the Goto button. PocketC will take you back to your text editor at the spot where it noticed the mistake. This point may not be where the actual mistake occurred—but it will usually be close. With some detective work and a little practice, you will be able to fix most errors without too much difficulty.

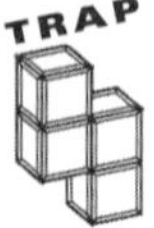

The most important advice is to enter your text very carefully. Make sure that if you are copying code from this book, you copy it *exactly.* Changing the case of a word can cause a disaster, as can replacing a forward slash (/) with a backslash (\). It is easy to make sloppy typing errors with a typical computer keyboard, but Graffiti input—the stuff you write in with your Palm stylus—is even more prone to error. You will probably need to enter program code much more carefully than you do normal text. If a character is incorrect in a memo, you can usually figure out what it should have been through context clues. The PocketC compiler will not be able to do this.

Running Your Program

Once the Hello World program appears in the PocketC main window, you can highlight it and click the Execute button to run the program. When you do so, the screen will look like the one in Figure 1.9.

Please note that the background of the program might be a little different if you have already run some PocketC programs on your particular device. Chapter 2, "Variables, Input, and Output: The Name Game," shows how to clear the screen and do a number of other fancier kinds of commands. At this point, your goal should be to get a program up and working. You should be very proud if you have managed to do so!

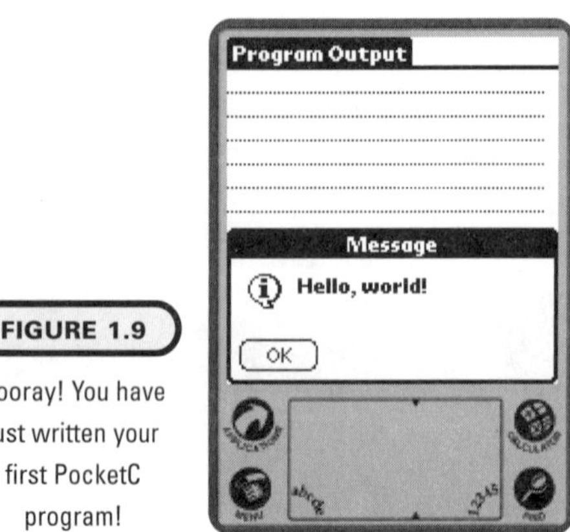

FIGURE 1.9

Hooray! You have just written your first PocketC program!

Writing Programs on the Desktop

One of the best things about PocketC is that it is as portable as the PDA itself. You can take it anywhere and program without a desktop computer. Still, you might find that there are times you would prefer to use your desktop computer, with its keyboard and much larger display, for typing in your programs. There are a number of ways you can integrate your computer with PocketC on your Palm.

Using a Desktop Text Editor

Perhaps the simplest solution is to use a plain text editor for writing your PocketC programs. If you already have a text editor you really like (such as Notepad or Emacs, for example), you can write your programs on the text editor and then copy them into Memo Pad via the Palm desktop program that came with your PDA. You will then have to synchronize your Palm and compile the program on the PDA. This solution is free, but it is also inconvenient. It can be a real pain to keep synching every time you have to change a character. Also, you should be careful about the size of your files if you use this approach. Most desktop editors can handle reasonably large files, but the Palm Memo Pad application cannot work with files larger than 4K. Still, this might be the best way to go if your program consists of a lot of text that would be tedious to enter by Graffiti, and you are on a very tight budget.

Compiling on the Desktop with PDE

Orbworks has released a desktop version of PocketC called the PocketC Desktop Edition (PDE). The PDE is an integrated text editor and compiler for the Windows environment. Figure 1.10 illustrates the Hello World program being edited with the PDE.

The PDE is basically a text editor optimized for writing PocketC code. It has syntax highlighting features, which automatically put all comments in green, all commands in black, and other text in blue. It also features automatic support for the built-in functions of PocketC. If you look carefully at Figure 1.10 you will see that the insertion point is on the `alert()` function, and the bottom of the screen shows a simplified version of the syntax for the function. The PDE also features an online help system that can be used to check the syntax of any built-in functions or operators you might use. The PDE does not have the 4K limit on source code files, which means it is much easier than a palm-based solution when you are working with large programs. The PDE also usually compiles larger code more quickly than the palm-based version.

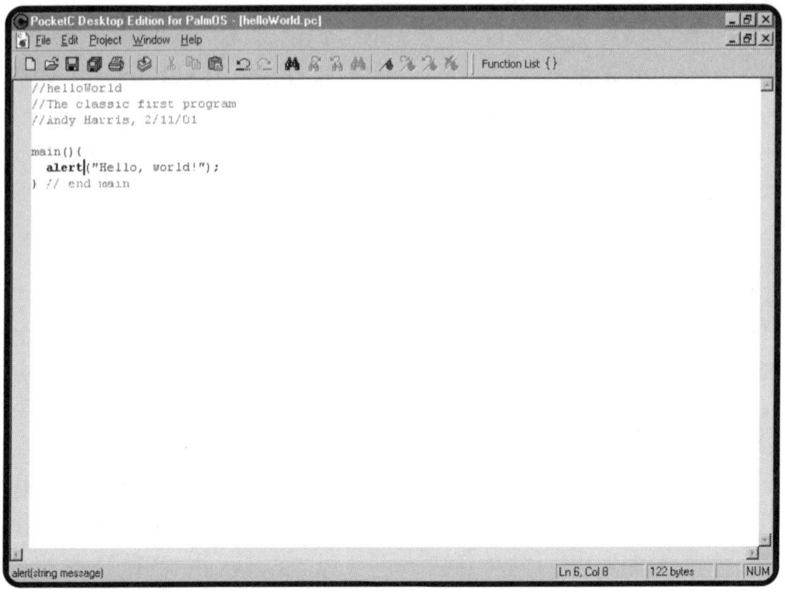

```
//helloWorld
//The classic first program
//Andy Harris, 2/11/01

main(){
  alert("Hello, world!");
} // end main
```

FIGURE 1.10

The PDE lets you edit PocketC programs on your desktop machine.

IN THE REAL WORLD

Although the PDE adds some nice features and allows the use of icons, it is not necessary. If you are feeling overwhelmed, feel free to concentrate on writing programs directly on the Palm. In fact, if you have a portable keyboard, you may not ever feel the need to use the PDE. Personally, I like to use the Palm-based version (with pedit pro to avoid the 4K barrier) when I'm away from my desktop machine. For more serious programming, I like the PDE. Most of the programs in this book (especially in the later chapters, when the programs get longer), were written with the PDE.

In addition to editing PocketC programs, the PDE will actually compile the programs to bytecode. If you choose Compile from the Project menu, the program will attempt to compile the code. You will receive the same types of error messages using the PDE that you see when compiling directly on the PDA.

Transferring Compiled Programs to the Palm

The PDE will let you compile programs, but you must have a Palm-capable device to test them. The compiler will generate a .pdb file, which you can install in your PDA. The next time you run PocketC, you will see the new program listed as a compiled PocketC applet.

IN THE REAL WORLD

To simplify this process, I downloaded Pilot Install, an excellent free program from Ralf Dietrich, and installed a shortcut to the program on my Windows desktop. This allows me to drag .pdb files onto the Pilot Install icon, and quickly install the programs without having to do a full hot-synch. This is a very easy way to test the programs. The Pilot Install program is available on the CD-ROM that accompanies this book.

It is very important that you test the program on the PDA, because it is possible that the program compiles perfectly but still has some problems.

Using Palm's Emulator on the Desktop

There is one more way to use a desktop computer to write PocketC code. You can use an emulator, which acts like a virtual Palm on your desktop. Palm Corporation offers a special program called POSE (Palm Operating System Emulator) that performs this task. A copy of POSE is included on the CD-ROM that accompanies this book.

IN THE REAL WORLD

POSE is designed with an interchangeable operating system, which allows you to test your programs on a number of different variations of the Palm OS.

For legal reasons, the version of POSE on the CD-ROM does not include the memory and operating system (called the ROM image). If you want to use POSE for testing your programs, you will either need to upload the ROM from your own Palm (instructions come with POSE) or request access to ROMs from Palm or Visor. Both companies release ROM images for developers, but you must sign a waiver promising to use the software appropriately.

Even if you can upload the ROM image from your own device, it isn't a bad idea to get some of the other ROMs from Palm and Visor so that you can test your program on different platforms. For example, you might want to write a program that uses color. You'll definitely need to check that the program works on both color-capable devices and those with a grayscale. If you have POSE installed on your machine, you can just replace the ROM with that of various devices to see how your program will work on them.

You can use POSE with PocketC installed on the virtual Palm, or you can use the PDE to write and compile a program, and then copy any resulting .pdb or .prc files to the emulator.

You can simply drag a Palm-appropriate file to the emulator to load it. This is probably the fastest way to test your programs on the emulator. (See Figure 1.11.)

FIGURE 1.11

POSE running on a Windows machine

Back to the Waiter Program

The Waiter program isn't much more complex than the Hello World program. It simply adds a few more dialogs and a couple of other interesting features. First, I wrote the joke program in the PDE. This wasn't absolutely necessary, but it is a nice option to have. I also added a couple of other commands to make the program just slightly more professional. Take a look at the code, and you will probably be able to guess at the meaning of the new commands even before I explain them to you:

```
//waiter
//a classic bad joke
//Andy Harris, 2/19/01

main(){
```

```
  clear();
  alert("customer: Waiter?");
  alert("waiter:   Yes?");
  alert("customer: There's a fly in my soup");
  alert("waiter:   and..?");
  alert("customer: What's it doing there?");
  alert("waiter:   I think it's the backstroke.");
  exit();
} // end main
```

Note that the Waiter program has essentially the same structure as the Hello World program. It consists of a series of comments and a `main()` function. The `main` function is encased in curly braces ({ }) and indented.

Note that I did not include parentheses behind the second occurrence of the word "main." This line is a comment. I am just telling myself that I'm ending the main function. If you want, you can put the parentheses there, but most programmers do not.

The `clear()` function clears the screen, erasing anything that happens to be there. If you do not use the `clear()` function at the beginning of your program, there may be information on the screen left over from the last PocketC program you ran. It's a nice idea to clear the screen first so you don't confuse the user with leftover information.

Most of the function consists of a series of alert statements, sending lines of the joke to the user. Note that each line stays on the screen until the user clicks on the OK button. Notice also that all lines except those that end with a brace end with a semicolon.

Finally, the `exit()` function closes the program. When the last statement is executed, the program will normally end, and return to the PocketC screen. The `exit()` function will return the user to the application screen. Generally, if you are expecting users to start your program from within PocketC it is no problem to let them return there when your program is finished. However, if you are letting users get to your program from the application screen, it's only polite to return them to the same place. The `exit()` function does this.

In the Real World

Any type of command is usually called a *statement*. In PocketC, most statements are also functions, so I might sometimes refer to exit as a statement and sometimes as a function. Both are correct.

Summary

This chapter took you through a major transition. You are no longer simply a user of your PDA; you now can write a program that will do what you want it to do. While your first programs are rather simple, you should still be proud. You know the basic format of all PocketC programs. You've met the `main()` function, and you have used the `alert()` function to send a message to the user. You know a number of ways to write and compile your programs, both on the PDA and on the desktop machine. Finally, you know how to attach an icon to a program so it can be run from the application screen.

CHALLENGES

1. Write a customized form of the Hello World program that tells the world that you are a great programmer-in-training.
2. Write some other joke using the same technique I used for the Waiter program.
3. Write a simple story that comes up to the screen one line at a time.

Variables, Input, and Output: The Name Game

Now that you have installed PocketC on your PDA, you are ready to write some programs that will do interesting things. In this chapter, you will learn a number of skills that form the foundation of computer programming in PocketC—and in any other programming language. Specifically, you'll learn how to deal with the following essential tasks:

- Creating variables for storing information in the computer's memory
- Determining which type of variable should be used to represent a piece of information
- Getting information from the user
- Changing variable from one type to another
- Sending information back to the user
- Using functions for manipulating text

The Name Game Program

This chapter shows you how to write an interactive program on your PDA. The program starts by asking for the user's full name, as you can see in Figure 2.1.

Once the computer has this information, it will return the user's name in a variety of formats, illustrated by Figure 2.2.

This may not be the most exciting computer game you have ever played, but it is still kind of cool. It demonstrates many of the essential concepts of computer programming, including how to get information from the user, how to store information in variables, and how to display information.

Basic String Variables

One of the characteristics that make computers stand apart from other machines is that they primarily work with information. Pretty much every interesting program manages information in some way. Programming languages like PocketC use a concept called *variables* as a technique for storing information in the computer's memory.

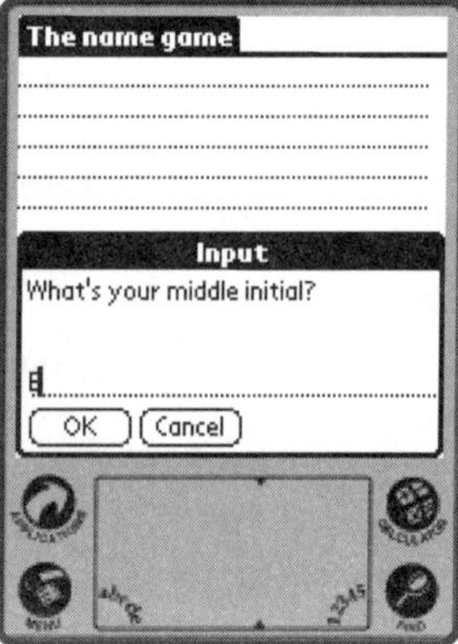

FIGURE 2.1

The program starts by asking for the first, middle, and last names of the user.

FIGURE 2.2

The user's name comes back in a variety of formats.

The Say Message Program

Examine Figure 2.3 and you will see a program that looks a lot like the Hello World program from the last chapter. However, this program has one significant difference, illustrated in Figure 2.4. It doesn't stop with a general announcement; it addresses one particular user.

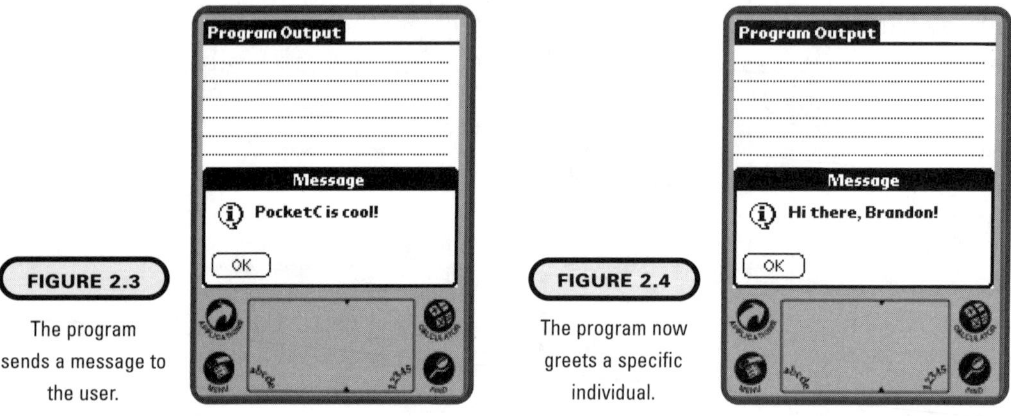

FIGURE 2.3

The program sends a message to the user.

FIGURE 2.4

The program now greets a specific individual.

Look at the code, and you'll see a new element:

```
//sayMessage
//illustrates a simple variable
//Andy Harris, 02/25/01

main(){
  string message;
  string person = "Brandon";

  message = "PocketC is cool!";
  clear();
  alert (message);
  alert ("Hi there, " + person + "!");
} // end main
```

The program starts with the comments you might expect, and it has a `main()` function, again just like Hello World. What is different is the way it handles messages. In the Hello World program, the message itself was sent directly to the alert statement—that is, it was typed into the parenthetical part of the `alert()`

function. In the Say Message program, information is stored in memory and then shown to the user. This line

```
string message;
```

creates a variable called `message`. The word *string* is used to denote that `message` will contain text values. The term *string* is used in most programming languages to refer to text values because computers tend to work with text as a series of attached characters, like beads on a string. In PocketC, you define a variable by starting with the variable type, and then you create the variable's name, so the phrase `string message` means "create a string (text) variable called 'message.'"

The process of creating a variable is called *declaring* the variable. Every variable must be declared before you use it. If you try to use a variable that has never been declared, the compiler will balk.

Most programs you create will have variables in them. PocketC requires you to create variables at the beginning of a function, before any other types of commands. If you create a variable after running some other command (such as an `alert()` function), the compiler will claim to be "confused" and will not compile your program.

The Say Message program features another variable, which is created in the next line:

```
string person = "Brandon";
```

This line is very similar to the preceding line. It creates another string variable, but this one is called `person`. The equal sign (=) is used to assign the value "Brandon" directly to the `person` variable. If you know what value you want a variable to have, you can assign that value directly to a variable as you create it.

In PocketC, as in most variants of the C language, the equal sign (=) does *not* refer to equality, as it does in mathematics. The equal sign refers to *assignment.* It might help to read it as *gets,* as in "person gets Brandon." Chapter 3, "Data and Decisions: The Morse Code Program," introduces another operator that is used to indicate equality.

Working with Strings

Once you have created the string variables, you can start working with them. It is very easy to give a variable a new value:

```
message = "PocketC is cool!";
```

That line assigns the value "PocketC is cool!" to the variable `message`. Assignment flows from right to left, so the value "PocketC is cool!" is assigned to the variable `message`.

Once the variable has a value, the value can be used in place of the variable. Look at the following line:

```
alert (message);
```

This looks like the alert statement you have seen before, but rather than a literal value, the parentheses contain the name of a variable. If the compiler sees a value in quotes, it outputs that value. If there is a variable name there instead (indicated by the absence of quote marks), it outputs the *value* of that variable. Since you have defined `message` to contain the value "PocketC is cool!" that message is what pops up on the screen when you run the program.

String Concatenation

Sometimes you might want to mix variables with literal values. The second greeting—"Hi there, Brandon!"—combines two literals and a variable. Here is the line that does the work:

```
alert ("Hi there," + person + "!");
```

You can see that the `alert` statement works with the literal value "Hi there." The plus sign (+) character tells the computer to combine that string with the upcoming string, which is the value of the variable `person`. Another plus sign is used to add the string value `"!"` to the end of the line. Using the plus sign in this way to add strings together is called *string concatenation.* Computer scientists *love* to come up with complicated names for simple concepts. Still, if you walk around muttering about "string concatenation" under your breath, people are bound to think you're smart.

String concatenation is used to take several string variables or literal values and combine them into one big string. Although this particular example is a bit contrived, the ability to combine literals and variables turns out to be a big deal. There are lots of uses for it. For example, this chapter's program involves getting the value for your variable from your user and including the value of that variable in your output.

Outputting Text to the Screen

Variables are a critical part of programming. Another element that is equally important is the ability to input and output values, so the program can communicate with the user. Output is reasonably straightforward, but you do have some choices in PocketC.

Output Demo

To explore some of the output techniques in PocketC, take a look at the program featured in Figures 2.5 through 2.7.

FIGURE 2.5

You're used to the alert function by now.

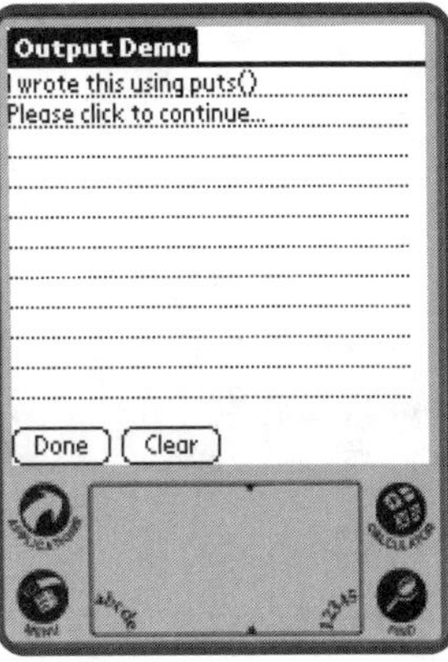

FIGURE 2.6

The program drew some text directly to the window.

FIGURE 2.7

After the user tapped on the screen, some more text appeared.

This program demonstrates a number of important ideas about output in PocketC. It illustrates some strengths and weaknesses of the alert dialog box. It introduces adding text directly to the screen, rather than through the alert statement. It demonstrates some characters used to control formatting on the screen, and it demonstrates a very simple form of pen input. Here is the code for the Output Demo program:

```
//OutputDemo
//Demonstrates output techniques
//Andy Harris, 02/27/01

main(){
  clear();
  title("Output Demo");
  alert("This is the alert function");
  puts("I wrote this ");
  puts("using puts()");
  puts("\n");
  puts("Please click to continue...\n");
  wait();
  puts("\n");
  puts("\n");
  puts("\t bye! \n");
  puts("click again to exit...\n");
  wait();
} // end main
```

Thoughts on the alert() Function

Until the Output Demo program, all of your output in this book has been through the alert dialog box created by the `alert()` function. While this practice is very useful for certain situations, the alert dialog box has some problems. It uses a lot of space on the screen, and you can't use it to put more than a line of text on the screen. It always shows up in the same place, and it requires pen input. It also halts the flow of the program, preventing any other code from executing until the OK button has been clicked. Users might find any of these behaviors annoying, especially if the alert dialog box is overused.

Most programmers prefer to use other output commands for garden variety output, and reserve the alert dialog box for those cases where it is important to get the user's attention.

Using the puts() Function

Once the alert dialog has been satisfied in the Output Demo, some text appears directly on the screen. This is accomplished via the `puts()` function. The term *puts* stands for "put string," and that's exactly what the function does. It takes a string value and types it onto the screen. Here's the first line of code to use the `puts()` function:

```
puts("I wrote this ");
```

This line writes the text directly on the screen. Because I had preceded it with a `clear()` function, the "I wrote this" line will appear at the top of an otherwise blank screen.

The next line of code executes immediately, because `puts()` does not wait for user input the way the alert statement does. It writes the rest of the sentence to the screen:

```
puts("using puts()");
```

The new text is typed on the screen exactly where the last line stopped, so the two lines together appear as one line of output. Of course, I could have combined the lines into one `puts()` function, but I wanted you to see the way that successive calls to the `puts()` function cause text to be written continuously to the screen without a pause for user input.

Using the Newline Character

Sometimes you will want to put new output on the same line as in the preceding section, and sometimes you'll want to indicate that the next output should occur on its own line. In standard text editing, you press the Enter key (or, of course, use a Graffiti input stroke) to indicate that you are ending a line, and the next thing typed should begin a new line. The Enter key is bound to a specific character (or series of characters, in some machines) which is actually embedded into the text. When you send output to the screen using the `puts()` function, you can simulate pressing the Enter key by embedding a special meta-character in your code. *Meta-characters* are special characters that denote a function that may be bound to a key but does not have a particular printable character associated with it. In the C-like languages, meta-characters begin with the backslash (\) character. The special string value "\n" is used to mean *newline,* or to simulate the *Enter* character.

Take a look at the following line:

```
puts("\n");
```

This command prints the newline character at the end of the text that had been written in the preceding `puts()` commands. The next output will appear on its own line. If you look at the output screen, you will see that this occurred. The next line of output is generated by this command:

```
puts("Please click to continue...\n");
```

Although you can't see the newline character on the screen, you can see its results. It's also worth noting that in this line ("please click to continue...\n"), I embedded the newline character into the string literal rather than writing it to the screen separately. The two approaches work equally well.

Using wait() to Pause the Program

Sometimes you might want to wait for the user to read something before continuing on (especially if you are planning to clear the screen). In these cases, you might want to use the `wait()` function, as I did in this program. The `wait()` function pauses the program and waits for the user to either tap the screen with the stylus or press a button. When either action happens, the next line of code will execute.

Note that the goodbye line appears to be indented. To get this effect, I used another meta-character. The Tab key is simulated by \t. This actually embeds a character meaning "put a tab here" into the text, and you will see the same effect as if you had pressed a Tab key (or input it through Graffiti).

Table 2.1 lists the output functions I've discussed so far.

TABLE 2.1 OUTPUT FUNCTION SUMMARY

Function	Description	Example
alert(string prompt)	Sends *prompt* to the screen in a dialog box. Halts program until OK button is clicked.	alert("Hello, world!!");
puts(string prompt)	Writes *prompt* to the screen at the end of the current screen text. Use "\n" and "\t" to format the text.	puts("Hello, world!!! \n");
clear()	Clears the screen immediately.	clear();
wait();	Halts program execution until the user taps the screen or clicks a button.	wait();

Using Dialogs for Input

PocketC supplies a number of techniques for getting information from the user. These techniques are referred to as *input* functions because they are used to input some value from the user to the program. Input functions are almost always used with a variable because the entire point of input is to get some value. It is important to have a variable ready to receive the value.

Input Demo

To illustrate various input techniques, take a look at Figures 2.8 through 2.11.

FIGURE 2.8

The first input function asks the user's name but does not provide a default value.

FIGURE 2.9

After the user enters a value and clicks OK, the demo replies with a customized greeting.

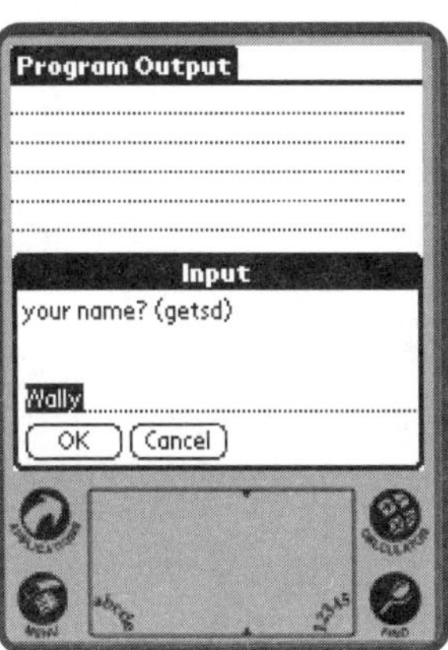

FIGURE 2.10

PocketC has another type of input function that supports a default value.

FIGURE 2.11

And still another type of input function allows you to make a smaller input box that can be placed anywhere on the screen.

The Input Demo program illustrates three different input functions. All three input functions have some elements in common—all have a way of sending information to the screen, all wait until the user clicks a button before running the rest of the program, and all return a string value that can be manipulated or stored in a variable. Here's the code for the Input Demo program:

```
//InputDemo
//Demonstrates various input methods
//Andy Harris, 2/27/01

main(){
  string userName;
  clear();

  userName = gets("your name? (gets)");
  alert("Hi, " + userName + "!");

  userName = getsd("your name? (getsd)", "Wally");
  alert("Hi, " + userName + "!");

  userName = getsi(10, 20, 80,"name? (getsi)");
  alert("Hi, " + userName + "!");
} // end main
```

Using the gets() Function

The most straightforward (but least flexible) form of input is the `gets()` function. The term *gets* is short for "get string," which is exactly what this function does. The `gets()` function expects one parameter, which is a string value to output. The string may be a variable, a literal string value, or some combination of values joined with the plus sign (+). It might seem strange that an input statement would require output, but it actually makes sense when you think about it. An input statement is generally used to get the user's response to some sort of query. The prompt is used to ask some kind of question.

Since the user is expected to enter some value, you must have a string variable in place to receive the value. In the following line:

```
userName = gets("your name? (gets)");
```

the prompt is the string value "your name? (gets)". This is the prompt that is sent out to the user. Note that you wouldn't usually indicate that the `gets()` function is being used. I added the gets indicator so it would be clear which input function is being used. The user usually won't know or care what input function you chose to use. In any case, the value inside the parentheses is the prompt that the user will see. If you wish, you can generate two lines of output by using the "\r" meta-character, which denotes the Return character. The "\r" meta character is much like the "\n", character, but in PocketC programming, "\r" is used primarily inside dialogs, where "\n" is intended for use in normal text.

Unlike the output functions (such as `puts()` and `alert()`) input functions such as `gets()` will always return a value. You will almost always assign the returned value to a variable. In this particular example, the results of gets ("your name? (gets)") will be copied to the `userName` variable. It is important to have a variable defined before you try to use an input statement, or you won't have a place to put the value. The program halts execution until either the OK or the Cancel button is clicked. If the user clicks the OK button, the variable will be sent whatever value the user typed into the dialog box. If the user clicks the Cancel button, an empty string ("") will be sent to the variable.

Using the getsd() Function

The `getsd()` function is almost identical to `gets()`. The only difference is that the `getsd()` function requires two parameters. The first parameter is a string prompt, just as in the standard `gets()` function. The second parameter is a *default value.* This is another string, which will be automatically entered in the dialog box and used as the value if the user doesn't choose to provide anything else. In the example, anybody who tries to remain nameless will be known as "Wally." You would generally use the `gets()` function if you don't have a suggested default value, and `getsd()` when you want to specify a default value. Otherwise, the functions operate in exactly the same way.

Using the getsi() Function

The `getsi()` function rounds out the input options (at least for now). It is a little different from the other choices. The `getsi()` function generates a dialog box, but unlike the other input functions, `getsi()` gives you some control over the size and placement of that box.

The syntax of the `getsi()` function is a little bit different from the other two, so as to accommodate the additional power. It has four parameters. The first two parameters indicate where the input box should go on the screen. PocketC uses a coordinate system that looks like the one you might remember from drawing graphs in school, but it doesn't start at the lower-left corner. Like most programming languages, PocketC puts the origin (0, 0) at the upper left-hand corner of the screen. As the *X* values increase, they move to the right-hand side of the screen, and as *Y* values increase, they move down to the bottom of the screen. The Palm screen is composed of a matrix of 160 by 160 little dots (or *pixels,* as they're usually called in computer graphics). Figure 2.12 illustrates the basic layout of the Palm OS screen.

You can place your dialog box at any legal location, but the coordinate you specify will be the upper-left corner of your dialog box. Be careful that you don't place the dialog where it will not show (if you put it too far to the right or too far down, the dialog will run off the end of the screen. PocketC is perfectly happy with this arrangement, but your users won't be).

The next parameter determines the width of the input dialog box. You'll want to ensure that the dialog box is wide enough to handle any values the user will input. You might want to use the screen width as a guide. Since the screen is 160 units across, a dialog box of width 80 will cover just over half of the screen. (The dialog box itself takes up some room, so it will be more than half the screen width.) These first three parameters are numbers, so they do not require the quote symbols ("") that string values need.

The last parameter is the default value to show in the dialog box. Notice that the `getsi()` function does not have a prompt—PocketC omits the prompt value to make the dialog as compact as possible. Most programmers simply put the prompt as the default text, as I did in the example. This provides a clue about what should go in the box. Since the default text is highlighted automatically, it will be overwritten when the user starts to enter a value. Unfortunately, this

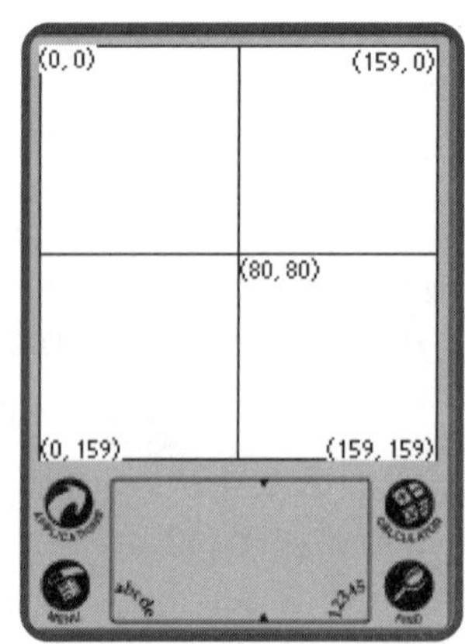

FIGURE 2.12

The screen layout with the corners and center of the screen labeled means that the cue disappears as soon as the user starts entering a value. If you want to keep a prompt on the screen, carefully design your screen so that your `getsi()` function pops up near some relevant text. (As a rough guide, each line of text appears to be about 15 pixels tall.)

In the following table, many of the function names begin with the term *string*. This is used to indicate that the function returns a string value. Frequently you will see this syntax in formal language definitions. You don't actually have to type the word *string* when you are using the function.

Table 2.2 lists the input functions discussed so far.

TABLE 2.2 INPUT FUNCTION SUMMARY

Function	Description	Example
string gets (string prompt)	Displays the value *prompt* in a dialog box with no default response. When the user presses OK, returns the value entered by the user	string guess; (guess = gets ("what is the answer?");
string getsd (string prompt, string default)	Displays the value *prompt* in a dialog box, and *default* as the default response. When the user presses OK, returns the value entered (or accepted) by the user	string guess; guess = gets("what is answer?", "42");
string getsi(int x, int y, i int w, string default)	Creates a dialog at (x, y) of width w. Display *default* as the default text. When the user presses OK, returns the value entered by the user	string guess guess = getsi(20, 20, 70, "what is the answer?");

String Functions

String variables are especially interesting because they can contain information that is meaningful to humans. Like most languages, PocketC supports a number of functions that work with string variables. The Name Game program you saw at the beginning of this chapter used a number of those functions.

String Mangler Program

The program featured in Figures 2.13 through 2.16 demonstrates a number of string functions. Essentially, the program takes a sample of text and runs it through most of the string functions supported in PocketC.

The code for this program is not complex, but it is longer than the programs you have seen so far. I'll show you the code one section at a time, rather than as one large listing, so that the explanations are close to the code they explain. Look on the CD-ROM to see the code in its entirety.

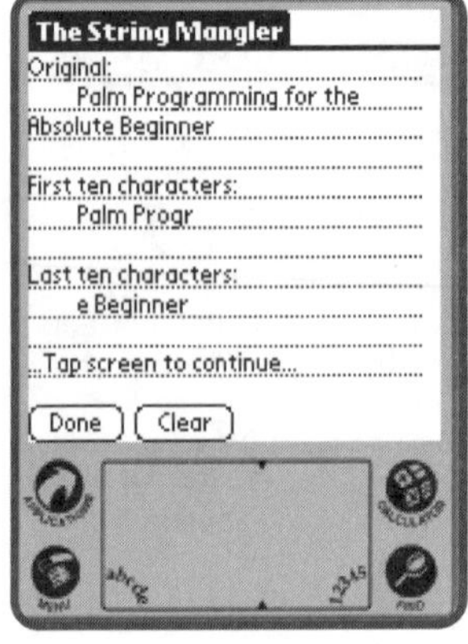

FIGURE 2.13

Finding the beginning and end of a string

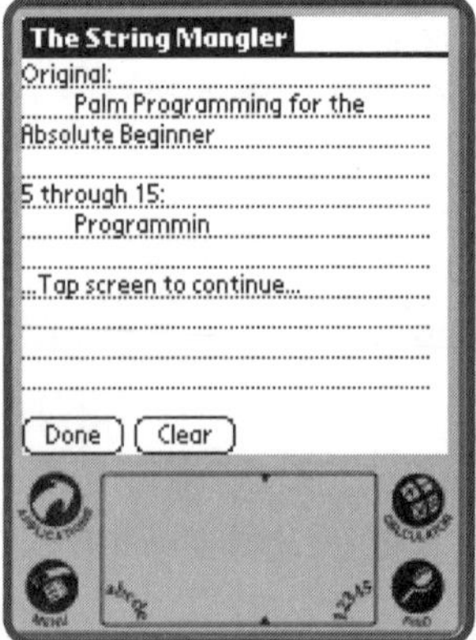

FIGURE 2.14

Finding characters in the middle of a string

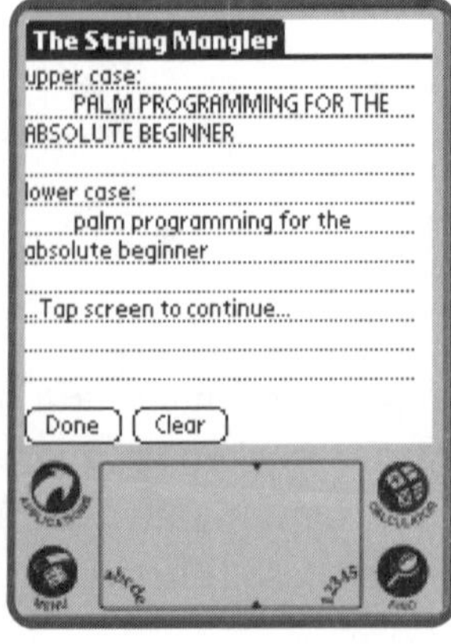

FIGURE 2.15

Converting a string entirely into upper- or lowercase

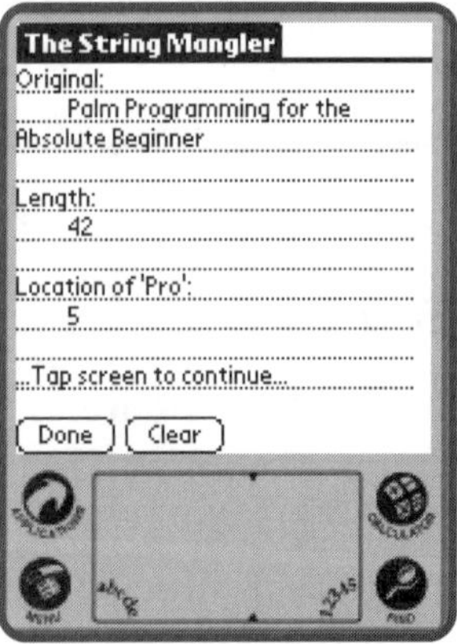

FIGURE 2.16

Extracting numeric information from a string

Starting Up the Program

The first page of the program finds the beginning and end of the string. Here's the code that sets everything up:

```
//stringMangler
//demonstrates various string functions
//Andy Harris, 3/02/01

main(){
  string book = "Palm Programming for the Absolute Beginner";
  string mangled;
  int number;
```

The program begins with the requisite comments, and the invocation of the `main()` function. I chose to use three variables for this program. The first is the string `book`. This variable contains the name of a well-regarded (I hope) book on computer programming. This is the string that I will be mangling in a number of ways throughout the program. Another string variable called `mangled` will contain the results of my various mutilations of `book`. By having two variables, I can make several changes to `book` without doing any permanent damage. The `mangled` variable will contain the results of my latest devious manipulations of the `book` variable.

Introducing the Integer

The `number` variable is a little bit different than the variables you already know and love. So far you have only seen string variables, because they are generally the easiest kind of variables for new programmers to tinker with. However, computers also work with numbers, and numeric values must be stored in the computer's memory in a completely different way than text. In fact, computers store different *types* of numbers in different ways. (Chapter 3 returns to this issue.) The keyword `int` stands for *integer*, which is the most common type of number used in computing. Integers, as you recall, are whole numbers—the ones with values like –3, –2, –1, 0, 1, 2, and 3. They are the numbers you normally count with, zero, and negative values.

The line

```
int number;
```

creates a new variable called `number`, which will be an integer variable. It will be used to store integer values. You'll see later on why I decided to add an integer variable to the program.

IN THE REAL WORLD

To be technically correct, everything in the computer is stored as *binary values,* which are easily converted into numbers. Text, images, videos, or any other media that can be manipulated by any type of computer is ultimately converted into numbers, then into base two numbers—that is, numbers in which the only symbols are 0 and 1 rather than 0 through 9. You can count as high as you please in binary, but it takes a lot of digits to do it.

Setting Up the Screen

Take a look at the next few lines:

```
clear();
  title("The String Mangler");

  //original
  puts("Original:\n");
  puts("\t" + book + "\n\n");
```

These lines do some necessary housekeeping. The `clear()` command clears the screen, so anything left over from a previous program will be swept away. The `title` command sets the title of the output screen to the program's name.

Note the comment that describes what will be happening in the next couple of lines of code. When a program starts to get long and involved, it's a great idea to sprinkle comments liberally through the code to remind you what is going on. It is surprising how often a programmer looks at code written just a few hours before and has no idea what it does. Good commenting will save you many hours of debugging.

The first `puts()` function tells the user that the original text is coming. The next line prints the value of the `book` variable. The \t character indents the output by inserting a tab character. The \n\n combination puts a blank line between the end of the book line and the next line to be printed. The first \n moves the focus to the next line of the screen. The next \n moves down another line, leaving a blank line. The newline character works just like pressing the Enter key on a keyboard. I used the tab and newline formatting tricks to make the screen easier to read. Liberal use of these characters can make your user's life much more pleasant. The Palm screen is very small, so you need to be exceptionally careful to make it as readable as possible.

Breaking Up Strings: substr(), strleft(), strright()

Now that the program is set up, you can start messing around with strings. Here is the code that produces the first page of the display:

```
//left and right
puts("First ten characters:\n");
mangled = strleft(book, 10);
puts("\t" + mangled + "\n");

puts("\n");

puts("Last ten characters:\n");
mangled = strright(book, 10);
puts("\t" + mangled + "\n");

puts("\n...Tap screen to continue...");
//next page
wait();
clear();
```

I started by announcing to the user that I was going to grab the first ten characters of the string. I did so by applying the `strleft()` function to the `book` variable. This function expects a string value or variable, and an integer. It then returns a string containing the appropriate number of characters from the beginning of the string. Since I specified ten characters from the `book` variable, the program returned "Palm Progr"—the first ten characters of "Palm Programming for the Absolute Beginner."

I had the result of the `strleft()` function copied over to the `mangled` variable. I then output `mangled` with a `puts()` function. Notice the use of the tab and newline characters to make everything look nice on the output screen.

Getting the last 10 characters is almost identical to getting the first 10. Instead of the `strleft()` function, I used `strright()`; doing so pulls the specified number of characters from the right, or end, of the string. I used the same type of formatting to make sure the results look good on the screen.

In the Real World

It might not seem terribly useful to be able to grab the beginning or ending parts of a string, but this functionality turns out to be very handy in a certain class of programs called *parsers.* The job of a parser is to examine text and extract some meaning from it. The text-based adventure games that were popular in the 1980s (and are still viable entertainment on the Palm—see http://www.pez.com) are one example of a simple parser. Such a program might expect two-word commands and needs to be able to examine the first or last word in isolation.

You might also use such a command to extract the domain name of an Internet address. (Just ask if the last three characters are "com," "edu," or "net.")

Getting a New Page

The screen on a PDA is very small; you can't squeeze much text onto it. I chose to implement a very rudimentary form of page handling in this program. The following lines will cause a new page to appear on command:

```
puts("\n...Tap screen to continue...");
//next page
wait();
clear();
```

The first line is simply a message to the user, announcing that tapping the screen will do something. This seems silly, but a user might not guess that there is more unless you say so. The `wait()` function temporarily halts the program until the user taps on the screen. After the user taps the screen, the next line in the program will execute. This is the `clear()` function, which will clear the screen. The subsequent `puts()` function calls will appear to be on a new page.

Extracting from the Middle of a String

The next screen shows ten characters from the middle (well, at least not on the left or right part of the string). It illustrates a way to extract a smaller string from a bigger one. Here's the relevant code:

```
//middle
puts("Original:\n");
puts("\t" + book + "\n\n");
```

```
puts("5 through 15:\n");
mangled = substr(book, 5, 10);
puts("\t" + mangled + "\n");

puts("\n...Tap screen to continue...");
//next page
wait();
clear();
```

Much of the code is repeated from the last section. The new part is the `substr()` function. The term *substr* is an abbreviation for substring. This function extracts a smaller string from a larger one, given two numeric parameters. The first numeric parameter refers to the starting character of the substring, and the final parameter refers to the length of the substring. The code fragment can be interpreted as meaning "get a substring from `book` starting at character 5 that is ten characters long."

If you've looked carefully at the results, you might be surprised. The program returns "Programmin," which is 10 characters long. However, the "P" in "Programming" is the sixth character of "Palm Programming for the Absolute Beginner," not the fifth. The reason for this seeming anomaly is that computers generally begin counting with zero rather than one. The "P" in "Palm" is actually considered character 0, not character 1!

Changing Strings: strupr(), strlwr()

The next page of the String Mangler program demonstrates converting a string value entirely into uppercase or lowercase values. Here is the code that performs these tricks:

```
//upper and lower case
puts("uppercase:\n");
mangled = strupr(book);
puts("\t" + mangled + "\n");

puts("\n");

puts("lowercase:\n");
mangled = strlwr(book);
puts("\t" + mangled + "\n");
```

```
puts("\n...Tap screen to continue...");
//next page
wait();
clear();
```

Most of this code is probably familiar to you by now. The only new parts are the two string conversion functions. The `strupr()` function takes a string and returns a copy of that string all in uppercase characters. The `strlwr()` function is similar, but makes a string all in lowercase characters.

Neither `strupr()` or `strlwr()` change the original string. They both generate a totally new value and leave the original string alone, just like all the other string functions you have seen so far.

IN THE REAL WORLD

Case conversion functions such as `strupr()` and `strlwr()` are often used to make a program *case-insensitive.* If you aren't terribly concerned about whether the user's input is uppercase or lowercase, you can use such a function to convert the string entirely into lowercase. Then when you try to examine the string, you won't have to worry about searching for uppercase characters.

Getting Information about Strings: strlen(), strstr()

There are a couple of other functions that operate on strings without returning string values. These functions are used to get some information about a string variable. The last page of the String Mangler program demonstrates the use of two such functions:

```
//length and substring
puts("Original:\n");
puts("\t" + book + "\n\n");

puts("Length:\n");
number = strlen(book);
puts("\t" + (string)number + "\n");

puts("\n");
puts("Location of 'Pro':\n");
number = strstr(book, "Pro", 0);
puts("\t" + (string)number + "\n");
```

```
    puts("\n...Tap screen to continue...");
  //next page
  wait();
  clear();

} // end main
```

The `strlen()` function is used to get the length of a string. This might be useful if you want to walk through a string one word or character at a time, or if you wanted to extract exactly half of a string. `Strlen` returns an integer value—this is why I declared the `number` variable as an integer way back at the beginning of this program. Since `strlen` is designed to return an integer value, I needed an integer variable to contain the results. The `strstr()` function also returns an integer. This function is used to search for a specific string inside another string, much like a find command in a text editor or Web browser. The `strstr()` function requires three parameters. The first is the string to be searched. The second is the substring you are looking for, and the third is a starting character. Here's the relevant line in the String Mangler program:

```
  number = strstr(book, "Pro", 0);
```

This line looks inside the string variable `book` for the substring value "Pro." It will begin at the beginning of the string, which is character 0. The function returns the character where the substring can be found, if it can be found at all. If it cannot find the substring, it returns a value of -1. To search for a second incidence of the substring, you might call the `strstr()` function a second time, but this time use the results of the first `strstr()` call as the starting position. This will search the rest of the string, ignoring the part you have already searched.

In the Real World

Functions like `strstr()` come in handy in a number of places. One such application that is currently in the news is the Web filter. Web filters are a class of programs that screen Web pages and prevent those with certain objectionable content from appearing in a browser. Many of these programs simply search the text of the page for any of a list of allegedly bad words and phrases using a somewhat more sophisticated version of the `strstr()` function. Of course, the weakness of such a program is that somebody must compile the list of bad phrases, and somebody decides what is bad or not—as with the early filter program that blocked access to the White House site because it mentioned bedrooms and beds.

Casting an Integer to a String

You might have noticed that the output lines for this last code fragment differed from the ones in the other parts of the program. Since both the `strlen()` and `strstr()` functions return integer values, the results are stored in an integer variable, `number`. The problem is that the `puts()` function that I'm using for output requires string variables. Fortunately, PocketC provides a very handy tool for converting one variable type into another. It is called the *cast operator.* Here's a line from the String Mangler program that uses it:

```
puts("\t" + (string)number + "\n");
```

By placing the name of a variable type in front of a variable, you are telling PocketC to convert the variable into the given type. In this case, I'm telling PocketC to take the value `number`, which is an integer, and convert it into a string value. You can use the same trick for converting all sorts of variables into different types.

Table 2.3 lists the string functions covered so far. The assigned string variable is `"MyVar"` throughout.

The Name Game Program

The String Mangler program is actually more complicated than the final program for this chapter. If you understood everything (or even most things) in the last program, you should have no problems with the Name Game that made its debut at the beginning of this chapter.

In the Real World

If you've looked at some of the sample code that comes with PocketC, or you've read the documentation, you might notice that the string cast that I did here was not absolutely necessary because PocketC will attempt to do automatic type conversions for you. Although this seems like a useful feature, I have found that it is a bad idea to trust such automatic conversions. It is easy enough to do the conversion yourself, and doing so will make it clear in the code that you intended to convert the value. Once you get more experienced, feel free to use automatic type conversions. While you're still a beginner, I'd suggest you do conversion by hand instead.

Table 2.3 String Function Summary

Function	Description	Example
string substr(string *orig*, int *start*, int *len*)	Extracts *len* characters from the *orig*, starting at character number *start*	myVar substr("Whoo Hoo!", 3, 5); //returns "o Hoo"
string strleft(string *orig*, int *len*)	Extracts *len* characters from the beginning of *orig*	myVar = strleft("Whoo Hoo!",4); // returns "Whoo"
string strright(string *orig*, int *len*)	Extracts *len* characters from the end of *orig*	myVar = strright("Whoo Hoo!", 4); // returns "Hoo!"
string strupr(string *orig*)	Makes a copy of *orig* entirely in uppercase characters	myVar = strupr("Whoo Hoo!"); //returns "WHOO HOO!"
string strlwr(string *orig*)	Makes a copy of *orig* entirely in lowercase characters	myVar = strlwr("Whoo Hoo!"); // returns "whoo hoo!"
int strlen(string *orig*)	Returns the number of characters in *orig*	alert(strlen("Whoo Hoo!")); //returns 9
int strstr(string *orig*, string *target*, int *start*)	If *target* string can be found in *orig* string, returns the character number in *orig* where *target* can be found. If *target* cannot be found, returns back -1. Begins counting at the *start* character of *orig*	string theString = "Whoo Hoo"; alert(strstr(theString, "oo", 0)); //returns 2 alert(strstr(theString, "oo", 4)); //returns 6, because the search started at the space between "Whoo" and "Hoo"
(string)*numVal*	Returns a string conversion of *numVal*	puts((string)7); // prints "7"

Setting Up the Game

The first part of the code involved setting up the screen and creating a number of string variables:

```
//nameGame
//Andy Harris
//01/12/01

main(){
   string fName;
   string lName;
```

```
string mi;
string fullName;
string mixedUp;
int numChars;
int qtrLength;
clear();
title("The Name Game");
```

The program could have been created with fewer variables, but having variables for everything made the program much more readable. You can probably guess what will go into each variable by its name. (That's a sign that the variable was named well: if you can't guess what kind of information a variable contains, the name should probably have been more descriptive.) The first three strings will contain parts of the user's name. The first name will go into `fName`, last name in `lName`, and middle initial will go into `mi`. The `fullName` variable will hold a couple of variations of the full name, put together in different orders. The `mixedUp` variable will contain the mixed-up version of the user's name that appears near the end of the program. The `numChars` variable is an integer, and it will contain the number of characters total in the user's name, and the `qtrLength` variable will be used to make the mixed-up version of the name.

I cleared the screen to clean up any junk left over from a previous program.

IN THE REAL WORLD

You might wonder how I knew which variables to create if I hadn't written the program yet. I didn't. I had to sketch out my ideas for the program first so as to know the kinds of values the program would require. This told me what variables I would need. Also, programs rarely get written from beginning to end. You will generally find yourself working on code, then going back to the top to add a variable when you need one. Chapter 4, "Repeating Behavior and Larger Programs: The Micro Football Game," goes into detail on a planning strategy to help you figure out what variables (and other tools) you'll need for a particular problem.

Getting User Input

All the user input in this program was done with the `gets()` function. I could have used some other functions, but `gets()` seemed to do what I wanted for this program. Here's the code that gets the various parts of the user's name:

```
fName = gets("What's your first name?");
lName = gets("What's your last name?");
```

```
mi = gets("What's your middle initial?");
```

Once these key variables have values, you can do some things to them.

The String Manipulations

First, I returned the user's name as a concatenated string:

```
fullName = lName + ", " + fName + " " + mi;
alert(fullName + "\n\n");
```

Note the use of literal spaces and the comma to make the string look correct. I built this first string so it would appear in last, first, middle order.

I then made another version of the full name using the more traditional order (first, middle, last):

```
fullName = fName + " " + mi + ". " + lName;
alert("usually called: " + fullName);
```

The next manipulation involved finding out the length of the string:

```
numChars = strlen(fullName);
alert("Your name has " + (string)numChars + " characters.");
qtrLength = numChars/4;
```

I used the `strlen()` function to determine the number of characters, which I then stored in a variable and reported to the user. I also used this value to generate the value of `qtrLength`. The slash character (/) is used to indicate division, so `qtrLength` contains one-quarter the length of the user's full name. I used this value to generate the mixed-up version of the name.

The next two lines simply generate uppercase and lowercase versions of the name:

```
alert("I'll shout it: " + strupr(fullName));
alert("Now I'll whisper: " + strlwr(fullName));
```

Note that it isn't absolutely necessary to assign the results of a function to a variable. In both of these lines, I simply used the specified function, knowing that it would return a string value which could legally be concatenated to the string being output.

The last part of the program generates a mixed-up version of the name.

```
mixedUp = strright(fullName, qtrLength);
mixedUp = mixedUp + substr(fullName, qtrLength, numChars - qtrLength);
```

```
mixedUp = mixedUp + strleft(fullName, qtrLength);
alert("mixed up: " + mixedUp);
```

I started by grabbing the last quarter of the user's name, and setting the `mixedUp` variable to that value. I then added the middle half of the name, and then finally the first quarter. I then output this value.

Summary

In this chapter you learned how to get information from the user. You learned about string variables, which are used to store text information in the computer's memory. You now have some experience with a number of functions for sending information to the screen, and you can format string output with metacharacters. You've experimented with a number of interesting functions designed to help you manipulate string values, and found out how to write a multiple-page output using the `clear()` and `wait()` functions. The next chapter shows you more about variables and ways to control the flow of a program.

CHALLENGES

1. **Change the Name Game program so that it uses some of the other input or output functions.**
2. **Add a new feature to the Name Game that changes the name in another way.**
3. **Ask the user for a word and convert that word into pig latin by extracting the first letter and adding it to the end of the word with "ay." For example, if the user enters "PocketC," the program should return "ocketCPay," Don't worry about words that begin with vowels.**
4. **Write a program that asks for the user's name, favorite color, and other information. Use the input to generate a story using the user's information.**
5. **Write a simple quiz program that asks the user a number of questions. (Don't worry about checking the user's answers yet.)**

Data and Decisions: The Morse Code Program

Now that you know how to get information from the user, you can use a number of simple but very important tools for making more interesting programs. The key to computer programs is the information that they work with. This chapter demonstrates several of the ways PocketC stores information. It also presents one of the most important kinds of structures for controlling the behavior of your programs, the *conditional* statement. With these ideas (and a few others) you will be well on your way to writing sophisticated programs.

In this chapter, you learn the following techniques:

- Using numeric variables to work with numbers
- Doing the basic mathematical operations on numbers
- Getting random numbers from the computer
- Using the `if`, `else`, and `end if` commands to make decisions
- Working with nested `if` statements and multiple `if` statement structures
- Making music on the PDA
- Storing commonly used code in functions
- Reading a character of Graffiti input

You've got a lot to learn in this chapter, but none of it is terribly hard. If you take it one step at a time, and make sure you understand each program before you look at the next one, you should have no problems.

The Morse Code Translator

This chapter shows you how to build the simple Morse code translator illustrated in Figure 3.1. Morse code is a special code, made up of dots and dashes, for encoding text. It was widely used in radio and military applications from the mid-1800s until close to the end of the 20th century. The program waits for you to input a Graffiti character, shows the Morse code sequence for the character, and plays the appropriate sequence of long and short tones through the speaker!

It's a silly example, but it is kind of cool to be able to see and hear a 19th-century communications technology on a 21st-century device like a PDA.

Using Numeric Values

The programs in the first two chapters work exclusively with text (string) values. I introduced these values early on because most people are more comfortable working with text than with numeric values, but computers actually prefer numbers. In fact, even the text values of a string variable are translated into numbers

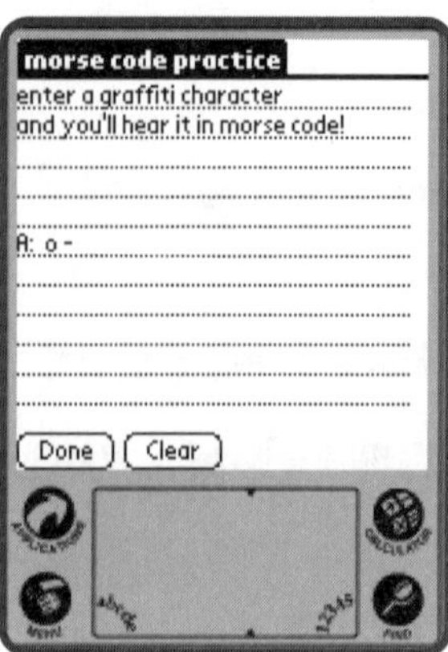

FIGURE 3.1

The user entered an **A**. You can see the Morse symbol for **A** on the screen. The speaker also played an appropriate tone.

by the computer. And of course, you will sometimes want to work with numbers as numbers in your programs, so numeric values are the natural next step in learning to program.

It's important to understand that computers store the numerical equivalent of text and numbers used as numbers very differently. In fact, different kinds of numbers are stored in different ways, as well. The computer has to work with numbers that have decimal points followed by fractional values in very different ways than it works with whole numbers. Although you can get along fine without knowing the exact details, you should be familiar with the kinds of variables you can use. Fortunately, PocketC has a small and straightforward set of variable types.

The Var Demo Program

The program featured in Figure 3.2 demonstrates several types of variables.

To write this program, I took one value and converted it repeatedly so that you can see how the various ways of storing information differ from each other. All four lines of the program represent *exactly* the same value, but the value looks very different when it is stored in different ways.

Variable Types in PocketC

PocketC has support for five types of data. Two of them work with characters, two work with numbers, and the fifth is a special type (pointer) that you'll have a chance to examine more closely in Chapter 8, "Using Arrays and Libraries."

Table 3.1 presents an overview of the various types of data.

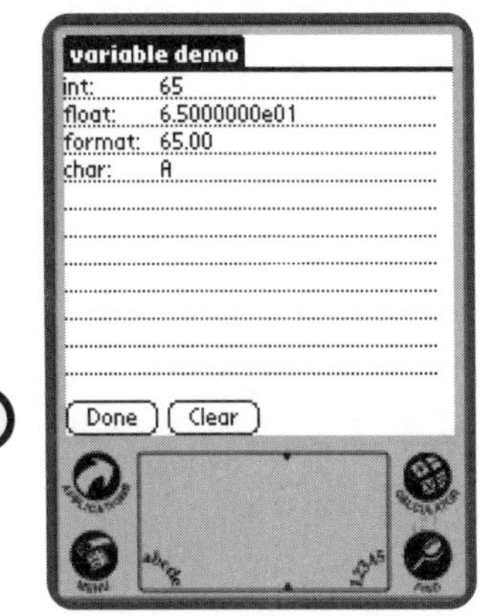

FIGURE 3.2

The number 65, cast into several different types

Table 3.1 Principal Data Types in PocketC

Type	Description	Values	Examples
int	integer values (no decimal point)	roughly 65,500 to -65,500	65 –4571
float	floating point decimal value	roughly 8 digits of accuracy times 10 to the +/– 37th digit	3.1415927 6.0200000e–23
char	one character of ASCII text	0–255 with some extra characters	'g' '4'
string	a series of characters	up to 255 characters long (longer with concatenation)	"PocketC rocks" "Rachel"

Each of these variable types deserves some discussion, because they all have characteristics that can make them useful for certain applications.

The `int` type is the most basic type of variable and one of the most commonly used. It refers to an integer. You may recall that integers are defined as any positive or negative number, as well as zero, but not fractional or decimal values. In computing, integer values have a limited range. The integer values in PocketC can range from –65,536 to 65,535. (Ask your friendly neighborhood computer scientist why the range is so strange. Nobody else probably cares, but it's still a limit you may need to be aware of.) If you try to store a value that is too large or too small, it will not work, and you will get an error. Still, most of the numbers you will work with in your programming will fit very nicely in this range. If you have a number that does not need a decimal point and isn't extremely large or small, an integer is usually a good choice.

If you are dealing with very large or very small numbers, or you need decimal values, you should probably consider the `float` data type. The term *float* stands for "floating point" representation. Floating point numbers are designed for scientific notation, and can work with very large or very small numbers. They are also suitable for fractional values.

By default, PocketC outputs all floating point values in scientific notation (some value from 1 to 10 raised to a power of 10). Later you will see a technique for converting the scientific notation form into something more readable for ordinary users.

IN THE REAL WORLD

The Palm OS supports a specialized form of ASCII that has a number of interesting characters including a key symbols for playing card suits, and fraction characters. I've included a program on the CD-ROM called "Make Chart" to demonstrate this. Install and run this program, and it will create a new Memo Pad document called "ASCII chart" that will show each number and the character associated with that number. You can use this memo to find the value of characters you might wish to use in your own program. In Chapter 09, "Memo Access," I will show you how I made the ASCII Chart program.

The `char` type represents one character. As I said earlier, computers even work with text as numbers. Most computers, including those using the Palm OS, use a form of notation referred to as ASCII (American Standard Code for Information Interchange). The ASCII codes are a series of integers between 0 and 255 that stand for letters and symbols that can be printed on the screen. A char constant is depicted inside single quote marks (').

The string variable type is used to hold text values. Actually, a string is just a bunch of chars attached together in the computer's memory. Most forms of C don't have a string variable type, because you can make a string out of characters. PocketC does supply the string type, which makes it easy to work with text values. You can define string values up to 255 characters long, and you can make strings even longer than that by *concatenating* strings—that is, by adding one to the next. Strings are enclosed inside double quote marks (").

Casting Variables

The Var Demo program illustrates the same value (65) being interpreted as an int, float, formatted float, and char variable. Here is the source code for the program:

```
//varDemo
//demonstrates variable types
//Andy Harris, 03/07/01

main(){
  int startVal = 65;
  float floatVal;
```

```
  char charVal;
  string stringVal;

  clear();
  title("variable demo");

  puts("int:\t\t" + startVal + "\n");

  floatVal = (float)startVal;
  puts("float:\t" + floatVal + "\n");

  puts("format:\t" + format(floatVal,2) + "\n");

  charVal = (char)startVal;
  puts("char:\t" + charVal + "\n");

  wait();
} // end main
```

The program starts by declaring four variables. I named the variables to indicate the type of value the variable would hold. I stored the integer value 65 into the int variable `startVal`.

The next few lines print out the value of `startVal`, to demonstrate how integers are displayed.

This line:

```
floatVal = (float)startVal;
```

generates a copy of the `startVal` variable in float format, and copies it to the `floatVal` variable. The (float) symbol is called a *cast* operator. It tells the compiler to cast the `startVal` value to a float type so it can be stored in a float variable.

If you look at the output for the program, the float value of 65 is output in scientific notation. It appears as 6.5000000e01. This can be expanded to "6.5 times 10 to the first power," that is, 65. Remember that floating point numbers work in scientific notation, which means they will return values in the same format. Fortunately, there is a special technique for turning a float value into something a little more readable.

The format function takes a floating point number and an integer as parameters. It prints out the number to a specified number of places. For example, `format(3.14159, 2)` would return `3.14`. As you can see from the screen shot, `format(floatVal, 2)` converts 6.5000000e01 into the much more readable 65.00. Most of the time, when you want to display a floating point value to the user, you will want to run it through the format command to turn it into something your user will be able to read easily.

Notice that you can also cast a variable to the char type, as I did in this line:

```
charVal = (char)startVal;
```

The cast operator formats the `startVal` as a char. If you look back at the output, you might be surprised to see that the value of `charVal` is the letter "A" and not a number at all. This is because 65 is the ASCII code for capital A. So when the value 65 is cast as a char, it is A, when it is cast as a float, it is 6.5000000e01, and when it is cast as an int, it is 65.

Table 3.2 lists the cast operators. Note that cast operators do not change the original values; they return a value in a new type, which can be output or copied to another variable.

TABLE 3.2 VARIABLE CONVERSION OPERATORS AND FUNCTIONS

Operator (function)	Description	Example
(int)*value*	Converts value to an int if possible. If thereis no obvious integer value, value, returns a 0	myInt = (int)3.1415; //myInt will contain 3.
(float)*value*	Converts *value* to a float if possible. If there is no obvious float value, returns a 0	myFloat = (float)3; //myFloat will contain 3.0000000e00.
(char)*value*	Convert *value* to a char if possible. If *value* is an int, returns the ASCII value associated with *value*	myChar = (char)65; //myChar will contain the value 'A'.
(string)*value*	Convert *value* to a string	myString = (string)3.14159; //mystring will contain "3.14159"
format(float *floatVal*, int *precision*)	Converts *floatVal* to a string with *precision* decimal places	puts(format(3.14159, 3)); // will output "3.141."

In the Real World

I used explicit type casting in this program to illustrate how the various types of variables work. However, PocketC is reasonably forgiving about variable types. It will often do cast conversions automatically without requiring you to put in the cast operator. However, it still might be a good idea not to rely on the automatic conversions until you completely understand how they work. I actually took advantage of automatic casting in this program because all of the output should really be in string values. I didn't want to add a string cast to the mix because that would have just confused things, but every time I had a variable inside a `puts()` function call, that variable was quietly cast to a string.

Don't let type casting freak you out. Most of the time, you won't have to worry about it all. Just keep in the back of your mind the idea that if you need to convert a variable to another type, you can use the casting operators to do so.

Doing Basic Math

Now that you know something about variables in PocketC, you can do all kinds of cool applications. One useful type of program allows you to do some calculations. Figure 3.3 illustrates a program that asks for two numbers and does a series of standard calculations on these numbers.

PocketC can use all the basic math operators and can do a few more advanced operations as well. This particular program illustrates the arithmetic operators that you will use most when writing programs.

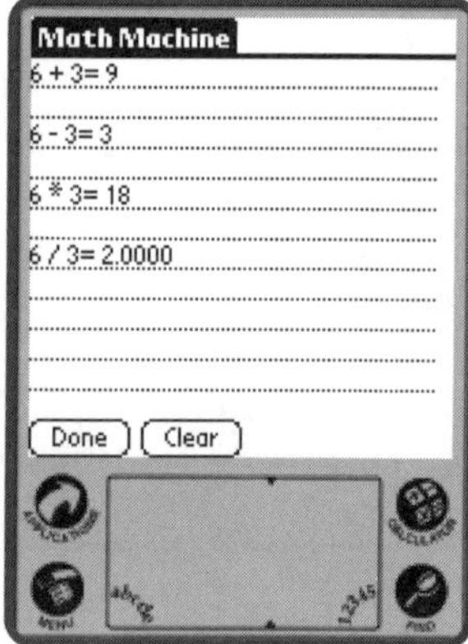

FIGURE 3.3

Given two numbers, the Math Machine program can do a set of basic operations and give you answers.

The Math Machine Program

The code for the Math Machine program is reasonably straightforward:

```
//mathMachine
//Demonstrates basic math operators
//Andy Harris, 03/10/01

main(){
  int x;
  int y;
  float result;

  clear();
  title("Math Machine");

  x = (int)gets("X value?");
  y = (int)gets("Y value?");

  //plus
  result = (x + y);
  puts(x + " + " + y + "= ");
  puts(format(result,0));
  puts("\n\n");

  //minus
  result = (x - y);
  puts(x + " - " + y + "= ");
  puts(format(result,0));
  puts("\n\n");

  //times
  result = (x * y);
  puts(x + " * " + y + "= ");
  puts(format(result,0));
  puts("\n\n");

  //divide
  result = ((float)x / (float)y);
  puts(x + " / " + y + "= ");
  puts(format(result,4));
  puts("\n\n");

  wait();
} // end main
```

I chose to define X and Y as int variables, so after I asked the user about them, I cast them into ints. (Note that this step wasn't strictly necessary. PocketC would have been able to make the conversion automatically, but I wanted to make it clear to myself that a type conversion is going on.)

Each of the calculations followed pretty much the same formula. I did a calculation, storing the answer in the `result` variable, and then I printed a line of output. Since I knew that the sum, difference, and products of integers would also have to be integers, I formatted the result to show no decimal points.

The division problem is where things get a little tricky. The first time I wrote the program, I wrote the division line like this:

```
result = (x / y);
```

This technique worked perfectly in all the other operations, but it caused a problem in division. PocketC saw that I was dividing two int values, so it assumed I wanted an int result, even though that result was being passed to a float variable. When I had set `X` to 6 and `Y` to 4, the result was reported as 0. When you divide 4 by 6 the answer is not 0, so there was definitely a problem. What I had to do was tell PocketC to convert `X` and `Y` to floating point values before dividing them. I did that with the line you now see in the code:

```
result = ((float)x / (float)y);
```

This caused the `X` and `Y` values to be considered float values before the division occurred, making a float value that can be passed to the result variable. Since the result of a division is often a floating point value with decimal values, I decided to format the result to four places. In this particular program I did not trap for division by zero, so if the user enters 0 for `Y`, the program will crash. A solution for that problem forms one of the challenges for this chapter. (It's pretty easy, and you'll have the tool you need by the time you get to it.)

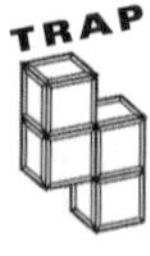

The solution for 4/6 that shows up when you do float arithmetic is still not exactly correct. Because computers do not have an infinite amount of memory, they cannot exactly handle values like 4/6, which repeat indefinitely. This phenomenon is well known in computer science, and it is called *round-off error.* It generally isn't a problem for most applications, but you have to be aware of it if you are writing programs that require extreme precision. Fortunately, programs that control spacecraft trajectories or nuclear reactors are rarely written on handheld devices.

Table 3.3 describes a number of other mathematical functions included in PocketC.

Table 3.3 Selected Math Operators and Functions

Function	Description	Example
cos, sin, tan, acos, asin, atan, cosh, sinh, tanh, acosh, asinh, atanh (float *angle*)	Perform trigonometry functions on *angle* (measured in radians)	x = sin(0).
float pow(float *a*, float *b*)	Returns *a* raised to the *b* power	x = pow(2,10); //x will get 1024.
float sqrt(float *a*)	Returns square root of *a*	x = sqrt(4); // x will get 2.
float log(float *a*)	Returns natural log of *a*	x = log(1); // x will get 0.
float exp(float a)	Returns e^*a*	x = exp(0); // x will get 1.float rand()
	Returns a random float from 0 to 1	x = rand(); // x will be anywhere from 0.0000000e00 to 1.0000000e00.
int random(int *elements*)	Returns a random integer from 0 to *elements* –1	x = random(5); // x will be 0, 1, 2, 3, or 4
int mathlib()	Returns a 1 if mathlib is present, a zero if it is not	x = mathlib; // will be 1 if mathlib is present.

You may not need all of these functions, but it is good to know they're there in case you do. Many of these functions require a special native library called mathlib. A native library is a specially constructed program that will allow the programmer to use new functions in the same manner as the included (built-in) functions. The mathlib library comes with PocketC, and you should definitely load it onto your PDA. The chances are good that it's already there, because many programs rely on it. You can use the `mathlib()` function to determine if the library is currently installed on your PDA. I describe the random functions in more detail throughout the rest of this chapter.

Getting Random Numbers from the Computer

Many of the most interesting things you can do with a computer involve random numbers. Almost every game involves random number generation, as do a number of more serious applications like business simulations and engineering models. Thus, the ability to generate random numbers is an important part of programming. Fortunately, PocketC makes it easy to get random numbers.

The Roll Die Program

In Figure 3.4 you will see a very simple program that rolls a die. At this point, I'll just display the numbers, but Chapter 5, "Using the Graphics Mode," shows you how to draw graphics on the screen.

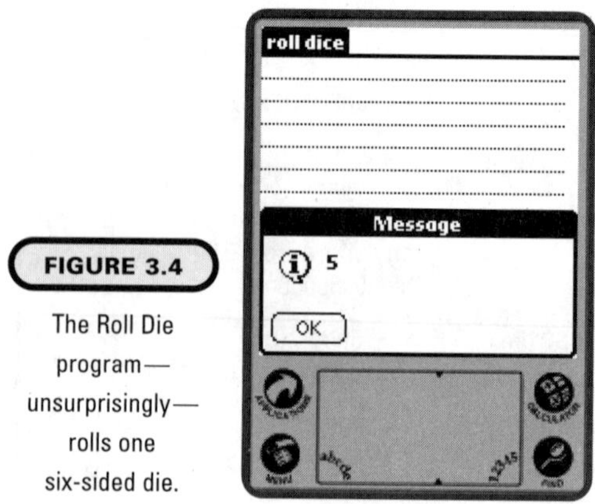

FIGURE 3.4

The Roll Die program—unsurprisingly—rolls one six-sided die.

This program may not be the most exciting thing you've ever seen, but it's an important step because it gives you the ability to add a sense of randomness to your games. More than that, you can control the level of randomness. A standard die is supposed to return values only from 1 to 6. This program shows you how to generate such a die, and also how to generate percentages, loaded dice (of course, *you* would never write a program that uses them), 20-sided dice, or just about any type of random value you could wish. Here's the code for Roll Die:

```
//rollDie
//Demonstrates random function
// Andy Harris, 03/07/01

main(){
  int roll;

  clear();
```

```
    title("roll dice");
    roll = random(6) + 1;
    alert(roll);
  } // end main
```

I created one int called "roll." The key line is this one:

```
roll = random(6) + 1;
```

The `random()` function is used to return a random integer value. It accepts one parameter, which is the number of values possible. `random(6)` will return an integer value from 0 to 5. (As you've seen, computers generally start counting at 0, not 1, so this is not too surprising.) Since I wanted a die that goes from 1 to 6, I just told it to make a 0–5 value, then add 1. Run the program several times until you are satisfied that the program generates random rolls in the correct range. You'll never see a value larger than 6 or smaller than 1.

Using the If Statement to Make Decisions

So far, all of your programs have been linear. They started at the first line and stepped through the instructions strictly in the order in which they appear in the program listing. This is fine, but sometimes you want the program's behavior to change based on some condition. For example, if you were making a dice game where rolling a 1 was a big deal, you might want the program to do something special whenever the die came up 1. Figures 3.5 and 3.6 illustrate exactly such a program.

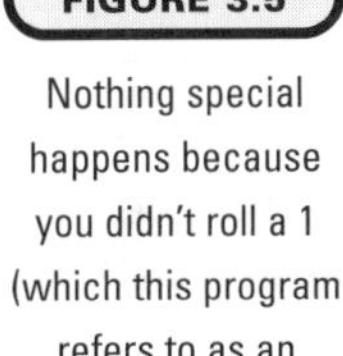

FIGURE 3.5

Nothing special happens because you didn't roll a 1 (which this program refers to as an *ace*).

FIGURE 3.6

This time it was an ace, so the program lavishly rewards you with a lovely and functional alert message.

The Find Ace Program

The Find Ace program is much like the Roll Die program, but it has one additional feature. Take a look at the code, and you'll see what it is:

```
//findAce
//Demonstrates if statement
//Andy Harris, 03/07/01

main(){
  int roll;

  clear();
  title("find ace");

  roll = random(6) + 1;

  puts(roll);
  if (roll == 1){
    alert("It's an ace!!");
  } // end if
  wait();
} // end main
```

The only part that is new is this segment:

```
  if (roll == 1){
    alert("It's an ace!!");
  } // end if
```

Conditions

The new segment of Roll Die contains the `if` keyword, followed by an expression in parentheses. The word *if* works in programming just as it does in English. Think of this example: "If you eat all your dinner, you can have dessert." The term *if* is followed by a condition (you must eat all your dinner). If that condition is met, you can have dessert. If the condition is not met, no dessert. The programming example is similar. The expression (roll == 1) is a condition, too. Conditions in programming tend to be a bit more formalized than in English, but the rules aren't too difficult. Conditions usually consist of a variable, a comparison operator from the list in Table 3.4, and a value. In this example, you are checking to see if the variable roll is equal to the value 1. Conditions must evaluate to true or false. If the roll is equal to the value 1, the condition will be true. If the roll is anything else, the condition is false.

As noted in Chapter 2, PocketC (like most variants of the C language) uses the equal sign (=) to refer to assignment rather than equality. When it needs to indicate that something has to be equal to something else—that is, to set a condition, it uses two equal signs strung together (==).

After the condition is a left curly brace ({) This indicates that a block of code will follow. All code between the left brace ({) and the right brace (}) will occur *only* if the condition is true. If the condition is false, control will jump to the next line of code after the right brace (}). It is traditional to indent the code between the braces, so you can tell that the code is part of a special structure. I also like to comment the right brace so I can tell what is ending. In the C-like languages, there are a lot of structures that use braces, so commenting and indenting can make your code a lot easier to follow.

TABLE 3.4 COMPARISON OPERATORS

Comparison Type	Operator	Example

equality	==	if(x==1){
		  alert("correct!");
		} // end if

inequality	!=	if(x != 1){
		  alert("that's not it...");
		} // end if

less than	<	if (x < 50){
		  alert ("too low");
		} // end if

greater than	>	if (x > 50){
		  alert ("too high");
		} // end if

less than or equal to	<=	if (x <= 50){
		  alert ("too low");
		} // end if

greater than or equal to	>=	if (x >= 50){
		  alert ("too high");
		} // end if

IN THE REAL WORLD

I said it back in Chapter 1, but it's worth saying again here: The way you use braces, indentation, and commenting to clarify your code make up your programming style. People get pretty passionate about their coding conventions. If you're in a class or writing programs professionally as part of a team, you'll usually be given some particular convention you'll be required to follow. If you're just programming for fun, you should still seek to develop a style that makes sense for you and makes your code easier to use and fix. The convention I adopt in this book is relatively straightforward and common, so it's not a bad place to start.

The Else Clause

The `if` statement is a very powerful tool. It has some other options that can make it even more powerful. As an example, look at the program illustrated in Figures 3.7 and 3.8.

Obviously, this is a kind of silly program, but it does illustrate one very important extension of the `if` statement. You can have one chunk of code that will occur if the condition is true, and you can have another chunk of code that will occur if the condition is false.

FIGURE 3.7

If the user gets an ace, the program says so.

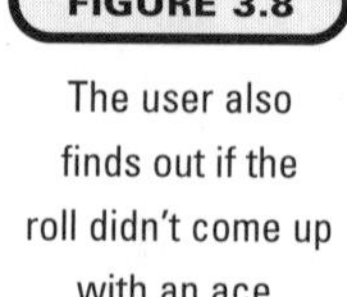

FIGURE 3.8

The user also finds out if the roll didn't come up with an ace.

The Ace Or Not Program

Here is the code listing for the Ace Or Not program, which demonstrates the `else` clause in action:

```
//aceOrNot
//demonstrates else clause
//Andy Harris, 03/07/01

main(){
  int roll;

  clear();
  title("ace or not");

  roll = random(5) + 1;

  puts(roll);
  if (roll == 1){
    alert ("Ace!!");
  } else {
    alert ("not an ace");
  } // end if
} // end main
```

It's a lot like the Find Ace program, but take a careful look at the `if` statement. The `if` statement is broken into two blocks of code. The first part occurs if the condition is true, and tells the user that an ace was found. The second part occurs if the condition was false. You can use an `else` clause like this to add code for when the condition is false. You can have as many lines of code as you need between `if` and `else`, and between `else` and `end if`.

Nesting If Statements

It is completely possible to have `if` statements inside other `if` statements. As an example, think about a program with two dice that should give a special bonus (I know, how about an alert statement?) when the user rolls 1 on each die. Such a program might look like Figure 3.9.

FIGURE 3.9

The user rolled snake eyes!

There are a couple of ways to get this kind of behavior, but my Snake Eyes program uses the notion of nested `if` statements. Look at the code to see what I mean:

```
//snakeEyes
//demonstrates nested if statement
//Andy Harris, 3/9/01

main(){
  int dieA;
  int dieB;

  clear();
  title("Snake Eyes");

  dieA = random(6) + 1;
  dieB = random(6) + 1;

  puts("A: " + dieA + "\n");
  puts("B: " + dieB + "\n");

  if (dieA == 1){
    if (dieB == 1){
      alert("snake eyes!");
    } // end dieB if
  } // end dieA if
  wait();
} // end main
```

This code looks a little more complicated than the earlier die-rolling programs, but most of the new material has to do with rolling two dice rather than one. The part that does the logic is at the very bottom of the code. The first `if` statement checks to see if dieA is 1. If it isn't a 1, the program moves on to the next line outside the "end dieA if" line, which pauses, then the program exits. If dieA is a 1, the condition is considered true, and the program checks dieB. If this condition is true, the player has snake eyes, so the program sends a colorful and elaborate message to that effect.

> **IN THE REAL WORLD**
>
> **Nested `if` structures like this are often used for error checking. If you are writing a program that analyzes an entire page of information, for example, you might want to run several checks on that information, and only proceed if every test comes out satisfactorily. You can generate a condition to test for each check, and put your code for processing the information inside all of the nested `if` statements. This will guarantee that the information is not processed if any of the conditions are not met.**

Comparing Multiple Values with Else If

The `else` clause is very useful, but sometimes you will want to check a variable against a number of possible values. To illustrate this point, consider the program illustrated in Figures 3.10 and 3.11.

This program takes the die roll and outputs the appropriate Spanish word for the number that appears. It has to check for each roll and set a value accordingly.

FIGURE 3.10

The roll is a 1, and the program says, "Uno."

FIGURE 3.11

The roll is a 5, and the program says, "Cinco."

Although this could be done with six different `if` statements, I did it with one long `if` statement. Take a look at the code, and you'll see how it works:

```
//dieSpanish
//demonstrates else if by typing out value of die
//Andy Harris, 03/07/01

main(){
  int roll;
  string dieVal;

  clear();
  title("Spanish Dice");

  roll = random(6) + 1;
  puts(roll);
  if (roll == 1){
    dieVal = "Uno";
  } else if (roll == 2){
    dieVal = "Dos";
  } else if (roll == 3){
    dieVal = "Tres";
  } else if (roll == 4){
    dieVal = "Cuatro";
  } else if (roll == 5){
    dieVal = "Cinco";
  } else if (roll == 6){
    dieVal = "Seis";
  } else {
    dieVal = "You must be cheating";
  } // end if
  alert(dieVal);
} // end main
```

This program works by creating a string variable that will hold the Spanish value for the die. I set up one large `if` statement with a number of `else if` clauses. Each invocation of `else if` allows me to test for a new condition. The `else` clause will be invoked if none of the other conditions were true. In this case, it should never happen, because I've carefully controlled the possible values. Still, I put in the `else` clause just to demonstrate how it works—and because it's a good habit for any programmer to have.

Comparing Multiple Values with Switch

It is possible to use `if` statements for all kinds of branching behavior, but PocketC supports another kind of branching statement that specializes in exactly the kind of situation you saw in the dieSpanish program. Often you will find yourself with one variable that has a number of possible values. In this situation, you might find the `switch` statement to be more useful. Here is another version of the Spanish Dice program that uses the `switch` statement. (I won't give you a screen shot because it looks exactly like the last program to the user—all the changes are internal.)

```
//dieSwitch
//illustrates how the switch statement works
//Andy Harris, 06/16/01

main(){
  int roll;
  string dieVal;

  clear();
  title("Spanish Dice (switch version)");

  roll = random(6) + 1;
  puts(roll);
  switch(roll){
    case 1:
      dieVal = "Uno";
      break;
    case 2:
      dieVal = "Dos";
      break;
    case 3:
      dieVal = "Tres";
      break;
    case 4:
      dieVal = "Cuatro";
      break;
    case 5:
      dieVal = "Cinco";
      break;
```

```
    case 6:
      dieVal = "Seis";
      break;
    default:
      dieVal = "You must be cheating";
      break;
  } // end switch
  alert(dieVal);
} // end main
```

The switch structure is quite easy to use. After the `switch` statement, you are expected to put the name of a variable or expression. PocketC allows you to switch on any type of variable, including strings. (Most versions of the C language only allow you to use switch on integers or characters). Once you have defined the variable you want to work with, use the `case` statement to describe the various values for which you are testing. Note that at the end of the case line is a colon(:), not a semicolon (;). After the case line, you can put as many lines of code as you wish. All the code between the `case` and the `break` statement will occur if the variable has the value associated with that case. The default case is a special case which works just like the `else if` clause in the previous program. If none of the other cases is true, the default case will get the program control. It's a good idea to put a default case in, just to anticipate strange new situations.

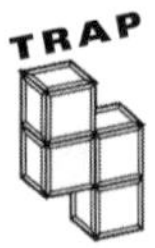

It is very easy to forget the break statements, particularly if you are familiar with Visual Basic, which does not require them. You must use the break statement to end each case, or the code will continue as if the next case were also true.

Getting Random Percentages

The `random()` function is very useful, but sometimes you want other kinds of random values, like when generating percentages. For example, you might write a game in which the user has a 50 percent chance of opening a treasure chest. The `rand()` function excels at exactly this kind of situation. To illustrate it, I'll write (another) silly and pointless program.

The weatherman has forecast a 40 percent chance of rain for tomorrow in my area. I decided to write a program that would predict rain 40 percent of the time, so I could really get a feel for the likelihood of rain. Figure 3.12 shows the output of the program.

FIGURE 3.12

Forty percent of the time, this program says it will rain.

Here's the source code that generates this admittedly useless program:

```
//willItRain
//demonstrates rand function and percentages
//Andy Harris, 03/07/01

main(){
  float roll;
  float chanceOfRain = 0.40;

  clear();
  title("will it rain?");

  roll = rand();
  puts(roll);
  puts("\n\n");
  puts(format(roll, 3));
  if (roll < chanceOfRain){
    alert("it will rain");
  } else {
    alert("it will not rain");
  } // end if
} // end main
```

Forty percent is also written as .40. I stored that value in a float called `chanceOfRain`. It would be great if there were a function that returned a floating point random value between 0 and 1, because that value would be equal to or less than .40 exactly 40 percent of the time, and the random value would be higher than .40 exactly 60 percent of the time. (Well, it *would* be exact if the routines were perfectly random, which they are not, but it's close enough for most applications.) It might not surprise you that PocketC does supply exactly such a function, called `rand()`. The `rand()` function generates a random percentage value, from 0 to 1.

In my code, I assigned the results of a `rand()` call to the roll variable. I then compared that roll variable to `chanceOfRain`. The roll will be less than `chanceOfRain` 40 percent of the time, so if roll is less than `chanceOfRain`, I'll tell the user it will rain.

Making Sound with the Tone Statement

Palm-based PDAs have a tiny but functional speaker installed. While you won't be producing any symphonies, you can control this speaker in your PocketC programs. PocketC supports the `tone()` function for producing sound. The `tone()` function takes two parameters, frequency and duration. Frequency refers to the pitch of the sound. A larger value for frequency is a higher sound. The frequencies of a number of notes appear in Table 3.5:

TABLE 3.5 FREQUENCIES OF NATURAL NOTES

Note	low	medium	high
C	262	523	1047
D	294	587	1175
E	330	659	1319
F	349	698	1397
G	392	784	1568
A	440	880	1760
B	494	988	1976

This table contains approximate frequencies for the natural (no sharps or flats) notes. If you want a sharp, get the average of the note and the next note higher (there is no B sharp or E sharp). To get a flat, find the average of the note and its next lower note (there is no C flat or F flat). If you are unfamiliar with music notation, don't worry. You can still have fun playing around with sounds by modifying the next program in the chapter.

The other parameter of the tone statement is the duration. Duration is specified in terms of milliseconds. That is, 1000 milliseconds is a second, 500 milliseconds is half a second. If you want a low A to play for one half-second, you would use this command:

```
tone(440, 500);
```

The Mary Program

The program featured in Figure 3.13 demonstrates use of the tone command to make music. Obviously you can't hear the figure, but it shows the screen you get while the program plays "Mary Had a Little Lamb." You'll need to run the program to get the full effect.

FIGURE 3.13

Pocket music: it sounds better than it looks. . . .

To see how this program works, take a look at the source code:

```
//mary
//demonstrates how to make sound using the tone function
//Andy Harris, 3/9/01
```

```
main(){
  clear();
  title("Mary Had a Little Lamb");

  //define notes
  int c = 262;
  int d = 294;
  int e = 330;
  int f = 349;
  int g = 392;
  int a = 440;
  int b = 494;

  //define lengths
  int q = 500;        //quarter note
  int h = 1000;       //half note

  clear();
  title("Mary Had a Little Lamb");
  puts("\n\n\n");
  puts("If you don't hear anything");
  puts("make sure sound is enabled ");
  puts("in your PDA preferences.");

  //play song
  //mary had a little lamb...
  tone(e, q);
  tone(d, q);
  tone(c, q);
  tone(d, q);
  tone(e, q);
  tone(e, q);
  tone(e, h);

  //little lamb...
  tone(d, q);
  tone(d, q);
  tone(d, h);

  //little lamb...
```

```
  tone(e, q);
  tone(g, q);
  tone(g, h);

  //mary had a little lamb whose
  tone(e, q);
  tone(d, q);
  tone(c, q);
  tone(d, q);
  tone(e, q);
  tone(e, q);
  tone(e, q);
  tone(e, q);

  //fleece was white as snow
  tone(d, q);
  tone(d, q);
  tone(e, q);
  tone(d, q);
  tone(c, h);

} // end main
```

The first thing the program does is define some notes. To make life easier, I decided to store the frequencies of some of my favorite notes into variables. That way, when I want to play a C, I can just put the variable `c` in the tone statement and won't have to remember that C is 262Hz.I also decided to encode two durations. I decided to set a quarter note to last half a second (500 milliseconds) and a half note to be one second long (1000 milliseconds). These are all the durations I will need for my elaborate composition.

The song itself turned out to be easy to write once I had set up the variables. I just translated each note from some written music to the appropriate tone statement. For example, the first note in "Mary Had a Little Lamb" is a quarter note E, so my first tone statement is

```
tone(e, q);
```

You can translate any music you wish to this type of format. If you are clever with math and music theory you can figure out how to transpose your music into another key without rewriting it, or how to change the speed of your music.

Storing Code in Functions

Now that you know how the computer stores information, it would be a good idea to see how it stores instructions. So far, you have built all your programs with only one function, called `main()`. When the program starts, it automatically executes any instructions found in the `main()` function. While this is fine for very simple programs, the single function can get so long that it is difficult to read. Programmers like to break their programs into segments that can stand somewhat alone because it is much easier to debug code that is subdivided.

The SOS Program

As a way to illustrate the use of functions, the program illustrated in Figure 3.14 automatically generates an SOS signal in Morse code. (It might come in handy if you're stranded on a desert island with your PDA, I suppose. . . .)

Morse code, if you recall, is a signaling scheme that uses a sequence of short and long signals to encode letters and other values. (You could think of it as a precursor to ASCII notation.) It would be fun to have the PDA actually produce tones for the dot and the dash, as Morse code was frequently used in radio and telegraph applications as an audio signal. Here is some code that will generate a dot:

```
tone(440, 200);
sleep(300);
```

The first line plays a short tone. The second command tells the computer to pause briefly. The `sleep` command accepts as its single parameter an amount of time in milliseconds to wait without processing. The `sleep` command is impor-

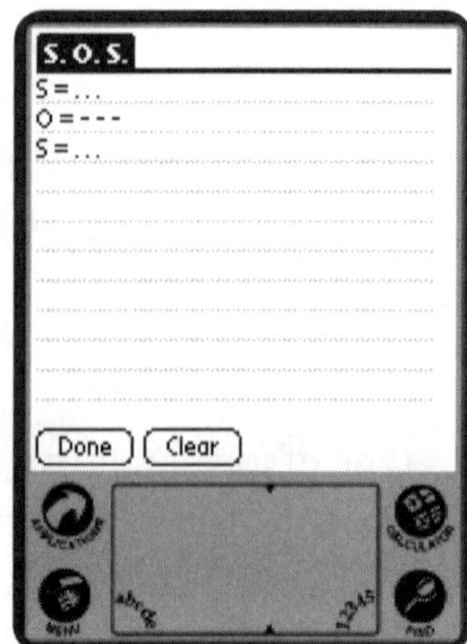

FIGURE 3.14

This program displays and plays the signal for SOS.

tant in Morse code—if the program just plays a series of dots immediately one after another, you might not be able to tell where one begins and another ends.

This similar pair of lines would play a dash:

```
tone(440, 400);
sleep(500);
```

The tone will be twice as long, and there is a somewhat longer pause, as well.

Each character in Morse code is made up of several dots and dashes. It would be very convenient if you could invent a new command which does both the tone and sleep command, so your program could simply say “make a dot” or “make a dash” and the appropriate lines of code would automatically occur.

In the following program, I created functions for dot and dash to do exactly that:

```
//sos
//Returns morse code for sos
//demonstrates function calls
//Andy Harris, 03/07/01

dot(){
  tone(440, 200);
  sleep(300);
} // end dot

dash(){
  tone(440, 400);
  sleep(500);
} // end dash

pause(){
  sleep(300);
} // end pause

main(){

  clear();
  title("S. O. S.");

  puts ("S = . . . \n");
  puts ("O = - - - \n");
```

```
    puts ("S = . . . \n");

    //S
    dot();
    dot();
    dot();
    pause();

    //O
    dash();
    dash();
    dash();
    pause();

    //S
    dot();
    dot();
    dot();
    pause();

} // end main
```

The exciting part of this program is that the code is *encapsulated.* To make an S, I need to make three dots. I don't really care at this point how an S is made, I just want to do it three times. At the top of the program, I have defined a new function `dot()`. The `dot()` function has all the code that actually plays a dot. In PocketC you have to define a function before you use it, so you'll usually write all your utility functions at the top of the program. Once I have defined the `dot()` and `dash()` functions, I can use them in my program just like the functions that are built into PocketC.

Reading Graffiti Input

To make a Morse code reader, you will need another input method. It would be nice to have some technique that can read just one character from the Graffiti area without popping up a dialog box at all. You actually already have such a technique at your disposal. The `wait()` method that you have been using all along has the ability to send some information back to the program. As you recall, `wait()` causes the program to pause until the user taps the screen or enters a keystroke. If the user enters a Graffiti stroke, that value is assigned to the `wait()` function and can be assigned to a variable. Here's a program that demonstrates this functionality:

```
//grafReader
//waits for a character of graffiti and repeats it
//Andy Harris, 03/13/01

main(){
  char myChar;

  clear();
  title("graffiti reader");

  puts("please enter a keystroke");
  puts("\n\n);

  myChar = wait();
  puts("You typed " + myChar);
  wait();
} // end main
```

In this program, I assigned the value of the first wait function call to the `myChar` variable. Before, I never really cared how the user indicated the end of input, but this time, if the user enters a character, the value of the `wait()` function will be passed to `myChar`. I then returned that value to the user.

Back to the Morse Code Program

The Morse code program turns out to be pretty simple. You already know all the programming you need. I won't have to introduce a single new programming concept. The only thing that you might not already know is the Morse code values themselves. Table 3.6 shows the main characters.

While the program itself is not very complex, it is long enough that the code would be easier to follow in smaller pieces. You still might want to examine the entire code from the CD-ROM that accompanies this book, though.

TABLE 3.6 MORSE CHARACTER EQUIVALENTS

Character	Morse	Character	Morse
A	0 -	N	- 0
B	- 0 0 0	O	- - -
C	- 0 - 0	P	0 - - 0
D	- 0 0	Q	- - 0 -
E	0	R	0 - 0
F	0 0 - 0	S	0 0 0
G	- - 0	T	-
H	0 0 0 0	U	0 0 -
I	0 0	V	0 0 0 -
J	0 - - -	W	0 -
K	- 0 -	X	- 0 0
L	0 - 0 0	Y	- 0 - -
M	- -	Z	- - 0 0

Defining Some Functions

The first part of the program sets up the normal comments, then defines a few functions I use throughout the rest of the program:

```
//morseCode
//Returns an input character in morse code
//Andy Harris, 03/07/01

dot(){
  tone(440, 200);
  sleep(300);
} // end dot

dash(){
  tone(440, 400);
  sleep(500);
} // end dash
```

```
pause(){
  sleep(300);
} // end pause
```

The `dot` and `dash` functions are copied directly from the SOS program. Since all the functionality of `dot` and `dash` are described here, I won't have to worry about them anywhere else. Also, If I decide to change how I make these tones, I only have to change it once in the function and that change will be reflected everywhere in the program.

Reading a Graffiti Stroke

The `main` function starts by setting up the screen and asking for a character. It then waits for input with the `wait()` method, and assigns the value of the keystroke to a variable.

```
main(){
  char theChar;

  clear();
  title("morse code practice");

  puts("enter a graffiti character \n");
  puts("and you'll hear it in Morse code! \n");
  puts("\n\n\n");

  theChar = wait();
```

Generating the Morse Code Signal

The next part of the code analyzes the value of the character with a large `if` and `else if` structure:

```
if (theChar == 'a'){
    puts("A:   o - \n");
    dot();
    dash();
  } else if (theChar == 'b'){
    puts("B:   - o o o \n");
    dash();
    dot();
```

```
    dot();
    dot();
  } else if (theChar == 'z'){
    puts("Z:   - - o o \n");
    dash();
    dash();
    dot();
    dot();
  } else {
    puts("Sorry, I don't know that one... \n");
    puts("Tap the screen to end the program\n");
    wait();
  } // end if
} // end main
```

Note that I didn't show the entire code because it is very repetitious, and you can see it in its entirety on the CD-ROM that accompanies this book. The `if` statement checks for each character, and if that was the character input, it generates the correct screen output and Morse code tones. Note that I have an `else` clause to catch any other kind of input. If the user tapped the screen or entered a punctuation character, the program doesn't have a way to generate the proper Morse code signal, so it explains this to the user.

Summary

This chapter covered some of the most important territory in programming: how computers work with various types of information, including integers, real numbers, characters, and strings; how computers make basic decisions using the `if` statement; and how to modify the `if` statement with `else` and `else if` clauses, as well as how to nest `if` statements to make even more powerful types of commands. It also covered the basic mathematical operations and functions, including how to generate random numbers, as well as how to play musical tones through the speaker, and how to read Graffiti input directly from the PDA. If you've got all that down, you should be very proud of your efforts. The next chapter shows you how to repeat parts of a program, giving you even more control of your Palm device.

CHALLENGES

1. Add an `if` statement to the Math Machine program so that it prints "error" if the user tries to divide by 0.
2. Add more functionality to the Math Machine program: Have it generate x raised to the yth power, or log(x), or the square root of x.
3. Write a program that does a basic conversion that you frequently need. For example, in some book designs one printed page is 350 words. When I want to know how many pages a chapter I'm working on will run, I'd like to have a program that reads in the number of words, divides it by 350, and returns the number of pages. That was one of the first PocketC programs I ever wrote.
4. Write a Math Quiz program that asks the user a couple of simple math questions and checks to see if the answers are correct.
5. Modify the Math Quiz program so that it randomly generates numbers for the user to figure out. (One hint: for division problems, randomly generate two numbers and multiply them together, then give the user one of the original numbers and their product. Have the user guess the other randomly generated number.)
6. Write a program that creates loaded dice that will show up as 1 half of the time. (Hint: create a random value 1 to 12.)
7. Write your own song. Use mathematical operations to generate any *accidental* (sharp or flat) tones you need, or to change octaves.

Repeating Behavior and Larger Programs: The Micro Football Game

By now you know how to store information in the computer using variables. You can get information in from the user and back to the user. You can manipulate various kinds of data, and you can implement basic decision-making using the `if` structure. Although these skills allow you to write some interesting programs, your programs still lack the ability to repeat. For example, the Morse Code Generator in Chapter 3 only generates the Morse code for one character—then the program stops. It would be better if the program continued waiting for new characters until somehow the user signaled the end of the message. In this chapter, you will look at ways to build more robust programs. Specifically, you'll learn the following techniques:

- Designing a program—rather than just falling into it
- Writing custom functions that can accept parameters
- Returning a value from a custom function
- Creating a function prototype
- Repeating a section of code based on a condition
- Repeating a section of code a certain number of times
- Working with variable scope
- Managing large programs that will not fit in one memo document

Introducing the Micro Football Game

This chapter's program simulates a (much simplified) game of American football. The basic premise of the game is that you want to move the ball to the other end of the field to score a touchdown. Figure 4.1 shows the first screen of the game, which provides some simple instructions.

The player must choose from a series of plays, which are shown in Figure 4.2.

The middle run is reasonably likely to succeed, but will result in low yardage. The long pass will be successful only a small percentage of the time, but when it does succeed it has the potential to gain some significant yardage. The punt play is used when the player wishes to punt the ball to the other team, and the field goal is used to attempt a scoring kick. The player chooses a play by entering a number into the input box. Figures 4.3 and 4.4 show the results.

If the play succeeds, the ball is moved forward some random amount. (In general, the riskier the play, the farther the ball is moved). If the play fails, the ball is not moved at all.

The player has four downs (turns) to move the ball at least ten yards. If the ball is moved ten yards, the player gets another four downs. If the player has not moved the ball forward ten yards the opponent gets the ball, and has a chance to score.

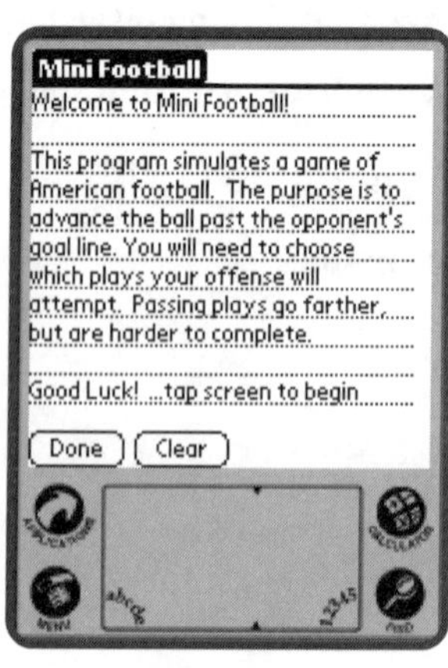

FIGURE 4.1

When the player starts the game, a page of instructions appears.

FIGURE 4.2

This menu shows the possible plays the player can choose.

FIGURE 4.3

The play might or might not succeed.

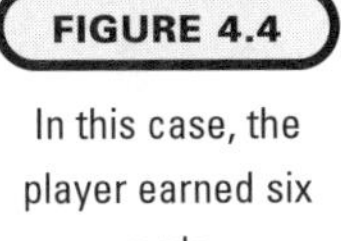

FIGURE 4.4

In this case, the player earned six yards.

When either side scores, the program posts the results as shown in Figure 4.5. The game lasts for what it calls "60 minutes," although each minute is considered the time needed to select and run a play.

This game is a reasonable (if highly simplified) facsimile of the rules of American football, and it provides an interesting diversion. The game is also interesting from a programming perspective because it is a little more complex than any of the programs you have seen before. The game has a number of component pieces, and the code is longer than what I've presented so far. Even an experienced programmer would probably encounter problems writing this program from scratch.

FIGURE 4.5

A scoreboard appears, describing the current (gloomy) situation.

Designing a Program: The STAIR Process

Computer programs are a combination of information and instructions; you are learning how to combine these elements to make programs. There is another side to developing programs that is equally important—experienced programmers have learned that the key to good programming is to have some kind of strategy in mind.

Of all the useful strategies for writing programs—and there are lots of them—the one I've found most successful for beginning programmers is the *STAIR technique.* Developed by a team from Indiana University in the mid-1990s, STAIR describes a process for moving from a general statement of some programming problem to a finished program. In a nutshell, here's what it involves:

- ***S*tatement**. You have to specify what you're trying to do before you can do it.
- ***T*ools**. You need to assemble tools for any job, whether they're hammers or programming routines.
- ***A*lgorithm**. Though it may be tempting to jump right in, the work goes better if you take the time to develop an algorithm—that is, a strategy—for using the tools to solve the problem.
- ***I*mplementation**. Once you've got an approach and a tool kit, you have to do the actual programming.
- ***R*efinement**. The first cut at a program almost never does exactly what was intended—you have to exercise it a bit and polish up the parts that don't work as planned.

In the Real World

When developing STAIR, we had a hard time finding an acronym that would work. One night I had a dream about climbing a set of stairs. I sat up in bed and said, "That's it!" out loud. After I told my wife that there was nothing wrong and she could go back to sleep, I wrote down the acronym on a notepad I keep by the bed for just such emergencies.

There actually is a programming lesson in this: Many times you will find the best solutions for your programming problems when your mind is relaxed and not directly thinking about the problem. If you find yourself getting frustrated, take a little break. The solution to one of your problems may come to you in a dream.

When you look at the code for the mini football game toward the end of this chapter, you will be able to see how it was written. You'll understand how the code works, but you may not really know how the program was imagined. It is one thing to look at code that already works, but it is quite a different process to write a program from scratch. Often you will find yourself staring at a blank computer screen, wondering what to do next, or you will be stuck with some strange error message and have no clue what to do next. A problem-solving method such as STAIR is the way past such obstacles. Since the goal is for you to write your own programs, not just be able to read mine, I'll go over how I started to think about the football game as an illustration of the STAIR process.

Stating the Problem

The "S" in STAIR is a reminder to *state the problem.* While this seems like a fairly obvious step, it is actually the most difficult part of programming. Programming is all about solving problems. It is essential to figure out exactly what it is you want your program to do, or you may not know when you have achieved your goal. Following are some characteristics of a well-defined problem statement:

- **It is unambiguous**. You have clearly stated all of the major goals of the problem, and identified things that you *do not* expect the program to do.
- **It is well defined**. You have thought about the scope of the program. You've picked a problem that you anticipate will be within your resources to write.
- **It is clear**. Your statement of the problem should *not* use technical jargon, or any programming words. The idea here is to make sure that you can say in English exactly what it is you want to do. It is very tempting to start describing in technical detail exactly what you plan to do. Resist the temptation. Start by describing what you *intend* to accomplish. Later you can concentrate on *how* you will do it.
- **It is written down**. When you start writing code, you are going to get frustrated and confused. This happens even to the pros, every day. As you write code, you'll be tempted to change things on the fly so much that at some point you may not even remember what you were trying to get done. That's when it's good to pull out the statement of the problem and reorient yourself.

Here is the original statement of the problem I used when I started to write the mini football game:

```
Write a game that simulates a much-simplified game of football. The
user will choose a play from a small menu, and the program will
determine whether that play was successful. The plays should work
something like real football; some plays are likely to succeed but
will result in short yardage. Other plays will be riskier, but more
rewarding when they succeed. If the player scores or reaches fourth
down without gaining at least 10 yards, the computer will get the
ball, and will be given a chance to score. The game should have a
time limit, and the game play must be challenging enough to be
interesting, but not so hard that the user never wins.
```

There might be better ways to state the problem, but that was the one I used; and since I succeeded in writing the program, it must have been pretty close. You will see that I did not anticipate everything, and I left a few elements pretty vague, but the general outline is there.

Tool Identification

The "T" in STAIR refers to the *tools* you'll need to use. As a programmer, you have access to a wide assortment of tools. In fact, it is sometimes this wealth of tools that can make your job so difficult. The next stage of the process is to identify a set of tools that might help you solve your problem. There are many different kinds of tools. The various commands and structures of your programming language are one obvious set of tools. The basic constructs in programming (such as variables and conditions) constitute another set. You might have other tools available such as online help, printed documentation, or this book. You might also be able to identify still other tools, such as software libraries, application programs (an image editor, for example), or prewritten code that you can modify.

For the mini football program, I had an unusual constraint. I could only use tools that I have already introduced to you or plan to show you in this chapter. That meant the program had to be written with the small but powerful set of programming concepts you have learned so far in this book. Following is the list of tools I identified, along with a preliminary list of the aspects of the program those tools would have to work on:

```
Tools I'll need:

Variables to handle the data of the game. Data include

  *  Player and computer score

  *  Down

  *  Position on field

A menu for determining which play the user wants to try. User inter-
action requires the following operations

  *  Clear screen

  *  Print choices on screen

  *  Get input from user

A way to calculate the results of a play choice. Elements include

  *  Some kind of random number technique

  *  Likelihood of success (determined by play choice)

  *  Yardage gained (also determined by play choice but randomized)

A technique for determining the computer's behavior when it has the
ball. Behavior

  *  May be very simple

  *  Random, but based on starting position

Some kind of scoreboard. Scoreboard maintenance requires

  *  Clear screen

  *  Print time left, score, down, and position

A timer of some sort. Timer action should

  *  Simulate the finite time in a football game

  *  Have either an actual time construct or maybe a loop
```

I started this list by thinking of a way I could organize the main parts of the game, and then I went through that list and thought about which programming constructs I might need to make that particular section of code work. Please note how inexact the solution is. When I started to write this program, I wasn't exactly sure how I was going to solve the problem I had stated. In fact, you will find that my final statement of the problem deviates slightly from this plan. However, the list of tools identified in this section got me a lot closer to a finished program than the statement of the problem did. In fact, you might think of the Tools step as a way of restating the problem in terms of a possible set of tools.

Generating an Algorithm

The term *algorithm* is just another word for a plan, or strategy. The "A" part of the STAIR process involves developing an algorithm. You might think of this as a way of looking more carefully at the tools you will need and fleshing out the details. If you look at every step of an algorithm and you can say "I can write code for that," your algorithm is ready to go. If you cannot do so, you might either need to refine your algorithm (maybe by breaking some complex task into smaller tasks) or learn a new skill. (The football program requires a loop, for example, and you haven't learned loops yet.)

Here's my algorithm for the football program. Note that it goes through the sections identified in the tools statement and provides much more detail on each one.

```
Main Variables. The first task is to create a series of variables
used throughout the program. The following table sets them out in
detail:

-----------------------------------------------------------------

Variable       Type   Description                           Start value
position       int    yards until touchdown. 80 is on           80
                      own 20-yard line, 0 is touchdown
play           int    number representing which play
                      user chose
yardsLeft      int    number of yards left until first
                      down                                      10
down           int    which down player is on (will
                      only be 1-4)                               1
playerScore    int    points player has earned                   0
oppScore       int    points opponent has earned                 0
timeLeft       int    time left until game is over              60
-----------------------------------------------------------------
```

I was actually only able to finish this list of variables after writing the rest of the algorithm. It's a great idea to start a table like this and keep posting elements to it so that you'll have a running idea about the main variables of your program.

The `main()` function. The main function will act as a controller.

* Make for loop with time going from 60 to 0
* Let player pick a play (**`choosePlay()`** function)
* Run the play (**`runPlay()`** function)
* Show the score (**`scoreBoard()`** function)

End the loop

* Congratulate user for victory if appropriate

The `choosePlay()` function. This function will generate a menu. The user will be able to choose which play from a list of choices presented on the screen.

* **`clear`** and **`title`** statements
* **`puts`** statements--one play choice per line
* **`getsi`** function to store user's play choice
* **`choosePlay()`** function returns choice

The `runPlay()` function. Given a particular play, this function will determine how likely it is that the play will succeed, and if it is successful, will determine how far the ball is moved.

* Define local variables as in the following table:

Variable	Type	Description	Start value
yardsWon	int	How many yards the play has won. Limited by yardMax.	
playResult	float	Random value used to determine if the play succeeds. Compared to difficulty.	
yardMax	int	Maximum yards gained if the play is successful. Determined by playChoice.	
difficulty	float	Percentage likelihood that play will succeed. Determined by playChoice.	

* Define normal plays:

  Set **yardMax** and difficulty based on play

  Calculate whether the play succeeded

  Determine new position if play succeeded

  check for touchdown

  check for first down

  check for "lost on downs"

* Set up field goal:

  Use random number generation based on position

  Field goal should be unlikely past 40-yard line

  Give ball to opponent

* Define punt:

  Move ball some random amount down the field

  Give ball to opponent

The oppBall() function. Set up the program to control opponent's ball.

* Move the position some random amount
* Display how far the opponent has moved
* Check for opponent score
* Return ball to player

The showScore() function. Display the score as needed.

* Determine field position from position (position 80 becomes "your 20-yard line")
* Print player, opponent scores
* Print position
* Print down
* Print yards to go until first down
* Print time remaining
* Pause until user taps screen

The algorithm for the football game is very detailed (although you will find it is still missing some steps). It is worth noting that all the most important programming is finished by the time you have completed the algorithm, and you haven't even turned the computer on yet! The best computer programming generally happens away from the computer, not at the keyboard.

Implementation

The "I" in STAIR stands for *implementation*. Once the algorithm is done, it is time to implement it. To implement the algorithm simply means to code it into the language in question. In this case, I will convert the football game to PocketC code. However, I could implement exactly the same algorithm in any other programming language that I know (or care to learn). Algorithms are relatively universal.

In the Real World

I once wrote a program that was used for a series of beginning programming classes. I used a language that only works on the Microsoft Windows platform (Visual Basic), because I knew the language well and because all of our labs used Windows. About a year later, I was asked to teach the same course in a television studio. I eagerly accepted the opportunity, but then I found out that the studio did not have a Windows machine. I'd have to teach using a Macintosh, and my program was written for Windows! Fortunately, I knew another language (Java) that works on Macintoshes, and I still had the algorithm from my first version. Developing the algorithm for the program in the first place was difficult, but translating it to a new language was not nearly as challenging as rewriting it from scratch. If I had not developed and stored my algorithm, however, I might well have had a hard time recreating the program for the new platform.

The nice thing about implementation is that it is a fairly simple process. All you should have to do is look at each block of the algorithm and translate it into a line or two of PocketC code. If you don't know how to translate the algorithm into code, you may need to rethink the algorithm or learn a new tool.

Refining Your Program

The last part of the STAIR process is *refinement*. Even if you plan your program with exceptional care, it is almost guaranteed not to work the first time. The refinement step generally involves looking at each aspect of the program that is not working. You then try to ascertain exactly what is going wrong and correct the error. Generally, this may involve looking back at all the other STAIR steps: Are you solving the right problem? Have you identified all the tools you might need? Did you develop your algorithm fully? Did you implement it correctly?

The refinement step is never easy, but if you have designed your program well, it is much less challenging than it would be if you just started coding and then tried to run the resulting beast.

Using Loops to Repeat

The football game will require a few new programming elements you have not seen before. Most importantly, the football game involves a lot of repetition. It is important to have a mechanism for repeating fragments of the program. PocketC actually includes two different mechanisms for repeating your code.

Using a While Loop to Repeat Behavior

Perhaps the most obvious need is to make a program repeat some of its behavior. PocketC provides a structure called a `while` loop, which is used for exactly this purpose.

The Keep Going Program

The Keep Going program is trivial, but it illustrates a very important point. The program, featured in Figures 4.6 and 4.7, demonstrates the new structure called a loop. You can write code so that a part of the code repeats for an indefinite amount of time.

FIGURE 4.6

This program asks the user whether to continue.

FIGURE 4.7

Since the user said "Y" the question appears again. This time the user does not wish to continue, and the program will end.

Conditions and Loops

Here is the code for the Keep Going program:

```
//keepGoing
//Demonstrates while loop
//Andy Harris, 03/19/01

main(){
  string keepGoing = "Y";

  clear();
  title("Keep Going");
  while (keepGoing == "Y"){
    keepGoing = gets("Keep going? (Y/N)");
    keepGoing = strupr(keepGoing);
  } // end while
} // end main
```

The part of the code that continues is enclosed inside braces following the statement while (keepGoing == "Y"). The `while` statement expects a condition, just as the if statement does. The code in the braces will be repeated as long as the condition is evaluated as true. As soon as the condition is evaluated as false, the condition ends. For example, when this program begins, the value of the keepGoing variable is "Y". When the `while` statement first occurs, the condition (keepGoing == "Y") is true, because the value of `keepGoing` is equal to the value "Y". Inside the loop, the program asks for a new value for `keepGoing` and translates that value into uppercase. The end of the `while` loop tells the computer to reevaluate the condition. If the user entered "Y" (or "y") the condition will still be true, and the code will execute again. If the user entered anything else, the code inside the loop will not execute; instead, program control will continue with the next line of code after the loop. In this case, there is no more code after the loop, so the program ends.

Preventing Endless Loops

Loops are very powerful. This power can lead to problems if you do not plan well. It is important to carefully design your loops so they have the behavior you are expecting. The condition used for a `while` loop is especially important, because if it does not work correctly, your program will have serious problems. Some parts of the code may never execute at all, and other parts may continue indefinitely.

Most conditions involve one key variable. The variable used to control a condition for a while loop is often called the *sentry variable.* In the real world, sentries are guards who prevent or allow access to some sensitive area. A sentry variable provides the same service to a loop. To ensure that your loop runs correctly, begin by identifying the sentry variable in your condition. In the Keep Going program, the sentry variable was also called `keepGoing`. The `keepGoing` variable is a string, and its starting value is "Y".

Think about what would have happened if I had not initialized the value of `keepGoing` to "Y". The default value of a string variable is "", so when the computer first encountered the condition statement, `keepGoing` would have the value "". That would make the condition (keepGoing == "Y") false. The program would obediently jump to the next line of code outside the loop and end without ever asking the user for input. You will generally want to initialize your sentry variable so the loop can occur at least once.

Inside your loop, you'll also want to ensure that the sentry variable can be changed in a way that will trigger the condition. Imagine if I had written the `keepGoing` code in this way:

```
//keepGoing
//Demonstrates while loop
//Andy Harris, 03/19/01

main(){
  string keepGoing = "Y";

  clear();
  title("Keep Going");
  while (keepGoing == "Y"){
    //  ******* I forgot to ask for a new value for keepGoing!!! *******
    keepGoing = strupr(keepGoing);
  } // end while
} // end main
```

The initial value of `keepGoing` is "Y", so the loop will occur at least one time. However, I forgot to ask for a new value for the `keepGoing` variable. The end of the while loop will revert to the beginning of the loop and check the condition again. The condition will still be true and the loop will continue. In fact, the loop will continue forever, because the condition can never be false. Obviously, this is a bad situation. If your PDA has ever frozen up and required a reset, it is likely that some form of an endless loop was to blame. Fortunately, if you write a program that contains an endless loop, you probably won't have to reset your Palm to get out of it. Instead, you can usually just click the Done button in the PocketC environment.

If you find yourself facing an endless loop, all you have to do is press the application button to exit your programs. Unlike most modern computers, the Palm OS does not (yet) support multi-tasking. This means that if you run any program, you will immediately kill the one currently running. This provides you a convenient way to get out of endless loops.

Endless loops are usually easy to prevent, but when your code gets complex you'll find that still you accidentally make them once in a while. The key to preventing endless loops is to ensure that it is possible for your condition to become false.

Note that I used the `strupr()` function to convert a string into uppercase. This prevents one possible user error. If the user enters lowercase "y", the character will be converted to uppercase, so the condition will still be true. There are some other tricks I could have done to improve the input even more (such as examine the first character of the input, so that "y," "Y," "Yes," and "yea" would all register as "Y").

Using a For Loop to Repeat a Given Number of Times

The `while` loop is the only kind of looping structure you really need, but often programmers encounter a special kind of looping situation that merits its own structure. Very frequently you will be called upon to repeat some code a certain number of times. The proper structure for such a situation is called the for *loop.*

The Racer program

To illustrate the `for` loop, I wrote a program that simulates a 10-lap race. Figure 4.8 demonstrates the racer in action.

FIGURE 4.8

The racer goes from lap 1 to lap 10. Note that I didn't show every single screen.

The code used to generate the racer program is straightforward. The only new element is the `for` loop.

```
//racer
//demonstrates for loops
//Andy Harris, 03/19/01

main(){
  int lap;

  clear();
  title("The Racer");
  for(lap = 1; lap <=10; lap++){
    alert("now on lap: " + lap);
  } // end for loop
} // end main
```

The `for` statement has three parts, separated by semicolon (;) characters. The first part is initialization. This segment initializes the sentry variable. In this particular case, I am using `lap` as a sentry variable, and initializing it to the value 1, because I want to start on lap 1.

The next part of the `for` loop is the condition. In `for` loops, you don't have to put the condition in parentheses, but it's just like a regular condition in every other way. I want to display the lap if it is less than or equal to 10, so my condition for this race program is lap <= 10. As soon as lap is larger than 10, I want the loop to end.

The third part of the for construct is the increment. Each time through the loop, I want lap to increment by 1. The ++ operator is a shortcut for "increment by 1." (There is a related decrement operator (—) that means "decrement by 1.") The statement lap++ could also be written as lap = lap + 1, but lap++ is easier to write.

If you want to increment by some value other than 1, you would just write something like **lap = lap + 5**.

IN THE REAL WORLD

When computer scientists decided to create a new programming language based on the C language, they decided to indicate that this new language was "better" than C, so the new language was called C++. Since PocketC is a little bit simpler than standard C implementations, maybe it could be called C--!.

The advantage of the `for` loop is that all the necessary components for a good loop are contained in the loop statement itself, so it is more likely that the loop will act correctly.

Counting Backward

With a minor modification you can make a loop that counts backward rather than forward. Here's a variation of the Racer program that does exactly that:

```
//backRacer
//shows stepping through a for loop backward
//Andy Harris, 03/19/01

main(){
  int lap;

  clear();
  title("Back Racer");
  for(lap = 10; lap > 0; lap-){
    alert("Now on lap: " + lap);
  } // end for loop
} // end main
```

The only difference is in the `for` loop statement. I started `lap` at 10, stayed in the loop as long as `lap` is larger than 0, and decremented `lap` by 1 on each pass through the loop.

Returning a Value from a Function

Chapter 3 introduced functions. Functions are generally used to break the code into smaller pieces.

Functions have some other very important potential uses. You can assign parameters to a function, and you can return values from a function. You are already familiar with this behavior: Most of the built-in functions of PocketC take some type of parameter and operate on that value. (Think of the `puts()` function, for example. It only works if you send a string value to the function.) Also, many functions return a value to the user. The `gets()` function is a good example of this behavior; it returns a value that you can assign to a variable or use in some other way.

The In-to-Cm Program

Your custom functions can have exactly the same behavior. To see an example, take a look at the In-to-Cm program in Figures 4.9 and 4.10.

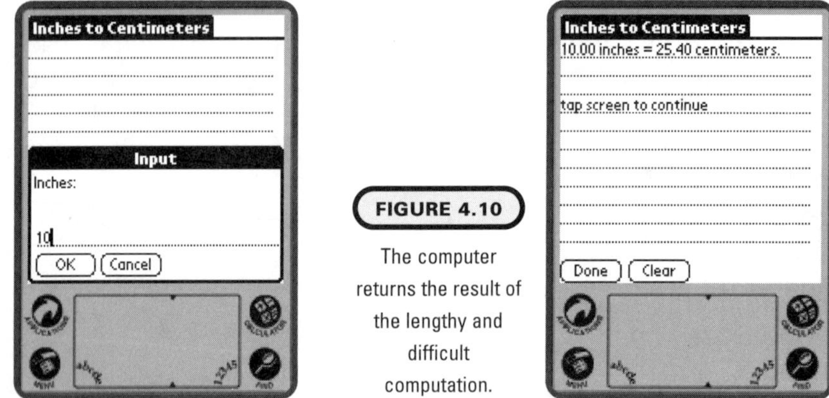

FIGURE 4.9 The user puts in a measurement in inches.

FIGURE 4.10 The computer returns the result of the lengthy and difficult computation.

Of course, this program can be written without a function, but the whole point of this example is to show how functions can be made more flexible. Here's some code that uses a function to manage the conversion:

```
//inToCm
//demonstrates functions with parameters
//and return values
//Andy Harris, 3/22/01

//function prototype
inToCm(float inches);

main(){
  float in;
  float cm;

  clear();
  title("Inches to Centimeters");
  in = gets("Inches: ");
  cm = inToCm(in);
  puts( format(in, 2) + " inches = ");
  puts( format(cm, 2) + " centimeters. \n");
  puts("\n");
```

```
  puts("\n");
  puts("tap screen to continue");
  wait();
} // end main

inToCm(float inches){
  return inches * 2.54;
} // end inToCm
```

The first thing to note in this program is the function prototype, which looks like this:

```
//function prototype
inToCm(float inches);
```

In earlier programs that used functions, the `main()` function was written last. This is because the `main()` function cannot call a function that it doesn't know exists. The basic rule is that you cannot call a function unless it has already been defined. Sometimes this causes problems in a complicated program because you might have two functions that call each other. Since they cannot both be defined first, you would seem to have an impasse. Fortunately, PocketC supports an idea called *function prototypes*. A function prototype is simply a line of code that describes what the function will look like. (It's usually the function's first line, but with the left brace replaced by a semicolon.) Some programmers prefer to simply generate a function prototype for every function in the program, so that they no longer need to worry about the order in which functions are written in the source code. Other programmers will only write function prototypes when one of the "chicken and egg" problems occurs. To keep the code simpler, I add function prototypes only when I feel they make the code flow in a more natural form.

Take a look at the `main()` function in the In-to-Cm program. It does the standard startup stuff, then gets a value of inches from the user. It then calls the `inToCm` function to figure out the centimeters. The actual code for the conversion is not in the `main()` function, but passed off to another function. This is nice because it allows the main function to concentrate on its primary job, which is getting information from and to the user. Whenever your programs start to get complicated, it's a good idea to encapsulate your code by packing some of the activity off to the functions.

Sometimes, as in this case, the function will need to communicate with the main program. First, the function will need to know how many inches to start with. Second, it will need to return a value (the number of centimeters) to the main program. Look again at the code for the `inToCm` function and you'll see how this is done:

```
inToCm(float inches){
  return inches * 2.54;
} // end inToCm
```

In your other function definitions, you've always left the parentheses empty. If you wish, you can place one or more special elements called *parameters* there. A parameter is simply a special variable declaration. Any program that calls this function is expected to send a float value to the function in parentheses. To set up a number of parameters to a function, just separate the variable declarations with commas. The code that calls the function must send the correct number of parameters, or the function will not be able to run.

You can also cause a program to send a value back to the calling program. The *return* statement has two main jobs. First, it immediately exits a function, without evaluating any other text in the function. Also, if it is followed by a value, that value is returned to the calling program, which can assign it to a variable.

Working in Multiple Files

PocketC is capable of working with reasonably large files, but you may sometimes run across limitations in the other software on your PDA. For example, the Memo Pad application built into the Palm software can only handle files of up to 4K (roughly 4,000 characters) long.

There are several ways around this limitation. Perhaps the easiest workaround is to use another editor, such as the desktop edition of PocketC or pedit. (Evaluation copies of both programs are available on the CD-ROM that accompanies this book.) Even if you are using the built-in text editor, the 4K limit poses no real problem, because you can write your code in multiple files. To see an example of this, look at the following program:

```
//incDemo
//demonstrates use of included files
//Andy Harris, 03/24/01

//function prototype
sayHi();

#include "otherFile"
```

```
main(){
  sayHi();
} //end main
```

The program looks extremely simple. Note that it does not include any `puts` statements, nor any output statements. Yet when the program is run, it produces the results shown in Figure 4.11.

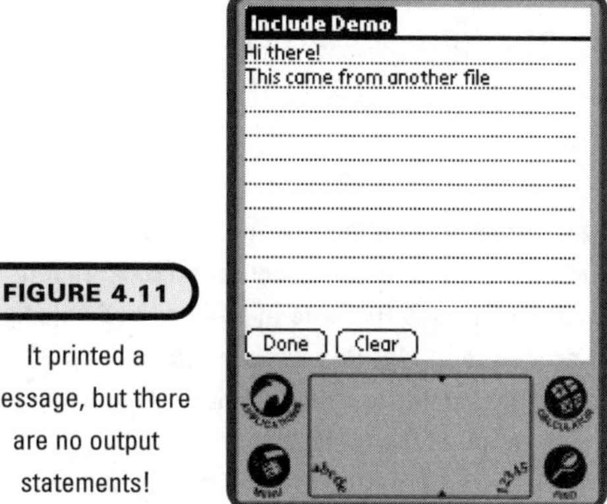

FIGURE 4.11

It printed a message, but there are no output statements!

The reason this program works is that there is a function available to it called `sayHi()`. The `sayHi()` function is stored in a totally different file on the PDA, called `otherFile`. Here's the code in the `otherFile` memo:

```
/$otherFile
//contains sayHi

sayHi(){
  clear();
  title("Include Demo");

  puts("Hi there! \n");
  puts("This came from another file");
  wait();
} //end sayHi
```

This memo contains the `sayHi()` function. There is nothing at all special about the `sayHi()` function. The only thing different at all about this file is the first line. Rather than starting with // as most PocketC programs do, it starts with /$. This special symbol still identifies the memo as a PocketC applet. However, the file is meant to be included in another program and not used as a stand-alone applet. It does not have a `main()` method, and it should not be compiled.

When you look back at the Inc Demo program, you'll see that I built a function prototype for the `sayHi()` function even though the function is in a different file. I then used this line to import otherFile:

```
#include "otherFile"
```

The #include statement is a special kind of command called a *preprocessor directive.* These commands do some special actions before the program is compiled. The #include command pulls in the contents of the other file and treats the program as if it were one large file.

The final version of the football game source code is provided in two different versions on the CD-ROM. The normal version of the program (MiniFB.pc) is too large to fit on one Memo Pad document, but it works fine in pedit or in the desktop edition of PocketC (I did most programming for this book in the desktop edition). If you are using Memo Pad as your text editor, take a look at MiniFBA.pc and the runPlay file. This is another version of the football game modified to fit in Memo Pad. I simply moved the `runPlay()` function to another file, and included that file into the main program.

Writing the Football Game

Now you are ready at last to write the football game. You have a solid plan, and you know a few more tools that may be of use. Although the program itself is a longer than others I've discussed, there is very little new information. Take a look at the code one chunk at a time, and it will make sense. Remember that the code you are looking at is the result of the implementation stage of STAIR, after some refinement. If you look at the code in this way, you can see how the implementation is nothing more than a further refinement of the algorithm translated into PocketC code.

The Variables and Function Prototypes

I started by defining function prototypes for all functions except `main()`. You don't have to declare a prototype for `main` because it's understood that your program will have a `main` function.

I then declared a set of variables that would be needed by every (or nearly every) function in the program. In all the earlier programs in the book, you have seen variable declarations only inside functions. Variables declared inside functions are called *local variables*. For the most part, it's a good idea to use local variables, because they will only have meaning when the function is running. As soon as the function has completed its job, the variable is destroyed. This eliminates the possibility that you might use the same variable name for two entirely different purposes. It also means that you don't have to keep track of all the variables in your program at once, just the ones used in the current function.

Local variables are good, but sometimes you have information that belongs to the entire program, not just to a function or two. If you declare a variable outside any functions, you are making a *global variable*. Global variables belong to the entire program, and can be accessed by any function of the program. In the football game, I use a series of global variables to handle the key information in the game. Here's the code that generates these global variables and function prototypes:

```
//MiniFB
//Demonstrates loops and conditions
//Andy Harris, 03/15/01

//function prototypes
splash();
int choosePlay();
oppBall();
runPlay(int play);
showScore();

//Global variable declarations
int position = 80;   //position on field (distance from goal)
int yardsLeft = 10;  //Yards left until first down
int down = 1;        //Which down the player is on
int playerScore = 0;//Player's score
int oppScore = 0;    //Computer opponent's score
int timeLeft = 60;   //Number of 'minutes' left in the game
```

The Splash Screen

I showed the game to a friend while testing it, and he had no clue how to get started. Therefore, though it wasn't included in the algorithm, I built a simple function to run at the very beginning, which explains the rules and sets up the stage. Programmers often refer to such a screen at the beginning of a program as a *splash screen.* It is quick and easy to code, and it adds a lot of professionalism to the program.

```
splash(){
  //generate a splash screen with instructions
  clear();
  title("Mini Football");
  puts("Welcome to Mini Football!");
  puts("\n");
  puts("\n");
  puts("This program simulates a game of American");
  puts(" football. The purpose is to advance the");
  puts(" ball past the opponent's goal line.");
  puts(" You will need to choose which plays your offense");
  puts(" will attempt. Passing plays go farther, ");
  puts(" but are harder to complete.");
  puts("\n");
  puts("\n");
  puts("Good Luck!  ");
  puts("...tap screen to begin");
  wait();
} // end splash
```

To build the splash screen, I just cleared the screen, added a title, and printed instructions to the screen.

The Play Selection Menu

The Play Selection menu is important because it provides the main input for the user. It involves printing out a screen full of choices, and accepting an input:

```
choosePlay(){
  //generate a menu to get the current play from the user
  //return a number representing the play chosen

  int localPlay;

  clear();
  title("Choose your play");
  puts("Choose your play\n\n");
  puts("  1) Middle Run \n");
  puts("  2) End Run \n");
```

```
  puts("   3) Screen pass \n");
  puts("   4) Long pass \n");
  puts("   5) Field goal \n");
  puts("   6) Punt \n");
  puts("\n\nYour play?");
  localPlay = getsi(65, 125, 15, "1");
  return localPlay;
} // end choosePlay
```

I decided to use the `getsi()` function to get user input, because it would integrate nicely into the screen.

Managing the Opponent's Behavior

The opponent's behavior is stored in a function called `oppBall()`. I decided to greatly simplify the opponent's behavior by making it a simple random number call whenever possible. I tried to figure out ways to make the opponent's behavior somewhat realistic while making the code as simple as possible. After playing the computer player a couple of times, you might be surprised at how simplistic the logic behind it is.

```
oppBall(){
  //manage opponent's turn

  int oppMove;

  //opponent has ball
  alert("Opponent has the ball");

  //move the ball some random number of yards
  oppMove = random(100);
  position = position +  oppMove;
  alert("Opponent moves " + oppMove + " yards");

  //check for opponent touchdown
  if (position > 100){
    alert("Opponent Scores!");
    oppScore = oppScore + 7;
    position = 80;
  } // end if
```

```
    //prepare to return ball to player
    down = 1;
    yardsLeft = 10;
} // end oppBall
```

All of the opponent's behavior is generated by a simple random number call. I generated a random number between 1 and 100, and added that to the value of position. If the resulting value is greater than 100, the computer scores a touchdown. I then reset the `down` and `yardsLeft` variables so they will make sense when the player receives the ball.

The runPlay Function

This function is the real heart of the program. Because it is a little longer and more involved, I will not show the code in one piece, but one section at a time.

The `runPlay()` function expects an integer, which will relate to the play the user chose. The function has a number of local variables that are used to determine the results of the play.

Local Variables in runPlay

```
runPlay(int play){
  //given a play, determine its results

  //local variables
  int yardMax;              //maximum yards. Higher for riskier plays
  float difficulty;         //percent likelihood play will succeed
  int yardsWon;      //number of yards won (random 0-yardMax)
  float playResult;     //whether play succeeded (random 0-1)
```

Checking the Play Type

The next section of the code simply examines the play number to see if it is one of the basic (nonkicking) plays:

```
//check for the play types
  if (play == 1){
    //Middle Run
    yardMax = 10;
    difficulty = 0.80;
  } else if (play == 2){
    //End Run
```

```
    yardMax = 15;
    difficulty = 0.60;
  } else if (play == 3){
    //Screen Pass
    yardMax = 30;
    difficulty = 0.50;
  } else if (play == 4){
    //Long Pass
    yardMax = 60;
    difficulty = 0.30;
```

For each play, I set two variables. The `yardMax` variable is used to determine how many yards the player will earn if the play succeeds. The average successful play will earn `yardMax` / 2 yards. I also set another variable called `difficulty`. This variable represents the difficulty of the play as a percentage. I decided to let the inside run succeed 80 percent of the time, but the long pass succeed only 30 percent of the time. I tried to balance the difficulty of the play with the potential reward. To change the difficulty of the entire game, you can manipulate these values.

Looking for Field Goal

Next the program checks to see if the player is attempting a field goal:

```
} else if (play == 5){
    //Field Goal
    if (random(60) > position){
      //50% successful on 30 yard line - farther away, less likely
      alert("field goal is good!");
      playerScore = playerScore + 3;
      //opponent starts on own 20 yard line
      position = 20;
    } else {
      alert("field goal is not good.");
    } // end if
    oppBall();
    return
```

I played around with a number of formulas for managing a field goal, and this one seemed to give the best balance of simple code and realistic results. I checked to see if a random (0–60) number was larger than the current position. The closer the player is to the opponent's goal line (where position is 0), the more likely it is that the random number will be larger than the position. I chose to use a value between 0 and 60 because this would mean that kicks from the 30-yard line would be good approximately 50 percent of the time. If the field goal is good, the program updates the score and resets the position.

Regardless of whether the field goal was good or not, the opposing team should get the ball, so I called the `oppBall()` function next. Finally, the code returns, which effectively ends the function. It is not necessary to continue running the function, because the results have already been determined.

Checking for a Punt

A punt works just like a long pass, but it is always successful (although it doesn't always go very far) and the player always loses the ball after a punt play. I simply generated another random number between 0 and 60, and moved the `position` variable that many yards. I checked for a punt that lands in the end zone and moved the position to the computer's 20-yard line.

```
} else if (play == 6){
    //Punt
    yardsWon = random(60);
    alert("punted " + yardsWon + " yards");
    position = position - yardsWon;
    if (position < 0){
      alert("touchback");
      position = 20;
    } // end if
    oppBall();
    return();}
```

At the end of the punt play, I gave the computer a chance to play, then used the `return()` command to exit the `runPlay()` function immediately.

Calculating the Normal Plays

If neither running play was selected, it is necessary to determine whether the play succeeded, and how many yards the player earned if it was.

```
//calculate regular plays
  playResult = rand();
  if (playResult < difficulty){
    alert("Play Succeeds!");
    yardsWon = random(yardMax) + 1;
    alert("You went " + yardsWon + " yards!");
```

```
} else {
   alert ("Stopped");
} // end if
```

I generated a 0–1 random value and assigned it to `playResult`. I then compared `playResult` to `difficulty`. If `difficulty` was set at .30, `playResult` will be less than `difficulty` roughly 30 percent of the time. The condition that compares these two variables is ultimately the key to the game because it determines how often a play is successful. By assigning different difficulty values to different plays, you give the player an opportunity to control the destiny of the game. However, to make the game more interesting, I added another random element. If the play succeeds, the number of yards earned is generated by another random call. The `yardsWon` variable will be filled with an integer value from 1 to `yardMax`. I assigned a high value for `yardMax` in the more difficult plays. This should encourage more daring play calling by the player.

To change the overall difficulty of the game, you can play around with the various values for `difficulty` and `yardMax`. You may also want to consider changing the basic formulas for game play. If the program totally breaks down, you can always reload it from the CD-ROM.

Checking for a Touchdown

Once a play has been run, the program checks to see if the player scored a touchdown:

```
position = position - yardsWon;
  if (position < 0){
    alert("touchdown!");
    playerScore = playerScore + 7;
    position = 20;
    oppBall();
    return();
  } // end if
```

This code is relatively straightforward. I start by subtracting `yardswon` from `position`. Remember that I defined a position value of 100 to be the player's own end zone, and a position value of 0 to be the computer's end zone. If the `position` variable has gotten smaller than 0, the player has scored a touchdown, so it is necessary to update the score, reset the position, and give the computer the ball. Once this happens, I exit the function because it will be time for the player to select a play again.

Checking for a First Down

A player who did not score a touchdown may still have earned a first down by moving more than 10 yards. The next piece of code checks for this situation:

```
yardsLeft = yardsLeft - yardsWon;
  if (yardsLeft <= 0){
    alert("First down!!");
    down = 0;
    yardsLeft = 10;
  } // end if
```

The `yardsLeft` variable tracks the number of yards necessary for a first down. The program subtracts `yardsWon` from `yardsLeft`. If the new value of `yardsLeft` is less than zero, the player has earned a new set of downs, so the `down` variable is reset to 0 and the `yardsLeft` variable is reset to 10.

Checking for a Fourth Down

If the user did not kick, score, or earn a first down, the program increments the `down` variable and checks to see if the player has had more than four downs. If so, the opponent gets the ball at the current position.

```
down++;
  if (down > 4){
    alert("ball lost on downs");
    oppBall();
    return();
  } // end if
} //end run play function
```

Displaying the Score

The `showScore()` function is used to show the current game status to the user:

```
showScore(){
  //shows the score
  int yardLine;
  string fieldHalf = "your ";

  //Figure field position variables
  if (position > 50){
    yardLine = 0 - (position - 100);
```

```
      fieldHalf = "your ";
    } else {
      yardLine = position;
      fieldHalf = "opponent's ";
    } // end if

    clear();
    title("Scoreboard                  ");
    puts("Player: " + playerScore);
    puts("\tOpponent: " + oppScore + "\n");
    puts("\n");
    puts("on " + fieldHalf + yardLine + " yard line \n");
    puts("down: " + down + "\n");
    puts("to go: " + yardsLeft + "\n");
    puts("Time left: " + timeLeft + " minutes \n");
    puts("\n");
    puts("tap the screen to continue");
    wait();

} // end showScore
```

Much of the code is straightforward, but one section may require explanation. As you have looked through the code, it has made a lot of sense to have the ball's position stored as a value from 100 (player's goal) to 0 (computer's goal). However, that's not how a football field is marked. The field is marked with a 50-yard line in the middle and decreasing numbers toward each goal line. Each goal is effectively the 0-yard line. The first part of the `showScore()` function is dedicated to converting the 0–100 value of the `position` variable to the "yard line" notation familiar to football fans.

It took some trial and error to get this formula right, but here's the way I did it:

```
If position is less than 50, the ball is on the opponent's half of
the field, so no special calculations are necessary to indicate the
opponent's half of the field. However, if the position is larger
than 50, the ball is on the player's side of the field. For example,
position 60 is the player's 40-yard line. If you subtract position
from 100, you get the negative of the correct yard line value
(60 - 100 = -40) so I just subtracted this value from 0 to get the
correct yard line (0 - -40 = 40).
```

The rest of the function simply involves printing out the scoreboard values to the screen.

The main() Function

In a well-designed program, the `main` function is often quite simple. As much as possible, the bulk of the code should be broken into smaller units. The `main` function should be primarily concerned with the primary flow of the program. This is the case in the football game:

```
main(){
  int thePlay;
  splash();

  //main loop for timer
  for (timeLeft = 60; timeLeft >= 0; timeLeft-){
    thePlay = choosePlay();
    runPlay(thePlay);
    showScore();
  } // end for loop

  //handle end of game
  alert("Game over!");
  showScore();
  if (playerScore > oppScore){
    alert("You win!!!");
  } else {
    alert("Maybe next time...");
  } // end if
  exit();
} // end main
```

The `main` loop starts by displaying the splash screen. It then generates a `for` loop to manage the number of plays. Essentially the user will get to choose plays 60 times. This makes an interesting game which lasts for a few minutes of real time. It's long enough to be exciting and feel like a real football game, but short enough to be appropriate for a handheld platform. This is not extremely realistic, but it's a good enough approximation that the player can get lost in the experience, and that's the goal. Inside the loop, I called the `choosePlay()` function, which returns a value stored in `thePlay`. I then pass `thePlay` to the `runPlay()` function. This function will automatically call `oppPlay()` when necessary. At the end of every play, I call `showScore()` so the player knows the status of the game.

When the `for` loop has run its course, the game is over. The last piece of business is to let the player know who won.

It's gratifying to see that the `main` loop is reasonably easy to read, because there are few details in it. In the main loop, you want to be thinking about the big picture of the program's behavior, and you don't want to be bogged down in details. The `main` loop calls the appropriate functions, and they do their jobs.

IN THE REAL WORLD

Programmers often like to take complex programs like this and break them into smaller pieces. This kind of "divide and conquer" approach to programming is often referred to as *modular* programming.

Summary

This chapter brings you around a major corner. You are continuing to learn important new syntax structures like the `for` and `while` loop, but you are also learning how to design original programs, and how to think through the complex task of writing a program. You have examined the STAIR process for writing computer programs. You have also learned a few new tools, like the `while` loop, which is a powerful tool for repeating certain code segments. The `for` loop is another type of loop that specializes in repeating things a specified number of times. You can now do more with functions, as you know how to pass values to a function, and how functions return values. You can now include code to overcome the Memo Pad program's text size limitation. You also have the notion of local and global variables. This chapter brings most of these elements together in simulation of a very complex event. In the next chapter, you will learn how you can add graphics and event-handling capabilities to your programs.

CHALLENGES

1. Add a loop to the Morse Code simulator from Chapter 3. Have the program continue accepting and translating characters until the user enters some special character (maybe *). You will need to inform the user on the screen how to end the loop.
2. Modify the behavior of the football game. There are many ways you could improve the program:
   - Add team names
   - Introduce special events (half time and quarters, injuries, interception) that appear at random
   - Add more play choices, or tune up the performance of the existing ones so they act more realistically
   - Improve the opponent's ball logic. Perhaps allow the user to select defensive plays as well, or have the opponent's yardage be based on whether the user chose appropriate plays on defense
3. Build the classic "I'm thinking of a number between 1 and 100" game. Have the computer generate a random number, and have the user guess the number. On each turn, have the computer tell the user if the guess was too high, too low, or correct.
4. Build the same game but have the computer guess the user's number.

Using the Graphics Mode: The Sketcher

In the earlier chapters of this book, you learned how to use the text mode to do some very powerful things. In this chapter, you begin to examine PocketC's graphics mode. Specifically, you learn the following techniques:

- Entering graphics mode
- Writing and manipulating text in the graphics mode
- Drawing lines, rectangles, and circles
- Using events to respond to user interaction
- Reading input from the pen
- Reading input from the Graffiti writing area

The Sketcher Program

In this chapter, you'll write a very simple sketchpad program that will allow you to draw simple figures on the screen using the pen. Figure 5.1 illustrates the sketcher program in action.

FIGURE 5.1

This chapter's Sketcher program allows me to give you this elegant self-portrait.

The user can draw using a variety of pen sizes, and in black, white, and a special "color" called *xor* (you'll learn more about that later in the chapter). There is also a clear screen function and a help screen. All of these options are chosen by entering a character in the Graffiti area.

This program has limited utility as a drawing program, but it is kind of fun, and you will be able to learn some very important ideas as you write it. Figure 5.2 lists the options the sketcher program offers.

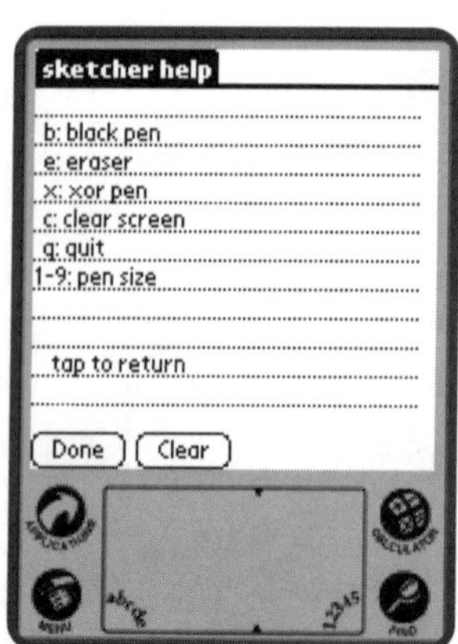

FIGURE 5.2

The help screen illustrates the various options available.

Using the Graphics Mode

The text mode is nice for the kinds of things you've done so far, but it does not allow you to put anything but characters on the screen. It also places limits on exactly where on the screen you place output. To move beyond these limitations, you need to explore the graphics mode.

The Hello Graphic Program

The Hello Graphic program you see in Figure 5.3 looks like your old friend Hello World, but under the hood, you will see that it works differently from the programs you have done so far.

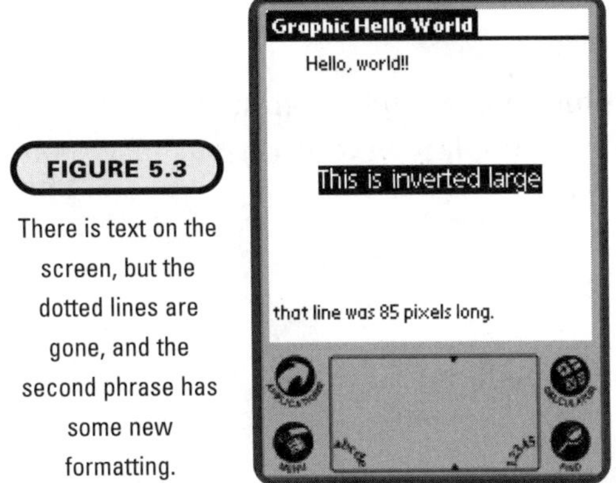

FIGURE 5.3

There is text on the screen, but the dotted lines are gone, and the second phrase has some new formatting.

You can still place text on the screen in graphics mode, but you have a little more control over exactly how the text looks and where it goes.

Here's the entire code for the Hello Graphic program. I explain each line in detail after the code.

```
//helloGraphic
//Andy Harris
//02-5.1

main(){
  int newLeft, newTop;
  string message = "This is inverted large";
  graph_on();
  clearg();
  title("Graphic Hello World");
```

```
    text(20, 20, "Hello, world!!");
    textattr(2,2,0);
    textalign(11);
    newLeft = 80;
    newTop = 80;
    text(newLeft, newTop, message);

    textalign(00);
    textattr(0,1,0);
    text(2, 140, "that line was " + textwidth(message) + " pixels long.");
    wait();
} // end main
```

Graphics Mode

The first order of business is to start graphics mode. The program starts by setting up a couple of variables that will be used to place text in various places on the screen, and to store a message. This line:

```
graph_on();
***PD: end code
```

is used to switch the computer from the text mode you have been using to a special graphics mode. The next line:

```
clearg();
```

is just like the `clear()` function you are used to in text mode, but it is a special version meant to clear the graphics screen. Now that you have the PDA set to graphics mode, you can no longer use the `puts()` function to write to the screen because that function is specific to text mode. The graphics mode supports an entirely different set of functions for displaying text.

In the Real World

Even though there is a distinction between the text and graphic modes in PocketC, most applications will use the graphic mode, which is the normal mode of the Palm OS. The text mode was created in PocketC to simplify quick and dirty text output.

The Graphics Screen

For the most part, you didn't have to worry much about where things were placed in text mode. The `puts()` function simply writes text at the next place on the screen, and it only requires the programmer to specify when to put in a carriage return. In graphics mode, you have a lot more control, but this also means you have a lot more responsibility. You can't just place text on the screen in graphics mode; you have to tell PocketC exactly where you want that text to go. The standard graphics screen in the Palm OS (at least version 3.5) consists of a 160-by-160 arrangement of dots. Figure 5.4 shows how the pixels are arranged on the screen.

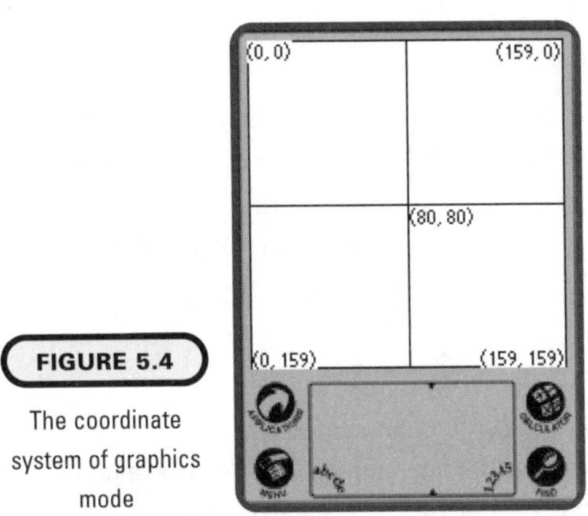

FIGURE 5.4

The coordinate system of graphics mode

As you can see, the top left corner of the screen is coordinate (0, 0), and the bottom right is (159, 159). You can place text (or later, graphics) anywhere on this screen that you wish. Whenever you need to refer to coordinates on the screen, you will be using values from 0 to 160.

Setting the Form Title

Most programs have a title bar. In graphics mode, you can set the title bar with the `title()` function, just as you do in text mode. In this program, I set the title with the following line:

```
title("Graphic Hello World");
```

It's important to know that the title bar takes up about 15 pixels of the top of the screen, so you shouldn't write to that part of the screen unless you have a good reason. It is a good idea to set the title to something, so the user knows what program is running.

Writing Text with the text() Function

The `text()` function is used to write text to the graphics screen. To use the text function, you must specify where the text should be placed, as well as the text that you wish to write to the screen. This line

```
text(20, 20, "Hello, world!!");
```

writes the text "Hello, world!!" beginning at pixel (20, 20), which is near the upper left-hand corner of the screen.

Changing the Text Characteristics with textattr(), textwidth(), and textalign()

If you look back at Figure 5.3 you will notice that the second line is a little bit different from the others. It appears in a slightly larger font, and the colors are inverted. Rather than the default black on white, the line is white on black. All these features were generated by the `textattr()` function. This function allows you to set certain characteristics of any `text()` statements that will follow. The `textattr()` function expects three parameters. The first one is the font. Table 5.1 lists the main fonts.

In chapter 9, "Memo Access: The Life Game" you will learn how to write a program that can be used to build an ASCII chart for any font that is available to PocketC. You may want to modify that program to see all the various ASCII symbols available to you.

Table 5.1 Fonts Supported by the textattr() Function

Font number	Font
0	Normal
1	Bold
2	Large
3	Symbol
4	Symbol11
5	Symbol7
6	LED
7	Large Bold

The symbol fonts are all used to represent various symbols available to the system. Symbol is the default symbol font, Symbol7 is a smaller version of the font, and Symbol11 is larger than the default version.

The second parameter of the `textattr()` function is the text color, represented by a number between 0 and 2, as shown in Table 5.2

Table 5.2 Colors Supported by the textattr() Function

Color number	Color
0	White
1	Black
2	Gray

The final parameter of `textattr()` represents underlining. You can specify three different styles of underline, as shown in Table 5.3.

Table 5.3 Underline Values Supported by the textattr() Function

Underline value	Type of underline
0	None
1	Solid
2	Dotted

In addition to the `textattr()` function, PocketC includes two other useful functions for manipulating text in graphics mode. The `textwidth()` function is used to determine the width of a text value in pixels given the current `textattr()` settings. This can be useful for determining the placement of text or as part of a function that automatically draws a rectangle around text (to make a button, for example).

The `textalign()` function is powerful, but it takes some getting used to. This function takes a single parameter, which is used to determine how the text will be placed on the screen.

Be careful of the terms used in the documentation. Although the help file describes the ability to left, right, and center align text, the terms are used differently in this context than you may have seen in the past. They refer to specified alignment points rather than to the screen as a whole. In the next section, I will show you exactly how the text alignment works in PocketC.

Recall that the `text()` function requires a pair of coordinates for placing the text. The default behavior of the `text()` statement is to use that point as the upper-left corner of the text to be placed. The `textalign()` function is used to modify how that point is related to the text on the screen. It uses a two-digit number to specify which part of the text should be placed at the point specified by the `text()` function. Please see Figure 5.5 to see the various values.

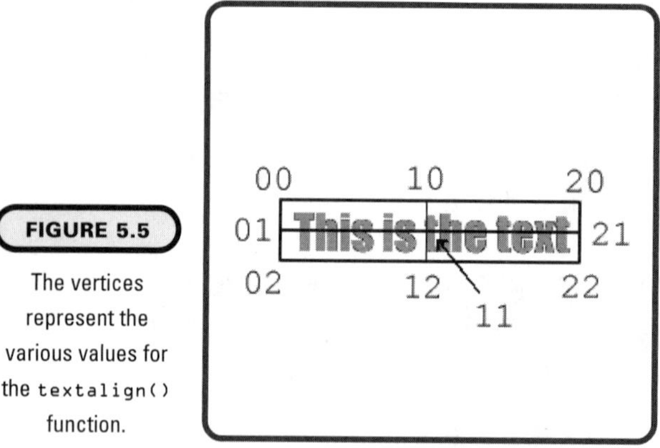

FIGURE 5.5

The vertices represent the various values for the `textalign()` function.

Most of the time, you won't need to worry about the `textalign()` function at all. It can be useful in certain circumstances, however. If you want to center some text completely in the screen (as I did in the Hello Graphic example), you can set `textalign` (11) to specify that whatever point you will use in the `text()` statement should be the middle of the string. Then, if you place the text at (80, 80), which is the middle of the screen, the text will be perfectly centered. Likewise, if you want some text to be aligned completely to the right of the screen, you might set the `textalign` value to 21. Then, when you perform the `text()` operation, you can specify the X value 159, which is all the way on the right edge of the screen. PocketC will calculate exactly where it needs to put the text to get the right-hand side of the text at pixel 159.

Drawing Basic Shapes in Graphics Mode

In addition to placing text, you can use a set of basic drawing commands to draw lines and rectangles to the screen. Figure 5.6 demonstrates a simple drawing made using these commands.

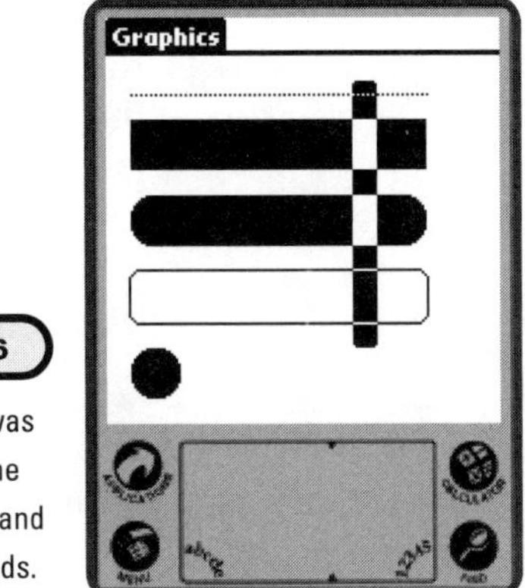

FIGURE 5.6

This drawing was made using the line, rectangle, and frame commands.

Look closely at this image, and you will see that the line is gray. You will also see rectangles with rounded corners, and frames (rectangles that are not filled in). You probably also noticed the vertical rectangle that seems to overlap the others in an interesting pattern. All these effects are achieved by changing some of the parameters of the `line()`, `frame()`, and `rect()` functions. These functions are very closely related, and they all have almost exactly the same syntax.

Here is the code for the program that drew Figure 5.6.

```
//graphDemo
//Demonstrates graphics primitives
//Andy Harris, 2/5/01

main(){
  graph_on();
  clearg();

  //draw a gray line
  line(2, 10,30, 130,30);

  //draw a rectangle with sharp corners
  rect(1, 10,40, 130,60, 0);
```

```
  //draw another rectangle with very rounded corners
  rect(1, 10,70, 130,90, 10);

  //draw a non-filled rectangle with soft corners.
  frame(1, 10,100, 130, 120, 5);

  //draw a vertical rectangle in XOR mode
  rect(3, 100,25, 110,130, 3);

  //the following line actually draws a circle(!)
  rect (1, 10,130, 30,150, 10);

  //wait for user input
  wait();
} // end main
```

The following sections describe the particular parts of this program in detail.

Drawing Lines Using the line() Function

The `line()` function (not surprisingly) draws lines on the screen. It takes five parameters: color, x1, y1, x2, and y2. The color can be one of the four choices given in Table 5.4.

TABLE 5.4 COLORS USED IN THE DRAWING FUNCTIONS

Color number	Color
0	White
1	Black
2	Gray
3	Xor

If you draw in white on the default white background, your new image will not appear. Gray looks like a dotted line. The line in the program was drawn in gray. All the horizontal rectangles were drawn in black. The vertical rectangle is drawn in the xor "color." When you specify xor, PocketC inverts whatever color is found on the screen, so if you draw a line in xor you get white whenever the background is black, and black whenever the background is white.

The `line` function draws a line from (x1, y1) to (x2, y2). Remember that (0, 0) is in the upper left-hand corner of the screen.

Drawing Rectangles with the rect() and frame() Functions

The `rect` and `frame` functions work very much like the `line` function, except they take one more parameter:

```
rect (color, x1, y1, x2, y2, radius);
rect (color, x1, y1, x2, y2, radius);
```

Both functions use the color, x1, y1, x2, and y2 parameters, just as the `line` function does. However, rather than drawing a line between (x1, y1) and (x2, y2), the `frame()` function draws an open rectangle and the `rect()` function draws a filled-in rectangle between the values. Both these functions presume that x1 is smaller than x2, and y1 is smaller than y2. In other words, you must describe the rectangle or frame from its upper left vertex to the lower right. The `rect` and `frame` functions have one parameter that the `line()` function does not. Both `rect()` and `frame()` require you to provide a parameter for radius. This parameter is used to round the corners of the rectangle or frame. If you set the radius to 0, the frame or rectangle will have completely square corners. If you set the value to half of the height of the shape, you will have completely rounded corners, as I do in the middle horizontal rectangle.

Note that the `rect()` function does not work with color 2 (gray). If you attempt to draw a rectangle in gray, it will be drawn in black (color 1) instead.

You may be surprised when you compare the code and the output of the Graph Demo program. Although there is clearly a circle on the screen, the Graph Demo program does not have a circle command, or anything like it. To make circles in PocketC, you actually use the `rect()` or `frame()` functions. This seems a little strange, but it isn't very difficult to do once you understand the radius parameter. To make a circle, simply make a rectangle or frame (depending on whether your circle should be filled in or not). Make sure that your shape is completely square—that is, the height is equal to the width. Then set the radius to half of the height of the shape, and you will have a circle. So, to make a (filled-in) circle of radius 10 with a center of (15, 15), you would use the following function call:

```
rect(1, 10,10, 20,20, 5);
```

Defining Constants

Every once in a while, you will encounter values that stay consistent throughout the run of a program. Sometimes you want to have a name for a value that makes the value easier to work with in code. PocketC has a feature that allows you to substitute a name for any type of value you might want to use in your code.

Look at the following program, and I'll explain what it does.

The Def Demo Program

```
//DefDemo
//Demonstrates the #define directive
//Andy Harris, 06/19/01

#define PHRASE "PocketC Rocks"
#define NUMDAYS 365
#define SIGNAL alert("Hey There!")

main(){
  alert(PHRASE);
  alert(NUMDAYS + " in a year");
  SIGNAL;
} // end main
```

The only part of this code that might surprise you is the #define lines that occurs at the top of the program. These statements are called *preprocessor directives*, because they are instructions to the compiler. All directives in PocketC begin with the pound (#) sign. The #define directive is used to name a value. In the first #define statement, I defined PHRASE as "PocketC Rocks." When the compiler reads the code, whenever it sees the text PHRASE, it will substitute the value "PocketC Rocks" before compiling the program. Although PHRASE might seem like a variable, it is not. PHRASE does not relate to any specific place in memory (as variables always do), and you cannot change the value of PHRASE while the program is running.

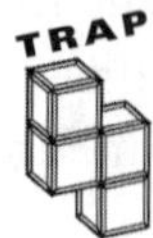

You cannot assign a value to a constant. The only way to set a constant's value is through the #define statement. For example, the line

PHRASE = "a new value"

would not work because PHRASE is not a variable, and you cannot assign a value to it.

Using Constants in Your Code

Inside the program you'll see the line:

```
Alert(PHRASE);
```

When the compiler sees this line of code it recognizes that PHRASE is one of the named entities it has stored, and it replaces the term PHRASE with the value "PocketC Rocks" before compiling the program.

Defined values such as PHRASE are often called *constants* because, unlike variables, the value of a constant will not change while the program is running. C programmers usually name constants in all uppercase letters to help them remember that the name corresponds to a constant, not a variable.

NUMDAYS is also a constant. It is not necessary to define a type for a constant or to add a semicolon after the constant definition line, because whenever the term NUMDAYS appears in the code, the PocketC compiler will simply replace it with the value 365.

Creating Macros with #define

To see the power of the #define directive, take a look at the last #define line. Rather than defining a variable-like entity, the term SIGNAL defines an entire line of code! Whenever the compiler encounters the term SIGNAL, it will replace it with the entire phrase alert("Hey There!"). Technically, this last use of the define statement is not called a constant, it's called a *macro*, because it is reminiscent of storing a keyboard macro in a text-editing program.

Although macros are very cool, they can cause a lot of problems for beginning programmers. Macros are never absolutely necessary, and they can be completely replaced by well-designed modular programming. On the other hand, constants can be an important part of good programming style, as they make your code much easier to read. As you read the rest of this book, you will see that most of the remaining programs include a constant definition section, but none of them use macros.

Handling Events

Graphics mode also gives you more flexibility (and responsibility) when it comes to getting information from the user. PocketC uses a system called *event-driven programming* to manage all the kinds of input that can come from the user. An event is basically a stimulus that the program can look for and respond to.

The Event Loop

This program demonstrates a pattern you will see again and again as a PocketC programmer. The general algorithm looks like this:

```
Set keepGoing to true
As long as keepGoing is true,
  *  Get an event
  *  Store it in the evt variable
  *  Check to see what type of event it is
       Handle the pen events (if any)
       Handle the key events (if any)
       Handle the button events (if any)
  *  Finish checking the event type
Finish the loop
```

This structure is called the *event-handling* loop, and it is common to event-driven programming environments. You will see a variation of this algorithm in almost every program you write for the rest of this book.

The Key Checker Program

This program demonstrates the basics of event handling by looking for keyboard input and copying it to the text screen. Figure 5.7 demonstrates the Key Checker program in action.

FIGURE 5.7

As the user writes in the Graffiti area, the text on the screen is automatically updated.

Key Checker introduces some important new concepts. Take a look at the code.

```
//keyChecker
//simple event monitor - checks for key input only
//Andy Harris, 02/07/01

#define EVT_KEY 1

main(){
  int keepGoing = true;
  int evt;
  char theKey;

  //set up the stage
  clear();
  puts("Type some keys \n");
  puts("Type 'q' to quit \n");

  //begin a loop
  while (keepGoing){

    //retrieve an event
    evt = event(1);

    //check to see if it was a key input
    if (evt == EVT_KEY){

      //respond to the key input
      theKey = key();
      puts((string)theKey);

      //check to see if it's the 'q' key
      if (theKey=='q'){
        keepGoing = false;
      } // end 'quit' if
    } // end 'key event' if
  } // end while
} // end main
```

The Key Checker program is a terrific example of a structure called an *event loop*. Basically, the program looks for some kind of action from the user. When input arrives, the program analyzes the input and acts on it. This process is repeated until the user signals the intention to exit the program.

This explanation will skip a few details to concentrate on how event handling works in general. The following example presents a more complete discussion of the various details.

I started by defining the EVT_KEY constant. EVT_KEY will be used to determine if the user tries to enter a key.

I created an `int` to keep track of the `keepGoing` value, another `int` (evt) to keep track of the type of event, and a char for keeping track of what character the user has entered.

After setting up the text screen, I created a standard loop based on the `keepGoing` sentry.

Note that this line:

```
while (keepGoing){
```

contains a legitimate condition even though it does not include a comparison operator. This is because the `keepGoing` variable itself is declared as boolean, meaning it will always have a value of true or false. Since this is also the main prerequisite for a conditional statement, a boolean variable can be used in a condition. This code:

```
//retrieve an event
evt = event(1);
```

waits indefinitely for an event to occur, and when it does, it stores a special numeric code in the `evt` variable. The code describes exactly what type of event has occurred. The next section includes a complete listing of the event types, but for now it is enough to know that `evt` will contain a 1 if the user entered some kind of keystroke.

The next order of business is to determine which kind of event occurred. That is done by checking the value of the `evt` variable.

```
//check to see if it was a key input
if (evt == EVT_KEY){
```

I used the EVT_KEY constant just because I think it makes the code much easier to read than the alternative.

```
if (evt == 1){
```

If a keystroke occurred, I want to repeat whatever character was entered onto the screen.

```
//respond to the key input
theKey = key();
puts((string)theKey);
```

The `key()` function returns the character that corresponds to the last keypress. This value is a char type, so it is a good idea to convert it to a string before using it in the `puts()` function.

I should also check for the “q” key, because that will signify that the program should end.

```
if (theKey=='q'){
  keepGoing = FALSE;
} // end 'quit' if
```

It is critical that there be some sort of mechanism for ensuring the program ends, or you could have an endless loop that could cause problems and require resetting the PDA.

All that is left is to close all the various structures.

```
} // end 'quit' if
     } // end 'key event' if
   } // end while
} // end main
```

The Event Demo Program

PocketC can handle a number of interesting events. Even when the event-handling seems to get very complex, it almost always follows the model you saw in the Key Checker program.

The program featured in Figures 5.8 and 5.9 demonstrates all the major event-handling features of PocketC.

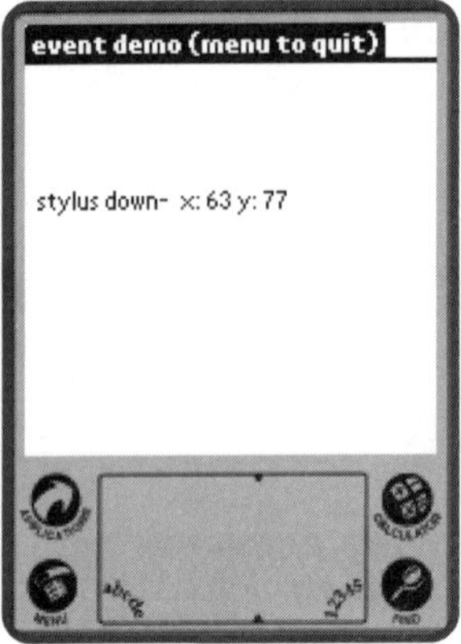

FIGURE 5.8

The user has tapped the stylus on the screen, and the program notes the details of the location.

FIGURE 5.9

Now the user has pressed the Calendar button. Again, the program notes this fact.

This program is simply an expanded version of the Key Checker program, but it looks at a number of different event types. Keystrokes are one of eleven types of events to which PocketC can respond. Table 5.5 offers a more detailed list of the events.

TABLE 5.5 THE EVENT CODES

Event number	Event that has occurred
0	Nothing
1	Key entered
2	Pen down
3	Pen up
4	Pen moved
5	Page Up pressed
6	Page Down pressed
7	Calendar button pressed
8	Address Book button pressed
9	To Do button pressed
10	Memo button pressed
11	Menu button pressed

As you can see, you will be able to write programs that can check for pen input, button input, and Graffiti input. The `event()` function will always return one of the 12 values in Table 5.5.

Although it's completely acceptable to use the actual numbers when looking at events, it is a great idea to create constants for the various events, so your code will be much easier to read. Here is the list of constants I prefer to use.

```
#define EVT_NONE 0
#define EVT_KEY 1
#define EVT_PEN_DN 2
#define EVT_PEN_UP 3
#define EVT_PEN_MV 4
#define EVT_PAGE_UP 5
#define EVT_PAGE_DN 6
#define EVT_BTN_CAL 7
#define EVT_BTN_ADD 8
#define EVT_BTN_TODO 9
#define EVT_BTN_MEMO 10
#define EVT_MENU 11
```

In the Real World

I like to begin every event constant with the term *EVT_* to help me remember it is a constant, and what kind of constant it is. If you define constants, you will find that your code is much easier to read and debug than if you just try to keep track of the numbers. For example, if you want to attach some code to the To Do button, it's much easier to remember `if(evt == EVT_TODO){` than it would be to remember that the To Do button is event number 9.

Variations of the event() Function

The `event()` function takes one integer parameter, which describes how long the program should wait for an event to occur. If you set this parameter to 0, the computer will immediately look for an event. If you set the parameter to 1, the computer will wait indefinitely for an event to occur. If you set the parameter to some value larger than 1, the computer will wait for that many milliseconds for an event to occur. For now, you will probably want to set the event parameter to 1 because you don't really want anything to happen until an event occurs.

Getting Information from the System

Once you have determined what type of event has occurred, you will probably want to know more about exactly what happened. For example, if you are looking at a pen event, you might want to know where the pen is on the screen, or if you're examining a keystroke event, you might want to know which key was entered. PocketC provides the functions listed in Table 5.6 for exactly this purpose.

The `key()` function is used to determine the last key input. Meanwhile, `penx()` and `peny()` return the coordinates of the pen during its last activity, `pstate()` returns a code for the current status of the pen, and `bstate()` returns a similar status for the Page Up and Page Down keys.

The last two functions in the table are a little different. You might recall that in many programs, the application buttons (Calendar, Address, To Do, and Menu)

Table 5.6 Selected Event-Handling Functions

Function	Meaning	Example
key()	Returns the last key entered (as a char)	thechar = key
penx()	Returns the x value of the pen	x = penx();
peny()	Returns the y value of the pen	y = peny();

pstate()	Returns 1 for pen down, 0 for pen up	if(pstate() == 1){
		alert("pen down!");
		} // end if

bstate()	Returns the value of the page button:
	0 = neither
	1 = page up
	–1 = page down
		if (bstate() == 1){
		alert("page up!");
		} // end if

hookhard(*n*)	Determines whether PocketC will interrupt button presses or pass them to the operating system.
	n = 0 pass button keys to OS (memo key starts memo program)
	n != 0 program can interpret button presses
		hookhard(1);
		evt = event(1);
		if (evt == 10){
		alert ("you want a memo?");
		} // end if

hookmenu(n)	Determines whether menu button will be passed to operating system or handled by PocketC *n* = 0 pass menu button to OS	hookmenu(1);
		evt = event(1);
		if (evt == 11){
		alert ("you want a menu?");
		} // end if

let the user go straight to those applications. (That is, press the Memo key and you will go directly to the Memo Pad or whatever other program you have bound to that key). In other programs (especially games) the meaning of these keys is changed. Sometimes you want to intercept the button press so that you can use buttons as an input device in your program. The `hookhard()` function gives you this capability. If you set its value to 0, the buttons will call the appropriate applications, and your program will not be able to use them. If you set `hookhard()` to any other value, you will be able to intercept the button keys for your program's use.

The `hookmenu()` function is very similar to the `hookhard()` function. It controls the behavior of the Menu button, determining whether a press of this button will activate the OS menu system or will be interpreted by your program.

Here is the code for the Event Demo program.

```
//eventDemo
//Demonstrates event handling in PocketC
//Andy Harris, 02/07/01

#define EVT_NONE 0
#define EVT_KEY 1
#define EVT_PEN_DN 2
#define EVT_PEN_UP 3
#define EVT_PEN_MV 4
#define EVT_PAGE_UP 5
#define EVT_PAGE_DN 6
#define EVT_BTN_CAL 7
#define EVT_BTN_ADD 8
#define EVT_BTN_TODO 9
#define EVT_BTN_MEMO 10
#define EVT_MENU 11

main(){
  int keepGoing = TRUE;
  int evt;
  string theMessage;

  graph_on();
  hookhard(1);
  hookmenu(1);
```

```
clearg();
title("event demo (menu to quit)");

while (keepGoing){
  evt = event(1);

  //check all possible events
  if (evt == EVT_KEY){
    theMessage = "Key pressed: ";
    theMessage = theMessage + (string)key();

  } else if (evt == EVT_PEN_DN){
    theMessage = "stylus down- ";
    theMessage = theMessage + " x: " + penx();
    theMessage = theMessage + " y: " + peny();

  } else if (evt == EVT_PEN_UP){
    theMessage = "stylus up- ";
    theMessage = theMessage + " x: " + penx();
    theMessage = theMessage + " y: " + peny();

  } else if (evt == EVT_PEN_MV){
    theMessage = "stylus move- ";
    theMessage = theMessage + " x: " + penx();
    theMessage = theMessage + " y: " + peny();

  } else if (evt == EVT_PAGE_UP){
    theMessage = "page up button ";

  } else if (evt == EVT_PAGE_DN){
    theMessage = "page down button ";

  } else if (evt == EVT_BTN_CAL){
    theMessage = "calendar button ";

  } else if (evt == EVT_BTN_ADD){
    theMessage = "address book button ";

  } else if (evt == EVT_BTN_TODO){
    theMessage = "to do button ";
```

```
    } else if (evt == EVT_BTN_MEMO){
      theMessage = "memo pad button ";

    } else if (evt == EVT_MENU){
      theMessage = " Menu button";
      keepGoing = FALSE;
    } // end if

    //write message to screen
    clearg();
    text(5, 60, theMessage);

  } // end while
} // end main
```

This code runs on for a lot of lines, but it is really almost identical to the Key Checker you saw in the last section. It consists of a while loop with an `event()` function call. After an event has occurred, the program checks to see which type of event it was. The program then responds to each type of event by sending an appropriate value to the `theMessage` string. Finally, it reports the message to the user.

Back to the Sketcher

You now have all the information you need to create the sketcher program. It is nothing more than a new combination of the elements you have already seen.

The Event Constants

The first part of the Sketcher program looks like this:

```
//Sketcher
//Demonstrates event handling
//Andy Harris, 02/07/01

#include "events.h"
```

The program relies on event handling, but I did not directly add the #define statements as I did in the eventDemo program. Since the event constants are going to be so useful, I decided I did not want to type them in every time I used event handling. I created a special file called events.h. Here are the contents of that file.

```
/$events.h

#define TRUE -1
#define FALSE 0

#define EVT_NONE 0
#define EVT_KEY 1
#define EVT_PEN_DN 2
#define EVT_PEN_UP 3
#define EVT_PEN_MV 4
#define EVT_PAGE_UP 5
#define EVT_PAGE_DN 6
#define EVT_BTN_CAL 7
#define EVT_BTN_ADD 8
#define EVT_BTN_TODO 9
#define EVT_BTN_MEMO 10
#define EVT_MENU 11
```

The /$ indicates that this is a file that should not be compiled on its own. When you try to compile programs, any files beginning with /$ will *not* be included. (Ending the file name with .h is a similar convention. Programmers used to working in more traditional C environments will find the .h convention familiar.) The events.h file is intended only to be included in other files. The rest of the file is familiar. It is simply the list of defines from the Event Demo program. Once you have created the events.h file, you no longer need to type in all the events definitions every time. You can simply add this line to the beginning of your program:

```
#include "events.h"
```

Like the #define command, the #include command is a preprocessor directive and it does not require a semicolon at the end. When the compiler encounters the include directive, it will read the contents of the included file just as if it were part of the program file.

The drawRect() Function

The heart of this program is a simple little function called `drawRect`. It looks like this:

```
drawRect(int size, int color, int x, int y){
  //given a size, color, and coordinates, draw a square
  rect(color, x, y, x+size, y+size,0);
} // end drawRect
```

It accepts four parameters and uses these parameters to draw a square. It is much like the built-in `rect()` function, but it always draws a square, and it always makes the corners perfectly square. I have basically encapsulated the `rect()` function inside a customized function that has exactly the parameters I want. Given an (x, y) pair and a size, it will automatically generate a square of that size by calculating x2 and y2. All the drawing in the entire Sketcher comes through this function.

The Help System

The program introduces a help system. It's pretty straightforward, but it still has a few features you might find interesting. Basically, the help system is just the text screen with some text written on it. However, if the user is drawing something on the screen, it would be nice if the drawing were preserved while the user looked at the help. This help system saves the current drawing screen to memory, then displays the help and waits for the user to tap the screen or enter a keystroke. When the user acknowledges reading the help text, the graphics screen is restored, and the user can continue drawing. Here's the code:

```
showHelp(){
  //show a help screen.
  //save the graphics screen, then switch to text mode
  saveg();
  graph_off();

  //write the help text on the screen
  clear();
  title("sketcher help");
  puts("\n");
  puts("   b: black pen \n");
  puts("   e: eraser \n");
  puts("   x: xor pen \n");
  puts("   c: clear screen \n");
  puts("   q: quit \n");
  puts("1-9: pen size \n");
  puts("\n\n     tap to return \n");

  //wait until user does something
  wait();

  //restore the graphics screen so user can continue drawing
  graph_on();
```

```
    restoreg();
    title("sketcher (h for help)");
} // end showHelp
```

There are a few functions here you might not be familiar with. The `saveg()` and `restoreg()` functions are used to save and restore the current graphics screen to memory. You can only store one screen using this technique, and the storage is temporary—but it's perfect for this situation. The `graph_off()` function turns off the graphics, returning PocketC to text mode. Notice that I changed the title to reflect the mode.

IN THE REAL WORLD

Adding online help is a crucial step when writing any complex program. This is especially true in the PDA world, where users *never* carry manuals. You must help your users learn how to use at least the most important features of your program. It's also a good idea to make the help system obvious (such as the title hint that I used in this example).

Starting the Event Loop

The Sketcher program uses exactly the same type of event loop you have seen throughout this chapter.

```
main(){
  //set up variables
  int evt;                       //holds event code
  int keepGoing = TRUE;          //sentry for main loop
  int penSize = 3;               //pen size 1-9
  int penColor = 1;              //pen color 0:white, 1:black,
                                  //           2:gray, 3:xor
  char theChar;            //holds command entered by user

  //set up the environment
  graph_on();
  clearg();
  title("sketcher (h for help)");
  while (keepGoing){
    evt = event(1);
```

I set up a number of variables and carefully commented them, so it is obvious what each one is meant to do. I then turned on the graphics mode, cleared the screen, set the title bar, and started the main loop. Whenever an event occurs, the event code will be stored in the `evt` variable.

Handling the Pen Events

If the user puts the pen down or moves it, something should happen on the screen. The first event handlers check for these two events.

```
//If pen down or moved, draw using current values
    if (evt == EVT_PEN_DN){
      drawRect(penSize, penColor, penx(), peny());
    } else if (evt == EVT_PEN_MV){
      drawRect(penSize, penColor, penx(), peny());
```

In either case, the program will call the `drawRect()` function. Exactly how the `drawRect()` function will behave depends on the variables. Pressing or moving the stylus draws something on the screen, but the color and size of the rectangle to be drawn will be changed by other code fragments.

Handling the Character Events

If a key event has occurred, the program checks to see if that keystroke is related to one of the commands that have been defined for the program.

```
//check for command requests
    } else if (evt == EVT_KEY){
      theChar = key();

      //help
      if (theChar=='h'){
        showHelp();

      //quit
      } else if (theChar == 'q'){
        keepGoing = FALSE;

      //eraser
      } else if (theChar == 'e'){
        penColor = 0;

      //black
```

```
        } else if (theChar == 'b'){
          penColor = 1;

        //xor pen
        } else if (theChar == 'x'){
          penColor = 3;

        //clear screen
        } else if (theChar == 'c'){
          clearg();

        //pen sizes
        } else if (theChar == '1'){
          penSize = 1;
        } else if (theChar == '2'){
          penSize = 2;
        } else if (theChar == '3'){
          penSize = 3;
        } else if (theChar == '4'){
          penSize = 4;
        } else if (theChar == '5'){
          penSize = 5;
        } else if (theChar == '6'){
          penSize = 6;
        } else if (theChar == '7'){
          penSize = 7;
        } else if (theChar == '8'){
          penSize = 8;
        } else if (theChar == '9'){
          penSize = 9;
        } // end character if     } // end event if
    } // end while loop
} // end main
```

Most of the keystroke commands are reasonably easy to follow. The "h" keystroke calls the `showHelp()` function, the "c" keystroke calls the `clearg()` command, and the various numeric values all change the pen size. Entering "e" causes the pen color to be white (or an eraser), and keying in "b" reverts the pen color to black. The xor pen is interesting. You might recall from the beginning of the chapter that xor behavior means that if the screen is currently black, the brush paints white, and if the screen is white, the brush paints black. If you set the brush to a large size and just press the stylus straight down without moving it, you will see this behavior. However, if you move the stylus around on the screen, you will see a somewhat random appearance of white and black pixels. This is because the pen is acting on itself. At first, I was disappointed in this behavior, but after playing with it, I decided I actually liked the effect. Maybe it's not a bug after all, but a feature.

Summary

In this chapter, you learned how to use the graphics mode to get better control of your PDA's output. You learned how to position text on the screen, and how to generate simple figures such as lines, rectangles, frames, and circles. You also learned how to harness the power of event-driven programming. Example programs generate an event loop, capture an event, determine what type of event occurred, and use the event manipulation functions to learn more about the event, such as what key was pressed or where the stylus was on the screen.

In the next chapter, you'll learn how to generate bitmap graphics. This will give you the ability to draw any kind of image you can imagine on the screen with relative ease.

CHALLENGES

1. **Generate a simple image using primitive shapes (circles, rectangles, and lines). Try to draw a house or a happy face, or some other design.**
2. **Write a program that moves your name around the screen. You may need a series of `for/next` loops, and you'll probably also want to investigate the `sleep()` command in the online help.**
3. **Change the paintbrush in the Sketcher program so it is round.**
4. **Add a calligraphy paintbrush (a diagonal slash) to the Sketcher program.**
5. **Add line, rectangle, and circle drawing features to the Sketcher program. For most of these commands, you'll need code to store a beginning (x, y) pair in the `pen down` event and code to draw the actual shape in the `pen up` event.**
6. **Create a button by drawing a rectangle on the screen. Trap to see when the user clicks on the button. (You'll have to compare the `penx()` and `peny()` values to the coordinates and size of the rectangle). If the user clicks on the button, alert some message to respond to the action.**
7. **Design a button-based user interface for the Sketcher program. (Note: Although you have all the tools you need to do this now, you'll learn a much easier technique in Chapter 7, "Adding a Graphical User Interface: The Mad Lib Game.")**

Creating Bitmap Graphics: The Space Rescue Game

You now have most of the key skills for writing interesting computer programs. However, you may be interested in adding to your program more sophisticated graphics than the simple shapes introduced in Chapter 5. The Palm OS can't do much with graphics (at least compared to modern desktop systems), but this can actually be a bonus when you are just starting out. PocketC supports a very simple form of black-and-white graphics. Nonetheless, the graphics system is still capable of some nice effects. In this chapter, you learn how to incorporate simple images into your PocketC programs, and how to build a basic arcade-style game. Specifically, the chapter covers the following techniques:

- Generating bitmap graphics with an editor
- Incorporating these graphics into a PocketC program
- Working with arrays for storing large amounts of data
- Building frame animations
- Moving objects around the screen
- Detecting collisions between objects

The Space Rescue Game

This chapter presents an arcade game called Space Rescue, which is illustrated in Figures 6.1 through 6.4. Like most arcade games, it has a simple premise: An accident in space has stranded an astronaut away from the space station he was working on. The player is a shuttle pilot who is trying to rescue the astronaut. The shuttle has one main engine and directional thrusters. The player must learn how to steer the shuttle close to the astronaut. If the shuttle gets close to the astronaut with a similar speed and direction, the astronaut is rescued.

FIGURE 6.1

The astronaut is moving around on the screen. The shuttle starts out stationary.

FIGURE 6.2

Pressing the Page Down key causes the shuttle to move forward.

FIGURE 6.3

The Phone and Checklist buttons rotate the shuttle.

FIGURE 6.4

Pressing the Page Down key again adjusts the shuttle's trajectory.

Although it may not be clear from these screen shots, the little astronaut is waving frantically. Simple elements like this can add tremendously to the appeal of a program.

The Space Rescue game is really just a starting point, but it does illustrate all the main principles of computer animation.

Bitmap Graphics

The most obvious new element you need is the ability to build more sophisticated graphics. Chapter 5 introduced the graphics functions needed to build some simple images, but these techniques may not be helpful in a program such as the space game.

Many languages give you some way to design an image in a graphics program and then import it into your project. Such images are usually referred to as *bitmap* graphics, because they are stored internally as a "map of bits."

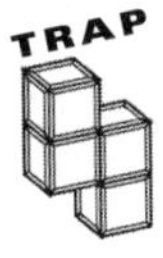

The term *bitmap* is a generic term for any kind of image generated by a series of numbers representing the color of each dot on the screen. The Microsoft .bmp format is also referred to as a bitmap, but it is only one example of a type of bitmap files. Although the Palm OS does not support the .bmp file format, you can still do a form of bitmapped imaging in PocketC. If you are interested in converting a Windows bitmap to a PocketC image, try the bmp2hex program included on the CD-ROM that accompanies this book.

PocketC offers a limited but still powerful version of bitmap graphics. It allows you to define an image mathematically, and then store the instructions for the image in a string variable.

The Show Smile Program

Figure 6.5 demonstrates a program showing a bitmap. Although this may look a lot like the image in Figure 5.1, it is a different kind of image. The image is a *bitmap,* that is, a file created with a special editor and retrieved through the PocketC language. PocketC treats bitmaps as a series of black and white dots. To save space, the series of black and white dots are compressed into a special format and stored in string variables.

The way the image information is stored involves some mathematical conversions, but fortunately that is just the kind of thing computer programs are great at doing. Rather than having to generate an image by hand, you can use a program that makes generating images easy.

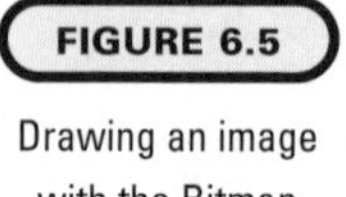
FIGURE 6.5

Drawing an image with the Bitmap Studio program.

Using the Bitmap Studio Program to Generate an Image

A number of excellent programs are available for generating PocketC images. The Bitmap Studio program, by Elucidata unLTD (included on the CD-ROM that comes with this book) allows you to draw an image on the screen, then store it to a memo file or the Clipboard. Figure 6.6 illustrates an image being drawn in Bitmap Studio. The image can be stored into a memo, where you can retrieve it for further editing, or you can copy it to the Clipboard so that you can paste it back into a string variable for later use in your program.

Once the image is stored in the special string format, you will be able to use it in your PocketC programs.

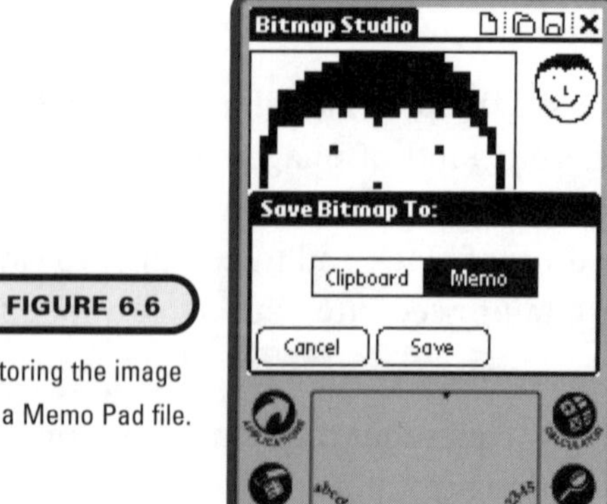

FIGURE 6.6

Storing the image to a Memo Pad file.

If you prefer to work with an image you already have on your Windows machine, you might want to investigate the bmp2hex program also included on the CD-ROM that accompanies this book. Be aware, however, that Windows images are much larger than their Palm counterparts, and support many more colors. Still, this might be a good way to convert some image (such as your company's logo) without having to redraw it in Bitmap Studio.

Using a Bitmap in a Program

Once the image is created, the next step is to write a program that can use the image. The Show Smile program does exactly that. Here's the program code:

```
//showSmile
//demonstrates drawing a bitmap
//Andy Harris, 04/07/01

main(){
  string smileImage =
"1e0000000000000000000000000000000087fc1e009ffe7f00ffffef80ffff9f00efff8c0
07cb58040600187f860009bf84000bf9c4204e8044000f00440009000404142102041c0002
061c000220100001119808011f28080080068c000804840008088770061 8c0c007fc40181ec
f303037ff98cc737e9ff0";

  graph_on();
  clearg();
  title("Showing a Bitmap");

  bitmap (30, 30, smileImage);
  wait();
} // end main
```

Most of the code in this program is very straightforward. The string variable `smileImage` contains a huge amount of information in a bizarre format. This is the way the Bitmap Studio reproduced the smile image as string data. It's okay for now if you don't know exactly how it works; the important thing is that the image you created in the bitmap editor can be stored as a string value. This is important because PocketC doesn't have a data type for images. Instead, you store all the image data into a string, and then tell PocketC to generate an image based on the information in the string. To make this particular image, I saved the image into the Clipboard, then started writing the program. I created the variable `smileImage`, and initialized the variable by pasting from the Clipboard into the string. Alternatively, I could have saved the data to a Memo Pad file, then copied and pasted the string data from the memo file into my program.

Once the image is stored into a string, it's a reasonably easy matter to put the image on the screen. Simply use the bitmap function to place a bitmap anywhere on the graphics screen.

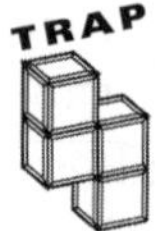

Bitmap Studio does not allow you to generate bitmap images larger than 40 by 40 pixels. This is not really a major problem because most of the time you will be animating bitmap images and moving them around on the screen. All the images in the Space Rescue program are actually smaller than 15 by 15.

Working with Arrays

The Space Rescue game appears to have two images (the shuttle and the astronaut), but actually the program features a lot of different images. I drew a shuttle image for each direction, and three astronaut images to produce the illusion of the astronaut waving for help. The eight shuttle images, although different, are still closely related, as are the three astronaut images. This kind of situation, where you might have several variables that are different but related, comes up frequently in many kinds of programming. The *array* is a structure designed for exactly such situations.

The Array Demo Program

The best way to understand arrays is to see them in action. Here is the source code for a program called the Array Demo:

```
//arrayDemo
//Demonstrates basic string array
//Andy Harris, 04/07/01

main(){
  string numeral[4];
  int i;

  numeral[0] = "zero";
  numeral[1] = "one";
  numeral[2] = "two";
```

```
  numeral[3] = "three";

  for (i = 0; i < 4; i++){
    alert(numeral[i]);
  } // end for
} // end main
```

The program prints the text values *zero* through *three* in succession. You could have done this several chapters ago, but take a look at how the information is stored here. Rather than having four completely separate variables for the different strings, I built one variable called `numeral` that has four possible values. If you create a variable with square brackets ([]) and a number after the variable name, you are creating an *array*. This means you are making one large string variable that can have four possible values. To tell the values apart, you'll use a numeric index. I loaded up values into the various numeral elements. Note that I had to include square brackets ([]) and an index whenever I referred to the `numeral` variable. This is necessary because there are now four different (but related) `numeral` variables in the program.

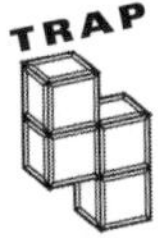

Although I created four elements in the numeral array, the largest one is "three." This is because computers commonly begin counting at 0. If I really wanted an array that went up to "four," I'd need to create an array with five elements.

The real advantage of using an array becomes evident inside the loop. I used a `for` loop to step through each possible index value, and output the appropriate string in turn.

Arrays can be used with any kind of variables, and they are frequently associated with `for` loops. Figures 6.7 and 6.8 illustrate the array demo in progress.

FIGURE 6.7

The array demo starts by displaying "zero."

FIGURE 6.8

The program steps through the array until the element "three" is on the screen.

Creating Shuttle Graphics

The Space Rescue program uses a number of images. Since images are stored as strings, you can easily generate an array of images by generating an array of strings containing the data used to build the images. I started working on the rescue program by building a series of ship images, and then writing a program that stores these images in an array.

The Ship Demo

Here is the first look at the shuttle. Figure 6.9 and Figure 6.10 show two of the eight possible directions in which the shuttle can go.

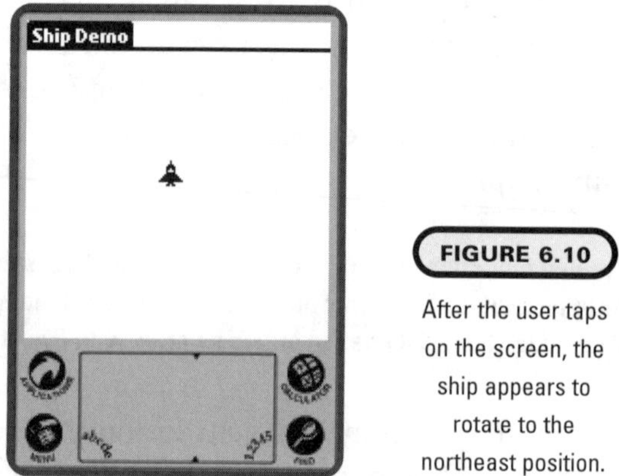

FIGURE 6.9

The ship is pointing north.

FIGURE 6.10

After the user taps on the screen, the ship appears to rotate to the northeast position.

As the demo proceeds, the ship will appear to rotate through all eight positions, and then the program will end. Of course, the ship is not really rotating. The program actually contains eight different images for the ship, and is showing these images one at a time.

The Ship Demo code may seem a bit long, but it isn't difficult to understand when you look at its component parts.

Setting Up Some Constants

The program begins by defining a series of constants for the directions the ship can point:

```
//shipDemo
//generate an array of ship objects
```

```
//andy Harris

#define NORTH 0
#define NORTHEAST 1
#define EAST 2
#define SOUTHEAST 3
#define SOUTH 4
#define SOUTHWEST 5
#define WEST 6
#define NORTHWEST 7
```

This will make the code easier to read and understand, because if I want to refer to the ship when it is pointing southwest, for example, I don't want to have to remember that southwest is 5.

Initializing the Ship Array

Next, the program creates a string array variable that will hold the definitions for the ship graphics, and it defines a function that initializes this array:

```
string ship[8];

init(){

  ship[NORTH] = "0d0200020007000f800d8008800f801fc03fe07ff0fff807000d80";
  ship[NORTHEAST] = "0d000800f0019003d0fff07fe03fc01f807f801f800b8009800080";
  ship[EAST] = "0d2000300038003c00bfc0fee07e38fee0bfc03c00380030002000";
  ship[SOUTHEAST] = "0d01000b000b001f007f001f807fc0ffe007f003d0019000f00008";
  ship[SOUTH] =  "0d0d800700fff87ff03fe01fc00f8008800d800d80070002000200";
  ship[SOUTHWEST] = "0d08000c800e800fc00ff00fc01fe03ff07ff85e004c0078008000";
  ship[WEST] = "0d0020006000e001e01fe83bf8e3f03bf81fe801e000e000600020";
  ship[NORTHWEST] = "0d800078004c005e007ff83ff01fe00fc00ff00fc00e800c800800";
} // end init
```

I used Bitmap Studio to generate all of the ship graphics. My ship was designed to be 13 by 13 bits large. I designed the ship on graph paper in both a horizontal and diagonal version, then I used Bitmap Studio to generate the various images. I stored all of these images as memos, then copied them into this program.

I made a special function called `'init()` to handle all this behavior.

The Main Loop

The next part of the program simply displays all the elements of the array in turn.

```
main(){
  int dir;
  init();

  graph_on();
  clearg();
  title("Ship Demo");

  for(dir=0; dir<8; dir++){
    bitmap(70, 70, ship[dir]);
    wait();
  } // end for loop
} // end main
```

The program begins with all the standard housekeeping functions. I also called the `init()` function, which will load up all the ship graphics.

The main body of the program is a `for` loop that steps through all eight possible directions. It displays a ship, and then waits for a key tap before continuing.

In the Real World

When trying to write a somewhat involved program like Space Rescue, you may run into problems figuring out where to start. It's a good idea to choose a small subset of the program and get it working cleanly before you worry about the other pieces. In this case, I have decided to make sure I have all the ship images loaded up and working as I expect them to. Once I'm sure this part is working, I'll add another element to the program.

Adding User Control

Now that you have established the ability to show all the versions of the ship image, it is time to add user input to the mix. Eventually, the rescue program will respond to four buttons. The Up, Down, Phone, and To Do buttons are often used for directional control on Palm-based game programs, so I'll continue the tradition. For now, all I'm concerned with is turning left, which will be signaled with the Phone button, and turning right with the To Do button. I'll also use the Memo button to end the game.

The Steer Ship Program

The Steer Ship program puts the direction of the shuttle craft under the user's control. By pressing the Phone and To Do buttons, the user can control the direction of the ship, as shown in Figures 6.11 through 6.13.

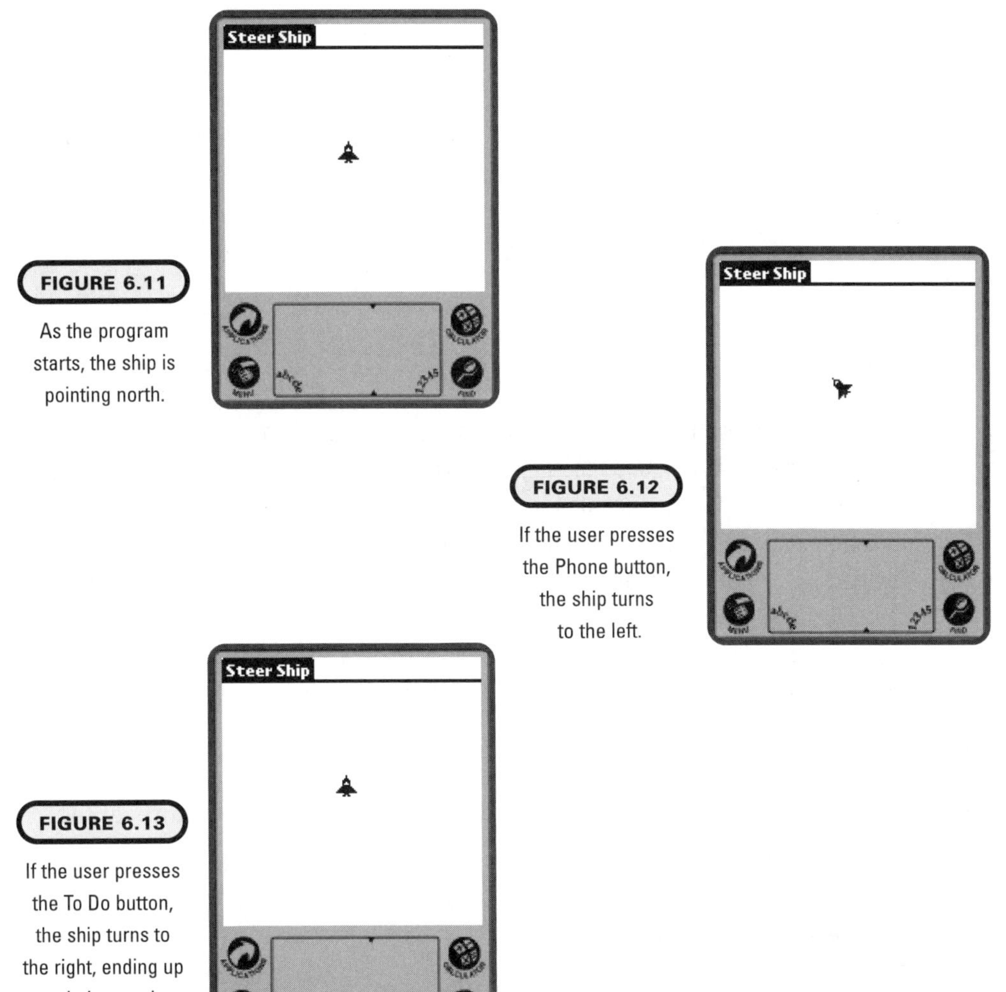

FIGURE 6.11 As the program starts, the ship is pointing north.

FIGURE 6.12 If the user presses the Phone button, the ship turns to the left.

FIGURE 6.13 If the user presses the To Do button, the ship turns to the right, ending up pointing north again.

Putting Some of the Code in a Library

The code for setting up the shuttle will be similar in all the rest of the programs in this chapter, so it might make sense to put it in a library rather than having to copy and paste it every time. I created a library called `shipLib.h` that copies a couple of key features of the ship demo.

```
/$ shipLib.h
//defines direction constants and ship graphics
//andy harris

#define NORTH 0
#define NORTHEAST 1
#define EAST 2
#define SOUTHEAST 3
#define SOUTH 4
#define SOUTHWEST 5
#define WEST 6
#define NORTHWEST 7

string ship[8];

setupShip(){

  ship[NORTH] = "0d0200020007000f800d8008800f801fc03fe07ff0fff807000d80";
  ship[NORTHEAST] = "0d000800f0019003d0fff07fe03fc01f807f801f800b8009800080";
  ship[EAST] = "0d2000300038003c00bfc0fee07e38fee0bfc03c00380030002000";
  ship[SOUTHEAST] = "0d01000b000b001f007f001f807fc0ffe007f003d0019000f00008";
  ship[SOUTH] =  "0d0d800700fff87ff03fe01fc00f8008800d800d80070002000200";
  ship[SOUTHWEST] = "0d08000c800e800fc00ff00fc01fe03ff07ff85e004c0078008000";
  ship[WEST] = "0d0020006000e001e01fe83bf8e3f03bf81fe801e000e000600020";
  ship[NORTHWEST] = "0d800078004c005e007ff83ff01fe00fc00ff00fc00e800c800800";

} // end setupship
```

This library is just like the beginning of the Ship Demo program, except I renamed the init function `setupShip`.

Importing the Libraries

The Steer Ship program will incorporate some of the features of the ship library and event handling, so I'll start by importing both.

```
// steerShip
// adds event handling and user control
// Andy Harris, 04/07/01

#include "shipLib.h"
#include "events.h"
```

When I imported the shipLib.h library, the code in that file was read by the compiler as if it were written in this main file. This means that all the variable and constant definitions I created in shipLib.h are now available to this program, as is the `setupShip()` function.

Setting Up the Program

The Steer Ship program does most of the normal setup, plus a few extra things:

```
main(){
  int dir = NORTH;
  int evt;
  int keepGoing=TRUE;

  setupShip();
  graph_on();
  clearg();
  title("Steer Ship");

  hookhard(1);
```

I begin by creating variables for direction, and a variable to hold an event. I also add a sentry variable called `keepGoing` to control when the main loop ends.

To set up the ship, all I needed to do was call the `setupShip()` function, which is in the shipLib.h library.

I then cleared the screen and turned on the graphics mode. Since this program will be responding to button presses, I told PocketC to trap for button presses with the `hookHard()` function. (Recall that by default, pressing a button will cause an application to launch immediately. I don't want the Phone button to launch the address book—the button should be interpreted by the program instead.)

The Main Loop

This program relies on an event loop to look for user events (in this case, only button presses) and respond to them. Here's the code for the main event loop:

```
while (keepGoing == TRUE){
    evt = event(0);
    switch(evt){
      case EVT_BTN_ADD:
        dir--;
        if (dir < NORTH){
          dir = NORTHWEST;
        } //end if
        break;
      case EVT_BTN_TODO:
        dir++;
        if (dir > NORTHWEST){
          dir = NORTH;
        } // end if
        break;
      case EVT_BTN_MEMO:
        keepGoing = FALSE;
    } // end switch
    bitmap(70, 70, ship[dir]);
  } // end while
```

The program continues as long as the `keepGoing` variable maintains the value TRUE. It looks for an event, and stores a value for the event in the `evt` variable. It then examines the event to determine what happened. I am only checking for button presses. I used a switch statement to compare the evt object to a number of constants. The use of constants makes the code much easier to read.

If the user pressed the Phone button, the program decrements `dir`. I set up the direction constants so subtracting one from `dir` would be just like turning to the left. The program then checks to see if the direction variable has gotten less than NORTH (which is 0). If so, the value of dir is set to NORTHWEST. This ensures that the `dir` variable always has a legitimate value.

The To Do button code is very similar. By pressing this button, the user has indicated that the ship should turn to the right, so the program adds 1 to `dir`, and checks to see that the direction does not get larger than NORTHWEST (which is 7).

Any time you increment or decrement a variable, you should think about trapping for a boundary value. Most of the time, you will want to reinforce an upper (or lower) limit for the variable.

The Memo button is used for the end of the game. If the user clicks on this button, however, the program doesn't immediately end. Instead, I set the value of `keepGoing` to FALSE. The next time through the program's while loop, the condition will be false and the loop will end, ending the program.

Flying the Ship around the Screen

The next incarnation of the program will give the ship wings. Now that the program can respond to keyboard input, it's time to add movement, as in Figure 6.14. I envisioned a movement system like the classic arcade game *Asteroids*. The player can add thrust only in the direction the ship is pointing. To change the ship's angle, the player can turn the ship and add more thrust. To slow down, the player should turn the ship in the direction opposite to the ship's motion and apply thrust. If this doesn't make any sense to you, just load the program on your PDA and play with it. It will all make sense with just a few moments' play.

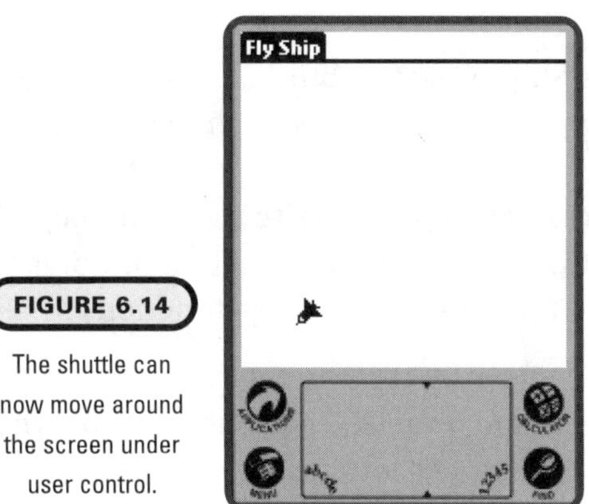

FIGURE 6.14

The shuttle can now move around the screen under user control.

Setting Up the Fly Program

The setup for the Fly program looks very similar to the others in this chapter, because it is based on them:

```
//fly
//moves ship around screen
//Andy Harris, 04/08/01
```

```
#include "shipLib.h"
#include "events.h"

deltaV();
moveShip();

int dir = NORTH;
int x=70;
int y=70;
int dx, dy;

main(){
   int evt;
   int keepGoing=TRUE;

   setupShip();
   graph_on();
   clearg();
   title("Fly Ship");

   hookhard(1);
```

Much of the code is taken from the Steer Ship program, but I'll highlight a few differences. First, I added function prototypes for the `deltaV()` and `moveShip()` functions. Recall that function prototypes are used so that the programmer can refer to a function in code before defining it. I wanted to write the main loop of this program before I wrote the two new functions, so I used function prototypes and wrote the functions later in the code. You'll get to see these functions in all their glory in a few moments.

I also added a couple of new variables. The `x` and `y` variables are used to note the shuttle's current position on the screen. (The upper left corner of the shuttle's position, to be precise.) The `dx` and `dy` variables are used to determine the difference in `x` and the difference in `y`. Mathematicians and scientists sometimes also refer to difference as *delta,* so this type of variable is also sometimes called `delta-x` and `delta-y`. Hey, if you're writing a space simulation, you should get to use some of the lingo, right?

The first part of the `main` function is very much like the other programs in this chapter. I changed the title, but all the other elements remained the same as in the Steer Ship example.

The Event Loop

The primary loop of this program is a standard event loop. Basically, it just gets an event handler, checks for button presses, and calls on various other functions to do the work:

```
while (keepGoing == TRUE){
     evt = event(20);
     switch(evt){
       case EVT_BTN_ADD:
         dir--;
         if (dir < NORTH){
           dir = NORTHWEST;
         } //end if
         break;
       case EVT_BTN_TODO:
         dir++;
         if (dir > NORTHWEST){
           dir = NORTH;
         } // end if
         break;
       case EVT_BTN_MEMO:
         keepGoing = FALSE;
       case EVT_PAGE_DN:
         deltaV();
     } // end switch

     moveShip();

  } // end while

} // end main
```

Adding a Delay to the Loop

I changed the event code slightly. In the earlier examples, I had the program act immediately upon an event, and then wait indefinitely for another event to occur—using the `event(0)` function call has this effect. Now that I'm adding movement, time becomes more important, so I changed the event function to `event(20)`. Setting the event to 20 causes the program to check for an event every 20/100th of a second, or five times a second. Setting this value to 25 will cause the loop to execute four times a second, and 500 will cause the loop to execute every five seconds. Table 6.1 lists the effects of the various settings for easy reference.

TABLE 6.1 SETTINGS FOR THE EVENT PARAMETER

Setting	Description	Example
n = 0	Event returns immediately	evt = event(0);
n = 1	Program waits indefinitely for an event to occur before moving on.	evt = event(1);

n > 1	Program waits for up to n 100ths of a second before moving on. n=50 means half a second, n = 300 means three seconds. If an event occurs before the time is up, the loop continues.	evt = event(50);
		// wait up to half a second
		evt = event(400);
		//wait up to four seconds

I set the event at 50, which means the program will loop twice a second. As I said before, if I put a smaller number in here, the program will execute more quickly; a larger number will cause the program to run more slowly. This is a terrific value to play around with if you want to change the difficulty level of the game.

Adding a Thruster Key

I added one more event to the loop. This program checks for the thruster, which I assigned to the Down key. The actions of the thruster are complex enough to warrant their own function, so I simply had the event handler call that function, `deltaV`. *Delta-V* is space talk for "change velocity," so I decided to give the function a NASA-like name. Again, you'll see this function in a few moments, but it's important to concentrate on the problem at hand right now, which is the event handler. My basic thinking here was this: When the user presses the Down key, the ship's velocity will change. The code for changing the ship's velocity will be called here, no matter what the details of that code.

IN THE REAL WORLD

It's good that the details of `deltaV` are hidden from view, because they constitute a very different problem from making sure the event handling works correctly. The first time I wrote this program, it contained only an alert statement saying, "I'm in `deltaV`." This let me focus first on getting the event handler working correctly. I only worried about the code for `deltaV` when I was sure it was being called at the right time.

Adding the moveShip() Function

After checking for every event that concerns me, I called the `moveShip()` function as the last action each time through the loop. Again, I'm only concerned about the big picture in the main loop, so I'll simply pass control to the `moveShip()` function, and not worry about its details until I'm actually writing that function.

The moveShip() Function

The `moveShip` function takes into account the current values of `dx` and `dy` to move the ship on the screen. The bulk of the function code rests in boundary checking—determining whether the ship has flown off the screen.

```
moveShip(){

  x = x + dx;
  y = y + dy;

  //check bounds
  if (x > 160){
    x = 0;
  } // end if

  if (x < 0){
    x = 160;
  } // end if

  if (y > 160){
    y = 0;
  } // end if

  if (y < 0){
    y = 160;
  } // end if

  //erase prev. Ship
  clearg();
  //draw the ship
  bitmap(x, y, ship[dir]);

} // end moveship
```

First, the function simply adds `dx` and `dy` to the current values of x and y. (See the next section to find out how `dx` and `dy` get their values.) Since it's conceivable that the ship could be moved off the screen, I had to check for the maximum and minimum screen values. (The Palm screen is 160 by 160 pixels, so x and y values cannot be smaller than 0 or larger than 160.)

I decided I wanted the world to wrap around because this would give the effect of a much larger space than the tiny Palm screen. If x became larger than 160, for example, I caused the value of x to be reset to 0, meaning that the next time the ship is displayed, it will be displayed at the left-hand edge of the screen.

Once I checked all the boundary conditions, I cleared the screen. This is necessary because the ship is not automatically removed from the screen when a new

In the Real World

There are basically four things you can do when an object hits a screen boundary:

* **Let the object keep moving off screen. Keep incrementing the appropriate variables but do not draw the object. This technique might be used when you're writing something like an air traffic control simulator that shows a limited amount of space, but can track traffic outside that space**
* **Stop the object at the edge of the screen. If x < 0, for example, set x to 0 or dx to 0. This is useful for situations where the object should not be allowed to leave the screen. (In a racing game, for example, the edge of the screen is probably the edge of the track. You might also want to write code that would somehow damage the car if it hit the walls, such as limiting its subsequent acceleration.)**
* **Bounce the object off the edge. This might be used in something like a billiards simulation. The easiest way to get bouncing behavior is to simply reverse the value of `dx` or `dy`. For example, the only way an object could bounce off of the right-hand wall is if `dx` is positive. When `x` is larger than 160, simply subtract `dx` from 0, which will give `dx` the same magnitude in the other direction. If you want to account for some give in the wall, subtract some value from `dx` before inverting it.**
* **Wrap the object to the other side of the screen. This is used when you want either to simulate a very large area as in the Space Rescue program, or simulate a cylinder or a globe. If you were writing a strategy game that took place on an entire planet, for example, you might allow wrap-around for the east and west borders to simulate circumnavigating the globe.**

one is drawn. Try taking the `clearg()` command out and you'll see what happens. You will get a series of leftover dots on the screen because each time the ship is drawn, it leaves little bits behind. The `clearg()` function clears the entire screen, which will be redrawn from scratch.

Redrawing the screen like this can take a lot of time, and can be troublesome when you have a lot of complicated graphics to draw. This simple program won't cause too many problems, but when you have a lot more objects moving around on the screen you'll start to see some noticeable flicker. See Chapter 11, "Using the Ptoolkit Library," for advanced techniques on how to correct for this problem.

The last part of the `moveShip()` function draws the current ship bitmap to the (x, y) coordinates.

The deltaV() Function

The purpose of the `deltaV()` function is to change the ship's velocity. The ship's speed and direction are determined by the variables `dx` and `dy`. Every time through the main loop, the ship's `x` variable will be incremented by `dx`, and the ship's `y` variable will be incremented by `dy`. If `dx` is positive, the ship will move to the right, and if `dx` is negative, the ship will move to the left. The `dy` variable works in a similar way; a negative value of `dy` moves the ship up, and a positive value moves the ship down.

The direction that the ship is currently pointing should determine what happens to `dx` and `dy`. If, for example, the ship is currently not moving and facing north when the thruster button is pressed, `dx` should be decremented, so the next time through the loop, the ship will move up one pixel. If the thruster button is pressed again, `dx` should be decremented again, causing the ship to move more quickly up the screen. To completely stop the shuttle, the player will need to turn the ship around so it's pointing south, then press the thruster twice.

This control scheme provides some very elegant behavior, because a player who's learned how to control the ship can give it pretty much any vector desired.

Here's the code that manipulates the ship's speed and acceleration:

```
deltaV(){

  //change the velocity
  switch (dir){
    case NORTH:
      dy-;
```

```
        break;
      case NORTHEAST:
        dx++;
        dy-;
        break;
      case EAST:
        dx++;
        break;
      case SOUTHEAST:
        dy++;
        dx++;
        break;
      case SOUTH:
        dy++;
        break;
      case SOUTHWEST:
        dy++;
        dx-;
        break;
      case WEST:
        dx-;
        break;
      case NORTHWEST:
        dy-;
        dx-;
        break;
    } // end dir switch

} // end deltaV
```

In every case, I simply translated the direction to appropriate changes in the `x` and `y` direction. I did not check for upper and lower bounds because it did not seem necessary. The player could achieve a ridiculous velocity, but it would not cause any problems except for making the game impossible to win.

Animating the Astronaut

Now the shuttle craft is basically done, and it's time to give the player someone to rescue. It would be easy to use a static bitmap here, but it isn't much more difficult to add animation of the type shown in Figure 6.15—and the animation adds a lot to the program.

FIGURE 6.15

The three frames of the astronaut (greatly enlarged).

I decided to draw an astronaut frantically waving for help. Again I called upon Bitmap Studio to assist in drawing the astronaut figures. Since all three figures are identical except for the arms, I drew one, saved it to a memo, modified it, saved that to a memo, and so on. Then I simply copied the bitmap strings from the memo documents to the Spaceman source code.

The Spaceman Program

So far the astronaut won't do anything but wave, so the program is easy to write:

```
//spaceman
//Animates an astronaut figure
//Andy Harris, 04/08/01

#include "events.h"

string man[3];

main(){
  int keepGoing = TRUE;
  int evt;
  int counter = 0;
  man[0]="0c0000644944942641f80f00f0060090090198";
  man[1]="0c0000624924922641f80f00f0060090090198";
  man[2]="0c0001602914922641f80f00f0060090090198";

  graph_on();
  clearg();
```

```
    title("space man");

    while (keepGoing == TRUE){
      evt = event(20);
      if(evt==EVT_BTN_MEMO){
        keepGoing = FALSE;
      } // end if
      counter++;
      if (counter > 2){
        counter = 0;
      } // end if

      //print the spaceman
      bitmap(70, 70, man[counter]);
    } // end while
  } //end main
```

I started by including the event-handling code in `events.h`. I then created a three-element array to hold the bitmap strings for the astronauts, and copied the code into the array elements. The rest of the code is a standard event loop that continues until the user presses the Memo button. Each time through the loop, the program increments counter by one, checking for counter to be larger than 2. I then simply print the element of the man array related to the current counter in the center of the screen.

It might be tempting to try to incorporate the astronaut directly into the evolving rescue code, but that may not be a smart idea. A lot of times it's better to test new concepts in smaller, more isolated programs. The programs with the ship in them have a lot of other elements going on, and it will be very easy to get confused. Also, it is possible that adding a new feature will mess up otherwise stable code. Once you know how to achieve some kind of effect (like animating the astronaut) in a small program, it is easy to incorporate the code into a larger program.

Collision Detection

Before the ship and the astronaut can be combined, you need one more technique critical to game programming, called *collision detection.* In 2-D arcade games, most of the action occurs when objects bump into each other. It's important to have some kind of code that can tell you when this has occurred. In the Space Rescue game, you'll need to know when the astronaut and the shuttle are touching. Before you tackle this in the game itself, it's a good idea to look at the problem in a simpler program. Several forms of collision detection are commonly used, but I'll show you one of the easiest to implement.

Looking for a Point in a Rectangle

The first thing you need to do is determine if a point is inside a rectangle. The program featured in Figures 6.16 and 6.17 demonstrates such behavior.

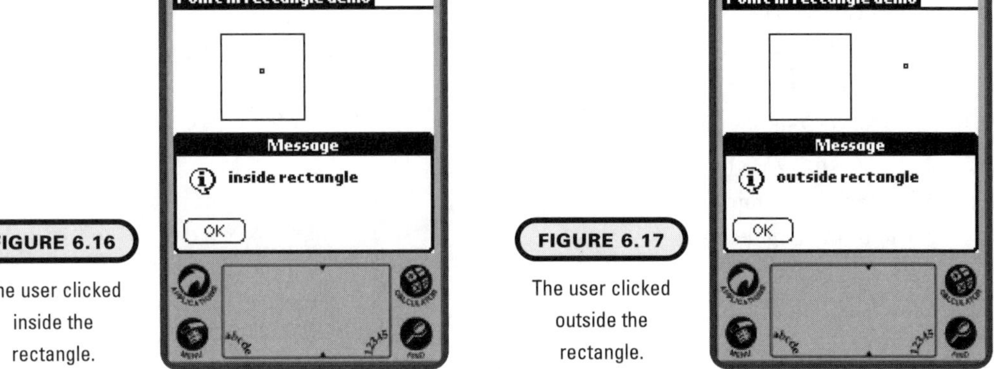

FIGURE 6.16

The user clicked inside the rectangle.

FIGURE 6.17

The user clicked outside the rectangle.

This functionality comes in handy all sorts of ways. If you want to simulate buttons on your graphics screen, you could draw a rectangle and check to see when a keypress occurs inside this rectangle. (In fact, this is exactly how command buttons work in the Palm OS, although the details are a bit more sophisticated. See Chapter 7, "Adding a Graphical User Interface: The Mad Lib Game," for more information.) Checking for a point inside a rectangle is also very useful when comparing two rectangles, as you will see.

The pointRec() Function

My strategy was to devise a function that could trap for a point inside a rectangle. I decided to write the function inside a simple program that would just check to see that the function works correctly. The function itself is the critical part of the program, so look at it first:

```
//pointRec
//determine if a point is in a rectangle
//Andy Harris, 04/04/01
```

```
int pointRec(int px, int py, int x1, int y1, int x2, int y2){

   //given point (px, py) and a rectangle (x1, y1) - (x2, y2),
   //return true if the point is inside the rectangle
   //otherwise return false

   int result = false;
   if (px > x1){
     if (px < x2){
       if (py > y1){
         if (py < y2){
           result = true;
         } // end y2 check
       } // end y1 check
     } // end x2 check
   } // end x1 check
   return result;
} // end pointRec
```

This function is designed to return a Boolean value (true or false). If the point is inside the rectangle, the function should return the value true. If the point is outside the rectangle, the function will return the value false. This function uses a lot of parameters. It expects the x and y coordinates of a point. It then expects the coordinates of two diagonally opposite points of a rectangle. Given these values, it can calculate if the point falls within the rectangle's boundaries.

I started by creating a variable called `result` that starts out with the value false.

I checked the points position with a series of nested `if` statements. The point is only inside the rectangle if every one of the if statements is true. By nesting the result = true line deep inside the `if` statement structure, I designed the program so the value of `result` will only be true if `px` is between `x1` and `x2`, and if `py` is between `y1` and `y2`.

The last line of the function returns the value of `result`, which will either be true or false.

The main() Function

The `main` function of this program is meant to test the `pointRec` function to make sure it does its job correctly.

I've said it before, but it's worth saying again: *It's a really smart idea to test new concepts in isolated environments before putting them in the larger context of a complex program.* By the time I incorporate `pointRec` into the Space Rescue program, I want to know for sure that it works as advertised.

The function draws a rectangle on the screen and waits for user input. It then checks to see if the pen input was inside or outside the rectangle drawn on the screen.

```
main(){

  graph_on();
  clearg();
  title("Point in rectangle demo");

  //draw the rectangle
  frame(1, 30, 30, 80, 80, 0);
  wait();
  //draw the point
  frame(1, penx(), peny(), penx()+1, peny() + 1, 0);

  if (pointRec(penx(), peny(), 30, 30, 80, 80) == true){
    alert("inside rectangle");
  } else {
    alert("outside rectangle");
  } // end if
} // end main
```

Once the `pointRec` function is mastered, you can look at another form of collision detection using rectangles.

Looking for Rectangle Overlaps: The Collision Detection Program

Rectangular collision detection is a staple of game programming, and there are many ways to do it. I'll show you a relatively simple form that is based on the `pointRec` function you've already learned.

The Collision Detection program demonstrates a function called `collision`. The `collision` function expects eight parameter values (the coordinates used to draw two rectangles) and returns a true or false value. If the rectangles intersect, the function returns the value true, and if the rectangles do not intersect, the function returns false.

To test the collision function, the program waits for the user to tap the screen four times. The first two taps are used to generate the first rectangle, and the second two taps are used to create the second rectangle. The x and y points gathered from these taps are then sent to the collision function, which determines whether a collision has occurred. Figures 6.18 through 6.20 illustrate different aspects of the behavior of the collision detection routine.

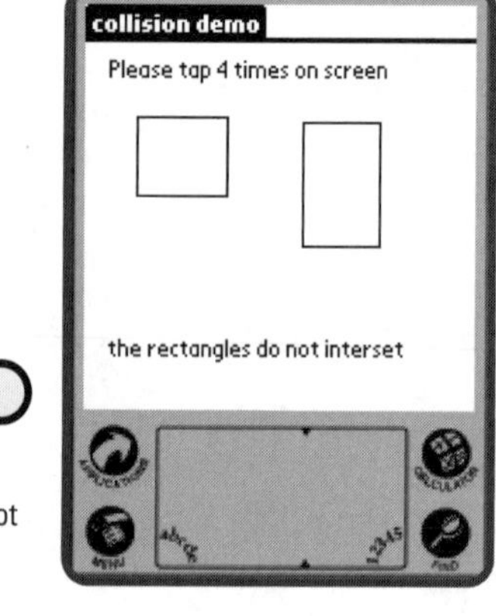

FIGURE 6.18

These two rectangles are not colliding.

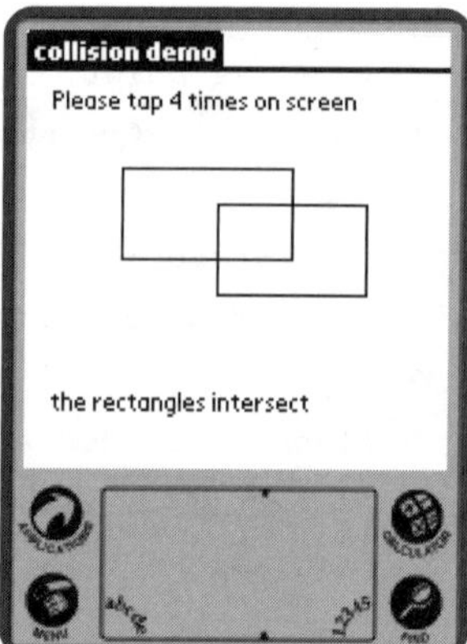

FIGURE 6.19

These two rectangles intersect each other.

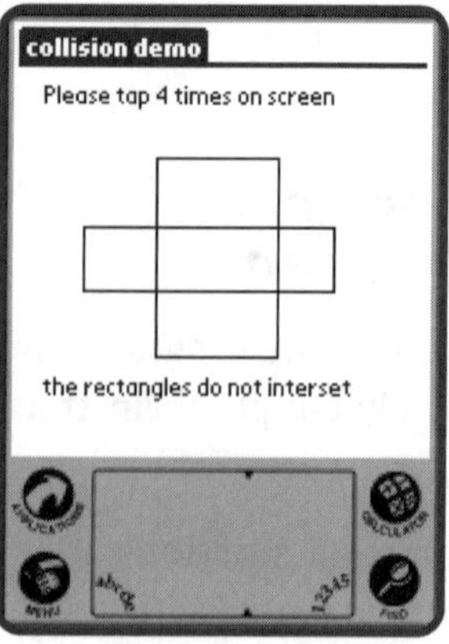

FIGURE 6.20

Here's a situation where the collision detection routine will not work correctly.

IN THE REAL WORLD

If the program doesn't work right, why use it?

It may surprise you to know that the collision detection program proves a case where the collision routine does not work correctly. This is precisely why you should test routines such as this one in programs that clearly let you see how the routine is working. At first, I was quite dismayed that my algorithm was incomplete, but upon further reflection I realized that the algorithm will work just fine for my program because the type of collision that the routine cannot handle should never happen in the Space Rescue program. As you examine that program later, I'll show you what I mean.

The Collision Function

The `collision` function works by calling the `pointRec` function twice. My basic reasoning was this: If I have two rectangles, A and B, the rectangles intersect if the upper left corner of A is inside rectangle B, or if the upper left corner of B is inside rectangle A. That should be reasonably easy to determine, because I can use the `pointRec` function to determine if any point is inside a rectangle:

```
int collision(int x1, int y1, int x2, int y2,
              int x3, int y3, int x4, int y4){
  //given rectangles (x1, y1)-(x2, y2) and (x3, y3)-(x4, y4)
  //determine if the rectangles overlap
  //requires pointRec function to be defined

  int result = false;

  //is (x1, y1) inside (x3, y3)-(x4, y4)?
  if (pointRec(x1, y1, x3, y3, x4, y4)){
    result = true;
  } // end if

  //is (x3, y3) inside (x1, y1)-(x2, y2)?
  if (pointRec(x3, y3, x1, y1, x2, y2)){
    result = true;
  } // end if

  return result;
} // end collision
```

The variable `result` is initialized to false. If the upper left point of rectangle A (x1, y1) is found inside rectangle B (x3, y3)-(x4, y4), result is changed to true. Likewise, if the upper left point of B (x3, y3) is found in rectangle A (x1, y1) - (x2, y2), the `result` variable becomes true. If neither of these conditions occurs, the value of `result` remains false. The value of the `result` variable is returned out of the function.

The main() Function of the Collision Detection Program

The Collision Detection program checks the `collision()` function to see if it is working correctly—something useful to know before incorporating the function into the Space Rescue game. The code is fairly straightforward:

```
main(){

   int x1, y1, x2, y2;
   int x3, y3, x4, y4;

   graph_on();
   clearg();
   title("collision demo");

   text(10, 20, "Please tap 4 times on screen");

   wait();
   x1 = penx();
   y1 = peny();

   wait();
   x2 = penx();
   y2 = peny();

   frame(1, x1, y1, x2, y2, 0);

   wait();
   x3 = penx();
   y3 = peny();

   wait();
   x4 = penx();
   y4 = peny();
```

```
frame(1, x3, y3, x4, y4, 0);

if (collision(x1,y1,x2,y2,x3,y3,x4,y4)){
  text(10, 130, "the rectangles intersect");
} else {
                              les do not intersect");
```

housekeeping, then waits for a pen tap. The x
l into x1 and y1. The program waits for another
ates into x2 and y2. This gives the program
ectangle, so it draws the first rectangle on the
taps and then retrieves the last four coordinate
feeds the coordinates to the `collision` func-
at function. If the collision came out true, the
priate message. If no collision is detected, that

Space Rescue

ace to build the Space Rescue program. Most of
various smaller programs. The only challenge
gether in a larger program.

e Rescue Game

f component pieces. The setup for the program
a number of steps, including creating several
and creating function prototypes for several of

```
//space rescue game
//illustrates animation concepts
//Andy Harris, 04/04/01

#include "events.h"
#include "rescueLib.h"
```

```
//function prototypes
deltaV();
moveShip();
setManDir();
moveMan();
checkRendevous();

//ship variables
int sdir = NORTH;
int sx = 70;
int sy = 70;
int sdx = 0;
int sdy = 0;

//man variables
int mx = 70;
int my = 70;
int mdx = 0;
int mdy = 0;
int counter = 0;
```

The Library Files

I decided to move several functions over to a library file. I was mainly interested in those functions I had already stored in the shipLib, and the utility functions. Since all of these routines had been tested separately and were reasonably well behaved, they seemed to fit in the library module.

The Rescue Library contains the `setupShip()`, `setupMan()`, `pointRec()`, and `collision()` functions. All of these functions have been described in other parts of the chapter, so I won't reproduce them here. Of course, you can look at them on the CD-ROM if you are curious.

Since I wrote this program with the desktop edition, I didn't have to worry about file sizes. If you write this program directly on the Palm device using Memo Pad, you may have to add more functions to the library or even add another library module. (However, if you find yourself consistently writing programs longer than the 4K limit of Memo Pad, you might be ready for the desktop edition or a more powerful text editor.) In addition to the rescue library, I chose to use the event library that has been so useful throughout this book.

Creating Function Prototypes

The Space Rescue game features a lot of functions. There are six functions in the main program, and another four defined in the rescue library. Since I imported the rescue library before starting the main program, all of the functions in that library were defined before they were used, and do not need function prototypes here. Generally, you will not need to define function prototypes for functions that you import in a library. However, because I didn't want to worry about function dependencies while I was writing the rest of the program, I defined a function prototype for every other function in the program.

Ship and Man Variables

I defined a set of variables that will be most critical to the operation of the program. I needed a set of variables to determine the direction, position, and speed of the ship, and a similar set of variables for the astronaut. To keep these variables straight, I started all the ship variables with the letter "s," and all the man variables with the letter "m." You might notice that I did not create a direction variable for the man, because the astronaut is shown in only one direction. I did create a counter to keep track of animating the astronaut.

The main() Function of Space Rescue

The `main()` function of the program is only slightly different from the main function of the Fly program:

```
main(){
  int evt;
  int keepGoing=TRUE;

  //int speed;

  setupShip();
  setupMan();

  graph_on();
  clearg();
  title("Space Rescue");

  hookhard(1);
```

```
    setManDir();

    while (keepGoing == TRUE){
      evt = event(50);
      switch(evt){
        case EVT_BTN_ADD:
          sdir--;
          if (sdir < NORTH){
            sdir = NORTHWEST;
          } //end if
          break;
        case EVT_BTN_TODO:
          sdir++;
          if (sdir > NORTHWEST){
            sdir = NORTH;
          } // end if
          break;
        case EVT_BTN_MEMO:
          keepGoing = FALSE;
        case EVT_PAGE_DN:
          deltaV();
      } // end switch
      moveShip();
      moveMan();
      checkRendezvous();

    } // end while

} // end main
```

The function begins by calling the `setupShip()` and `setupMan()` functions. These functions (not surprisingly) create and set up the string arrays for the ship and astronaut animations.

I added a call to the `setManDir()` function, which sets the position and direction of the man randomly.

The event loop looks just like that of the Fly program, but I added a couple of additional function calls to the end of the loop. Each time through the loop, the program moves the ship, moves the man, and checks for a rendezvous.

In the Real World

The practice of putting as much functionality as possible into well-named functions really pays off here. Even though you haven't seen all of the details of all of the functions, by reading the `main` function you have a pretty good idea of everything the program will do.

The deltaV Function

I borrowed the `deltaV` function from the Fly program. The only change is modifying the variables to specify that they refer to the ship.

```
deltaV(){

  //change the velocity
  switch (sdir){
    case NORTH:
      sdy-;
      break;
    case NORTHEAST:
      sdx++;
      sdy-;
      break;
    case EAST:
      sdx++;
      break;
    case SOUTHEAST:
      sdy++;
      sdx++;
      break;
    case SOUTH:
      sdy++;
      break;
    case SOUTHWEST:
      sdy++;
      sdx-;
      break;
```

```
      case WEST:
        sdx--;
        break;
      case NORTHWEST:
        sdy--;
        sdx--;
        break;
  } // end dir switch

} // end deltaV
```

The moveShip() Function

Moving the ship is also very similar to the code from the Fly program, except for changing a few variable names:

```
moveShip(){

  sx = sx + sdx;
  sy = sy + sdy;

  //check bounds
  if (sx > 160){
    sx = 0;
  } // end if

  if (sx < 0){
    sx = 160;
  } // end if

  if (sy > 160){
    sy = 0;
  } // end if

  if (sy < 0){
    sy = 160;
  } // end if

  //erase prev. Ship
  clearg();
  //draw the ship
  bitmap(sx, sy, ship[sdir]);

} // end moveship
```

The setManDir() Function

This `utility` function is used to randomly assign a position and a vector to the astronaut figure.

```
setManDir(){
  //randomly sets the man's position and direction
  mx = random(160);
  my = random(160);
  mdx = random(11)-5;
  mdy = random(11)-5;
} // end setManDir
```

I set the coordinates for the astronaut to random values between 0 and 160. The `mdx` and `mdy` variables are used to determine the speed and direction of the astronaut. I wanted the value to be somewhere between 5 and –5 for the delta variables, but the `random` function does not generate negative numbers. I compensated by creating a random number between 0 and 10, and subtracting 5 from that number.

The moveMan() Function

The `moveMan()` function calculates the position of the astronaut on the screen.

```
moveMan(){

  mx = mx + mdx;
  my = my + mdy;

  //check bounds
  if (mx > 160){
    mx = 0;
  } // end if

  if (mx < 0){
    mx = 160;
  } // end if

  if (my > 160){
    my = 0;
  } // end if
```

```
    if (my < 0){
      my = 160;
    } // end if

    //draw the man
    bitmap(mx, my, man[counter]);

    //increment counter
    counter++;
    if (counter > 2){
      counter = 0;
    } // end if
  } // end moveMan
```

The function adds `mdx` to `mx` and `mdy` to `my`, moving the man in the direction specified by (`mx`, `my`). It then checks for boundaries, wrapping the astronaut around the screen if he leaves the visible area. It then increments the counter so that the man figure will be animated, resetting the counter if necessary.

The checkRendezvous() Function

The `checkRendezvous()` function checks to see if the shuttle craft and the astronaut have made contact. The `collision` function will determine if the shuttle and the astronaut images are overlapping, but the conditions for a successful rescue are a bit more exacting. The shuttle should be going at approximately the same speed and direction as the astronaut in order to effect a rescue.

```
checkRendezvous(){
  //check to see if a rescue has occurred
  if (collision(sx, sy, (sx + 13), (sy + 13), mx, my, (mx + 12), (my +
12))){

    if ((mdx - sdx) > -3){
      if ((mdx - sdx) < 3){
        if ((mdy - sdy) > -3){
          if ((mdy -sdy) < 3){
            alert("Rescue!");
            setManDir();
            return();
          } // end if
        } // end if
```

```
      } // end if
    } // end if
    alert("You weren't supposed to crash into him!");
    setManDir();
  } // end if
} // end checkRendevous
```

The first thing the function does is check for a collision. Since I defined the ship to be a 13x13 image and the man to be a 12x12 image, the collision function compares the rectangles containing the astronaut and the ship. You might wish to adjust the difficulty of the game by making the comparison rectangles a little larger or smaller.

The function checks to see that the velocities are similar. A set of nested `if` statements performs this task. A rescue will occur only if the difference between `mdx` and `sdx` is between 3 and –3, and if the difference between `mdy` and `sdy` is also between 3 and –3. This is another place you could adjust the difficulty of the game. By testing for a wider range of velocities, you will make the game easier.

If all the velocity checks come out okay, the program tells the user that a rescue occurred, resets the man's position and velocity, and exits the function. If any of the velocity checks fails, but the collision check is true, the function complains about the driving skill of the player.

This function would be the natural place for some scorekeeping.

In the Real World

The way this game works, the potential flaw in the collision function is not a problem. There are only two ways that the kind of overlap the collision algorithm can't catch will occur:

- **If the relative velocity of the two objects is similar, a normal overlap will have to happen first, which will be caught by the collision function. Since the `checkRendezvous()` function always resets the astronaut's position and velocity after any collision, you won't get two collisions in a row that could cause the overlapping behavior.**
- **If the relative velocity of the two objects is very large, it is conceivable that they could overlap in one turn without the corner of one being inside the corner of the other, but a large difference should be considered a crash anyway.**

Summary

This chapter has taken you quite a long way. You can now build bitmap images using a simple editor, and use arrays to deal with any kind of multiple values. You have learned how to use string variables and arrays to generate bitmap images, how to move objects on the screen, and how to flip between array elements to create the illusion of animation. You've seen what goes into developing a mildly involved program, and how to use collision detection algorithms.

CHALLENGES

1. **Give the astronaut a limited amount of oxygen. If the ship does not rescue the astronaut before the time runs out, the astronaut is lost.**
2. **Add scorekeeping. Give the player a score for the number of astronauts caught and the speed with which they were retrieved.**
3. **Limit the number of astronauts, so the game will have an ending place.**
4. **Add random space junk that the pilot has to avoid.**
5. **Change the program so it gets progressively more difficult as the player advances.**
6. **Use the techniques in this chapter to build an entirely different game or animation.**

Chapter 7

Adding a Graphical User Interface: The Mad Lib Game

You know enough about PocketC programming to write many kinds of programs. You can get input from the user in various ways including Graffiti, button presses, and stylus taps. You can also send information out to the user in text mode and through various devices in graphics mode. While these capabilities are all you need to build any type of program, modern users and programmers have gotten used to the use of higher-level graphic tools. Modern programming languages often employ a *graphical user interface* (GUI). As a user, you have probably encountered programs that had text boxes for entering text, drop-down list boxes, radio buttons and check boxes, tables and buttons. These GUI elements (collectively called *components* or *controls*) are good for the user because they are familiar. Most users know how to use a drop-down list box or a set of check boxes to select some information from the screen. PocketC itself does not have direct support for GUI components, but a number of free libraries do provide this functionality. In this chapter, you'll examine one of these libraries and use it with your programs. The chapter also covers the following topics:

- Using graphical user interfaces
- Examining the main types of controls available in a GUI
- Installing and running the Ccontrols library
- Building some GUI forms by hand
- Responding to GUI events
- Using the Ceditor to quickly build a framework

The Mad Lib Game

As an illustration of GUI concepts, this chapter shows you how to build a simple game that you might recall from your middle-school days. As illustrated in Figure 7.1, the program begins by displaying a form with several elements on it.

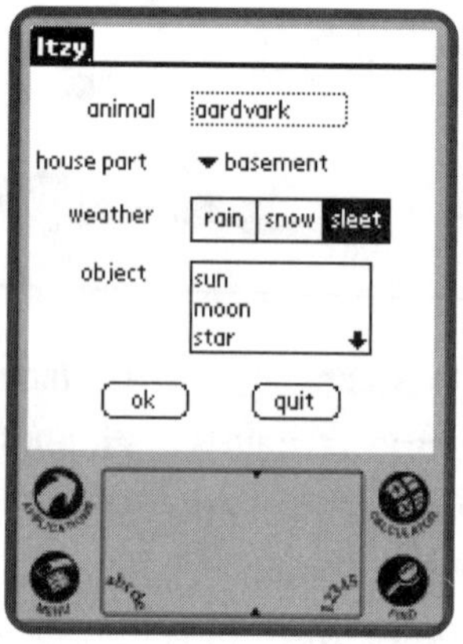

FIGURE 7.1

The Mad Lib game lets the user enter information in a number of ways.

The program allows several types of user input. A user who clicks the box next to the word animal will get the opportunity to edit the text in that box, as shown in Figure 7.2. A box that can be edited like this is usually called a *text box.*

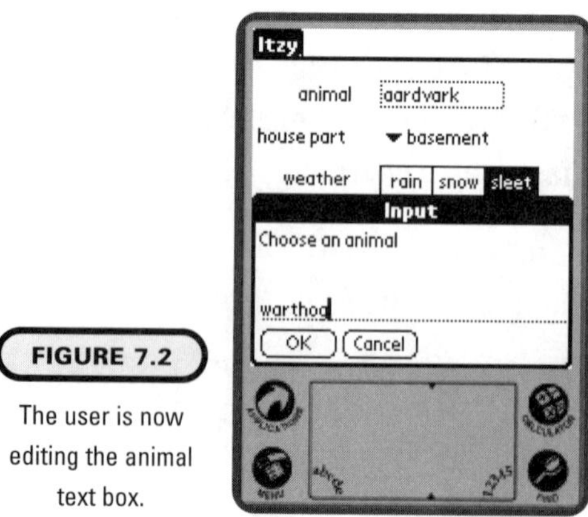

FIGURE 7.2

The user is now editing the animal text box.

The program features some other kinds of input. Figure 7.3 shows what happens if the user clicks on the text next to the words house part.

FIGURE 7.3

When the user clicks on the house part, a little menu drops down.

The house part is retrieved by a device called a *dropdown list box*. Not surprisingly, this is a list box that drops down when the user clicks on it.

The program also features a standard list box. This is like the dropdown list, but it displays on more than one line.

At the bottom of the screen you see two buttons. One button quits the program, and the other will process the information on the form. If the user clicks on the OK button, the story shown in Figure 7.4 appears.

Clicking anywhere on the screen takes the user back to the form. At that point, the choices are to change the values again or quit.

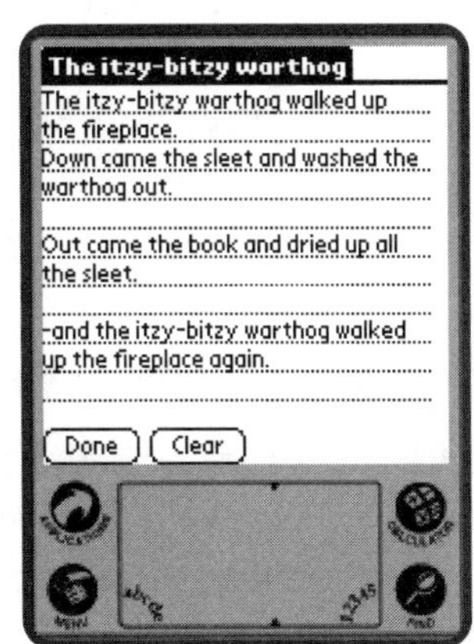

FIGURE 7.4

The user has generated a new version of a classic nursery rhyme. (The itzy-bitzy warthog?)

Using Ccontrols

Native PocketC (programmer-speak for PocketC in its basic form, without add-ins) does not support GUI objects such as buttons, list boxes, and labels. However, all such components can be built using the normal PocketC functions. A number of developers have created third-party libraries to add graphical interface design to PocketC. I've chosen to describe Ccontrols—one of the more popular libraries—in this book, but the others are very similar. This library was originally written by Mario Schlesinger, and has been updated by a team of volunteers led by D. Stéphane Thibault.

Ccontrols features all the major types of GUI objects that programmers and users are used to, including the ones you have seen in the Mad Lib program and a few others. Ccontrols also comes with an editor that helps you generate the visual layout of your interface.

The Basics of Graphical User Interface Design

Graphical user interfaces are popular for a number of reasons. Users generally are familiar with the various types of controls, so they can jump right into a program without a lot of help. GUI elements can be much more efficient ways to communicate with the program than is Graffiti input. This is especially important on Palm-based devices. Graffiti is slow and tedious compared to simply tapping on the screen. Palm programs should encourage quick and easy input when possible.

Programmers like GUIs for other reasons. It can be very difficult to anticipate user input; by using a GUI you can limit the user's input to legitimate values, saving you a lot of error checking. Many GUI systems (like Ccontrols) support a rapid application development (RAD) tool. These tools are editors that greatly simplify the creation of GUI programs. Under appropriate circumstances, using an RAD tool can help you write programs very quickly because the RAD tool will automatically write most of the code, freeing you to concentrate on the specific code necessary for your program.

Installing and Running the Ccontrols System

The Ccontrols package is included on the CD-ROM that accompanies this book. The package includes a number of components. Install the Cedit.prc file in the normal way. This program is a stand-alone program that allows you to draw controls on the screen. The Ceditor program also has the ability to generate the library files needed for Ccontrols. Run the Ceditor program, then click the menu button to see the program's menus. Choose Install Ccontrols from the Form menu. This function will automatically generate three memos with the Ccontrols library in them. If you wish to use Ccontrols with the desktop edition, hotsynch your Palm and copy the Ccontrols memos to text files. You will need to have the Ccontrols memos created in order to write programs that use the Ccontrols system. However, you do not have to write your program using the Ceditor. Once you have Ccontrols installed, you can incorporate the library into your program with an include statement. You will see later how to write programs using Ccontrols, but for now, take a look at some of the controls you can build using the library.

The Types of Controls Available

Ccontrols supports a number of different graphic controls. Figure 7.5 demonstrates some of them. Take a look at the program to see the various controls at your disposal.

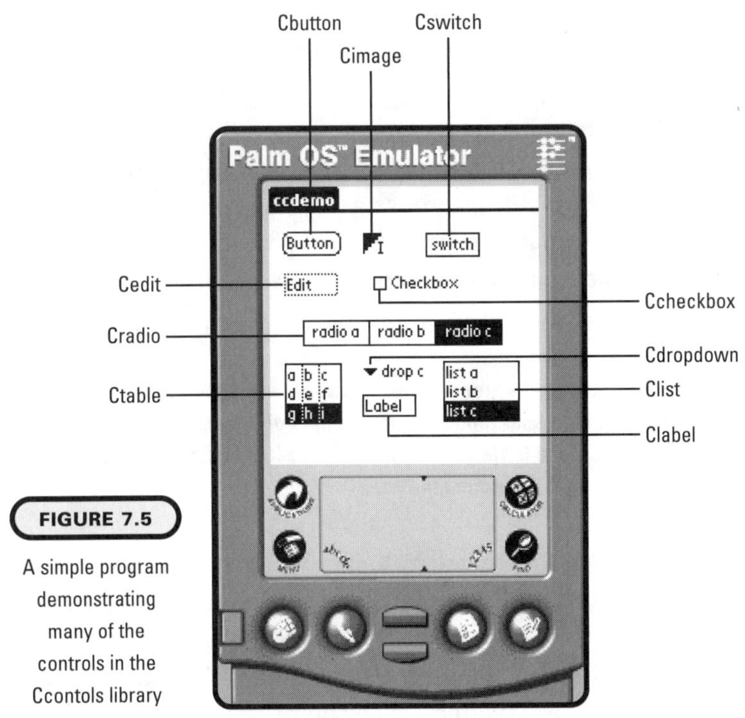

FIGURE 7.5

A simple program demonstrating many of the controls in the Ccontols library

All the objects in the Ccontrols library begin with the letter "C" to avoid confusion with other variables and functions you might create in your programs.

- **Cbutton**. The Cbutton control gives you a classic button. When the user clicks on the button, it briefly changes color (to white text on a black background). You will generally write code to respond to a button click.
- **Cimage**. The Cimage control works a lot like a button control, except it allows you to specify a bitmap image instead of text. The image is a normal bitmap string just like the regular PocketC bitmap command. When the user clicks on the image, it inverts colors, just like the button. As with the button, you will often write code that is intended to act whenever the user clicks on the Cimage object.
- **Cswitch**. The Cswitch control also gives you an element that looks like a button, but it stays on or off. You will generally use this control when you want the user to be able to turn some kind of value on or off.
- **Cedit**. The Cedit control allows you to place a text box on the screen. When the user clicks on the text box, an input dialog automatically pops up. Whatever the user enters into that dialog will be the new value of the text box.
- **Ccheckbox**. The Ccheckbox control gives you the classic labeled check box, which is usually used to indicate some type of value that can be turned on or off.
- **Cradio**. The Cradio control gets its name from old car radios—the ones where you pushed in a button to select a radio station, and another button would pop out. You will often use a Cradio group to allow the user to choose one option from a number of choices. Cradio switches are very easy to use, but they take up a lot of room on the screen.
- **Ctable**. The Ctable control lets you display data in a tabular fashion.

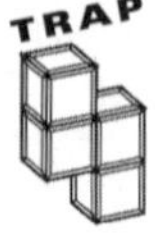

The table control is great for displaying data in a tabular format, but it is very difficult to use for user input. The developers of Ccontrols are looking at improving the design of the table control, but for now it is best to use other controls when you want to get input from the user.

- **Cdropdown**. The Cdropdown control gives you another way to let the user choose from a number of elements. When the user clicks on the control, a list of possible choices drops down. This control is a good choice when you want to save real estate on the screen because it only takes up a large part of the screen when it is activated. Once the user has made a selection, the

Cdropdown list requires only one line on the screen.

- **Clist**. The Clist control gives you still another way to allow the user to choose from a number of options. Unlike the Cdropdown, all the elements in the Clist control are generally available on the screen all the time.
- **Clabel**. The Clabel control just displays text inside a rectangle. Labels make useful output devices, but they don't have any direct way to pick up user input.

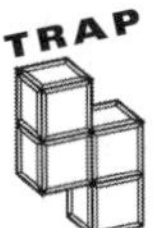

Ccontrols also supports a number of other interesting techniques, including menus, pop-up screens, and data-bound tables. I cover some of these controls later in this book, but feel free to look over the documentation that came with Ccontrols and experiment on your own.

Designing a GUI by Hand

Later in this chapter you will learn how to use the Ceditor program to assist in building a complete program. Although the Ceditor program helps you build a program, it is important that you understand how to use components in your own programs. Once you are sure you know how the controls work in a completely original program, you can use the editor to build fancier applications.

The Hi World GUI Program

As usual, it makes sense to start with a very small program and then build from it. Take a look at Figure 7.6, which shows the classic Hello World program as it is written with Ccontrols.

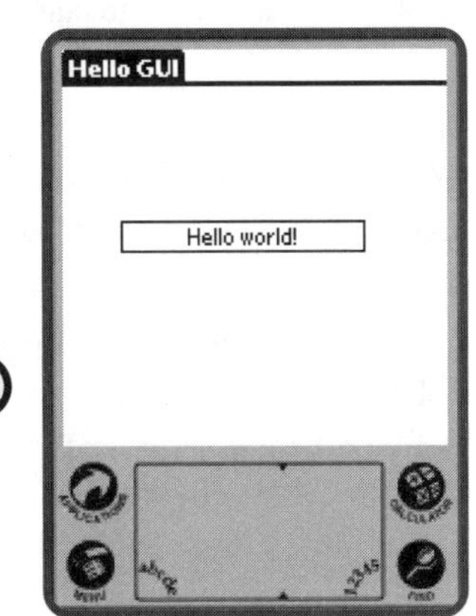

FIGURE 7.6

It looks like any other Hello World program, but the text is in a box.

I built the Hi World GUI program using Ccontrols, so it looks a little bit different from the way it would if it had been written without a GUI.

Initializing the Program

The first part of setting up the program is making a link to the Ccontrols library and setting up a variable to manage the label object.

```
//HiWorldGUI
//The simplest GUI I can think of
//Andy Harris, 04/21/01

#include "Ccontrols.c"

Chandle lblOutput;

main(){

  graph_on();
  clearg();
  title("Hello GUI");
```

This part of the code has an include statement that brings in the Ccontrols library.

For this to work, you must have the Ccontrols installed. Install them from the Ceditor (as described earlier in this chapter) if you haven't already done so.

You might be surprised that you only have to include one memo, because the Ceditor program generates three memos. The Ccontrols.c memo contains includes to the other memos needed, so you don't need to (and cannot) directly include those files.

The `Chandle` is a special custom variable type defined by `Ccontrols`. It will contain a reference to a control object. You must make a `Chandle` for each control you will be using in your program. A new variable of type `Chandle` called `lblOutput` refers to the label object I'll be creating soon. If all this confuses you, don't worry. All you really need to know is that you must create a `Chandle` variable for all components. The only control in this program will be a label, so I made a `Chandle` for it.

It's a good idea to name objects in a way that helps you remember what they are. I use "lbl" for labels, "txt" for text boxes, and so on. This technique is called *Hungarian notation.* It is very popular among programmers who use GUI tools, because the various objects can get very hard to keep track of otherwise.

Creating and Displaying the Label

Once you have defined a `Chandle`, you will need to make a label. Here's the code that generates and displays the label:

```
  lblOutput = Clabel(25, 70, 100, 1, 2, 1);
  Csetcontent(lblOutput, "Hello world!");
  Cdraw(lblOutput);

  wait();
} // end main
```

The first order of business is to create a label object. The `Chandle` can refer to any type of control. To make it a label, you must call the `Clabel` function. This function expects the six parameters shown in Table 7.1.

TABLE 7.1 PARAMETERS OF THE CLABEL FUNCTION

parameter	values	description
x	0–160	x location of label
y	0–160	y location of label
width	0–160	width of label
line	0 = white, 1 = black, 2 = gray	what color line to draw around (or under) label
style	0 = plain, 1= underlined, 2= boxed	whether line is drawn at all, under, or all around label
alignment	0 = left, 1 = centered, 2 = right	How text will be aligned inside label

I chose to put the label at coordinates (25, 70) and to make the label 100 pixels wide. I surrounded the label with a black box, and centered the text inside the label. When you're deciding which coordinates to use, it helps to lay out the screen on a grid like the one shown in Figure 7.7.

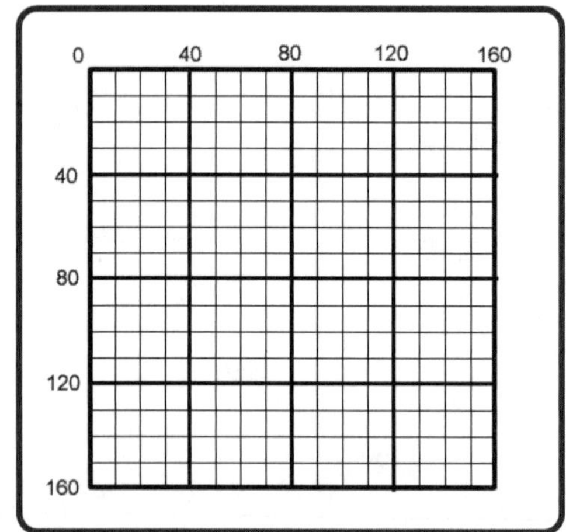

FIGURE 7.7

You can use this grid (available as a PCX image on the CD-ROM) to help lay out your controls.

I then set the label's contents with the `Csetcontent()` function. This function is used to set the content of most Ccontrols objects. It requires two parameters, the object's handle and the text to be added.

Finally, I used the `Cdraw()` function to draw the label itself. You can use this function to draw any of the Ccontrols objects on the screen. If you do not use the `Cdraw()` function, the object will not be visible.

Responding to GUI Events

GUI objects can also respond to events. It is important to know how this works, because almost all programs written to use a GUI also use an event-driven paradigm. This is not really new to you, because most of the code you've seen in this book also follows an event-based model. Many of your programs have involved a main loop that repeats indefinitely, waiting to respond to user events. To illustrate how events work in Ccontrols, look at the program illustrated in Figure 7.8.

The buttons are placed on the screen much like labels, but buttons are different in that they are intended to respond to an event. The only reason to put a button

FIGURE 7.8

This program features three buttons. Two are traditional, and one is an image.

on the screen is to give the user something to click. You need to be able to do some action when the button is clicked. All three buttons in this program have some code associated with them, as illustrated in Figures 7.9, 7.10, and 7.11.

FIGURE 7.9

When the user clicks the About button a simple dialog pops up.

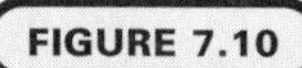

FIGURE 7.10

When the user clicks on the little image, another dialog shows up.

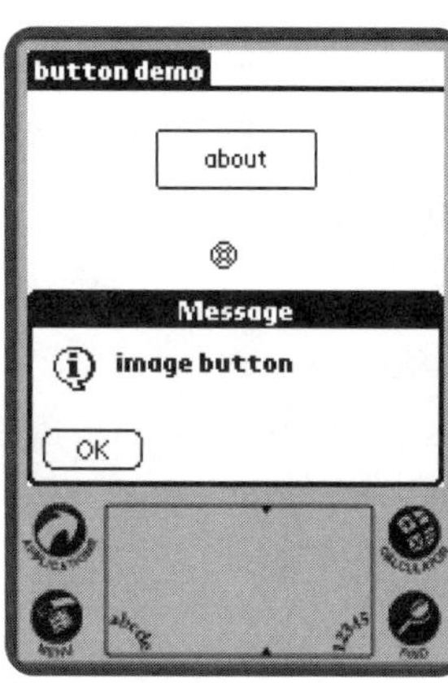

FIGURE 7.11

When the user clicks on the Exit button, the program says goodbye and then ends.

Initializing the Button Demo

It makes sense to divide programs that use controls into at least two major parts. The first part is initialization. Look at the starting code for the Btn Demo program, which includes a function called `init()`:

```
//btnDemo
//Demonstrates buttons in Ccontrols
//Andy Harris, 04/20/01

#include "Ccontrols.c"

Chandle btnAbout, btnQuit, img;

init(){
  graph_on();
  clearg();
  title("button demo");

  btnAbout = Cbutton(50, 30, 60, 20, 1, 2);
  Csetcontent(btnAbout, "about");
  Cdraw(btnAbout);

  img = Cimage(70, 70, 10, 10);
  Csetcontent(img, "0a1e0210528ad4924924ad45282101e0");
  Cdraw(img);

  btnQuit = Cbutton(50, 100, 60, 20, 1, 2);
  Csetcontent(btnQuit, "quit");
  Cdraw(btnQuit);
} // end init
```

The program starts with a reference to the Ccontrols library and a handle for each of the buttons I'll need. I'll be using two regular buttons plus a special-purpose button called the Cimage.

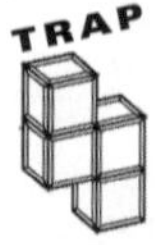

I purposely created the references for the various buttons outside of any function definitions. The objects I'm dealing with here should be accessible to the entire application, so they should be global to the entire program.

Buttons are created with the `Cbutton` function. This function is similar to the `Clabel` function, and uses the parameters listed in Table 7.2.

TABLE 7.2 PARAMETERS OF THE CBUTTON FUNCTION

parameter	values	description
x	0–160	x location of button
y	0–160	y location of button
width	0–160	Width of button
height	0–160	Height of button
line	0 = white, 1 = black, 2 = gray	What color line to draw around button
border	0 = square corners, height/ 2 = round corners	Radius of border corners (as in frame statement)

After creating each of the Cbutton objects, I set its contents and drew it on the screen. The `Csetcontent()` and `Cdraw()` functions work exactly the same way for buttons as for labels.

The Cimage object is much like a button, but it allows you to define an image rather than text. The parameters of the Cimage object are x, y, height, and width.

The setContent method of the Cimage object expects a bitmap string like those you created with Bitmap Studio in Chapter 6.

You must ensure that the height and width of the Cimage object are the same as the height and width of the bitmap that the string describes.

In all other ways, Cimage objects are just like buttons. They even invert when the user clicks on them.

Responding to Button Events

The main loop in the BtnDemo program is modified slightly to handle button events. In addition to the normal events, Ccontrols has a special function called `Cevent()`. You can use this function to determine if a particular control has been clicked, and write code to respond to the event. Here's the `main()` function of the BtnDemo program, illustrating the modified event loop:

```
main(){
  int keepGoing = true;
```

```
  int evt;

  init();

  while(keepGoing){
    evt = event(1);
    if(Cevent(btnAbout, evt)){
      alert("button demo");
    } else if (Cevent(img, evt)){
      alert("image button");
    } else if (Cevent(btnQuit, evt)){
      alert("goodbye!");
      keepGoing = false;
    } // end if
  } // end while
} // end main
```

The main program starts by calling the `init()` function, which will set up all the controls. It then sets up a standard while loop, assigning an event to the `evt` variable. It checks each button to see if it has been clicked by calling the `Cevent()` function. `Cevent` takes two parameters. The first is the handle of the object you want to check. The other value is the event variable for the program itself. If the object has been clicked, `Cevent()` returns the value true. Otherwise, it returns the value false.

Following is the general strategy for Ccontrol event handling:

- Set up a normal event loop.
- Use an if-else if clause to check for each of the objects' event handlers.
- Be sure that some event triggers the sentinel variable and ends the loop.

Building a More Complex Example

Most programs that use a GUI involve a combination of various types of controls. Often, such a program will use labels to output messages to the user and buttons to indicate that some action should occur. The other types of controls are generally used to allow the user to input information easily. In Figure 7.12 you will see a simple example of such a program.

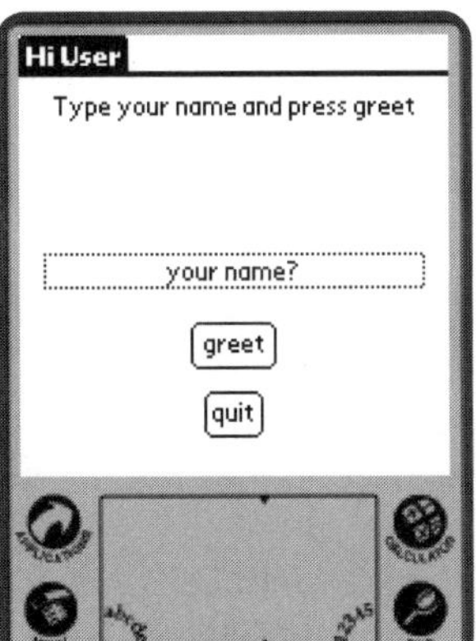

FIGURE 7.12

This program features an edit field and two buttons.

IN THE REAL WORLD

This program also has two labels, but the presence of labels is not always obvious to the user. Often (as in this case) the programmer will deliberately create the labels so that they will blend into the background. The reason you might use a label instead of simply a text function is that you can easily change the text in the label with the `Csetcontent()` function, and you can easily change other characteristics of the label, such as its border, size, and position.

Since PocketC does not allow the user to enter text at an arbitrary place on the screen, the Ccontrols edit field pops up a `gets()` dialog whenever the user clicks on an edit field. Once the user dismisses the dialog, the resulting string is copied automatically to the edit field. Figures 7.13 through 7.15 illustrate the program in action.

FIGURE 7.13

When the user clicks on the edit field, a dialog pops up to ask the user's name.

FIGURE 7.14

After the user dismisses the dialog, the text field has changed.

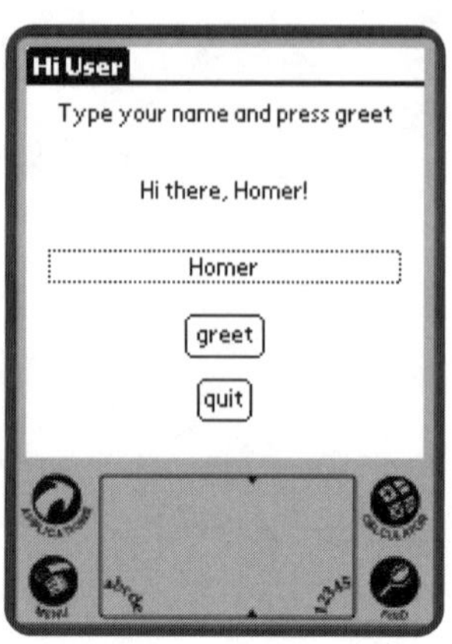

FIGURE 7.15

When the user taps the Greet button, a new message will appear with a personalized greeting.

The Main Variables in Hi User

The Hi User program may be simple, but it demonstrates all the main principles of GUI programming. Look at the source code for the global variables and program startup:

```
//HiUser
//Demonstrates using Ccontrols
//Andy Harris, 04/21/01

#include "Ccontrols.c"

Chandle lblInstructions, lblOutput, txtInput;
Chandle btnGreet, btnQuit;

init(){
  graph_on();
  clearg();
  title("Hi User");
```

The program incorporates the Ccontrols library in the normal way, then generates a number of `Chandle` objects. You might be surprised to see two labels. The first one, lblInstructions, will contain the (brief) instructions for the program. The second, lblOutput, starts out blank but will eventually contain the greeting.

The txtInput handle will refer to an edit box that will receive the user's name. The btnGreet and btnQuit handles will refer to the appropriate button objects on the screen. The program has an `init()` method, that starts by switching to graphics mode, clearing the screen, and setting the title.

Note that I used a form of Hungarian notation to describe all the `Chandle` variables. This makes it clear what I intend each component to be. You might be curious why I used "txt" for the edit box. Most GUI languages (including Java, Visual Basic, and JavaScript DOM) refer to this type of control as a text box, so I decided to keep my notation consistent across languages. Of course, you can develop your own coding conventions, as long as you stay consistent.

Initializing the Hi User Components

The main job of the `init()` function is to build components and place them on the screen:

```
    //create labels
    lblInstructions = Clabel(10, 20, 140, 0, 0, 1);
    Csetcontent(lblInstructions, "Type your name and press greet");
    Cdraw(lblInstructions);

    lblOutput = Clabel(10, 50, 140, 0, 0, 1);
    Csetcontent(lblOutput, "");
    Cdraw(lblOutput);

    //create text box
    txtInput = Cedit(10, 80, 140, 2, 2, 1);
    Csetcontent(txtInput, "your name?");
    Csettopic(txtInput, "please enter your name:");
    Cdraw(txtInput);

    //create buttons
    btnGreet = Cbutton(65, 105, 30, 15, 1, 3);
    Csetcontent(btnGreet, "greet");
    Cdraw(btnGreet);

    btnQuit = Cbutton(70, 130, 20, 15, 1, 3);
    Csetcontent(btnQuit, "quit");
    Cdraw(btnQuit);

} // end init
```

I created each object using the appropriate function, set its content, and drew it on the screen. All of the objects are familiar except the edit box. It has a very familiar set of parameters, shown in Table 7.3.

TABLE 7.3 PARAMETERS OF THE CEDIT() FUNCTION

parameter	values	description
x	0–160	x location of edit box
y	0–160	y location of edit box
width	0–160	Width of edit box
line	0 = white, 1 = black, 2 = gray	What color line to draw around (or under) edit box
style	0 = plain, 1= underlined, 2= boxed	Whether line is drawn at all, under, or all around edit box
alignment	0 = left, 1 = centered, 2 = right	How text will be aligned inside edit box

The parameters of the `Cedit()` function are just like those of the Clabel object.

I used one other function (`Csettopic`) with `txtInput`, allowing me to set a topic value for the control. The topic is the prompt that will appear in the `gets()` dialog when the user clicks on the text box. It's a good idea to set the topic so the user has some idea what to type into the dialog box.

The `Csettopic()` function requires two parameters, a control handle and a string of text.

Responding to the Hi User Events

The main method of the Hi User program sets up a standard event loop. This loop checks for button presses and responds appropriately:

```
main(){
  int keepGoing = true;
  int evt;
  string userName;

  init();

  while(keepGoing){
    evt = event(1);
    if (Cevent(btnQuit, evt)){
```

```
        keepGoing = false;
      } else if (Cevent(txtInput, evt)){
        //do nothing, but I must have the Cevent here
      } else if (Cevent(btnGreet, evt)){
        userName = Cgetcontent(txtInput);
        Csetcontent(lblOutput, "Hi there, " + userName + "!");
        Cdraw(lblOutput);
      } // end if
    } // end while
} // end main
```

The `main` function begins by declaring a sentry variable (`keepGoing`) and an event variable (`evt`). It then calls the `init()` function, which sets up the controls on the screen.

The `main` loop continues as long as the `keepGoing` variable has the value true. The program queries the event system and stores an event response into the `evt` variable.

I used an `if-else if` structure to query each of the relevant controls. I had to trap for events on three controls. If the user clicks the Quit button, the program should exit. This is easily managed by setting the value of `keepGoing` to false. The next time through the loop, the program will end.

The main program code does not need to do anything if the user clicks on the text box, but you still need to call the `Cevent()` function with the text box for it to work properly.

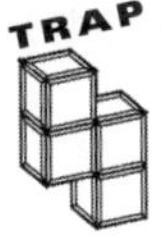

In most GUI languages, you don't have to do anything to make text boxes work correctly. In Ccontrols, you *must* remember to call the `Cevent()` function with your edit field as a parameter, or the dialog will not automatically pop up. You don't need to write any other code when the text box is clicked, but you do need to explicitly call the `Cevent()` function.

The real action happens in the Greet button. If the user clicks on this button, the program will copy the current value of the edit field (txtInput) to a variable, and use that variable to make a custom greeting in the output label (lblOutput).

I used the `Cgetcontent()` function to retrieve a control's content and to set another control's content to a new value. Note that you have to redraw the control with the `Cdraw()` function for the change to take effect.

In the Real World

Even in very complicated GUI programs, it is very common for all the code to be in one or two buttons. Most of the objects don't require event-handling code at all. For example, I did not even check to see if the labels responded to events, because I don't expect the user to click on them. Buttons and edit fields should always have event-handling code, but most other controls do not need such code most of the time.

Working with Ceditor

If you have looked at the help system that accompanies the Ccontrols library, you might be overwhelmed by the complexity and variety of the controls. Although it's good to know how to build a program using Ccontrols by hand, it can be very tedious getting the layout correct. It's also quite difficult to remember all the different options for the various objects. Happily, the Ccontrols package comes with a nifty editor that greatly simplifies adding controls to your programs.

Figure 7.5 illustrated a program that featured several of the key controls in the Ccontrols library. I actually wrote that program without entering a single line of code! Instead, I used the Ceditor program to generate the graphical user interface.

Adding Components

The Ceditor program starts with a blank screen and a minimal (but still very useful) set of controls on top, as shown in Figure 7.16.

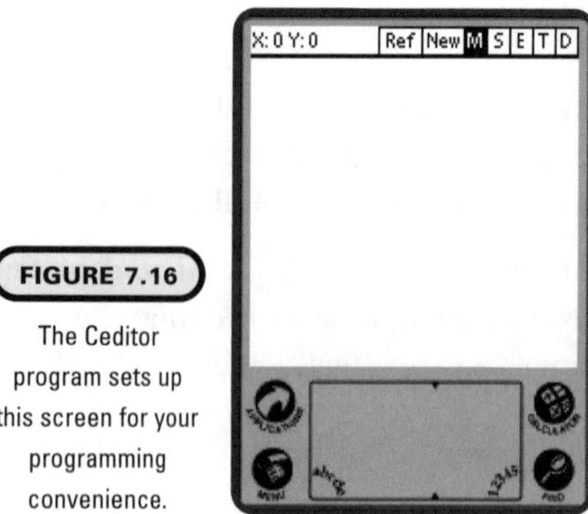

FIGURE 7.16

The Ceditor program sets up this screen for your programming convenience.

All the main functions of Ceditor are available from the set of buttons across the top. Here's what the various buttons mean:

- ***Ref.*** Refresh the screen. Sometimes things get jumbled on the screen. Pressing this button redraws every control on the screen immediately.
- ***New.*** Create a new component. Pops up a list of possible components, and then gives you a special dialog box for editing that component's main characteristics.
- ***M.*** Move a component. After you click this option, you can click on a component that you want to be able to move around the screen. This function is very handy for fine-tuning the layout.
- ***S.*** Resize a component. In this mode, you can change the size of any component by clicking on it and dragging its lower right-hand corner.
- ***E.*** Edit a component. In this mode, you can edit any component by clicking on it. Selecting a component brings up a dialog screen specific to this component. You can use this command to rename your components and determine their other characteristics, such as border, alignment, and so on.
- ***T.*** Test the controls. This mode allows you to see the controls as they will operate in the program. Clicking on a control in this mode gives you its normal behavior. You can edit the text in a text field, select from a set of radio buttons, and so on.
- ***D.*** Delete a component. This command allows you to delete a control. Any component you tap after selecting the D option will be deleted.

Adding a Label to the Screen

To demonstrate the Ceditor program, this section will show you how to add a label to the screen.

Tap the New button to create a new object, and then select label. A crosshair appears, letting you choose the upper left corner of the new label. Once you click the screen, you automatically go into edit mode for the new label. Figures 7.17, 7.18, and 7.19 trace this process.

The Ceditor program makes it very easy to create controls because you don't have to remember all the details of all the control-creation functions. Simply type the appropriate values in the editor, and the control will be created automatically for you. If you don't like the position or size of the control, you can use the move and size modes to change these values visually.

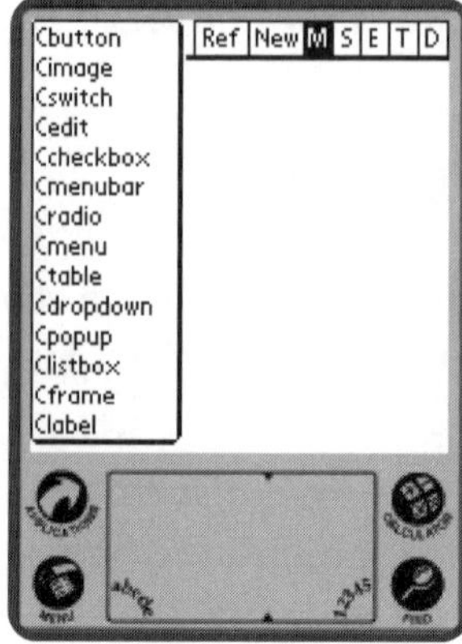

FIGURE 7.17

After you click the New button, a list of components appears.

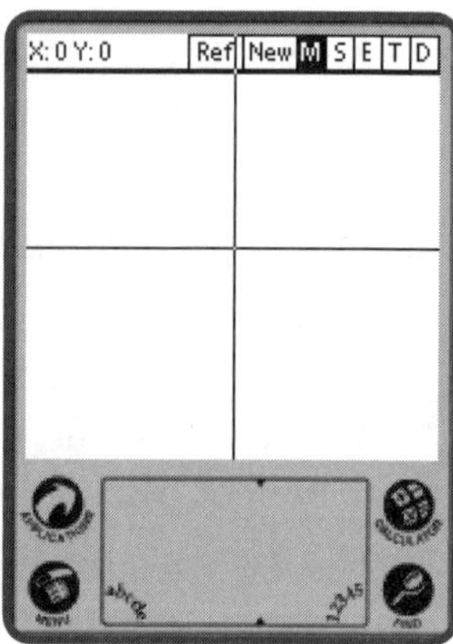

FIGURE 7.18

Once you choose a control, you can place its upper left corner via this screen.

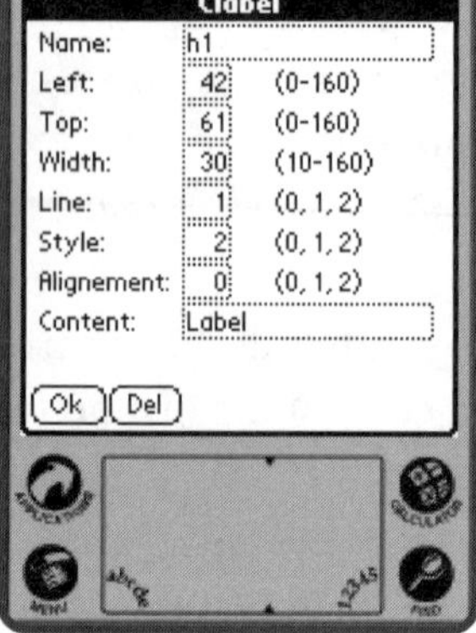

FIGURE 7.19

A new screen pops up with all the various characteristics of the label object available.

It's easy to get a rough feel for the size and placement of controls using the move and size modes, but it is very difficult to get components lined up exactly. Use the move and size modes to get close, and then edit the x, y, height, and width values directly to fine-tune the placement of your controls.

Play around with a number of different controls. You will find that each type of control has an edit screen appropriate to the details of that particular type of control.

Generating Source Code

You can save and load various layouts with the Ceditor program, but the real strength of the editor is its ability to generate working PocketC code. Figure 7.20 shows a simple screen layout I generated with the editor.

FIGURE 7.20

This screen offers one label and one button—don't you wish you could click it?

When you choose the Generate Code command from the Form menu, the program asks you for a name for the program, and then it generates three memo files. I named my program Don't Click (or rather, dontClick, in PocketC terms), and the editor created three memos: //dontClick main (Ceditor), /$dontClick controls (Ceditor), and /$dontClick methods (Ceditor). You can compile dontClick main (Ceditor) and it will work, but it won't do anything interesting until you add some functionality.

Examining the Main Memo Created by Ceditor

The strategy is to use Ceditor to build an outline for your program. You can use it to generate all the code for generating your objects. The program also builds a very simple form of the main event loop that you can modify for your own needs. The main memo includes the other two files and calls a series of functions that are defined in the other memos. Following is the main memo created by the Don't Click program:

```
// DontClick main (CEditor)
include "DontClick controls (CEditor)"
include "DontClick methods (CEditor)"
main(){
graph_on();
title("DontClick");
initcontrols();
initcontents();
inititems();
drawcontrols();
messageloop();
}
```

When you examine this code you can see that the main program imports the other two memo files. It then has a main function consisting entirely of calls to other functions. Fortunately, it's reasonably easy to guess what all the functions do. The `initcontrols()` function initializes all the controls according to the settings specified in the editor. The `initcontents()` and `inititems()` methods set up the contents of the controls. The `drawcontrols()` method (unsurprisingly) draws all the controls on the screen. The `messageloop()` method runs the main loop of the program. It's interesting that the main program of every single program generated by Ceditor looks exactly like this (except of course for the title). Everything that makes a particular program different occurs in the other two memos.

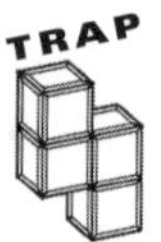

You might have noticed that this code (and all the code that comes out of the Ceditor program) is written in a different style than you have seen elsewhere in the book. Ceditor does not add many comments, and does not indent the code. This was done to help write very small programs, but the resulting code can be difficult to read and modify. You might want to consider adding your own comments and formatting to the code if you will be making any changes to it. Fortunately, you will generally only have to make changes in a couple of places, and these changes are usually very straightforward.

Examining the Controls Memo

All of the code for initializing and drawing the controls is placed in the memo called "DontClick controls (CEditor)." Here's the code generated for the Don't Click program:

```
/$ DontClick_controls (CEditor)
include "Ccontrols.c"
Chandle  btnClick, lblOutput;
initcontrols(){
btnClick=Cbutton(45,80,70,25,1,4);
lblOutput=Clabel(25,40,110,1,0,1);
}
initcontents(){
Csetcontent(btnClick,"Don't click me!");
Csetcontent(lblOutput,"Don't click the button!");
}
inititems(){
}
drawcontrols(){
```

```
Cdraw(btnClick);
Cdraw(lblOutput);
}
```

When this memo is included in the main file, it generates the Chandles for the two elements in the program (remember that this program consists only of a button and a label). The `initcontrols()` function creates the control functions necessary to create the two controls. The `initcontents()` function sets up the contents of the controls. The `inititems()` method is used for objects such as tables and lists that have multiple items, so it is left empty for this program. The `drawcontrols()` function calls Cdraw on the respective control objects.

Managing Events in the Don't Click Program

The last file that Cedit generates is called "DontClick methods (CEditor)." This file contains all the event-handling procedures. For most simple programs, this file is all you will need to modify:

```
/$ DontClick methods (CEditor)
on_btnClick(){
}
on_lblOutput(){
}
messageloop(){
int e;
while(1){
e=event(1);
if(Cevent(btnClick,e)) on_btnClick();
else if(Cevent(lblOutput,e)) on_lblOutput();
}
}
```

It actually makes sense to look at this file from the bottom up. With the curly brackets uncommented, it's somewhat harder to follow than the code I wrote myself, but the variable names make it possible to understand what's going on. The `messageloop()` function is an event loop much like the ones you have seen earlier in the chapter. It was automatically created by the editor. The `messageloop()` function is a little sneaky. Rather than doing any actual work, it simply checks for each component's event to occur. If that event occurs, it calls an appropriate function. These functions, which all begin with "on_", start out empty. If you want to add any functionality to a program written with Ceditor, generally all you have to do is write code in these event handlers. If you don't want anything to happen when a particular component is clicked, just leave the function for that component blank.

For this program, all that's needed is for the program to complain and then exit when the user clicks on the button. To do that, I'll simply modify the `on_btnClick()` function like this:

```
on_btnClick(){
   Csetcontent(lblOutput, "ouch!");
   Cdraw(lblOutput);
   alert("I wish you hadn't done that.");
   exit();
} // end on_btnClick
```

This change to the code causes the program to snarl at the user, just as it should. Figures 7.21 and 7.22 show the interchange.

IN THE REAL WORLD

If this is so easy, why would you ever do it by hand?

The Ceditor does simplify the creation of GUI forms tremendously. You can quickly generate a program skeleton with almost no coding. The editor is especially comforting for those programmers who are familiar with other GUI tools, such as Microsoft Visual Basic. However, a number of programmers who use Ccontrols (including me) prefer not to use the editor for most programs. I find the code produced by the editor to be very awkward and difficult to read. If I have to spend a lot of time cleaning up the editor's code, maybe using the editor didn't save much effort after all. I also think the file names generated by the editor are long and complicated. They are especially troublesome when you are trying to work with the desktop environment. Most file management systems are very unreliable when given file names with spaces in them, so I ended up changing the files to get them on the CD-ROM.

Finally, I sometimes find that the editor can be overkill. For simple programs, it is just be easier to write the code by hand. If I want a lot of controls, or complex controls (menus or tables, for example), I might use the Ceditor, but often I do so just to see how the code will be written. There's nothing wrong with using the editor, but you should decide for yourself when it makes sense to use it and when you will be better off writing your own control code.

FIGURE 7.21

So what happens if the user can't resist?

FIGURE 7.22

What did you expect?

Back to the Mad Lib Game

For the Mad Lib game, I relied heavily on Ceditor to build the program. I then tweaked the code considerably to make it work the way I wanted. My basic strategy was to take a familiar nursery rhyme ("The Itzy-Bitzy Spider") and allow the user to change key words, hopefully to humorous effect. Since this program was also meant to be a demonstration of GUI controls, I decided to use several different types of controls for user input.

Designing an Input Form

I designed the input form with the Cedit program. The design of most of the components was very straightforward. The drop-down box for the house part is a little more involved because I had to initialize the list with some starting elements, as shown in Figure 7.23.

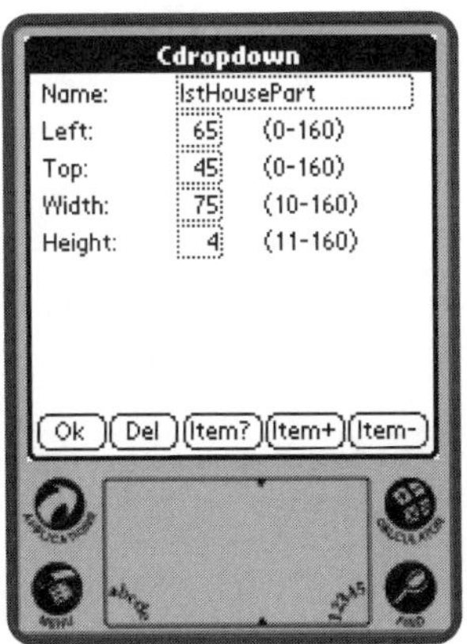

FIGURE 7.23

When you edit a drop-down list (or similar multi-item component), you get some new buttons on the bottom of the screen.

In addition to the familiar OK and Del buttons, you will encounter three new buttons when you edit a drop-down list or other multi-element component (including the list box, the radio buttons, and the table). The Item? button gives you a list of the items you have currently added to the component. The Item+ button lets you add a new item to the component, and the Item- button lets you delete an item from the component. I added a bunch of semi-random house parts to the drop-down list control to come up with the selection shown in Figure 7.24.

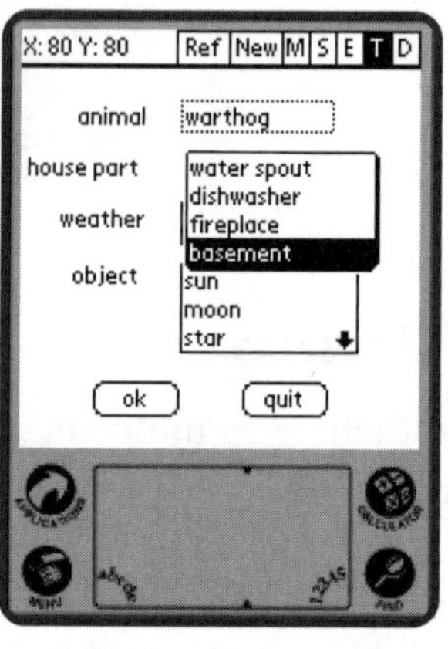

FIGURE 7.24

When the user clicks on the list box, it drops down, showing all the options.

The list box for the object is edited in much the same way. The only difference between lstHousePart and lstObject is that lstHousePart is a *drop-down* list box, and lstObject is an ordinary (multi-line) list box. The edit forms for the two types of list boxes are almost identical.

After I designed the form I saved it and told Ceditor to generate code for the form.

Saving the form is different from generating code, and you should do both. When you save the form, you are saving data that the Ceditor program uses to describe the form information. You should always save the form in case you discover a mistake. If you don't, all additional changes will need to be made by hand.

Modifying the Code

The code that results from Ceditor is reasonably sound, but it does not yet do anything interesting. I made a few changes.

```
// Itzy
// Creates a Mad lib based on "Itzy Bitzy Spider"
// Demonstrates use of Ccontrols, Cedit
// Andy Harris, 06/26/01
```

```
//function proto
makeStory();

//include auto-created files
include "Itzy2.pc"
include "Itzy3.pc"

main(){
graph_on();
title("Itzy");
initcontrols();
initcontents();
inititems();
drawcontrols();
messageloop();
}
```

The long file names gave me trouble when I used the desktop version of the PocketC compiler, so I changed the name (first line) of the main file to Itzy.

Almost all of the actual work of the program can be done in one function that will be called when the user clicks the OK button. I decided to define that function (called `makeStory`) in my main file so it would be easier to find later. Just to avoid any problems, I created a function prototype for the function before the include statements.

I changed the names of the other two files to Itzy2.pc and Itzy3.pc. Itzy2 contains the control creation stuff and Itzy3 contains the event-handling code. Since I changed the names of the files, I also had to change the include statements.

The rest of the main function is taken exactly from Ceditor, with no changes whatsoever—meaning no formatting and comments.

The makeStory() Function

Almost all the original code in the Itzy program should happen when the user clicks the OK button. I decided to store all the relevant code in a function that I'll later attach to the button click event. Here's the code for the `makeStory()` function, defined in the Itzy main memo.

```
makeStory(){
  string animal;
  string weather;
  string housePart;
```

```
    string object;

    //get values from screen
    animal = Cgetcontent(txtAnimal);
    weather = Cgetcontent(optWeather);
    housePart = Cgetcontent(lstHousePart);
    object = Cgetcontent(lstObject);
  saveg();
    graph_off();
    clear();
    /*  Test code:
    puts("Animal: ");
    puts( animal + "\n");
    puts("Weather: ");
    puts( weather + "\n");
    puts("House Part: ");
    puts(housePart + "\n");
    puts("Object: ");
    puts(object + "\n");
    */

    title("The itzy-bitzy " + animal);
    puts("The itzy-bitzy " + animal);
    puts(" walked up the " + housePart);
    puts(". \nDown came the " + weather);
    puts(" and washed the " + animal );
    puts(" out. \n\n");
    puts("Out came the " + object);
    puts(" and dried up all the " + weather);
    puts(".\n\n-and the itzy-bitzy " + animal);
    puts(" walked up the " + housePart);
    puts(" again.\n");
    wait();
    graph_on();
    restoreg();
} //end makeStory
```

The `makeStory` function essentially queries the screen for information from the user. I created a series of variables to represent the various terms the user will input. I then used Ccontrols functions to extract the values from the screen components.

Here is the pseudocode plan for the control access functions.

Function	Parameters	Notes
Cgetstate (handle)	handle: handle of a control	Used with Cswitch, Ccheckbox, returns 0 (off) or 1 (on).
Cgetcursel (handle)	handle: handle of a control	Returns the index of the selected item in a list-style item (Cradio, Cmenu, Ctable, Cdropdown, Clistbox). Returns -1 if nothing is selected. First item is 0.
Cgetcontent (handle)	handle: handle of a control	Returns the content of the current control. Used with all controls but Ctable and Cswitch.

In most cases, you can simply use the `Cgetcontent()` function to retrieve the value of a particular control.

Once all the variables have data in them, it is a simple matter to print the story to the screen. Note that I stored the graphics screen and switched to text mode, then printed the story on the screen. I then waited for a keystroke, switched back to graphics mode, and restored the graphics screen.

You might also notice the commented `puts` statements (the passage between /* and */). While I was debugging the program, I started with a simpler text screen that would clearly indicate which of the variables were correctly receiving values. When the variables were all being read correctly, I commented out that simple printing code and replaced it with the actual story. I decided not to eliminate the debugging code in case I needed it again.

Examining the Control-Building Code

The Ceditor program does a very good job of building the actual controls. You will not need to change this code at all, but you still might want to look at it so you can see what's going on:

```
/$ Itzy2
include "Ccontrols.c"
Chandle  h1, h2, h3, h4, txtAnimal, lstHousePart, optWeather, lstObject,
btnOk, btnQuit;
```

```
initcontrols(){
h1=Clabel(10,25,40,0,0,2);
h2=Clabel(7,45,40,0,0,2);
h3=Clabel(10,65,40,0,0,2);
h4=Clabel(7,87,40,0,0,2);
txtAnimal=Cedit(65,25,60,2,2,0);
lstHousePart=Cdropdown(67,45,75,4);
optWeather=Cradio(65,65,80,15);
lstObject=Clistbox(65, 89, 70, 3);
btnOk=Cbutton(30,135,33,12,1,4);
btnQuit=Cbutton(90,135,33,12,1,4);
}
initcontents(){
Csetcontent(h1,"animal");
Csetcontent(h2,"house part");
Csetcontent(h3,"weather");
Csetcontent(h4,"object");
Csetcontent(txtAnimal,"aardvark");
Csettopic(txtAnimal,"Choose an animal");
Csetcontent(btnOk,"ok");
Csetcontent(btnQuit,"quit");
}
inititems(){
Cadditem(lstHousePart,"water spout");
Cadditem(lstHousePart,"dishwasher");
Cadditem(lstHousePart,"fireplace");
Cadditem(lstHousePart,"basement");
Cadditem(optWeather,"rain");
Cadditem(optWeather,"snow");
Cadditem(optWeather,"sleet");

Cadditem(lstObject, "sun");
Cadditem(lstObject, "moon");
Cadditem(lstObject, "star");
Cadditem(lstObject, "book");
Cadditem(lstObject, "pan");
Cadditem(lstObject, "door");

}
drawcontrols(){
```

```
Cdraw(h1);
Cdraw(h2);
Cdraw(h3);
Cdraw(h4);
Cdraw(txtAnimal);
Cdraw(lstHousePart);
Cdraw(optWeather);
Cdraw(lstObject);
Cdraw(btnOk);
Cdraw(btnQuit);
}
```

When you look at this code, you will see that it is much like the Don't Click program, but with more controls. The `initcontrols()` function creates all the various control objects according to the settings determined in the Ceditor. The `initcontents()` function sets up the contents of all the simple (non-list) controls. The `inititems()` function sets up the content of the controls that can contain more than one item. Finally, the `drawcontrols()` function draws all of the controls onto the screen.

It is not necessary to modify the code in this memo at all. Anything you need to change in this memo can usually be done in the editor itself.

Modifying the Event Loop

The `makeStory()` function is defined in the main memo, but you will need to modify the rest of the code somehow for `makeStory` to occur at all. Also, the program will need to respond to the Quit button. The Itzy3 memo has the event-handling code:

```
/$ Itzy3
// methods (CEditor)


on_h1(){
}
on_h2(){
}
on_h3(){
}
on_h4(){
}
on_txtAnimal(){
```

```
}
on_lstHousePart(){
}
on_optWeather(){
}
on_lstObject(){
}
on_btnOk(){
  makeStory();
}
on_btnQuit(){
  exit();
} // end btnQuit
messageloop(){
int e;
while(1){
e=event(1);
if(Cevent(h1,e)) on_h1();
else if(Cevent(h2,e)) on_h2();
else if(Cevent(h3,e)) on_h3();
else if(Cevent(h4,e)) on_h4();
else if(Cevent(txtAnimal,e)) on_txtAnimal();
else if(Cevent(lstHousePart,e)) on_lstHousePart();
else if(Cevent(optWeather,e)) on_optWeather();
else if(Cevent(lstObject,e)) on_lstObject();
else if(Cevent(btnOk,e)) on_btnOk();
else if(Cevent(btnQuit,e)) on_btnQuit();
}
}
```

Again, I left most of this code alone. The `messageloop()` function simply calls the event-handling functions, so it is unnecessary to modify `messageloop()` at all. Most of the event functions do not require code either. The only time you need to add code is when you want some action to happen when a control is pressed. As a general rule, all buttons will have some sort of code attached to them, and almost nothing else will. In this program, the only controls that need event code are the two buttons. When the user clicks on the OK button, the program should make the story by calling the `makeStory()` function. When the user clicks on the Quit button, the program should exit. I simply added an exit statement to the `on_btnQuit()` function to exit the program.

Summary

This chapter adds a powerful new ability to your programming skill set: you can now generate graphical user interfaces using familiar elements such as text boxes, buttons, drop-down lists, and tables. You have learned how to build programs using the Ccontrols library by hand, and you have also learned how to use the Ceditor program to quickly build a code skeleton for your programs. Doing so allows you to create programs with a professional look—and programs that have the potential to ease input for the user and to cut down on input problems.

CHALLENGES

1. Write a more involved version of the Mad Lib program using your own ideas.
2. Design a currency converter (or something similar for a problem you frequently have to solve). Use text fields and buttons to control the form.
3. Investigate using a Cdialog to add multiple forms to your programs.
4. Add a GUI element to the drawing program in Chapter 5. Perhaps use a switch control for the pen size and another for pen color.
5. Add button input to the Space Rescue game from Chapter 6. Place Left, Right, and Accelerate buttons at the bottom of the screen.

Creating a Smart Opponent: The Tic-Tac-Toe Game

In most of your programs so far, the user did most of the real work. In this chapter you'll get a glimpse at how you can write programs that appear to think. As you know, it is possible to write computer programs that perform very well at certain strategy games. The classic example of this is an IBM computer called Big Blue, which beat Gary Kasparov, a sitting Grand Master chess player. This event rocked both the chess and computing worlds, signaling that it is possible for a computer to outperform even an exceptional individual.

The practice of writing programs that can appear to think like humans is called *artificial intelligence* (AI). AI can be a daunting topic, but the basic principles are not beyond the grasp of a talented beginner. In this chapter, I show you how to use some basic AI principles to build a tic-tac-toe game that is unbeatable. Specifically, you'll learn how to:

- Think about a game or task in terms of its underlying data
- Use arrays to store information
- Create and use a two-dimensional array
- Incorporate a native library into your code
- Build a user interface as a game foundation
- Use *heuristics* to choose an optimal solution

The Tic-Tac-Toe Game

You're probably familiar with the game of tic-tac-toe. It is played on a three-by-three grid with two players. The players alternate drawing symbols in squares on the board. One player draws an X in any empty square, and the other player draws an O in a remaining empty square. The object of the game is to get three of your symbols in a row.

Some tic-tac-toe strategies can help you win every time—or at any rate, a skilled player can play the game and never lose. While human players understand the winning strategy very well, it is a challenge to translate this strategy into a computer algorithm. Many beginning programmers start to write a version of tic-tac-toe thinking it is very simple. Such programmers are often surprised at the complexities involved in implementing a computer opponent smart enough even for this simple game.

The program featured in Figures 8.1 and 8.2 demonstrates a tic-tac-toe program with an effective computer opponent.

The computer opponent is very capable. It will win or tie most games. If the computer starts play before the human player, it will never lose.

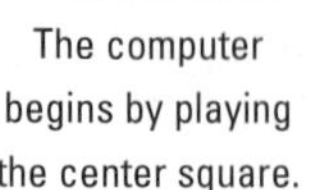
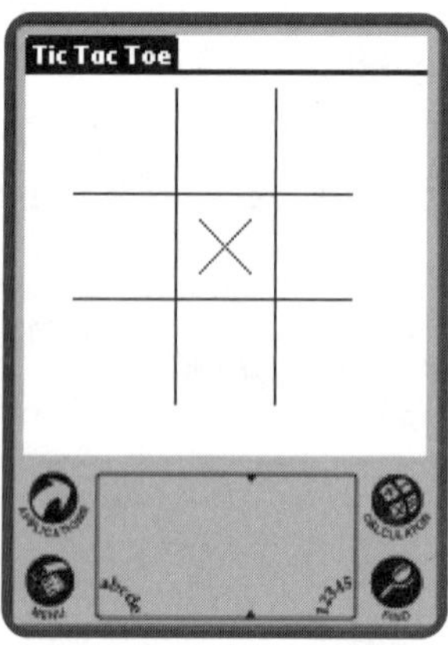

FIGURE 8.1

The computer begins by playing the center square.

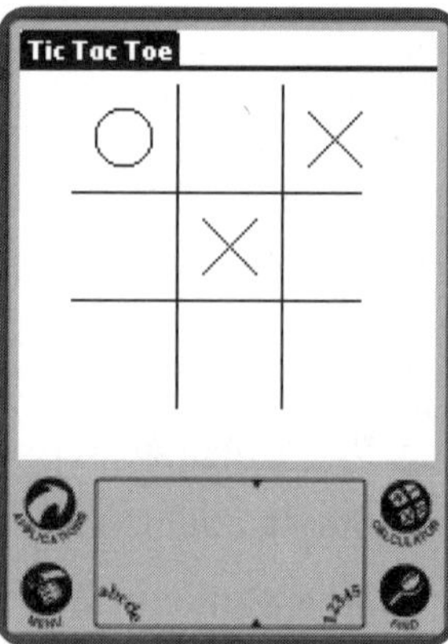

FIGURE 8.2

When the user clicks a square, the computer responds by choosing another square.

Strategy for the Tic-Tac-Toe Game

Most of the visible mechanics of the game are very straightforward. The visual design of the game and the user input functions use skills presented earlier in this book. The key to this game is the artificial intelligence scheme. To program an interesting computer opponent, you first must carefully analyze the environment in which the program will operate. In this case, the rules of tic-tac-toe are exceptionally simple, and the game board is very small. You can easily identify a number of winning combinations, and the patterns for a winning combination are well known. Still, it is quite difficult to translate ideas that are obvious to human players (for example, if two squares in a row are filled and the third is empty, you should play in that third square) into a working computer algorithm.

Creating a Heuristic

There are many ways to develop a computer player. The easiest would be to let the computer choose which square it will play totally by chance. This would be reasonably easy to implement, but the computer player would make bizarre moves and would not be fun to play against.

A *heuristic* is a device used to help the computer make more informed decisions. The basic idea of a heuristic algorithm is to evaluate a number of possible moves. The program then analyzes the playing board and assigns a score to each move based on how well that move might further the computer player's goals (or frustrate the human player's goals). Once all the possible moves have been ranked, the computer chooses the highest-ranking move and executes it. To use a heuristic algorithm, you must figure out a way to calculate the available moves, and also define a strategy for ranking the moves.

Creating Input for the Game

The visual interface for this program could be designed in several different ways, but I decided to keep the interface simple so I could focus on the artificial intelligence aspects. The game board is a series of lines, and each X and O is drawn with a graphics primitive. Users will input moves by tapping on the square they wish to use next. I chose to communicate with the user through alert dialogs. The first version of the Tic-Tac-Toe program concentrates on the visual elements and the user input.

The Stripped-Down Game

As usual, I'll start with a simple subset of the final game and test it one small part at a time. The first part to work on is the visual interface. Figures 8.3 and 8.4 illustrate a very simple version of the program—tic-tac-toe for two human players (or one who's very easily amused).

This version of the Tic-Tac-Toe program does not have any artificial intelligence at all. It cannot even tell if one player or the other has won the game. Still, it is an important step toward the final game.

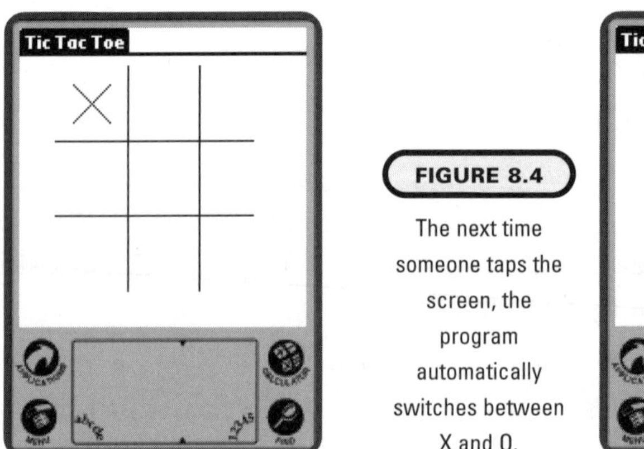

FIGURE 8.3

If the user taps in a square, the program draws an X there.

FIGURE 8.4

The next time someone taps the screen, the program automatically switches between X and O.

Drawing the Game Board

The game board is simply a grid of four lines that separate the screen into a three-by-three grid. Figure 8.5 illustrates the basic screen layout.

> **IN THE REAL WORLD**
>
> **It is a very good idea to have a drawing like this. Programmers often need to think about coordinates of various parts of the screen, and having a diagram makes it much easier to determine where things should go. You don't have to use a graphics program like I did here. You can simply draw your screen on paper. However, I like to use a graphics editor to draw such images because I can draw the screen grid in one layer, and then overlay any of the drawings or coordinates in a new layer. You will need a higher-end graphics program (my personal favorite is the Gimp, because it is powerful and free) to do your graphics planning.**

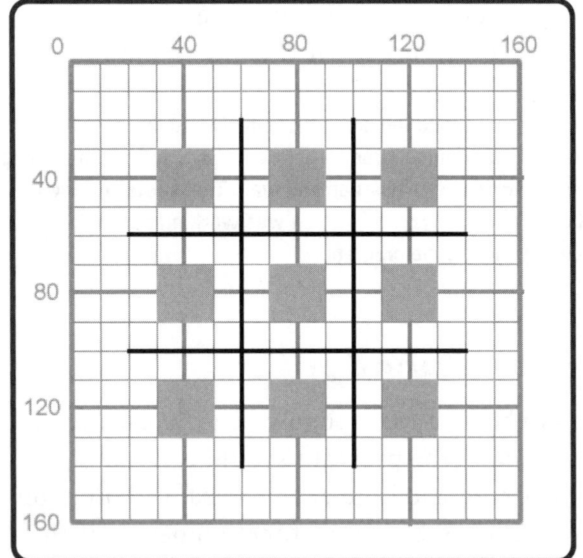

FIGURE 8.5

The game board: the squares are where the X and O characters will be drawn.

I wrote a function called `drawScreen()` to draw the basic game board.

```
drawScreen(){
  //draw the tictactoe board

  graph_on();
  clearg();
  title("Tic-tac-toe");
  line(1, 60, 20, 60, 140);
  line(1, 100, 20, 100, 140);
  line(1, 20, 60, 140, 60);
  line(1, 20, 100, 140, 100);

} // end drawScreen
```

The programs in this chapter are fairly long, so to save space I will only show one a function at a time. As usual, the best way to understand what is happening in the chapter is to look at the actual code from the CD-ROM and try to modify it yourself.

As you can see, this function clears the screen, switches to graphics mode, and draws the lines on the screen. Since I had already determined the line placement in my sketch, it was very easy to figure out exactly how the lines should be drawn. Still, you may find that you need to play around with your original placement to make sure the screen turns out the way you want.

When I first wrote the program, I simply had the `drawScreen()` and a `main()` function defined. The `main()` function did nothing but call the `drawScreen()` function and wait. This strategy allowed me to quickly see if the `drawScreen()` function was working correctly before I added other functionality to the program.

The checkHits() Function

The program needs to be able to respond when the user clicks on the screen. If the user clicks on a square, the program should print an X or O symbol on that square. If the user clicks outside the game board, the program should respond appropriately as well. The `checkHits()` function performs this task:

```
checkHits(int x, int y){
  int shapeX, shapeY;

  if (checkNW(x,y)){
    shapeX = 30;
    shapeY = 30;
  } else if (checkN(x,y)){
    shapeX = 70;
    shapeY = 30;
  } else if (checkNE(x,y)){
    shapeX = 110;
    shapeY = 30;
  } else if (checkW(x,y)){
    shapeX = 30;
    shapeY = 70;
  } else if (checkC(x,y)){
    shapeX = 70;
    shapeY = 70;
  } else if (checkE(x,y)){
    shapeX = 110;
    shapeY = 70;
  } else if (checkSW(x,y)){
    shapeX = 30;
    shapeY = 110;
```

```
  } else if (checkS(x,y)){
    shapeX = 70;
    shapeY = 110;
  } else if (checkSE(x,y)){
    shapeX = 110;
    shapeY = 110;
  } else {
    alert("please click in a square");
    return();
  } // end if

  //draw the appropriate shape
  if (turn == "X"){
    drawX(shapeX, shapeY);
  } else {
    drawO(shapeX, shapeY);
  } // end turn if

} // end checkHits
```

This function expects two integer parameters. These integers will be the X and Y coordinates of the last pen tap. The `shapeX` and `shapeY` variables will contain the X and Y coordinates of the X or O character to draw on the screen. Each square has an appropriate place to start drawing the character, which can be determined by the sketch drawn earlier in the design process. The `shapeX` and `shapeY` values will determine the upper-left corner of the shape. The bulk of the `checkHits()` function is a large `if-else if` structure that examines each square in turn to see if the square has been clicked. (The next section presents the functions that perform this role.) If none of the squares were clicked, the program informs the user of this fact.

The last part of the function checks to see whose turn it is, and then calls a function to draw the appropriate shape on the screen.

Reusing the pointRec Function

The most natural form of input for this program is pen input—the user should simply tap on a screen to place a symbol in a square. The program will need some way to determine where on the screen the user tapped. Fortunately, the `pointRec()` function developed in Chapter 6 performs this function admirably.

It's always a good idea to reuse working code when you can, so I decided to recycle this bit. Just to refresh your memory, here is the `pointRec()` function:

```
int pointRec(int px, int py, int x1, int y1, int x2, int y2){

  //given point (px, py) and a rectangle (x1, y1) - (x2, y2),
  //return true if the point is inside the rectangle
  //otherwise return false

  int result = false;
  if (px > x1){
    if (px < x2){
      if (py > y1){
        if (py < y2){
          result = true;
        } // end y2 check
      } // end y1 check
    } // end x2 check
  } // end x1 check
  return result;
} // end pointRec
```

You may recall that the `pointRec()` function expects six integers. The first two numbers determine the coordinates of a point. The next four numbers describe opposite corners of a rectangle. If the point is inside the rectangle, the function returns the value `true`. If the point is outside the rectangle, the function returns the value `false`.

The Square Checking Functions

Although the `pointRec()` function is handy, it is a little tedious, so I decided to build a series of Boolean functions that would automatically call it. In this way, my program will no longer need to think about the exact coordinates of a square, but can simply call an appropriate function to determine if any square has been clicked:

```
int checkNW(int x, int y){
  return pointRec(x,y,20,20,60,60);
}
int checkN(int x, int y){
  return pointRec(x,y,60,20,100,60);
}
```

```
int checkNE(int x, int y){
  return pointRec(x,y,100,20,140,60);
}
int checkW(int x, int y){
  return pointRec(x,y,20,60,60,100);
}
int checkC(int x, int y){
  return pointRec(x,y,60,60,100,100);
}
int checkE(int x, int y){
  return pointRec(x,y,100,60,140,100);
}
int checkSW(int x, int y){
  return pointRec(x,y,20,100,60,140);
}
int checkS(int x, int y){
  return pointRec(x,y,60,100,100,140);
}
int checkSE(int x, int y){
  return pointRec(x,y,100,100,140,140);
}
```

All these functions are very simple. They all expect X and Y as inputs, and check to see if that point is inside the rectangle defined for that square. All the functions will return the value from the `pointRec()` function, which is a Boolean (true or false) value. Functions that return Boolean values are very useful in conditions, because they often make the code more readable.

Drawing the X and O Characters

The `checkHits()` function does not explicitly draw the X and O characters; it calls special functions to do so. These functions are very straightforward, and they are designed to be flexible.

```
drawX(int x,int y){
  //given x,y coordinates, draws an X
  line(1, x,y, x + 20,y + 20);
  line(1, x + 20,y, x,y + 20);
} // end drawX
```

```
drawO(int x, int y){
  //draws an O at (x,y)
  frame(1, x,y, x+20, y+20, 10);
} // end drawO
```

The drawX function expects an X and Y coordinate parameter. It draws a 20 by 20 X using two line commands.

The drawO function also expects X and Y coordinates, but it draws a circle instead.

Remember that the PocketC default graphics functions do not have an explicit circle command. You can use the radius parameter of the frame function to build a circle.

The houseKeeping Function

The houseKeeping function describes a series of tasks that should happen at the end of each turn:

```
houseKeeping(){
  //manage stuff that should happen each turn
  if (turn == "X"){
    turn = "O";
  } else {
    turn = "X";
  } // end turn if

  counter++;
  if (counter > 8) {
    alert("Game Over!");
    keepGoing = false;
    return();
  } // end if

} // end houseKeeping
```

The first thing to do is change the turn variable. This variable will contain an "X" or a "Y" based on which player's turn it is. The function also increments a turn counter, which will end the game. Since there is currently no way to tell if a player has won, the program will simply proceed for nine turns.

The main() Function

All the critical code for this program is stored in the functions you have just seen. All that remains is to put all the elements together in order and tie them together with a `main()` function.

In the following code listing, I have taken out all the function bodies except for the `main()` function because you have already seen the functions described earlier in the chapter. This listing is intended to demonstrate the larger design of the program and how it fits together. I did leave the function definitions in the code listing so you can see the order in which they were defined. Of course, if you use function prototypes, the order of function definition does not matter. Examine the code listing on the CD-ROM to view the entire program at once.

```
//tttNoScore
//Screen input - no scorekeeping
// Andy Harris, 05/02/01

int keepGoing = true;
int counter = 0;
string turn = "X";

int pointRec(int px, int py, int x1, int y1, int x2, int y2){

  //given point (px, py) and a rectangle (x1, y1) - (x2, y2),
  //return true if the point is inside the rectangle
  //otherwise return false
 . . .
} // end pointRec

drawScreen(){
  //draw the tictactoe board
  . . .
} // end drawScreen

drawX(int x,int y){
  //given x,y coordinates, draws an X
 . . .
} // end drawX
```

```
drawO(int x, int y){
  //draws an O at (x,y)
  . . .
} // end drawO

int checkNW(int x, int y){
  . . .
}
(other checking routines)

checkHits(int x, int y){
  //checks each square for pen input.
  //draws the appropriate shape in the square
  . . .
} // end checkHits

houseKeeping(){
  //manage stuff that should happen each turn
  . . .

} // end houseKeeping

main(){
  drawScreen();
  while(keepGoing){
    wait();
    checkHits(penx(), peny());
    houseKeeping();
  } // end while
} // end main
```

This version of the Tic-Tac-Toe program has three global variables. The `keepGoing` variable is used in the normal way, to determine if the main loop should continue. The counter variable is used to indicate the end of the game. The `turn` variable indicates whether player X or Y is currently playing.

The `main` function is extremely simple. It begins by drawing the screen, then the program starts a loop that continues until the value of `keepGoing` is changed (which will happen in the `houseKeeping` function). It then waits for an input, checks the pen input with the `checkHits()` function (which calls a number of other functions), and calls the `houseKeeping` function.

IN THE REAL WORLD

A well-built `main` function like this one simply contains a bunch of other function calls. This makes it easy to see the overall flow of the program without cluttering the `main` function with details that properly belong in other functions. This type of code delegation is especially important in a complex program that is doing a lot of different things. By carefully designing the initial form of the program, I have made it much easier to add functionality later. A sloppier design will cause you problems later, because it will be more difficult to integrate new code with the existing program.

Looking for a Winner with If Statements

All the basic functionality of the Tic-Tac-Toe program is there, but the code is very simple. It cannot determine if a player has won the game. Of course, you could write a series of `if` statements to test all the possible ways a player could win. However, you will quickly find that this approach is unwieldy. There are nine possible winning combinations—each of these combinations would require a minimum of three `if` statements to recognize. This means that the structure to determine if a player has won the game will involve at least 27 `if` statements. Each `if` statement will take 2 or 3 lines of code to implement, meaning that just this part of the program will approach 100 lines of code. If there is a problem in the algorithm, you will have to debug all 100 lines of that code. You will need a similar set of code fragments later on to implement an artificial intelligence algorithm, meaning another 100 lines of code.

Clearly, it would be good to have some other way to think about the winning conditions. The secret to efficient code is the use of effective data structures. If you can think of an effective way to manage the information about a problem, you can save yourself a lot of work in the long run.

The Winning Combination

In tic-tac-toe, there are two extremely important pieces of information. First, is the game board itself. Somehow it would be good to store information about the game board, so you can figure out which player has clicked on which square. You should be able to go back and analyze the game board to determine the winner.

The other critical piece of data in tic-tac-toe is the winning combinations. In this particular game, there are a number of identifiable winning combinations. If the program has a way of storing them, it should be relatively easy to determine if a player has won the game or not by comparing the status of the game board to each of the winning combinations. The next version of the game—illustrated in Figure 8.6—is a more complete version of the two-player game, with the ability to determine if a winning combination has occurred.

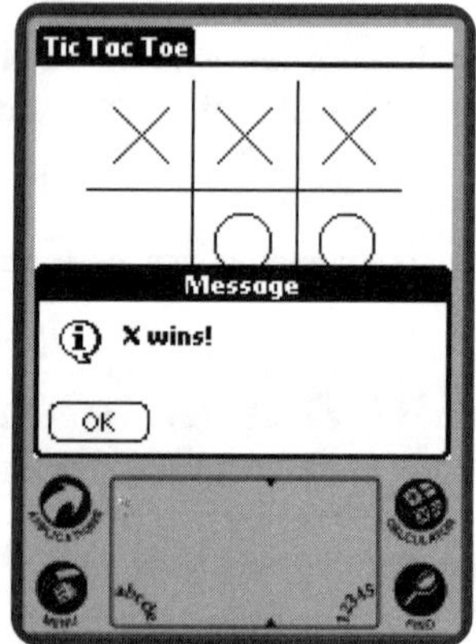

FIGURE 8.6

Now the program can detect a winning pattern.

The Game Board Array

As I said, the first data element to consider is the game board itself. Although there is a visual representation of the board on the screen, the program could still use a more efficient way of tracking which player has placed a marker in which square.

Creating an Array for the Game Board

You may recall arrays from Chapter 6, which describes building an array of images to handle animation. Arrays are simply variables that can hold multiple values of the same type. The various elements of an array are indicated by a numeric index. The game board is a perfect candidate for this type of array. There are nine squares in the game board, and they can be numbered as indicated in Figure 8.7.

Remember that computers usually begin counting with 0, so the numbers should go from 0 to 8 rather than 1 to 9.

To make an array data structure, I simply built an array of strings. Since the game board will be accessed from many different places inside the program, I chose to define it as a global variable:

```
string board[9];
```

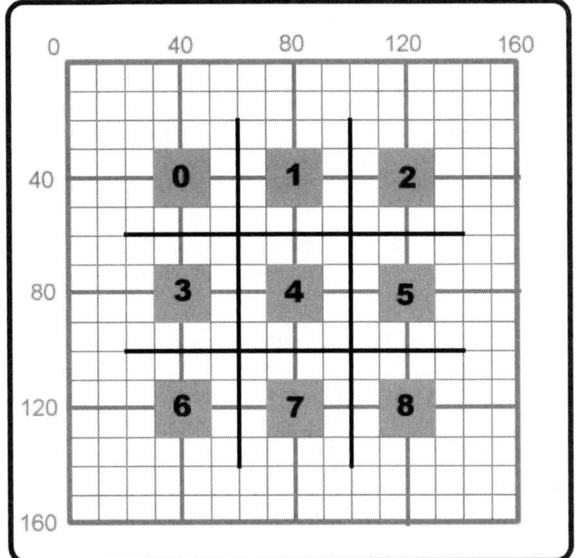

FIGURE 8.7

Each square in the game board is assigned a number from 0 to 8.

Initializing the Board Array

As with any variable, it makes sense to initialize an array to some starting value. Arrays are frequently initialized as one entity by using a loop. It's often convenient to do this with a function, so I added a `clearBoard()` function to the program:

```
clearBoard(){
  int i;
  for(i = 0; i < 9; i++){
    board[i] = i;
  } // end for loop
} // end clearBoard
```

The function simply steps through the array, assigning a value to each item. Note that each item in the array gets its own index as a starting value. This is a little unusual. Most of the time when you initialize an array, you set each element to the same starting value (often 0 or a null string). Later on it will be critical that the elements of the array all start out with different values, because I will be checking for equality to determine a winner. For example, if square 0, square 1, and square 2 all contain the value `X`, then player X is the winner. If the cells all start out with equivalent values, the program will falsely indicate there is a winner even before play begins!

Updating the Board in the checkHits() Function

Once there is a data representation of the playing board, it is necessary to update the array every time a player selects a cell. The easiest way to do this is to make a small modification to the `checkHits()` function:

```
checkHits(int x, int y){
  int shapeX, shapeY;

  if (checkNW(x,y)){
    board[0] = turn;
    shapeX = 30;
    shapeY = 30;
  } else if (checkN(x,y)){
    board[1] = turn;
    shapeX = 70;
    shapeY = 30;
  } else if (checkNE(x,y)){
    board[2] = turn;
    shapeX = 110;
    shapeY = 30;
  } else if (checkW(x,y)){
    board[3] = turn;
    shapeX = 30;
    shapeY = 70;
  } else if (checkC(x,y)){
    board[4] = turn;
    shapeX = 70;
    shapeY = 70;
  } else if (checkE(x,y)){
    board[5] = turn;
    shapeX = 110;
    shapeY = 70;
  } else if (checkSW(x,y)){
    board[6] = turn;
    shapeX = 30;
    shapeY = 110;
  } else if (checkS(x,y)){
    board[7] = turn;
    shapeX = 70;
    shapeY = 110;
```

```
  } else if (checkSE(x,y)){
    board[8] = turn;
    shapeX = 110;
    shapeY = 110;
  } else {
    alert("please click in a square");
    return();
  } // end if
  if (turn == "X"){
    drawX(shapeX, shapeY);
  } else {
    drawO(shapeX, shapeY);
  } // end turn if

} // end checkHits
```

In each square's conditional code, I copied the value from the `turn` variable (which will be `X` if it's X's turn) to the appropriate element of the array. The board array will contain a number (the square's index) if the cell has not been selected. If the cell has been chosen, the board will contain an X or an O depending on which player selected the square.

Viewing the Board

The board array does not have a visual representation, but you might want to see how it looks. Here's a utility function that lets you see exactly what the status of the board array is:

```
showBoard(){
  //shows the current status of the board

  saveg();
  graph_off();
  clear();
  puts("0: " + board[0] + "\t");
  puts("1: " + board[1] + "\t");
  puts("2: " + board[2] + "\n");
  puts("3: " + board[3] + "\t");
  puts("4: " + board[4] + "\t");
  puts("5: " + board[5] + "\n");
  puts("6: " + board[6] + "\t");
```

```
    puts("7: " + board[7] + "\t");
    puts("8: " + board[8] + "\t");

    wait();
    graph_on();
    restoreg();
} // end showBoard
```

The program saves the graphics screen, prints up the values of the various board elements, waits for input, then returns to the graphics screen. You might leave such a function in your program for testing purposes, but you probably wouldn't let the end user see it.

If your program is not acting properly (which is very likely, as you are debugging it) you can call this function within your code to see exactly what is happening inside the board array, as shown in Figures 8.8 and 8.9.

You might be familiar with the concept of *Easter eggs*—special surprise code fragments found in commercial programs. Many of these elements began life as testing code much like the `showboard()` function. These functions were often embedded into the program to assist programmers in debugging, then disconnected (or assigned to some arcane keystroke combination that typical users would not know). Of course now a lot of programmers put Easter eggs into their programs simply for fun. Still, it's interesting to know that these code fragments often served a utilitarian purpose.

FIGURE 8.8

When the screen looks like this . . .

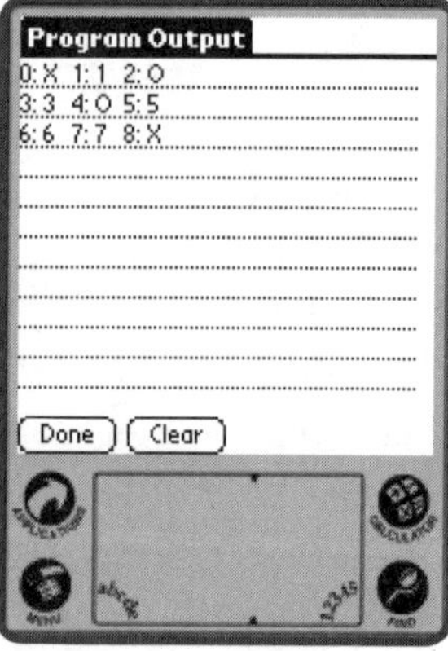

FIGURE 8.9

. . . the showBoard function displays these results.

Working with the Winning Combination Array

In addition to the game board itself, the Tic-Tac-Toe program can use another data structure. A key problem is to figure out when either player has won the game. When you know in advance all the winning combinations, you can figure out a way to store them in memory and compare the board's configuration to all the possible winning combinations. Given the board design (cells numbered 0–8, with 0 in upper left), the following are all the possible winning combinations.

```
-------------------------------------------------------------
Winning Combinations in Tic-Tac-Toe
0    1    2      top row
3    4    5      middle row
6    7    8      bottom row
0    3    6      left column
1    4    7      middle column
2    5    8      right column
0    4    8      top left-bottom right
2    4    6      top right-bottom left
-------------------------------------------------------------
```

If any of these combinations contain the same value at all three points, one player or the other has won. For example, if board[0], board[1], and board[2] are all "O", the O player has won. To check all the possible winning combinations, you could look at each row of the table above and check if the associated cells in the board array have the same values.

Multi-dimensional Arrays

Tables such as this come up frequently in many types of problem solving. Programming languages have a special structure for encoding this type of table in memory. The arrays you have used so far (such as the board array) are lists of data. Traditional arrays are also called *single-dimension* arrays. Many programming languages also allow you to define arrays with multiple dimensions. Two-dimensional arrays are extremely handy when working with data in a table. Unfortunately, PocketC does not directly support two-dimensional arrays. There are a number of very helpful libraries that do, however.

Introducing PToolboxLib

On the CD-ROM that accompanies this book, you will find a package called PToolboxLib. Joe Stadolink wrote this special library mainly to support game programming, but it is very handy for most kinds of PocketC programming because it extends the functionality of PocketC in some very powerful ways. Later chapters explore many of the other features of PToolboxLib, but for now, Tic-Tac-Toe takes advantage of its ability to create multiple-dimension arrays.

PToolboxL ib is not source code, like all the other programs you have used or imported so far in this book. It is a library file, and it is imported into your code with the library statement.

The library statement is much like the include statement you have used before, but different in that include files are simply PocketC source code that is to be added to the file. You can edit the contents of include files directly, and they will be compiled when you compile the program. (This is obvious on the spot—when you compile a program that uses the Ccontrols library, for example, it takes a long time to compile the program because every function in Ccontrols is being recompiled.) A library file is a file that has already been compiled. Most library files are written in a more powerful version of C (usually not on the Palm itself). The code in a library file is often more efficient than code written in PocketC because it has already been compiled and does not need to be run through the PocketC interpreter. Joe Stadolink chose to compile his library externally to get better performance in graphics-intensive programs.

For now, the only implication of PToolboxLib's being a library rather than an include file is that it is installed as a .pdb file, and you use the `library` statement rather than the `include` statement to import it.

Creating the Winning Combo Array

To facilitate finding a winner (and the upcoming artificial intelligence code), I need a two-dimensional array to store the winning combination data. The PToolboxLib supports this behavior, but it differs from the other libraries you have used earlier in this book:

```
library "PToolboxLib"
```

Once the library has been defined, you can access its functions as if they were built into PocketC itself.

To hold the array, I created a special type of variable called a *pointer*. Pointers are just like other variables, except that they refer to a memory address rather than an actual variable. Since an array is not just one value but several, arrays are generally stored as pointers rather than directly as variables. Most arrays are actually pointers, but in regular arrays (like the board array you saw earlier in this chapter) the fact that the variable is a pointer is hidden from you. If you're confused, don't worry. Most of the time pointers are not an issue in PocketC. Since the array function I'll be using in a moment returns a pointer, I'll need a pointer, but once that's done, the variable will feel pretty much like any other array.

To create an array, you invoke PToolboxLib's `array()` function:

```
winCombo = Array("i, 8, 3");
```

This array function expects one string parameter, but this is often broken into several pieces. In this case, the first value ("i") indicates that this will be an array of integers. The `8` and `3` values indicate that it will be a two-dimensional array of eight rows and three columns. Each row will represent a winning combination, and the three columns represent the three cells in each winning combo.

Setting Up the Wining Combo Array

It is useful to set up the entire array in a function. This function starts by creating a two-dimensional array. It then adds values to each element in the array.

```
setupWinCombo(){
  winCombo = Array("i, 8, 3");
  winCombo[0][0] = 0;
  winCombo[0][1] = 1;
  winCombo[0][2] = 2;

  winCombo[1][0] = 3;
  winCombo[1][1] = 4;
  winCombo[1][2] = 5;

  winCombo[2][0] = 6;
  winCombo[2][1] = 7;
  winCombo[2][2] = 8;

  winCombo[3][0] = 0;
  winCombo[3][1] = 3;
  winCombo[3][2] = 6;
```

```
  winCombo[4][0] = 1;
  winCombo[4][1] = 4;
  winCombo[4][2] = 7;

  winCombo[5][0] = 2;
  winCombo[5][1] = 5;
  winCombo[5][2] = 8;

  winCombo[6][0] = 0;
  winCombo[6][1] = 4;
  winCombo[6][2] = 8;

  winCombo[7][0] = 2;
  winCombo[7][1] = 4;
  winCombo[7][2] = 6;
} // end winCombo
```

Note that elements in a two-dimensional array have two indices. The first index refers to the row, and the second index refers to the column. (If it helps, think of a spreadsheet. A cell in a spreadsheet is identified by a row designator and a column designator—usually a letter and a number rather than the pair of numbers used here, but it's the same concept.)

The spacing helps to separate each row in this function. While creating and filling this array may seem tedious, you will see shortly how useful it can be.

Debugging the Winning Combo Array

Since winCombo is not a visual element, it can be hard to know if the function correctly generated the data. Just to be sure, I wrote a quick function to display all the elements in the winCombo array:

```
showWinCombo(){
  int row, col;

  saveg();
  graph_off();

  clear();
  for(row = 0; row < 8; row++){
    for (col = 0; col < 3; col++){
      puts(winCombo[row][col]);
      puts("\t");
```

```
    } // end col for
    puts("\n");
  } // end row for
  wait();
  restoreg();
  graph_on();
} // end showWinCombo
```

The showWinCombo code prints out the results of the winCombo array, as shown in Figure 8.10, so you can see that it is working correctly. It uses a pair of nested `for` loops to step through every element in the array—a technique that's very commonly used for the purpose. It works like the basic `for` loop introduced in Chapter 6 to examine all the elements in a normal array, with an extra loop to handle the added dimension. This type of stop-and-check code is very useful in programming—the time it takes to do is nothing compared to the time it saves by revealing problems before the program starts mysteriously dying later in the process.

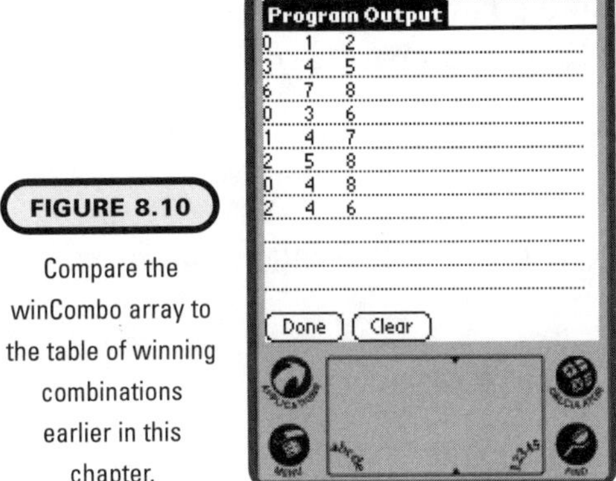

FIGURE 8.10

Compare the winCombo array to the table of winning combinations earlier in this chapter.

Checking for a Winner

Once all the data structures (the board array and the winCombo array) are in place, it becomes reasonably easy to determine if either player has won the game:

```
string checkWinner(){

  int row;
  for(row = 0; row < 8; row++){
    if (board[winCombo[row][0]] == board[winCombo[row][1]]){
      if (board[winCombo[row][1]] == board[winCombo[row][2]]){
```

```
        return(turn + " wins!");
      } // end if
    } // end if
  } // end if
  return("none");
} // end checkWinner
```

The function steps through each row of the winCombo array. The most difficult part of this function is the various code fragments that look like this:

```
board[winCombo[row][0]]
```

This code is not as crazy as it might look. Recall that each row of winColumn represents a possible winning combination. The values in the winCombo array represent which cells of the board should have the same value if it is a winning combination. As a concrete example, here is the first row of the winCombo array:

winCombo[0][0] is 0
winCombo[0][1] is 1
winCombo[0][2] is 2

Remember, if board[0] is equal to board[1] and board[2], whatever player entered those cells is the winner. To simplify, just think of comparing cells 0 and 1 of the game board. You could do so with this line:

```
if (board[0] == board[1])
```

Since `winCombo`[0][0] is 0, and `winCombo`[0][1] is 1, you could replace that line with this one:

```
if (board[winCombo[0][0]] == board[winCombo[0][1]])
```

The only difference is rather than directly comparing board[0] and board[1], I'm going to the winCombo array to figure out which two cells to compare. The advantage of this is that by changing the value of row, I can check any winning combination, because they are all stored in the winCombo array.

The `checkWinner` function checks for the first two columns of the winCombo array. If they are the same, it then compares the middle column with the last. If these two columns are also equal, all three cells have the same value, and there is a winner. The only thing left to do is determine who that winner is, which is determined by the turn variable. The `checkWinner` function will always return a string, which will be `X` or `O` if there is a winner, or `none` if neither player has won yet.

The TicTacTwo Game (Two Players, Tracks Winner)

The addition of these elements and some small changes to the code lead to a program that enables two players to play tic-tac-toe with each other on the same Palm. The computer will recognize if either player wins, and it will also recognize a cat's game (tie).

The code listings in this segment just point out the parts of the code that changed from the program in the "Stripped-Down Game" section earlier in this chapter. Look at the entire source code on the CD-ROM to see the program in its entirety.

Here are the global variables for the TicTacTwo program:

```
//tictactwo
//tictactoe program
//two - player version
//checks for winning score
//Andy Harris, 05/02/01

library "PToolboxLib"

int keepGoing = true;
int counter = 0;
string turn = "X";
pointer winCombo;
string board[9];
```

The only additions are the pointer for the winCombo array, and the board array.

The `main` function has also changed a bit:

```
main(){
  int evt;
  int x, y;

  clearBoard();
  setupWinCombo();
  //showWinCombo();
  //wait();

  drawScreen();
```

```
    while(keepGoing){
      wait();
      checkHits(penx(), peny());
      //showBoard();
      houseKeeping();

    } // end while

} // end main
```

The new elements all refer to the arrays. The program calls the `setupWinCombo()` function to initialize the winning combo array. Just to check the program, I had a call to `showWinCombo()` in the function, but I commented it out. Likewise, the `showBoard()` call is used for debugging, but commented out of the way when it is not needed.

The `houseKeeping` function is modified to add the winner checking function:

```
houseKeeping(){
  if(checkWinner() != "none"){
    alert(checkWinner());
    keepGoing = false;
  } // end if

  if (turn == "X"){
    turn = "O";
  } else {
    turn = "X";
  } // end turn if

  counter++;
  if (counter > 8) {
    alert("Cat's game!");
    keepGoing = false;
    return();
  } // end if

} // end houseKeeping
```

If `checkWinner()` is found to be true, the winner is reported, and `keepGoing` is set to false, which will end the program.

Adding a Hint Function

It might seem like a daunting task to develop an interesting computer opponent, but the effort spent on managing the data will pay off in a big way. If any two elements of a winning combo are the same, and if the third element of that combination is empty, that empty element should get the attention of the computer player. While this is not a foolproof strategy, it is quite effective. If the computer player goes first, it will never lose. Before implementing the complete player strategy, I have decided to write a version of the game that will always tell the user which square it thinks is best. This is a good way to test out the algorithm, because I can try a number of strategies to see how well the computer reacts. The Figure 8.11 illustrates a complete game that demonstrates the power of the artificial intelligence. Note that the number in the lower right-hand corner of each screen is the AI's suggested next square. If I always click on the indicated square—as I did in the sequence shown in Figure 8.11—a tie is guaranteed. (Nobody has ever explained to me why a tie in tic-tac-toe is called a cat's game, but that's what it's called.)

Creating the findBest() Function

The key to the artificial intelligence in this program is the `findBest()` function. The purpose of this function is to scan the board looking for the best possible play. The function will return with a recommendation of the square to play. The `findBest()` function has two main components. The first checks to see if there are any empty squares that will lead to a win or a block. The other evaluates all the squares to see which is the most promising, and returns that square. The `findBest()` procedure uses a special kind of algorithm called a *heuristic*. The basic idea of a heuristic is to determine some set of rules for ranking the various options available, so that the computer appears to make better decisions. Games with varying difficulty levels usually have multiple algorithms defined, so when the game is on the hardest level, the computer is using the most sophisticated heuristic in the program.

Comparing the Board with the Winning Combos

To track the various squares on the board, I added another array called rank. This array corresponds with the board array. Each element in the rank array has a score associated with it.

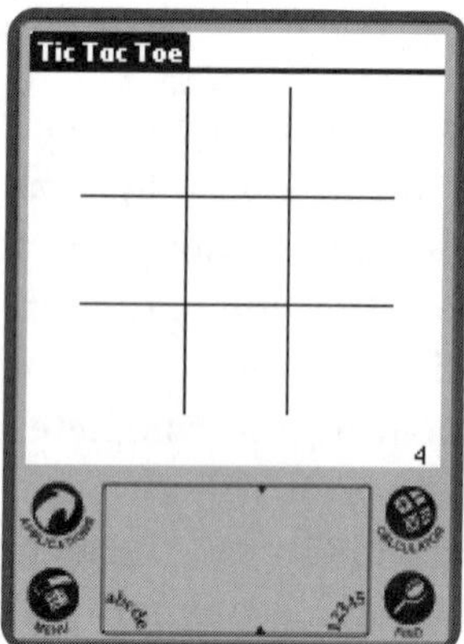

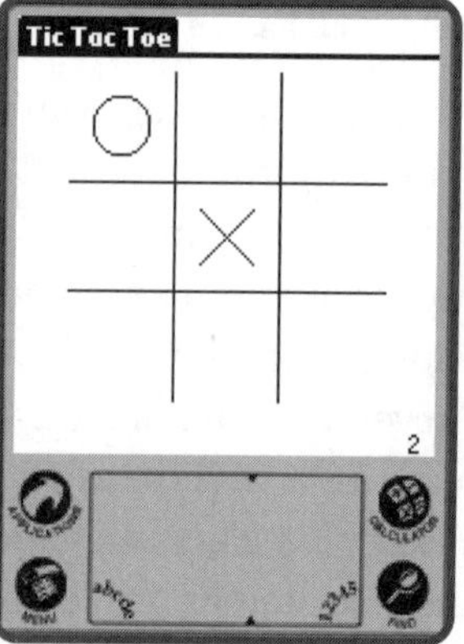

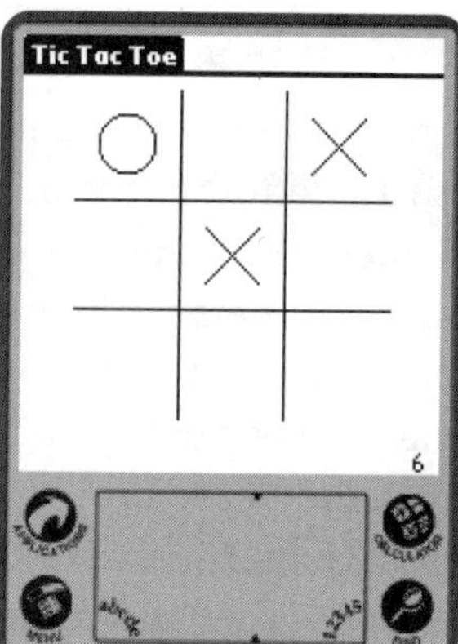

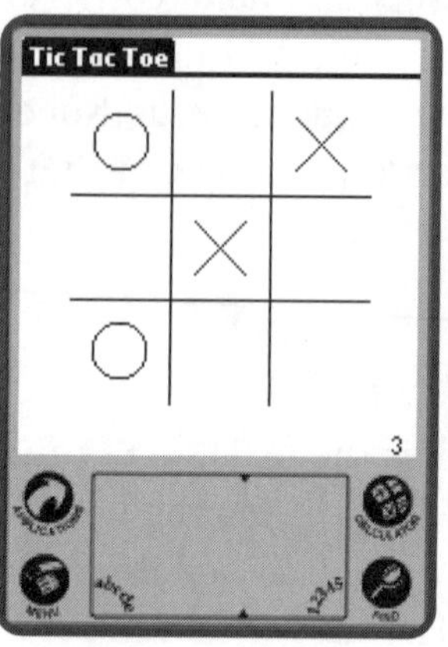

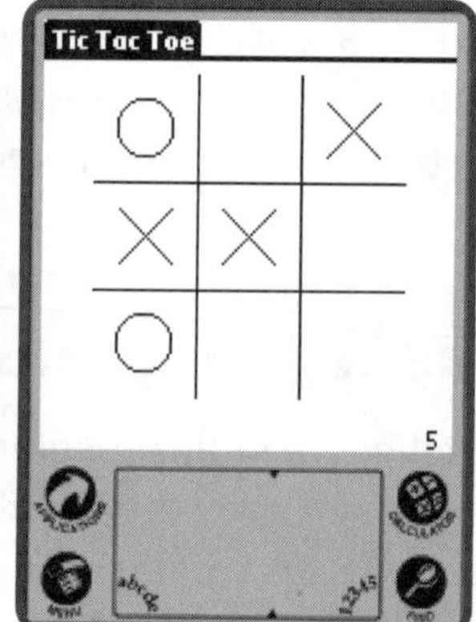

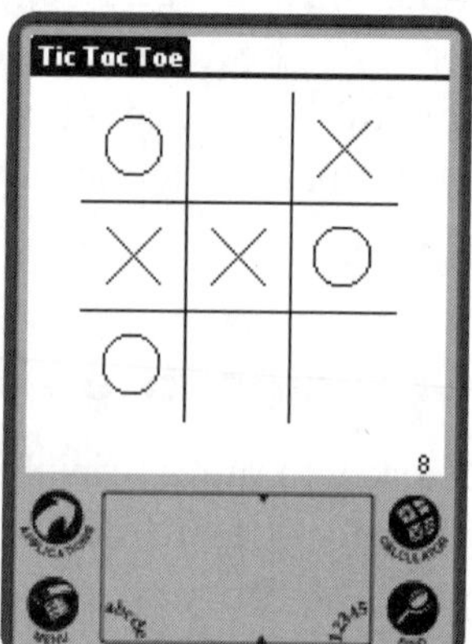

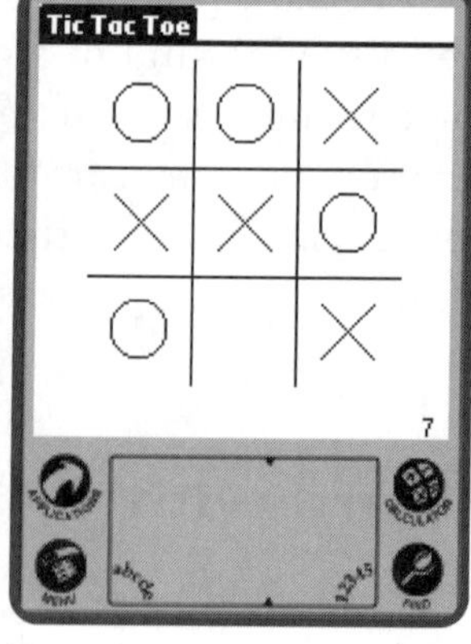

FIGURE 8.11

A complete game with the hint code activated. I followed the computer's suggestion in every case.

Table 8.1 gives the starting ranks.

Table 8.1 Starting Ranks of the Cells

3	2	3
2	4	2
3	2	3

Each cell was given a base score based on the number of winning combinations that go through that cell. Since there are four winning combinations that include the center cell, it has the highest default ranking. The corners are the next highest with rankings of three, and the remaining cells all have a rank of two. When you know the starting values of all elements in an array, you can assign the elements all at once, like this:

```
int rank[9] = {3,2,3,2,4,2,3,2,3};
```

By assigning a rank to each square, I have given the computer a guideline as to the relative importance of the squares. The computer will always choose from the cells with the highest score.

As the game progresses, the value of the cells will change. If a cell is needed to win the game or block the opponent from winning, it becomes much more valuable and should be chosen on the next turn. If either player has used a cell, that cell should be removed from consideration. Here is the code that checks for a winning or blocking cell:

```
int findBest(){
  //returns the index of the best choice
  int i;
  int row;
  int bestSquare = 0;
  int highestRank = -999;
```

```
//showBoard();
for (row = 0; row < 8; row++){
  if (board[winCombo[row][0]] == board[winCombo[row][1]]){
    rank[winCombo[row][2]] = rank[winCombo[row][2]] + 5;
  } // end if
  if (board[winCombo[row][0]] == board[winCombo[row][2]]){
    rank[winCombo[row][1]] = rank[winCombo[row][1]] + 5;
  } // end if
  if (board[winCombo[row][1]] == board[winCombo[row][2]]){
    rank[winCombo[row][0]] = rank[winCombo[row][0]] + 5;
  } // end if
} // end for
```

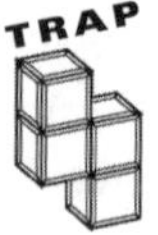

Because of the way multi-dimensional arrays are created, it is possible to access a value that you haven't explicitly defined. For example, the first time I wrote this program I accidentally set the `for` loop for the row to repeat nine times, even though there are only eight rows. The program happily accessed the last row of data, returning whatever happened to be in the next few cells of memory. Be very careful that you do not move beyond the bounds of a multi-dimensional array, or you will have unpredictable results.

The function steps through all the winning combinations. It then compares the board's values for the first two items in the winning combination. Again, an illustration might make this simpler. Remember that the first row of winCombo is {0, 1, 2}. The first `if` statement checks to see if the value in board[0] is equal to the value in board[1]. If the values are equal, then board[2] is an extremely important cell, and its rank should be increased. It doesn't really matter which player has the 0 and 1 cells occupied, because the number 2 cell is now critical in either case.

The next `if` statement checks to see if board[0] and board[2] have the same value. If they do, the rank of the 1 cell is increased. The last `if` statement checks to see if board[1] and board[2] have the same value, and increases the rank for cell 0 if this is the case.

Since all of the `if` statements are inside a `while` loop, the loop continues repeating the process for all the winning combinations.

This is one place in which you might wish to improve the algorithm. It is possible that both a winning and blocking solution would present themselves. In this situation, the program should favor the winning solution.

Returning the Best Square

Once any possible winning or blocking squares are identified, the function looks at all the squares and reduces the rank of any square that has an X or an O in it:

```
for (i = 0; i < 9; i++){
    //drastically reduce the score of a square with x or o in it
    if (board[i] == "X"){
      rank[i] = rank[i] - 99;
    } // end if
    if (board[i] == "O"){
      rank[i] = rank[i] - 99;
    } // end if

    //see if the current cell has a good rank
    if (rank[i] > highestRank){
      highestRank = rank[i];
      bestSquare = i;
    } // end if
  } // end for loop
  return(bestSquare);
} // end findBest
```

The function checks each cell of the board, and if it contains an X or an O, the rank of that cell is reduced by 99. This will make the cell extremely unattractive to the computer player. Finally, the rank of the current cell is compared to the highest rank (which is initialized to a ridiculously low value). If the current cell has the highest rank encountered so far, the rank of that cell is transferred to the `highestRank` variable, and the `bestSquare` variable receives the current value of i. As the function ends, it returns the value of `bestSquare`.

Presenting the Best Square

All that remains for this version of the program is to indicate the suggested best square. This can be done in the `main` function:

```
main(){
  int evt;
  int x, y;

  clearBoard();
```

```
  setupWinCombo();
  //showWinCombo();
  //wait();

  drawScreen();

  while(keepGoing){
    text(150, 150, findBest());
    wait();
    checkHits(penx(), peny());
    //showBoard();
    houseKeeping();
  } // end while

} // end main
```

The only new line is the one that calls the `findBest()` function and writes the resulting value to the screen with a `text()` command.

Adding the Computer Opponent

Once the heuristic is tested, it is reasonably easy to add the computer opponent. I added a function called `aiPlay()` as follows:

```
aiPlay(){
  //artificial intelligence makes a play

  int bestSquare;
  int shapeX, shapeY;

  bestSquare = findBest();
  switch(bestSquare){
    case 0:
      shapeX = 30;
      shapeY = 30;
      break;
    case 1:
      shapeX = 70;
      shapeY = 30;
      break;
```

```
    case 2:
      shapeX = 110;
      shapeY = 30;
      break;
    case 3:
      shapeX = 30;
      shapeY = 70;
      break;
    case 4:
      shapeX = 70;
      shapeY = 70;
      break;
    case 5:
      shapeX = 110;
      shapeY = 70;
      break;
    case 6:
      shapeX = 30;
      shapeY = 110;
      break;
    case 7:
      shapeX = 70;
      shapeY = 110;
      break;
    case 8:
      shapeX = 110;
      shapeY = 110;
      break;
  } // end switch

  if (turn == "X"){
    drawX(shapeX, shapeY);
    board[bestSquare] = "X";
  } else {
    drawO(shapeX, shapeY);
    board[bestSquare] = "O";
  } // end turn if

} // end aiPlay
```

The aiPlay() function calls on the findBest() function to determine where the computer player should move. The function uses a switch statement to set up the location of the next move, much like in the checkHits() function described earlier in this chapter. Then the program draws the appropriate shape on the screen and sets the board array so that it will recognize the move. Once the bestMove() function is working correctly, it is easy to get the computer player to work.

Alternating between Human and Computer

A small change in the main() function is necessary so that the human and computer players will alternate:

```
main(){
  int evt;
  int x, y;

  clearBoard();
  setupWinCombo();
  //showWinCombo();
  //wait();

  drawScreen();

  while(keepGoing){
    aiPlay();
    houseKeeping();
    if (keepGoing){
      wait();
      checkHits(penx(), peny());
      houseKeeping();
    } // end if
  } // end while

} // end main
```

Each time through the loop, the computer player will go first by calling the aiPlay() function. The main program then calls the houseKeeping() function to check for winning conditions. It's possible that the game is over. If so, keepGoing will be false, and the next part of the loop will be skipped, ending the game. If keepGoing is still true, the computer waits for human input, then calls the checkHits() function to determine where the human user wants to play. Once again, the program calls the houseKeeping() function.

In the Real World

The code in this chapter works, but there is always room for improvement. When I showed the programs in this chapter to a friend, he had a number of suggestions for improvements:

Parts of the code could be shortened using arrays and a few tricks.

For instance, the `aiPlay()` and `checkHits()` functions have "hardcoded" values for the x and y positions of the start drawing area. You could put these in an array, thereby avoiding all the `if – else if` statements. So `aiPlay` would become:

```
bestsquare = findBest();
shapex = boardShapeX[bestsquare];
shapey = boardShapeY[bestsquare];
```

which would avoid the whole switch statement.

The other technique would be to have `checkHits()` return the square number, as opposed to checking each square individually.

Also, there can be little tricks used to get around "hard coding" everything. To give a semi-algorithmic example of a new `checkHits()`:

```
x = penx(); y = peny();
```

Check once to see if the user has tapped inside the whole playing area.

```
PointRec( x, y, 20, 20, 140, 140 )
```

If successful, calculate the square position based on x, y within the play area.

```
x = x–20; y = y-20;
x=int(x/40); y=int(y/40);
square = x+(y*3)
```

Assuming the previous is a function `getSquare()`, `checkHits()` becomes:

```
sq = getSquare();
board[sq] = turn;
shapex = boardShapeX[sq]; // using technique from my previous example
shapey = boardShapeY[sq];
/* draw X or O as original */
```

I showed you these comments to illustrate some very useful points. First of all, it's a great idea to show your programs to other programmers, because they will often have ideas for improvement. (Especially if your friends are as smart as the guy who gave me this advice). Secondly, there is always room for improvement. Even after you feel your code is working, there is always some way to make it more extensible or perform better.

Summary

This chapter covered some very important ground. You now know how to generate a simple heuristic that enables the computer to play a simple game very well. You've followed a program all the way from the conceptual stage through a number of iterations—a path that will be useful in any programming project—and you can use the PToolbox library as well as single-dimension and multiple-dimension arrays.

CHALLENGES

1. **Change the program so that it asks if the user wants to play again.**
2. **Alternate between the user and the computer taking the first turn.**
3. **If the human player is allowed to go first, the AI has a weakness that can be exploited. Use the tttHint program to determine this weakness, and fix the AI so that it is no longer a problem.**
4. **Improve the AI so that if the computer sees both a blocking and a winning option, the winning combination will take precedence. (This is NOT the weakness I mentioned in the last exercise.)**
5. **Allow for different difficulty levels. Maybe use an entirely random AI for the easy level, then allow for more sophisticated heuristics at higher levels.**
6. **Make the game board a four-by-four grid.**

Memo Access: The Life Game

Computer programs can be used to explore a variety of interesting phenomena. In this chapter, you'll build a special type of program that shows how a simple set of rules can be used to generate complex and beautiful patterns. The program in this chapter is more of a toy than a game, but it is still fascinating.

This chapter's program simulates a colony of bacteria. Each individual bacterium is uninteresting, but the colony will grow according to a very simple set of rules that results in beautiful patterns. The program you will write is an example of a *cellular automaton.* This class of programs looks at a series of entities and simulates simple decision-making behavior in them. Most of the programming skills for the game are already part of your repertoire. However, you'll need to learn how to let the user load or save various favorite patterns. In this chapter, you will learn the following techniques:

- Writing a basic cellular automaton program
- Storing data to a memo file
- Loading data from a memo file
- Designing a program for maximum flexibility

Conway's Game of Life

The mathematician John Conway devised the Game of Life in the late 1960s. The game board is much like a checkerboard, with each square capable of holding an organism. The organisms on the board live and die according to a very simple set of rules:

- Any cell with exactly three neighbors will become (or remain) alive.
- If an organism is alive and has exactly two neighbors, it remains alive.
- All other cells will die off.

During every turn, Conway would examine each square in the board and determine if it would live or die according to these rules. Conway originally played this game on a Go board using small stones. Although it was unwieldy to manage the game in this way, some very interesting patterns emerged. He found that some patterns remain stable indefinitely, that some go through a sequence of patterns, and some die off completely after a while. In 1971, Martin Gardener featured the game in his puzzle column in *Scientific American.* The Game of Life quickly became a popular subject of computer programs, because the computer can manage all the details of calculating the next generation much more quickly and accurately than a human player can. Once computer programs were employed in this way, even more interesting patterns emerged. Some patterns emerged that appeared to move around the screen; they were called "gliders" and "spaceships." Other patterns repeatedly shoot out new gliders, or move around on the screen leaving "puffs." Extremely lifelike behavior arose from a very simple set of rules.

For more information on the Game of Life, and a Java Applet that allows much faster and more elaborate patterns, see http://www.math.com/students/wonders/life/life.html

How the PocketC Version Works

In this chapter you learn how to implement a limited version of Conway's Life in PocketC. Figures 9.1 through 9.6 illustrate the program in action.

FIGURE 9.1

The starting screen is a blank space with some buttons along the bottom.

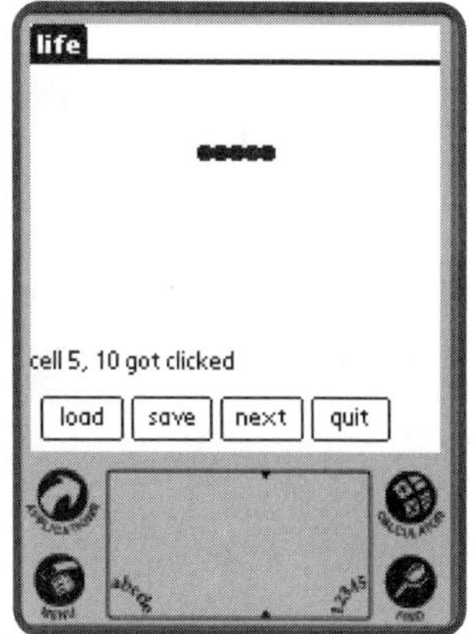

FIGURE 9.2

Here is a simple starting pattern.

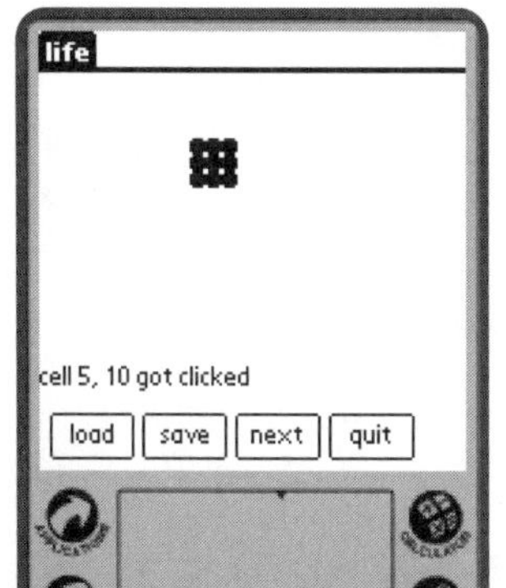

FIGURE 9.3

When the user clicks Next, the computer calculates the next generation.

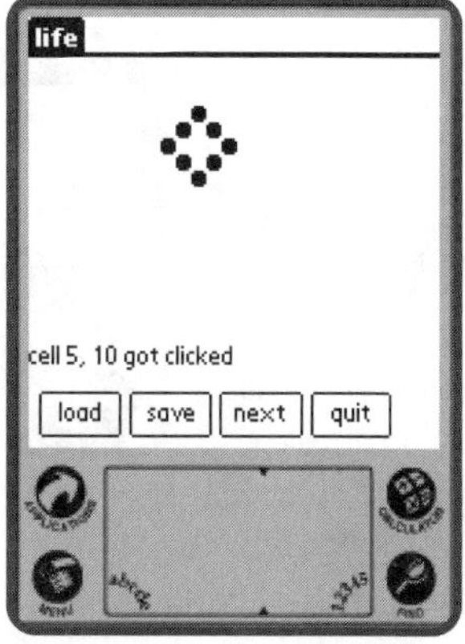

FIGURE 9.4

This pattern generates another pattern.

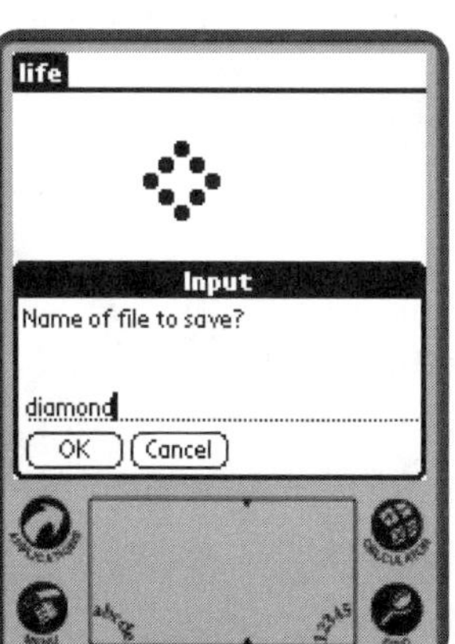

FIGURE 9.5

A pattern can be saved into a memo file.

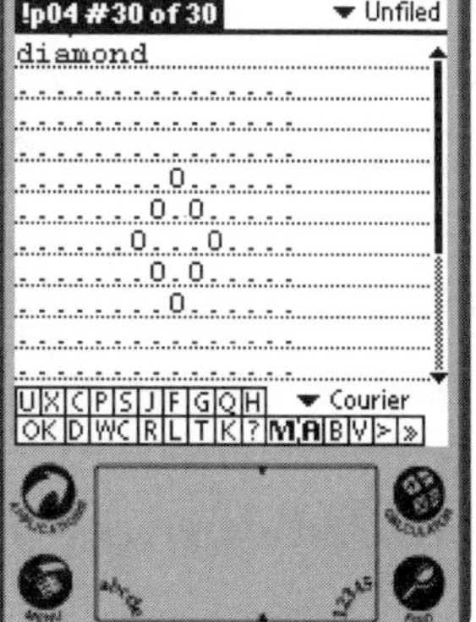

FIGURE 9.6

The user can edit or view the file with Memo Pad or another editor.

It's much easier to edit the files in a fixed-width font. A higher-end memo program such as pedit will add this functionality. I used pedit in Figure 9.6, but the memo editor that comes with the Palm OS will also work. You'll just have to be more careful with it because the period is much narrower than the 0 character in Memo Pad's only font. Ultimately though, you won't need a text editor at all because you'll be using the Life program itself to save, edit, and load your files.

In the example in Figure 9.7, the program is loading a famous pattern called the "r Pentamino" pattern.

FIGURE 9.7

The Life program also features a load function.

While the PocketC version of the program is not blazingly fast, it does provide you with a framework for exploring the fascinating world of cellular automata. The default rules of Conway's Life are interesting enough, but when you write your own program, you can have even more fun by changing the rules, the size of the world, and other parameters.

Creating a Memo

The ability to store and retrieve information in memos is an important feature in this game. Memos in the Palm operating system operate much like text files in traditional computers.

How Memos Work on the Palm

The Palm operating system has a unique way of storing information. Traditional computers use files on disk drives as the primary way to store information. Most

Palm-based devices do not have disk drives available. Instead, all information is stored in the Palm device's memory. As I discussed in Chapter 1, the Palm supports two types of files. Palm program files end in .prc, and they contain instructions for the computer to execute. The other type of file in the Palm world is the Palm database file. All the information stored by any Palm program is goes into a Palm database (.pdb) file. Each of the built-in programs on the Palm uses a specific type of .pdb file, including the Memo Pad application. PocketC allows direct access to this file. In effect, you can read and write memos from your PocketC applications. This is a very useful feature, because it means your programs can store information directly on the Palm. If your program needs to keep track of information between multiple runs, say for a grocery list or a high score table, the Memo Pad format is a good way to do this. Memos are especially convenient to work with because they can be manipulated by other programs. Any memos you create in a PocketC program can be read directly by the Memo Pad program that came with your PDA. If you have another editor (such as pedit), you can use that editor to read and write memo files as well.

Some memo editors (such as pedit) feature multiple modes. Be sure that you are writing in the standard 4k memo mode if you want to be able to read your memo in PocketC.

Disadvantages of Memos

Although memos can be very useful, they do have some disadvantages. First, since the user can edit memos, the data can be corrupted very easily. If your data need a very specific format (as the data for the Life game will) and the user changes the memo file by hand, there may be some strange results. Also, Memo Pad data is extremely insecure. It wouldn't be a good idea to use a memo to store passwords, for example, because the memo data will be accessible to anybody who can use Memo Pad on the Palm Pilot. In Chapter 10, "Databases and Pointers: The Password Keeper," you will learn how to create your own .pdb formats to prevent these problems.

The Make Chart Program

For an example of memo creation, recall the Make Chart program on the CD-ROM, which you first saw way back in Chapter 3. Figures 9.8 and 9.9 illustrate the program in action.

FIGURE 9.8

The Make Chart program creates a memo with ASCII values of various characters.

FIGURE 9.9

Once the Make Chart program has run, you can view the new ASCII Chart document in the Memo Pad program.

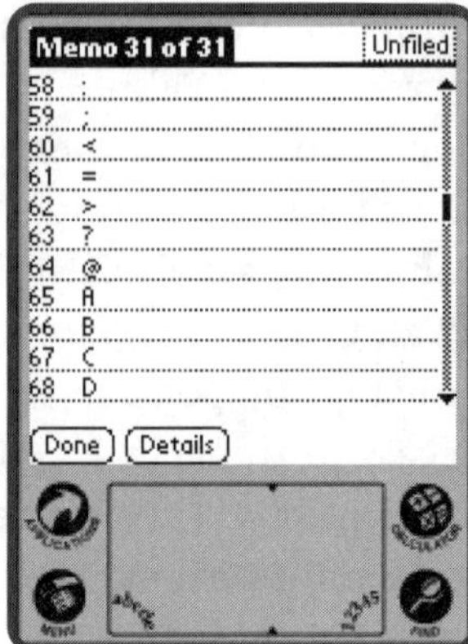

Make Chart is a utility program that helps you work with ASCII characters. It generates a memo with a series of ASCII values and the related symbols. You can use this document to determine the value of various characters, such as the playing card symbols or the Yen sign.

The design of the Make Chart program is actually very simple:

```
//makeChart
//Creates an ASCII chart memo pad document
//Andy Harris, 3/9/01

main(){
  string theChart;
  int i;
  clear();
  puts("please wait... \n");
  for(i=0; i<=165; i++){
    theChart = theChart + i;
    theChart = theChart + "\t";
    theChart = theChart + (char)i;
    theChart = theChart + "\n";
  } // end for loop
  puts(theChart);

  //create a memo
  mmnew();
  mmputs("ASCII Chart \n");
```

```
  mmputs(theChart);
  mmclose();
  alert("Created a new memo called ASCII Chart");

} // end main
```

The program has a string variable called `theChart`. All the chart information will be added to `theChart`, which will then be written to a memo. The program features a `for` loop that steps through the first 165 characters.

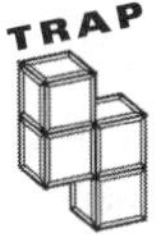

You might recall that ASCII stands for "American Standard Code for Information Interchange." ASCII is the encoding set used on most computers. The Palm operating system uses a slightly customized version of ASCII. For example, the ASCII value 7 was originally meant to sound the bell on teletype machines, so it is ignored by the Palm OS, which has more sophisticated sound routines. Also, the Palm version of ASCII features some symbols that are not found in standard ASCII, such as character 22 (the Graffiti control character) and character 23 (the Graffiti shortcut symbol).

There are 256 characters in the main ASCII character set, but many of them do not print properly in the Palm environment. I decided only to include the first 165 characters, because these values include all the characters that are printable in the default fonts given in the Palm OS.

I copied `i` (the `for` loop counter) to `theChart`, then cast `i` to a char, which returns the ASCII value corresponding to `i`.

I used the Tab character to separate the numeric value and the character, and the Newline character to place each pair on a new line.

Even the Tab and Newline characters are actually ASCII values. If you look closely at the ASCII chart produced by this program, you'll see that there is an extra tab after value 9, because the Tab character is actually the ASCII value 9. When you use the "\t" sequence in your programs, PocketC automatically replaces "\t" with ASCII character 9. Likewise, the Newline("\n") character is generally some combination of the ASCII values 10 and 12. You'll see an extra carriage return between lines 10 and 11 of the ASCII chart memo because the program printed ASCII 10, which the Palm OS interprets as the carriage return.

Once the loop is finished, the program creates a memo using built-in PocketC functions. All the memo functions in PocketC begin with mm. The `mmnew()` function is used to build a new memo. Use `mmputs()` to write a string to the open memo, and `mmclose()` to close the memo. You can write many times to the memo. Each new call to `mmputs()` writes at the end of the memo.

IN THE REAL WORLD

The memo-creating features of PocketC are heavily used in the Ceditor program that comes with Ccontrols. You might recall that the program can automatically generate the Ccontrols header files, and it also generates PocketC source code. All these files are memo files, created using exactly the techniques described here.

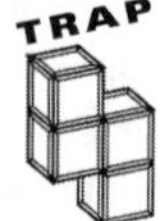

If you are used to sequential file handling in traditional languages, use of the memo looks similar, but it is not identical. Memo files don't have names! Instead, the first line of the file is used to denote the file name. Also, each memo is not a separate file, but a new entry to one large database. (All the memos on your Palm are stored in one .pdb file.) There is no such thing as opening for input or output. It's up to you to keep track of which type of file access you are doing. You may not have more than one memo open at a time. These restrictions are not really a problem, because for the most part it is easier to access a memo on the Palm than it is to use sequential access files in traditional languages.

Memo Functions

PocketC comes with a number of useful functions designed to help you work with memo files. Table 9.1 gives you a list for ready reference.

Reading a Memo

It can also be useful to read information in from a memo. Generally, you will read information in from a memo one line at a time. Since the number of lines in a memo is a dynamic thing, programmers generally use a `while` loop to get all the lines in the memo file. The `mmeof()` function is used to determine if the program is at the end of file or not.

The Surferspeak Program

To illustrate Memo Pad input and output, I'll show you a completely silly program. The Surferspeak program prompts for the name of a memo file, and then translates it into "surfing talk," as in Figures 9.10 through 9.12.

Table 9.1 Functions Used to Work with Memos

Function	Description	Example
mmnew();	Creates a new empty memo. The title will be defined by the first line you write to the memo.	mmnew();

int mmfind(string *title*);	Finds and opens the memo with *title* as its first line. If the *title* memo cannot be found, function returns the value 0 (false).	if (mmfind("ASCII chart") == 0){
		puts("Please run the makeChart program");
		} // end if

mmputs(string *text*);	Writes *text* to the end of the memo	mmputs("Hi, Mom!");
string mmgetl();	Returns the next line of text. Usually used inside a loop	string theLine; theLine = mmgetl();

int mmeof();	Returns false if not at end of file. Usually used when reading a file.	while (!mmeof()){
		puts(mmgetl());
		} // end while

mmrewind();	Resets pointer to the beginning of the file	mmrewind();
mmclose();	Close the file.	mmclose();
mmdelete();	Close and delete the current memo.	mmdelete();
int mmcount();	Count the number of memos in the PDA.	mmcount();

FIGURE 9.10

The program asks for the name of a memo file.

FIGURE 9.11

The program has finished its serious and weighty calculations.

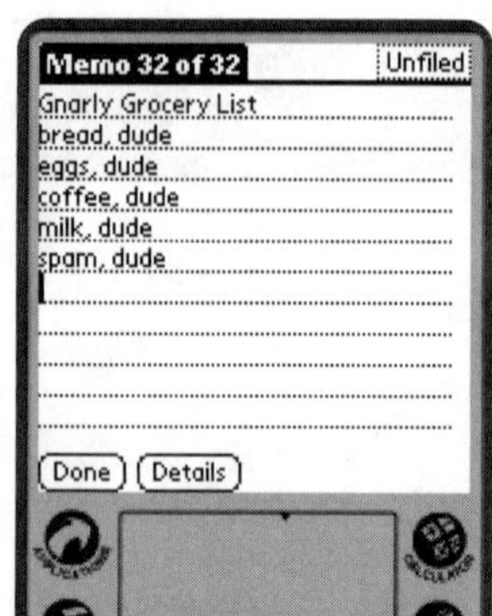

FIGURE 9.12

The new memo

This may not be the most important program you have on your PDA, but it does demonstrate all the key features of memo file manipulation in PocketC.

Here's the code:

```
//surferSpeak
//demonstrates memo handling
//opens a memo
//adds ', dude' to the end of each line
//creates a new memo
//Andy Harris, 05/09/01

main(){
  string fileName = "";
  string newFile = "Gnarly ";

  graph_off();
  clear();
  title("Surfer Translation");

  //open the file
  fileName = gets("Memo to translate?");
  if (mmfind(fileName)){
    //translate the name
    newFile = newFile + mmgetl() + "\n";
    puts("please wait: .");
```

```
    //read the other lines
    while (!mmeof()){
      newFile = newFile + mmgetl();
      newFile = newFile + ", dude \n";
      puts(".");
    } // end while
    mmclose();

    //create a new file
    mmnew();
    mmputs(newFile);
    mmrewind();
    fileName = mmgetl();
    mmclose();
    alert(fileName + " now created, dude.");

  } else {
    alert(fileName + " not found.");
  } // end if
} // end main
```

The program begins by defining two string variables. The `fileName` variable will be used to hold the first line of the file, which serves as a file name. The `newFile` variable will contain the entire modified memo before it is written to the memo.

I began by asking the user for a memo name. This is a risky operation, because it's quite possible that the user will type the value incorrectly or with the wrong capitalization. The `mmfind()` function serves two purposes. First, it attempts to open the file if it can find it. Also, `mmfind()` returns a Boolean value. If the memo file is successfully opened, `mmfind` will return the value `true`. Otherwise, it will return the value `false`. The bulk of the program will execute only if the file was successfully found. If the program could not find the file, it exits gracefully. It's critical to do this kind of error checking whenever you work with user input, especially when you are also working with file manipulation.

Once the file is open, I add "Gnarly" to the beginning of the first line. The value "Gnarly" is the initial value of the `newFile` variable, and I simply add the first line to it via the `mmgetl()` function. Note that the `mmgetl()` function does not preserve the carriage return characters, so I added them myself. The first line of the file when it gets saved will be "Gnarly" and then whatever the first line was before. "Grocery List" becomes "Gnarly Grocery List," for example.

The rest of the file should just be a copy of the original with the phrase ", dude" at the end of each line. I started a loop that will continue as long as the program is not at the end of the file—the exclamation point (!) means *not*, so that's what the `while (!mmeof())` line is doing. I added each line to `newFile`, added the ", dude" phrase, and added a Newline character.

IN THE REAL WORLD

You might also notice the `puts()` lines in the code. Since a large file might take some time to process, I decided to add a visual indicator that something is going on. A user who sees no evidence of progress is likely to shut the computer down while it's still processing.

Once the loop is finished, I rewound the pointer back to the first line, and copied the new title to the `fileName` variable. Finally, I told the user about the new file, and closed the file.

Writing the Life Game

File handling is the only new PocketC syntax in the Life program, but the program is involved enough to merit careful study on its own. I wanted the program to follow the basic rules of the Life game as defined by Conway. However, I wanted to build in some flexibility, like the ability to save and load patterns, the ability to change the size of the game board, and the ability to change the rule sets to see what would happen. Also, I felt the program required a combination of Ccontrols buttons and straight graphics primitives, and that gave me a chance to illustrate how those features can be combined in the same program.

Global Variables

The program code starts in the usual way, with comments, importing various libraries, and declaring some critical global variables.

```
//life
//Conway's game of life
//demonstrates combining controls with graphics
//saving and loading memo files
//Andy Harris, 05/09/01

#include "Ccontrols.c"

library "PToolboxLib"
```

```
pointer board;    //the main game board
pointer neighborhood;   //used to calculate next generation

int ROWS = 15;   //number of rows in the board
int COLS = 15;   //number of columns in the board
int cellHeight, cellWidth;   //width and height of one cell

//buttons
Chandle btnLoad, btnSave, btnNext, btnQuit;
```

I included the Ccontrols library and PToolboxLib. Recall that these are different kinds of files. Ccontrols is source code, so it is imported with the #include directive. PToolbox is a predefined library, so it must be imported using the library statement. I'll be using Ccontrols to simplify the creation of buttons, and I'll use PToolbox for the two-dimensional array like in the last chapter.

The `board` and `neighborhood` variables will both be two-dimensional arrays, so I declared the variables as pointers. ROWS and COLS determine the size of the game board. I carefully designed the code so I could put any value for these two variables and have the program still function. The `cellHeight` and `cellWidth` variables will be used to determine the size of one cell.

Finally, I created a bunch of Chandle objects to point to the buttons I'll be creating along the bottom of the screen.

Reusing the pointRec() Function

The `pointRec()` function that you've seen throughout the book makes yet another appearance in this program. I'll use it to determine if the user has clicked on any particular cell in the playing board. Just to refresh your memory, here's the `pointRec()` function again:

```
int pointRec(int px, int py, int x1, int y1, int x2, int y2){
  //given point (px, py) and a rectangle (x1, y1) - (x2, y2),
  //return true if the point is inside the rectangle
  //otherwise return false

  int result = false;
  if (px > x1){
    if (px < x2){
      if (py > y1){
        if (py < y2){
```

```
          result = true;
        } // end y2 check
      } // end y1 check
    } // end x2 check
  } // end x1 check
  return result;
} // end pointRec
```

As you recall, the function is given a point and a rectangle. It returns `true` if the point is inside the rectangle, and `false` if the point falls outside the rectangle.

Setting Up Buttons

The Life program uses a number of buttons as the primary user interface. I created these buttons using the Ccontrols library. Since the buttons are a secondary part of the program, I found it easier to design the buttons by hand than to use the Ceditor program. Besides, I find the code generated by Ceditor to be difficult to read. I set up the buttons in a function called (surprise) `setupButtons()`:

```
setupButtons(){
  //create buttons for user interface.
  //buttons are drawn in showBoard

  btnLoad = Cbutton(5,140,30,15,1,2);
  Csetcontent(btnLoad, "load");

  btnSave = Cbutton(40,140,30,15,1,2);
  Csetcontent(btnSave, "save");

  btnNext = Cbutton(75,140,30,15,1,2);
  Csetcontent(btnNext, "next");

  btnQuit = Cbutton(110,140,30,15,1,2);
  Csetcontent(btnQuit, "quit");

} // end setupButtons
```

This function simply creates a series of buttons and places them along the bottom of the screen. I sketched the screen for an approximate placement, and then I used some trial and error to situate the buttons more exactly. Note that I did not draw the buttons here, because they will be drawn as part of showing the screen.

Creating the Board

The game board is a two-dimensional array created with the `Array()` function of PToolboxLib. I created and initialized the array in a special function:

```
createBoard(){
  //generate the starting board
  int row, col;

  cellHeight = 100/ROWS;
  cellWidth = 100/COLS;

  //create an array of ROWS by COLS values.
  board = Array("c, " + (string)ROWS + ", " + (string)COLS);
  for (row = 0; row < ROWS; row++){
    for (col = 0; col < COLS; col++){
      board[row][col] = '.';
    } // end col loop
  } // end row loop
} // end createBoard
```

This function is meant to be called one time at the beginning of the `main()` function. It has three tasks.

- First, it calculates the height and width of each cell. These values will be used in later functions to determine how to draw the organism on the screen, and how to determine where the user has clicked.
- Second, the `createBoard()` function creates a two-dimensional array to hold the game board information. Remember that PocketC doesn't support two-dimensional arrays directly, so I used the `Array()` function from PToolboxLib to build the array. The `Array()` function expects one string parameter. To create an array that is ROWS by COLS, I had to interpolate the string values of ROWS and COLS to the function parameter. Notice that the array is of type 'c', which is a character type.
- The third task of the `createBoard()` function is to initialize the board array. As usual, I used a pair of nested loops to step through each element of the array, and set the cell to a starting value of "." so as to start up with a board full of something.

I decided to use a character array to store the game board to simplify testing. I used a "." to denote a blank cell, and an "O" (the letter O) to indicate a live organism. This way, I could edit and view boards in Memo Pad and get an approximation of how they would look in graphics mode. This strategy also let me test the functionality of the program before I got the graphics completely working.

Showing the Board

Once the board is created, you need a function for displaying it. This function is called whenever the board needs to be updated.

```
showBoard(){
  int row, col;

  for (row = 0; row < ROWS; row++){
    for (col = 0; col < COLS; col++){
      //text((col * cellWidth) + 15, (row * cellHeight) + 15,
board[row][col]);

      if(board[row][col] == "O"){
        rect(1,
            (col * cellWidth) + 15,
            (row * cellHeight) + 15,
            (col * cellWidth) + 15 + cellWidth,
            (row * cellHeight) + 15 + cellWidth,
            cellHeight/2);
      } else {
        rect(0,
            (col * cellWidth) + 15,
            (row * cellHeight) + 15,
            (col * cellWidth) + 15 + cellWidth,
            (row * cellHeight) + 15 + cellWidth,
            cellHeight/2);

      } // end if
    } // end col loop
  } // end row loop

  //show the buttons
```

```
  Cdraw(btnLoad);
  Cdraw(btnSave);
  Cdraw(btnNext);
  Cdraw(btnQuit);

} // end showBoard
```

The `showBoard()` function is not as complicated as it looks. Essentially, it steps through the board array, printing out the value of each element. While I was initially testing the program, I printed the actual contents of the board array, with the following line:

```
text((col * cellWidth) + 15, (row * cellHeight) + 15, board[row][col]);
```

This line invokes the `text()` function to draw some text on the screen. The `text()` function requires three parameters, x, y, and text, to print. Each of these parameters must be calculated. The X position is calculated by multiplying the current column number by cellWidth, so, if cellWidth is 20, the 0th column values would get an X value of (0 * 20) + 15, or 15. The 5th column will be placed at (5 * 20) + 15, which is 100. I added 15 to each value to move the board off the left-hand border of the screen. The Y value is calculated in a similar way. The text to print is pulled from the board array.

Once I got the program working well in text mode, I decided to use graphics to represent the organism. Graphics mode is preferable for this sort of thing for the following reasons:

- You have more control over the appearance.
- Graphics can automatically change scale to cope with a larger or smaller board.
- There might be some speed advantage.

The large `if` structure in the middle of the function draws graphic images in place of the text-based output. The drawing is done via a `rect()` function call. If you look closely, you will see that both of the calls to the `rect()` function are nearly identical. If the board value is ".", the function draws a white (invisible) circle. If the board value is "O", the function draws a black circle. To get the circle drawn on the right spot on the screen, I had to do some calculations. Table 9.2 gives a summary of the calls to the `rect()` function.

The last part of the `showBoard()` function uses the `Cdraw()` function to display all the buttons.

Table 9.2 Creating the Circles: Parameters of the rect() Function

Parameter	Value	Description
color	0 or 1	0 draws white circle, 1 draws black circle
x1: x coordinate of upper left corner of rectangle	(col * cellWidth) + 15,	Multiply the column number by the width of one cell. Add 15 for left margin
y1: y coordinate of upper left corner of rectangle	(row * cellHeight) + 15,	Multiply the column number by the width of one cell. Add 15 for left margin
x2: x coordinate of lower right corner of rectangle	(col * cellWidth) + 15 + cellWidth,	x1 + cellWidth
y2: y coordinate of lower right corner of rectangle	(row * cellHeight) + 15 + cellHeight,	y1 + cellHeight
radius: radius of corners	cellHeight/2	Perfectly rounded corners, making a circle

Loading a Pattern from a Memo

Loading and saving patterns are critical parts of this program. The Life program is able to load a board from a Memo Pad file. Here is the code for the `loadPattern()` function:

```
loadPattern(){
  //loads a pattern from a text file
  string fileName;
  int row, col;
  string theLine;
  char theChar;
  fileName = getsd("file to load?", "rPent");
  if (mmfind(fileName)){
    theLine = mmgetl();  //grab and ignore the title line
    for (row = 0; row < ROWS; row++){
```

```
      theLine = mmgetl();
      for (col = 0; col < COLS; col++){
        theChar = (char)substr(theLine,col,1);
        board[row][col] = theChar;
      } // end col loop
    } // end row loop
    mmclose();
  } else {
    alert ("could not find " + fileName + ".");
  } // end 'found file' if
} // end loadPattern
```

This function requests a memo name from the user. If the memo file is not available, an appropriate message is sent to the user and the function quits. If the memo file is located, the function begins by requesting the first line with a `mmgetl()` function call. The first line will contain the title of the file, which is no longer important, so the program does not do anything with it. All the later lines are expected to contain data.

A `for` loop steps through the number of rows. It gets a line for each row. That line is analyzed to extract each character, and the individual characters are stored in the board array. After both `for` loops are finished, the function closes the memo and exits.

If the Memo Pad file is not in exactly the right format (for example, if it does not have the correct number of rows or columns) this function will have unpredictable (but almost certainly unpleasant) results. It's safest to use the Life program itself to create the memo, because the `save` function is designed to create exactly the type of file that the load function is expecting.

Saving a Pattern to a Memo

Saving a pattern to a memo file is even easier than loading the file.

```
savePattern(){
  //saves a pattern to a memo file
  string fileName;
  int row, col;

  fileName = gets("Name of file to save?");
  mmnew();
```

```
    mmputs(fileName + "\n");

    for (row = 0; row < ROWS; row++){
      for (col = 0; col < COLS; col++){
        mmputs(board[row][col]);
      } // end col loop
      mmputs("\n");
    } // end row loop
    mmclose();
  } // end savePattern
```

The function asks the user for the name of the file to create. It then generates the memo and writes the specified name to the first line. The function then steps through a pair of `for` loops to examine each cell of the board array. It writes each element to the memo. At the end of every row, the function adds a Newline character to the memo. After the loops have finished, the function closes the file and exits.

Editing a Pattern

Another important function in the Life game is the one that allows the user to edit the pattern on the screen. This function works by calculating the position of every square on the board, and then making a call to `pointRec()` to see if the pen has tapped in that square. If so, it changes the value of the cell in the board array, and it updates the screen accordingly.

```
editPattern(){
  //Allow user to edit any square with a pen tap

  int row, col;
  int x, y;
  //wait();

  x = penx();
  y = peny();

  for (row = 0; row < ROWS; row++){
    for (col = 0; col < COLS; col++){
      //check cell for a tap
      if (pointRec(x,y,
```

```
          (col * cellHeight) + 15,
          (row * cellWidth) + 15,
          (col * cellHeight) + 15 + cellWidth,
          (row * cellWidth) + 15 + cellWidth)){
        text(0,120,"cell " + row + ", " + col + " got clicked");

        //change the board value
        if (board[row][col] == '.'){
          board[row][col] = 'O';
        } else {
          board[row][col] = '.';
        } // end if

        //print out (in text mode)
        //text((col * cellHeight) + 15, (row * cellWidth) + 15, "   ");
        //text((col * cellHeight) + 15, (row * cellWidth) + 15,
board[row][col]);

        //graphic print of cell value
        if (board[row][col] == '.'){
          rect(0,
            (col * cellHeight) + 15,
            (row * cellWidth) + 15,
            (col * cellHeight) + 15 + cellWidth,
            (row * cellWidth) + 15 + cellWidth,
            cellHeight/2);
        } else {
          rect(1,
            (col * cellHeight) + 15,
            (row * cellWidth) + 15,
            (col * cellHeight) + 15 + cellWidth,
            (row * cellWidth) + 15 + cellWidth,
            cellHeight/2);
        } // end '. or O' if
      } // end pointRec if
    } // end col loop
  } // end row loop
} // end editPattern
```

The entire `editPattern()` function is housed in a pair of `for` loops. The location of the current cell is calculated, much as it was in the `showBoard()` function. The last position of the pen and the current cell's position are sent to the `pointRec()` function to determine if the user tapped on the cell. If not, no further processing is needed on this cell, and the function proceeds to the next cell. If the user did tap on the cell, it is necessary to change the value of the board array for that cell. As before, I began by writing a version of the program that printed out the text in the board array directly. Once I was certain that the logic of the function was working correctly, I commented that code out and added code to draw the organisms as circles. This circle-drawing code is exactly like that used in the `showBoard()` function.

Showing the Neighborhood

All the functions you have examined so far have set up the environment so that you can work with and modify a pattern, but the most critical element is still missing. Somehow, the program needs to be able to implement Conway's rules so that the patterns can emerge. One of the stipulations of the original rules is that all the changes in a generation happen at exactly the same time. To make this happen, and to simplify the analysis of the board, I created a new array called *neighborhood*. This array will be slightly larger than the board array, because its purpose is to contain the entire playing board with a border of empty squares all around. Take a look at Figures 9.13 and 9.14, which show how the neighborhood will look as graphics and as text, and then I'll explain why I created it this way.

Remember that the survival or death of a cell is completely dependent on the number of neighbors that cell has. The next function you see takes a cell and

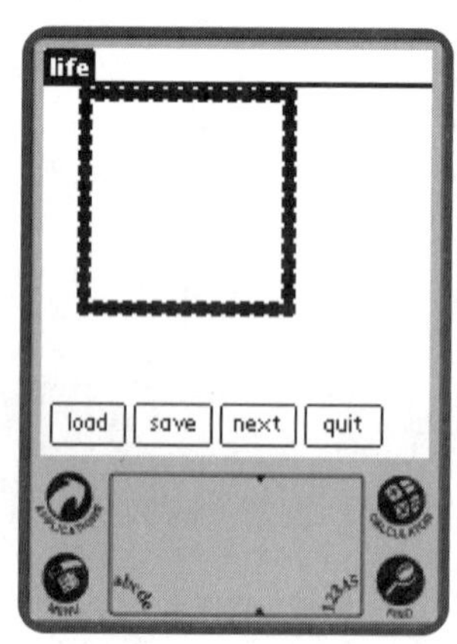

FIGURE 9.13

Here's a pattern that has cells all along the edges.

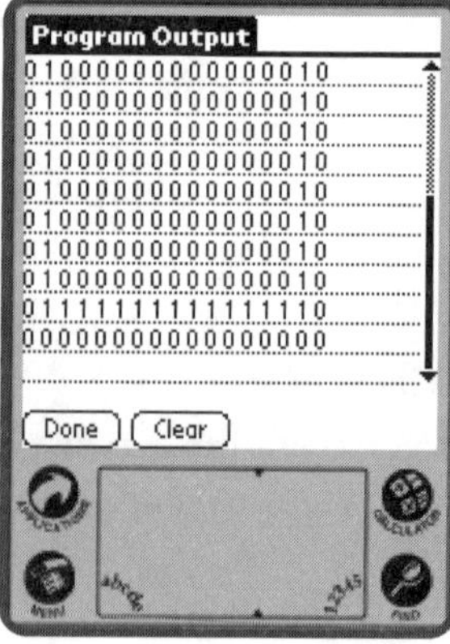

FIGURE 9.14

The neighborhood array for the border pattern is based on the original, but different. (Note that only the bottom of the neighborhood pattern is visible, because the text screen does not have enough lines to display it all in one page.)

counts that cell's neighbors. As you can imagine, this won't be terribly difficult for those cells in the middle of the board, but it is more difficult to figure out how to count the neighbors of the cells at the edges or in the corners. The easiest way past this problem is to generate a new array with a border of all empty elements. Essentially, I'm making a copy of the board array and surrounding it with a frame of empty elements. Then I only have to check the neighbors of those cells that were part of the original board. To make the counting easier, I also ensure that the neighborhood array is an array of integers. If a cell has an organism in it, it will contain the value 1. Otherwise, it will contain the value 0. The user will never see the neighborhood array, but I added a function for viewing the array just so I could be sure it is working correctly:

```
showNeighborhood(){
  //utility function to check neighborhood array

  int row, col;
  saveg();
  graph_off();
  clear();
  for (row = 0; row < ROWS+2; row++){
    for (col = 0; col < COLS+2; col++){
      puts(neighborhood[row][col] + " ");
    } // end col loop
    puts("\n");
  } // end row loop
  wait();
  graph_on();
  restoreg();
} // end showNeighborhood
```

This function is called only when you are debugging the program. It steps through the neighbors array and prints the current element of this array onto the screen.

Counting a Cell's Neighbors

It is important to know how many neighbors each cell in the board array has, because this indicates whether an organism there will be born, live, or die. The `checkNeighbors()` function is designed to perform exactly this duty. Given a row and column of the board array, the `countNeighbors()` function will generate a new larger copy of the board array with a border of blank cells all around the original board. This new array will also convert the "O" and "." symbols used in the original board to the integers 1 and 0 to simplify counting.

```
int countNeighbors(int row, int col){
  //given a row and column of the board,
  //returns the number of neighbors that cell has

  //neighbors is larger than board (a border of zeros)
  //nRow and nCol are row and column plus one

  int nRow;
  int nCol;
  int neighbors = 0;

  nRow = row + 1;
  nCol = col + 1;

  neighbors = neighbors + neighborhood[nRow - 1][nCol - 1];
  neighbors = neighbors + neighborhood[nRow - 1][nCol];
  neighbors = neighbors + neighborhood[nRow - 1][nCol + 1];
  neighbors = neighbors + neighborhood[nRow][nCol - 1];
  neighbors = neighbors + neighborhood[nRow][nCol + 1];
  neighbors = neighbors + neighborhood[nRow + 1][nCol - 1];
  neighbors = neighbors + neighborhood[nRow + 1][nCol];
  neighbors = neighbors + neighborhood[nRow + 1][nCol + 1];
  return(neighbors);
} // end countNeighbors
```

The `countNeighbors()` function is given the `row` and `col` values of a cell in the board array. Since the neighborhood array is larger, a local row and column value (nRow and nCol) are used. Each of these values is one larger than the original `row` and `col`, to compensate for the padding of zeroes around the original board.

And now a word about capitalization among constants and variables. ROWS and COLS, which refer to the number of rows and columns in the board, are in capital letters because they are constants, and all-caps is the standard convention for constants. These two values will not change during the run of the program. The `row` and `col` variables really are variable. They are used in various parts of the program to refer to the current row and column that is being operated on.

The `neighbors` variable is used to hold the number of neighbors that a given cell has. It checks all the cells around the current cell and adds the integer value of these cells to the `neighbors` variable. At the end of the function, it returns the value of neighbors.

Calculating the Next Generation

It is a reasonably simple matter to calculate the next generation of cells once the `countNeighbors()` function is in place:

```
next(){
  //calculates the next generation
  int row, col;
  int neighbors;
  neighborhood =   Array("i0, " + (string)(ROWS + 2) +", " + (string)
(COLS + 2));
  for (row = 0; row < ROWS; row++){
    for (col = 0; col < COLS; col++){
      if (board[row][col] == "0"){
        neighborhood[row+1][col+1] = 1;
      } // end if
    } // end 'col' for loop
  } // end 'row' for loop

  //if a cell has three neighbors, it is alive
  //if a cell is alive and has two neighbors it is alive
  //in all other cases, the cell dies
  for (row = 0; row < ROWS; row++){
    for (col = 0; col < COLS; col++){
      neighbors = countNeighbors(row, col);
      if (neighbors == 3){
        board[row][col] = "0";
      } else if ((neighbors == 2) && (board[row][col] == "0")){
        board[row][col] = "0";
      } else {
        board[row][col] = ".";
      } // end if
    } // end col loop
  } // end row loop
  showBoard();
} // end next
```

The function begins by creating the neighborhood array. This array is large enough to contain a border of zeros around the board array, so it must be ROWS +2 by COLS +2 cells large. Each element of the board array is examined, and then a corresponding cell in neighborhood is modified. The value of cell (0, 0) of board will be used to indicate the value of cell (1, 1) in neighborhood. This ensures that all of the cells of the board array have eight neighbors in neighborhood, which greatly simplifies the design of the `countNeighbors()` function. Also, the values in the neighborhood array are integers rather than characters. The program uses 1 to indicate a cell with an organism, and 0 to indicate an empty cell. This use of integers also simplifies the `countNeighbors()` design.

Once the neighborhood array is filled, the function steps through each element in the board array again. It calls the `countNeighbors()` function with the board's current row and col. The `countNeighbors()` function counts the neighbors in the corresponding cell in the neighborhood array.

If any cell has three neighbors, that cell should contain an organism, so this rule is implemented via an `if` statement. If a filled cell has exactly two neighbors, the organism should survive. I chose to implement this rule with a compound if statement:

```
} else if ((neighbors == 2) && (board[row][col] == "0")){
```

This version of the `if` statement has two conditions joined by the && operator, which stands for *logical and*. It is used to mean that both conditions must be true for the `if` statement to return true. So, if neighbors is 2 and if the current cell (board[row][col]) is filled, then the cell should stay alive.

In any other situation, the current cell should die, which is handled by the `else` clause.

The main() Function of the Life Game

The `main()` function of the Life game is actually very simple, because most of the work in the program is delegated to other functions. It simply handles the main program flow and event checking.

```
main(){
  int keepGoing = true;
  int evt;
```

```
  graph_on();
  clearg();
  title("life");

  createBoard();
  setupButtons();
  showBoard();
  while(keepGoing){
    wait();
    editPattern();
    evt = event(1);
    if (Cevent(btnLoad, evt)){
      loadPattern();
      showBoard();
    } else if (Cevent(btnSave, evt)){
      savePattern();
    } else if (Cevent(btnNext, evt)){
      next();
    } else if (Cevent(btnQuit, evt)){
      keepGoing = false;
    } // end event if
  } // end while loop
} // end main
```

The `main()` function begins by defining the standard `keepGoing` and `evt` variables. It does the standard screen setup, then calls functions to create the board, set up the buttons, set up the board, and show the board. The bulk of the function is filled with a standard `while` loop. This loop waits for input, and then calls the `editPattern()` function to analyze the input when it arrives. It also checks the buttons. If any of the buttons are clicked, the program calls the appropriate function. If the user clicks on the Quit button, the value of `keepGoing` is set to `false`, which exits the loop and ends the program.

Summary

In this chapter you developed a cellular automaton system, and in the process learned how to integrate controls with ordinary graphics. You used two-dimensional arrays to manage complicated data, and you learned how to load and save information in Memo Pad files.

CHALLENGES

1. Change the board to another size. (This should actually be very simple.)
2. Experiment with other rule sets. For example, what if the cell remains alive with four neighbors?
3. Add an auto-increment feature that displays several generations in a row, like a movie.
4. Write a shopping list program that accepts data from a series of screens drawn with Ccontrols, then saves the resulting shopping list as a memo.
5. Add a high score list to any of the games from earlier in the book. Keep the high scores in a memo.

Databases and Pointers: The Password Keeper

Most novice programmers quickly grasp the control structures like looping and branching statements. Heavy use of these elements is appropriate for the types of programs that beginners work with. As you get interested in more elaborate programs, however, you find that the amount of information you are dealing with grows tremendously. Using control structures alone to handle all this information becomes more and more difficult.

This chapter presents a powerful tool in the Palm programming universe: the special database files the Palm OS supports. Your program can use these files to store any kind of information you want. In this chapter, you get some experience working with simple databases. You will also learn how you can compile your programs so that they have their own icons on the PDA, and no longer need to be run from within PocketC on the Palm. Specifically, the chapter covers the following techniques:

- Storing and retrieving sequential information from a Palm database (.pdb) file
- Using pointers to refer to variables
- Designing and using a random access database
- Creating menus using the Ccontrols library
- Responding to menu requests
- Creating stand-alone programs with the desktop edition

The Password Keeper Program

Unlike the other chapters, which mostly use games as their primary examples, this one works with something a little more practical—a password-keeping program of the sort I always wanted on my PDA. Like most technical people, I tend to accumulate accounts and passwords. I have four unix accounts, three NT accounts, and countless message board memberships, instant messaging accounts, and customer support accounts. Each one has its own login procedure and password. For example, I enjoy flight simulators, so I subscribe to an online message board about flight simulators. Every time I go to that site, it prompts me for my user ID. I also often visit the excellent Web message board at http://www.orbworks.com for PocketC programmers. (This is a terrific place to go if you are ever stuck on a PocketC problem.) Of course, this message board also requires a login. Each site seems to have different rules about what is an appropriate user ID and password, so it becomes very difficult to keep track of them. I resorted to keeping all my login information in a Memo Pad memo, but this had some obvious security problems. Anybody who got hold of my PDA could get into all my accounts. I could use the Palm security features, but they are very tedious when you're dealing with just one memo.

I planned accordingly:

```
I wanted a program that would run on my Palm so it is always with
me. It should be reasonably secure, so only I can get into it. It
should allow me to quickly look through all my accounts. It should
support searching for a password, and it should be reasonably easy
to add another account to the system.
```

Figure 10.1 shows Password Keeper's opening screen.

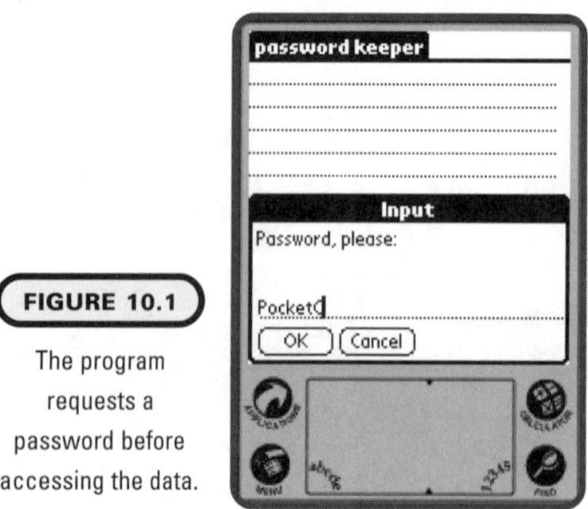

FIGURE 10.1

The program requests a password before accessing the data.

It's a little ironic that a program intended to free you from memorizing passwords requires you to learn one more, but this is the easiest kind of security to invoke, so I decided to use it here. Figure 10.2 through 10.9 walk you through various stages of Password Keeper operations.

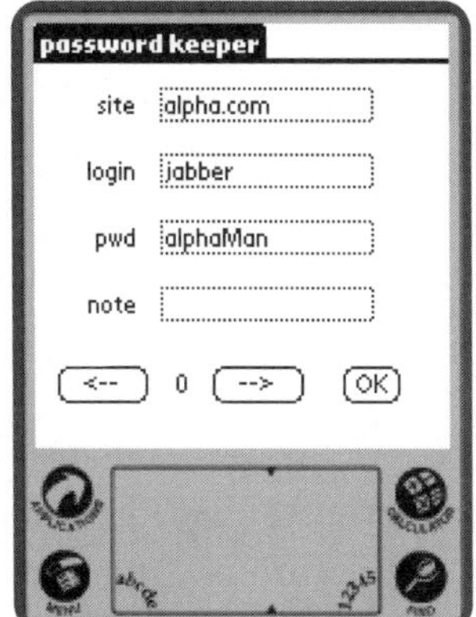

FIGURE 10.2

The main screen features information about one account.

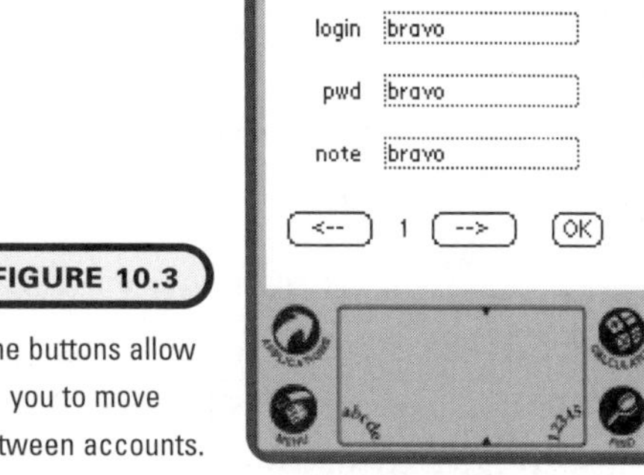

FIGURE 10.3

The buttons allow you to move between accounts.

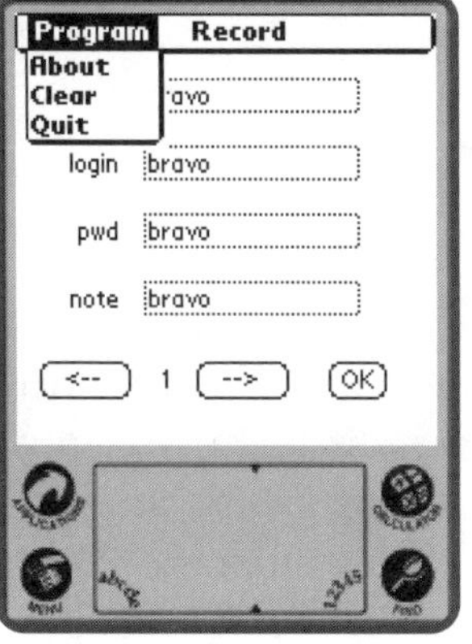

FIGURE 10.4

When you click on the Menu button (the one you commonly use to invoke menus in your palm programs), a menu pops up in the expected place.

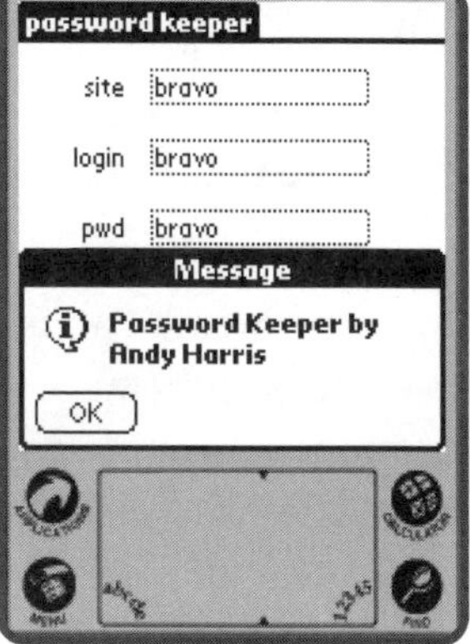

FIGURE 10.5

The program has the mandatory About box. (But this one will feature your name!)

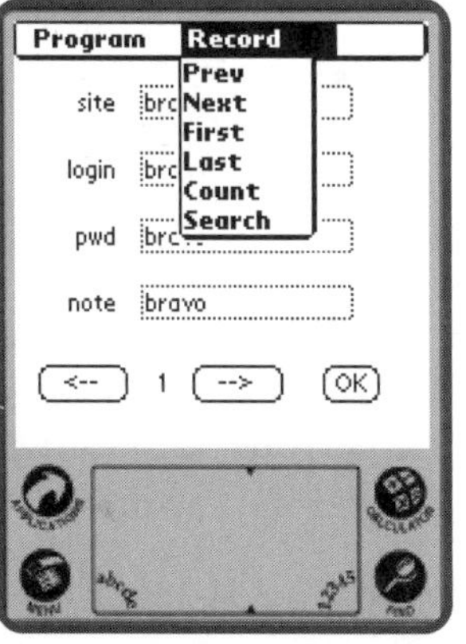

FIGURE 10.6

The Record menu features more sophisticated commands for moving between accounts.

FIGURE 10.7

The user can search for a particular site.

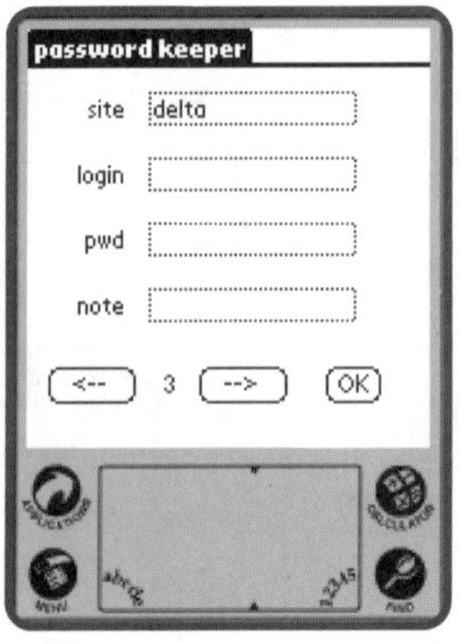

FIGURE 10.8

If the site has a record on file, its information will be displayed.

FIGURE 10.9

The program also has the ability to clear out the database if necessary.

As you can see, Password Keeper provides a number of tools designed to help the user maintain and access password data. This application is the custom program I most frequently use on my own PDA. Once you have written it, you will be able to modify it so that you can store any kind of data you wish in a custom application on your PDA.

Sequential Data Access

You learned in Chapter 9 how to store information in Memo Pad documents. Using the Memo Pad is easy, but it is highly insecure. Anybody who has physical access to your Palm or your desktop environment will be able to read all of your passwords. Also, Memo Pad documents have very little intrinsic organization to them. They are just long streams of text. It would be good to have a more sophisticated way of storing information into the Palm's memory. The Palm OS provides a feature called Palm database (.pdb) files for exactly this purpose. A .pdb file can be used to store any kind of information the PDA can hold.

There are actually two very different ways of storing data. One technique is called *sequential access,* and the other is called *random access.* Since sequential access is a little easier to understand, I'll start by showing you an example that uses the sequential approach. Later in the chapter, I cover the use of random access files.

Sequential access files work much like audiotapes. If you are listening to the first song on a cassette tape and you want to hear the last song immediately, you have to fast forward past all the other songs. There's no way to go directly to a specific song without moving through the others. Likewise, in a sequential file all the data are stored in one continuous stream. This makes sequential access data storage simple to implement—you just tack anything new onto the end of the file—but it can be very difficult to work with if there is a large amount of information. Still, for small amounts of information, sequential files are the way to go.

The Memo Pad files written in Chapter 9 are a specialized example of sequential access. Memo files have a couple of disadvantages. The data is publicly accessible, it all goes to one database (the Memo Pad db), and you can only write string data. The next example lets you overcome all those shortcomings.

The Database Demo Program

Here is a very simple program that writes some data to a .pdb file and then retrieves it.

```
//dbDemo
//Simplest possible database example
//Andy Harris, 5/12/01

main(){
  dbcreate("practiceDB");
  dbwrite("I'm from a database!");
  dbclose();
  dbopen("practiceDB");
  alert(dbread('s'));
  dbclose();
} // end main
```

This program creates a database, writes to it, and closes it. It then reopens the database, reads some information from it, and closes the database. It is a reasonably straightforward application, but it is heavily dependent on the basic database functions built into PocketC. Table 10.1 presents the built-in functions for ready reference.

Creating a Database

To create a database, you simply use the `dbcreate()` function, supplying the name of the database you want to create. The name of the database will be hidden from the user, but you can see any databases you have created in the PocketC main window, as shown in Figures 10.10 and 10.11.

Table 10.1 Basic Database Functions

Function	Description	Example

dbopen(string *dbname*)	Opens an existing database called *dbname*. If the open was not successful, returns a 0.	int success;
		success = dbopen(myDB);
		if (!success){
		alert("couldn't find the db");
		} // end if

dbcreate(string *dbname*)	Creates a new database called *dbname*. If *dbname* already exists, it is overwritten. Returns 0 on failure.	dbcreate(myDB);
dbwrite(*data*)	Writes *data* (which can be any type) to the currently open database.	dbwrite("Hi there");
dbread(char type)	Reads data from database as specified type. Types can be 's' (string), 'c' (char), 'i' (integer), or 'f' (float).	string myString; myString = dbread('s');

dbpos()	Returns position in the file, or –1 if at the end of the file.	while (dbpos() != 1){
		alert(dbread('s'));
		} // end while

dbclose()	Closes the currently open database	dbclose();

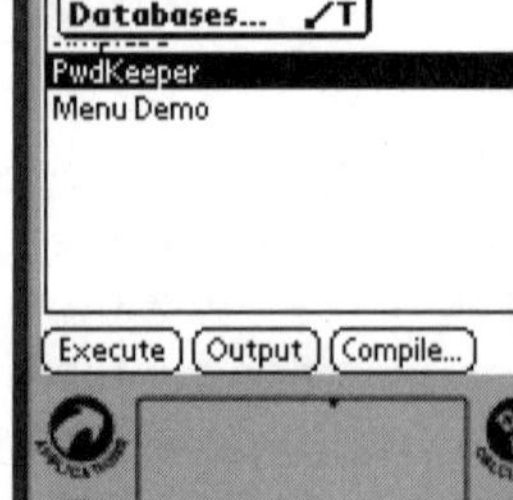

FIGURE 10.10

You can choose databases from the menu.

FIGURE 10.11

These are the databases on this PDA. I created "PracticeDB" in this example.

It's good to know about this database list (and delete) screen when you are working with databases, because sometimes things go wrong, and you'll want to delete your database and start over. It's also good to be able to check this screen when you aren't sure if a database has been created correctly, or if you don't remember exactly how its name was spelled.

If you call `dbcreate()` with a database name that is already in use, the new database will overwrite (and destroy) the old one. You will generally use `dbcreate()` only one time on any particular database.

The `dbcreate()` function returns a value that tells you if it succeeded in opening the database. This value will be `false` if the database failed to open.

Opening an Existing Database

It is more common to open an existing database. One of the most important reasons to have databases is to support *persistence.* Any information you have stored in variables will be destroyed as soon as your program ends. If you want information to be stored between runs of a program, you should store it in a database. You'll generally create a new database only if the database does not exist already. The `dbopen()` function is used to open a database. It also returns a Boolean value that describes whether the open succeeded or failed. Usually, the database will fail to open if the name is spelled incorrectly, or if the database does not exist. In this small program, I had already created the database a line or two ahead, so it wasn't necessary to check for the existence of the database. Later examples use an `if` statement to handle the situation where the database doesn't already exist. (Usually in this situation, you want the code to create the database.)

Writing to a Database

The `dbwrite()` function is simple and powerful. It allows you to write any kind of data you wish to the currently open database. Of course, there must be a database currently open. The data is written to the end of the file, much like in the memo access you did in Chapter 9. You can write integer, character, float, or string data to the database. However, you need to keep track of the type of data you have sent, because you must know the type when you retrieve the information with the `dbread()` function.

Reading from a Database

You can retrieve any information written to the database using the `dbread()` function. This function takes one parameter, a character describing the type of data to read, as shown in Table 10.2.

You must read in your data in exactly the same type it was written to the database. If you wrote it as integer and read it as float or string, your data will be corrupted.

To avoid conversion problems, you might want to consider storing all data as strings, and then using casting to convert numeric data back to its appropriate type once you have pulled it from the database.

Each call to the `dbread()` function retrieves one piece of data written by `dbwrite()`. You can use the `dbpos()` function to determine which piece of data the database is currently pointing to. If you are not sure how many records are in the database, you can loop through until `dbpos()` returns -1, which will happen at the end of the file.

Closing the Database

It is a good idea to close the database with the `dbclose()` function when you finish using it. The `close` function will ensure that the database is stored properly in memory.

Table 10.2 Character Codes for the dbread() Function

code	data type
'i'	integer
'f'	float
'c'	character
's'	string

Problems with Sequential Access

The design of a sequential access database is quite simple, but it can be problematic when you are dealing with large or complex information. What happens, for example, if you want to store integer and string information with the data? You'll have to be able to figure out what type the data is. More important, what if you have a large database with information about hundreds of things? In a sequential access database, you'd have to look all the way through the file to look for any particular piece of data. This isn't a huge problem at first, but it can quickly turn into a big drain on your PDA as the amount of information grows.

Random Access Databases

Most of the pitfalls of the sequential storage scheme can be overcome by another style of data storage called *random access.* If sequential access reminds you of an audio tape, random access is more like a CD. The term *random* means that you can go to any particular spot in the file directly, without having to go through the rest of the data to get there.

To see how this works, you need to know a bit of terminology from the random access data world. Random access databases are designed around entities called *records.* A record is a particular entity that you are keeping track of. Each screen of the Password Keeper represents one record in the database. Records are made up of *fields.* Fields are much like variables—they each have a name and a value. It's important to keep track of the type of data in a database, for reasons you'll see in a moment. The entire collection of records is called a *table* or *file.* In the Password Keeper program, the entire database is the file, each screen is a record, and *site*, *login*, *pwd*, and *note* are all fields.

A random access database works by calculating the starting position of each record in the file. That means all the records must be exactly the same length. This requires some care, but it isn't really all that difficult. In any computer system, most of the data types are predictable—the amount of space taken up by a character is always the same. The same is true of integers and floats. The problem comes when you are working with strings.

The Problem with Strings

The basic amount of memory required to store a string depends on the length of the string. For example, *Hi* takes three bytes (the basic unit of measurement in computer memory) of storage. The first byte contains the value H, the second

IN THE REAL WORLD

To tell the truth, PocketC is much more forgiving about the size of random access records than most programming language. For example, one test program I've seen used the first rec of a db to store global settings, password, etc, the next two recs stored category titles, then the rest of the db contained the "standard" data records. As long as you are pointing to the right record, and you always read back in the same format as was written, there's no problem. A lot of Palm programming sites advocate a single db per application. I assume this is for simple apps—besides, an app needing more complex databases is probably better suited to something other than PocketC. One last point: the least number of support files used by the app, the easier it is to clean up or uninstall.

However, I still think it makes sense for you to think about random access records as being generally the same length, as this *is* true for the vast majority of programming languages you will encounter.

contains the value i, and the last byte contains the null character. The string "Hello, there, world!" takes up 21 bytes; 20 for the characters in the string, and the last byte contains the null value. These are examples of *null-terminated* strings. The computer keeps reading characters until it encounters the null character, which signifies the end of the string.

This discussion actually explains the term *string.* Many versions of C don't have string variables at all! Internally, the computer works only with characters. A string is just a bunch of characters put together like beads on a string. PocketC (like many other programming languages) automatically takes care of converting strings to arrays of characters in memory for you.

For most purposes, null-terminated strings are great. You generally aren't concerned about the details of string storage. In random access databases, however, null-terminated strings can give you huge headaches because they do not have a determined length. In a random access database, the amount of room allocated for each field must be fixed. You must allocate exactly the number of characters that will be occupied by each field in the database.

If you've ever created a database in a program like Microsoft Access, you have encountered this phenomenon. Whenever you define a record, you must determine the length of every text field in the database. You aren't required to determine the length of numeric values, because the length of these variables is defined by the variable type.

Fixed-Length Strings

Fortunately, you can specify a particular length for a string even if it doesn't contain that many characters if you understand a little more about how data works inside the computer. There should be a way to specify where in memory a string exists. Then you should be able to tell the computer to take only the next *n* bytes of information. If you can do this, you will have a string of exactly *n* bytes long, which would be ideal for a random access database. PocketC has a feature for storing fixed-length strings in databases, but this feature requires you to understand a little more about pointers.

Understanding Pointers

C programming is famous for its support of a special type of variable called the *pointer.* Pointers have gotten a reputation for being difficult to work with, but they really aren't as bad as you might have heard. You've already encountered pointers when you created multi-dimensional arrays, but now it's time for a closer look at them. A pointer is simply another way of looking at a variable. A variable, as you know is a location in memory that stores some information. Most of the time, you are concerned about the *contents* of the variable; the location of the variable in the computer's memory is usually of no interest to you, because the computer handles it automatically. However, there are a few situations in which it's handy to know where a particular variable is in memory. A pointer is not concerned with the contents of memory but with the *location* of data in memory. Pointers are usually used in conjunction with regular variables. PocketC treats pointers as a separate data type.

This simple rule will help you past your pointer confusion. Whenever you see a variable name that starts with an asterisk (*), read that as "value at." So `*myPointer` should be read as "value at myPointer." Likewise, read an ampersand (&) at the beginning of a variable name as "address of." Thus `&myVar` should be read as "Address of myVar." If you get into this habit, you'll find that pointers aren't difficult at all.

The Pointer Demo Program

The best way to understand pointers in action is to look at a program that uses them.

```
//pointerDemo
//illustrates basic pointer concepts
//Andy Harris, 05/15/01

main(){
  int number;
  string message;

  pointer pNumber;
  pointer pMessage;

  number = 1;
  pNumber = &number;

  alert("Number: " + number);
  alert("pNumber: " + pNumber);
  alert("*pNumber: " + *pNumber);

  *pNumber = 2;
  alert("Number: " + number);

  message = "Hi there!";
  pMessage = &message;
  alert(message);
  alert("*pMessage: " + *pMessage);
} // end main
```

This program has two normal variables and two pointer variables. Remember that normal variables refer to content and pointer variables refer to addresses. Also recall the convention that * means "value at" and & means "address of." With those conventions in mind, this program is not difficult to understand. The first thing I did was assign the value 1 to the normal int number. There's nothing at all surprising about that. You can also assign values to pointers, but you never assign literal values to them, because you don't know exactly where things are stored in memory. Here is the line that assigns the pointer pNumber a value:

```
pNumber = &number;
```

If you read that line as "pNumber gets address of number," you have a pretty good idea of what is going on. The program figures out the address of the number variable and assigns that address as the value of the pointer `pNumber`. After this line executes, `pNumber` will contain the address of the `number` variable. (To keep things more clear, I started all pointers with the character p in this example.)

The next part of the code has several alert statements. The first simply outputs the value of `number` variable, as shown in Figure 10.12.

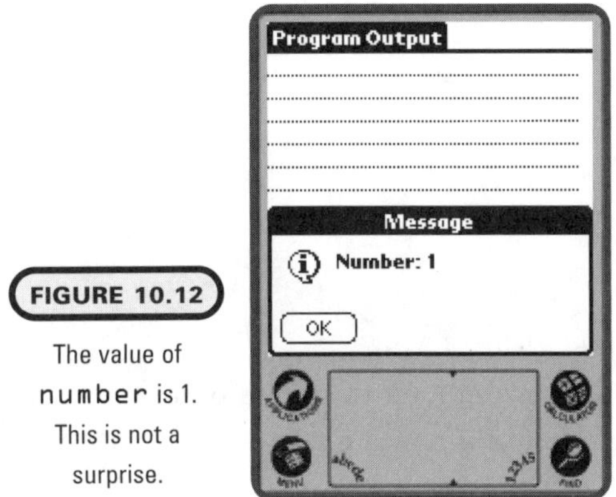

FIGURE 10.12

The value of `number` is 1. This is not a surprise.

The second outputs the value of `pNumber`, which looks like a random string of digits, as shown in Figure 10.13.

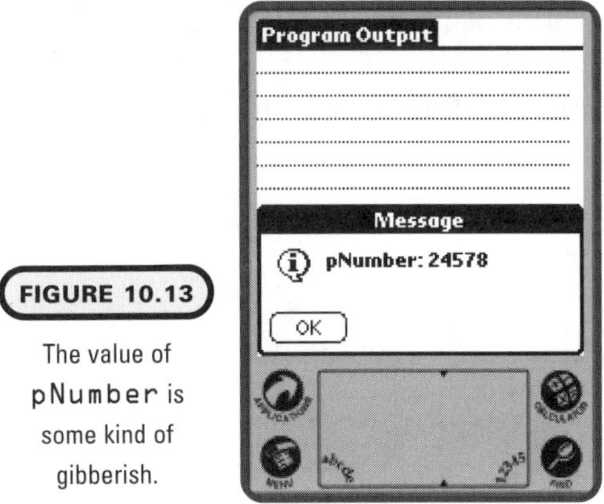

FIGURE 10.13

The value of `pNumber` is some kind of gibberish.

The value of a pointer is not generally useful to the user. It refers to the location in memory of a particular variable. Figure 10.14 shows the relationship between number and pNumber more clearly.

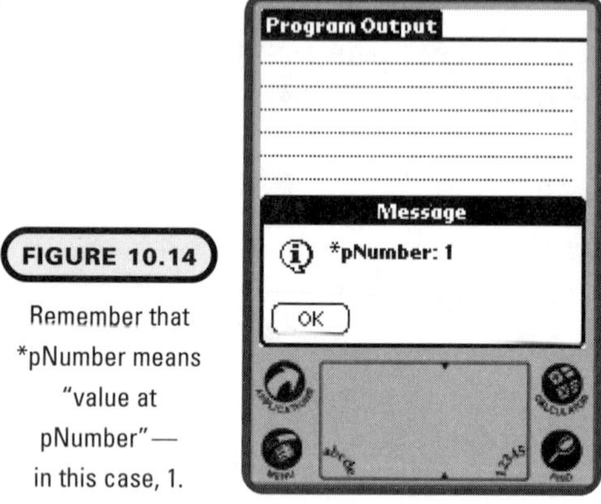

FIGURE 10.14

Remember that *pNumber means "value at pNumber"— in this case, 1.

This statement returns the value of the address referred to by the pointer. Since `pNumber` is a pointer to `number`, the value at `pNumber` is the same as the value of `number`.

The next line shows an interesting characteristic of pointers:

```
*pNumber = 2;
```

This should be read as "the value at pNumber gets 2." When the computer encounters this instruction, it stores the value 2 to the location referred to by `pNumber`. Since `pNumber` is a reference to the location of `number`, the value of `number` has changed by the time the next alert statement gets to it, as shown in Figure 10.15.

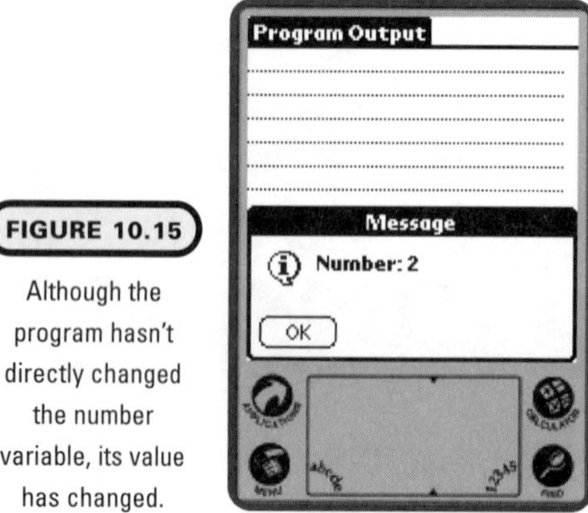

FIGURE 10.15

Although the program hasn't directly changed the number variable, its value has changed.

Pointers allow indirect access to variables. The rest of the program illustrates that exactly the same techniques can be applied to string variables.

PocketC is unique in the way it handles pointers to strings. In most versions of C, a pointer to a string is the address of the first character of that string. The dereferenced (*) version of that pointer is usually a single character. PocketC actually returns the entire string. This is convenient, but you should be aware that it is not the usual behavior of C.

Pointers come in handy in a number of situations. They are commonly used to pass arrays as parameters in a function call or to allow access to a variable from within another function. In this chapter, I use pointers to simulate a fixed-length string for a random access database.

Creating Random Access Data

PocketC supports random access as well as sequential access data. A random access database is characterized by a series of records, each of the same length. PocketC provides a number of database functions designed to facilitate random access data, as shown in Table 10.3.

Table 10.3 Random Access Database Functions

Function	Description	Example
dbrec(int *recnum*)	Sets the database to record # *recnum*. If *recnum* is past end of database, a new record will be added.	dbrec(2); // move currently open database to record # 2.
int dbnrecs()	Returns the number of records in the database.	alert(dbnrecs() + " records.");
dbwritex(pointer *ptr*, string *format*);	Writes the data referred to by *ptr* using the type referenced by *format*. See Table 10.4 for valid formats.	dbwritex(&userName, "s20"); //stores userName as a 20-character string.
dbreadx(pointer *ptr*, string *format*);	Reads from the database and stores into variable referred to by *ptr*. Stores data according to *format*.	dbreadx(&userName, "s20"); //reads userName as a 20-character string

You can still use all the other database functions, but these additional functions allow for true random access. The `dbrec()` function is used to set the database to a particular record. This is used to move quickly between records in the database. The `dbnrecs()` function is used to determine how many records are currently in the database. The most critical new functions are variants of the `dbread()` and `dbwrite()` functions. Both `dbreadx()` and `dbwritex()` provide more control over how information is written to and read from the database. Specifically, both functions work by specifying a pointer and a format. The pointer should be the address of a variable you want to store or modify. The format determines what type of variable the pointer is referring to, as listed in Table 10.4.

TABLE 10.4 TYPE FORMATS FOR DBREADX() AND DBWRITEX()

code	data type
'c'	Character
'i2'	2-byte value
'i4'	Integer
'f'	Float
'sz'	Null-terminated string. ('normal' strings in PocketC. Dynamic length)
's#'	String of # characters. Used for fixed-length strings

To see how these functions work, here's a preview of the Password Keeper code:

```
//write info to database
dbrec(recNum);
dbwritex(&site, "s30");
dbwritex(&login, "s30");
dbwritex(&pwd, "s30");
dbwritex(&note, "s30");
```

As you can see, the program sets the record number, then writes several variables to the database. I chose to make all my variables 30-character strings. The function to read the data is surprisingly similar:

```
dbrec(recNum);
dbreadx(&site, "s30");
```

```
dbreadx(&login, "s30");
dbreadx(&pwd, "s30");
dbreadx(&note, "s30");
```

Later in this chapter I use these code fragments in context, but still, you should get the idea that readx and writex are used to transfer values from variables to the database in a format that will encourage random access.

Creating Menus in Ccontrols

The only other part of the Password Keeper program that is new is the menu system. Menus are easily created with the Ccontrols library. The menus you create in PocketC look and behave much like any other menus you have used in your Palm travels. You start up the menu by clicking on the menu button (It's the menu icon to the lower left of the Graffiti area.) Figures 10.16 through 10.18 illustrate a simple program that demonstrates menus in action.

FIGURE 10.16

Nothing happens until the user clicks on the Menu button.

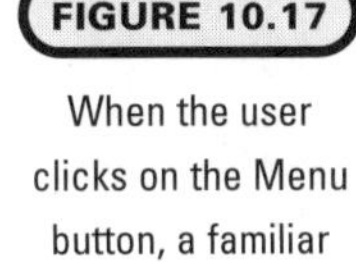

FIGURE 10.17

When the user clicks on the Menu button, a familiar type of menu shows up.

FIGURE 10.18

When the user clicks on the Two element, the program responds with the Japanese term for "two."

Creating Menus and the Menu Bar

Memos can be created via the Ceditor program, but they are reasonably easy to build by hand as well. Here's the initialization part of the Menu Demo program:

```
//Menu Demo
//Demonstrates memo access in Ccontrols
//Andy Harris, 04/20/01

#include "Ccontrols.c"

Chandle mnbMain;
Chandle mnuDemo, mnuProgram;

init(){

   graph_on();
   clearg();
   title("Menu Demo");

   //set up menu bars
   mnbMain = Cmenubar();

   //Demo menu
   mnuDemo = Cmenu(5, 40, 40);
   Csettopic(mnuDemo, "Demo");
   Cadditem(mnuDemo, "One");
   Cadditem(mnuDemo, "Two");
   Cadditem(mnuDemo, "Three");
   Caddmenu(mnbMain, mnuDemo);

   //program
   mnuProgram = Cmenu(45, 40, 50);
   Csettopic(mnuProgram, "Program");
   Cadditem(mnuProgram, "About");
   Cadditem(mnuProgram, "Quit");
   Caddmenu(mnbMain, mnuProgram);

   text(10, 70, "Please press menu button");
} // end init
```

The program begins by creating Chandles for the menu bar itself, as well as the two menus. CControls considers the menu bar (the thing across the top of the screen) and the two menus (in this case Demo and Program) as three distinct entities. You can create them all just like the more traditional controls. Use the `Cmenubar()` function to create the menu bar, and the `Cmenu` function to create each menu object. The `Cmenu` function requires three parameters. The first one refers to the x position of the topic. The second parameter is the width of the topic in the menu bar. The third parameter refers to the width of the menu when it is pulled down.

You determine the name of each menu by invoking the `Csettopic()` function on that menu. You can then add specific elements to each menu with successive calls to the `Cadditem()` function. Finally, you add each menu to the menu bar, using the `Caddmenu()` function. If you create a menu and don't specifically add it to the menu bar, it won't appear.

Accessing Menu Events

You can write code to respond to menu events much like the other objects in the Ccontrols system. However, only the menu bar itself responds to the `Cevent()` function. You need to do some other manipulation to determine exactly which element was selected. Here's the `main` function of the Menu Demo program:

```
main(){
  int keepGoing = true;
  int evt;
  string command;

  init();

  while(keepGoing){
    evt = event(1);
    if(Cevent(mnbMain, evt)){
      if(Cgetcursel(mnuDemo)!= -1){
        command = Cgetcontent(mnuDemo);
      } else if (Cgetcursel(mnuProgram) != -1){
        command = Cgetcontent(mnuProgram);
      } // end if
      switch (command){
        case "One":
          alert("Ichi");
```

```
          break;
        case "Two":
          alert("Ni");
          break;
        case "Three":
          alert("San");
          break;
        case "About":
          alert("Menu Demo");
          break;
        case "Quit":
          keepGoing = false;
          break;
        default:
          alert(command);
      } // end switch
    } // end menu if
  } // end while loop
} // end main
```

Though the code is a bit long, it isn't really very difficult. All the key action happens near the beginning of the function:

```
if(Cevent(mnbMain, evt)){
   if(Cgetcursel(mnuDemo)!= -1){
     command = Cgetcontent(mnuDemo);
   } else if (Cgetcursel(mnuProgram) != -1){
     command = Cgetcontent(mnuProgram);
   } // end if
```

The program checks to see if the menu bar has received an event. If so, it is necessary to see which of the menu objects has been activated. The `Cgetcursel()` function returns the value of the currently selected menu item. If nothing in the menu is currently selected, the function will return the value –1. If Cgetcursel of mnuDemo is not –1, then something on mnuDemo was selected, so I use `Cgetcontent(mnuDemo)` to figure out what was selected. I then copy the value to the command variable. I then do a similar check of the mnuProgram menu. If you have more menu items, just check them all. Once this code is finished, you'll have the text of whatever menu element was selected in the `command` variable. The rest of the function simply looks at the various possible values of `command` with a switch statement, and performs the appropriate actions for each situation.

The Password Keeper Program

As usual, you know everything you need to know to write the final program in the chapter. It's just a matter of putting all the pieces together in a new way.

Global Stuff

The program listing begins in the typical way, by importing needed libraries, defining function prototypes, and creating global variables:

```
//PwdKeeper
//Keeps a database of passwords
//Andy Harris, 05/15/01

//function prototypes
getRec();
putRec();

//main variables
string site, login, pwd, note;
int recNum = 0;

include "Ccontrols.c"

//control handles
Chandle  lblSite, lblLogin, lblPwd, lblNote;
Chandle  txtSite, txtLogin, txtPwd, txtNote;
Chandle  btnPrev, lblRecnum, btnNext, btnOk;
Chandle mnbMain, mnuProgram, mnuRecord;
```

I defined function prototypes for `getRec()` and `putRec()`. It was reasonably easy to find a way to write all the other functions without dependency problems, but these two gave me some trouble, so I prototyped them.

The entire program revolves around five key variables. Each record has four parts: the site name, the login (or user ID) of the site, the password for the site, and a note. I defined a variable for each of these elements. These variables will be used throughout the program to refer to the various fields in the database. The other principal variable is `recNum`. This int is used to determine which record is being displayed. The user could conceivably have several records in the database, but only one will be visible at a time. The `recNum` variable keeps track of the current record.

I included Ccontrols, because it provides an easy way to handle controls, buttons, and menus.

I created a bunch of Chandle objects. I began with a label for each record, and I also made a text field for each record. The program also requires three buttons and a label to refer to the current record. Finally, I made handles for all the necessary menu items.

There is no way I could have just dreamed up all these controls. I began with a sketch on paper, which gave me a rough idea which controls would be needed. In fact, I used Ceditor to build the interface from my sketch, but I don't like the code it generates so I used Ceditor to get a look that I liked, then copied the values from the editor into my own code.

Initializing the Database

This program is all about the database, so it's a good idea to initialize the data well. There's a small problem, though. The first time this program runs, it should create the data from scratch. During subsequent runs, it should open the database rather than creating it, because a call to `dbcreate()` would destroy the existing data. Here's the code that makes sure the database gets created once and only once:

```
initdb(){
  //if the database exists, open it
  if (!dbopen("pwds")){
    //if it doesn't exist, create it
    dbcreate("pwds");
  } // end if
  recNum = 0;
  getRec();
} // end initdb
```

This function takes advantage of the fact that dbopen returns 0 on failure. If the result of the `dbopen` call is anything but 0, that indicates the database was successfully opened. The condition (!dbopen("pwds")) will be true if the database did not exist, and false if it did. If the database did not exist during the call to `dbopen`, the function creates it. The program can handle either contingency. If the database is there, it will be opened. If it is not there, it will be created. Regardless, the database should start by displaying record number 0. I set recNum to 0 and called the `getRec()` function. Later in the program the `getRec()` function gets the current record from the database and displays it on the screen.

Creating the Controls

The visual interface of this program gives the application a lot of appeal. It is a clean interface, with all the most important elements visible on the screen. There is support for more powerful features, but these less prominent commands are hidden in the menus. This is a reasonably good design strategy. You should try to have the most important controls available on the screen, but you should avoid cluttering the display if possible. The Palm screen is tiny enough to start with, so you need to be judicious about screen design.

IN THE REAL WORLD

My initial plan was to use Ceditor to design the screen. It was very easy to get the screen design I wanted, but I personally find Ceditor code distracting and hard to read. I used the Ceditor program to get a prototype of the screen, because the editor makes it easy to resize and move elements around on the screen. Once I found the display I wanted, I used the data from the editor to build my own controls by hand.

The Ccontrols are convenient, but they can slow your program down. If you find that your program is acting sluggishly, you may want to selectively remove some of your controls. For example, the field names didn't really need to be labels at all, because they won't really do anything in the program. Replacing them with ordinary `text()` statements might improve the speed of the program. You can use whatever technique suits you, of course.

Here is the function that generates all the visible controls:

```
createControls(){
  //create the visual interface for the program
  //except the menus

  //site
  lblSite=Clabel(10,25,30,0,0,2);
  Csetcontent(lblSite,"site");
  Cdraw(lblSite);

  txtSite=Cedit(50,25,80,2,2,0);
  Csetcontent(txtSite," ");
```

```
Csettopic(txtSite,"Site?");
Cdraw(txtSite);

//Login
lblLogin=Clabel(10,50,30,0,0,2);
Csetcontent(lblLogin,"login");
Cdraw(lblLogin);

txtLogin=Cedit(50,50,80,2,2,0);
Csetcontent(txtLogin," ");
Csettopic(txtLogin,"Login?");
Cdraw(txtLogin);

//Pwd
lblPwd=Clabel(10,75,30,0,0,2);
Csetcontent(lblPwd,"pwd");
Cdraw(lblPwd);

txtPwd=Cedit(50,75,80,2,2,0);
Csetcontent(txtPwd," ");
Csettopic(txtPwd,"Password?");
Cdraw(txtPwd);

//note
lblNote=Clabel(10,100,30,0,0,2);
Csetcontent(lblNote,"note");
Cdraw(lblNote);

txtNote=Cedit(50,100,80,2,2,0);
Csetcontent(txtNote," ");
Csettopic(txtNote,"Note?");
Cdraw(txtNote);

//prev
btnPrev=Cbutton(10,130,33,12,1,4);
Csetcontent(btnPrev,"<-");
Cdraw(btnPrev);

//recNum
lblRecnum=Clabel(50,130,15,0,0,1);
```

```
  Csetcontent(lblRecnum,"0");
  Cdraw(lblRecnum);

  //next
  btnNext=Cbutton(70,130,33,12,1,4);
  Csetcontent(btnNext,"->");
  Cdraw(btnNext);

  //ok
  btnOk=Cbutton(120,130,20,12,1,4);
  Csetcontent(btnOk,"OK");
  Cdraw(btnOk);

} // end createControls
```

The function is long but very straightforward. For each control, I use the appropriate Ccontrols function to create the control. I then use the `Csetcontent()` function to apply some text to each of the controls. Finally I use the `Cdraw()` function to draw each control on the screen.

Creating the Menus

To create the menus, I just repeated the basic outline of the Menu Demo program from earlier in this chapter. I wanted a two-menu design, with one menu to handle main program functions and another to deal with functions of the data, like navigation and searching commands.

Try to design your menus around some kind of sensible scheme. As a user, you've probably been frustrated by commands that were not logically placed in the appropriate menu. Try to help your users avoid that frustration.

Here's the function that creates the menus:

```
createMenus(){
  //generate and populate the menus

  //main menu bar
  mnbMain = Cmenubar();

  //program menu
  mnuProgram = Cmenu(5, 50, 50);
```

```
    Csettopic(mnuProgram, "Program");
    Cadditem(mnuProgram, "About");
    Cadditem(mnuProgram, "Clear");
    Cadditem(mnuProgram, "Quit");
    Caddmenu(mnbMain, mnuProgram);

    //record menu
    mnuRecord = Cmenu(65, 50, 60);
    Csettopic(mnuRecord, "Record");
    Cadditem(mnuRecord, "Prev");
    Cadditem(mnuRecord, "Next");
    Cadditem(mnuRecord, "First");
    Cadditem(mnuRecord, "Last");
    Cadditem(mnuRecord, "Count");
    Cadditem(mnuRecord, "Search");
    Caddmenu(mnbMain, mnuRecord);

} // end createMenus
```

I started by creating the menu bar. I then created each menu, set its topic, and added all of the menu items.

Getting a Record from the Database

Now that the program has all the necessary interface items, you can start to get information to and from the database. The purpose of the `getRec()` function is to grab the current record from the database and display it on the screen:

```
getRec(){
  //read information from databae
  dbrec(recNum);
  dbreadx(&site, "s30");
  dbreadx(&login, "s30");
  dbreadx(&pwd, "s30");
  dbreadx(&note, "s30");

  //copy information to controls
  Csetcontent(txtSite, site);
  Csetcontent(txtLogin, login);
  Csetcontent(txtPwd, pwd);
  Csetcontent(txtNote, note);
```

```
  //refresh controls
  Cdraw(txtSite);
  Cdraw(txtLogin);
  Cdraw(txtPwd);
  Cdraw(txtNote);

} // end getRec
```

The function begins by setting the database to the current record with the `dbrec(recNum)` command. I then use a number of `dbreadx()` calls to read values from the database to the appropriate variables. I read all the variables as 30-character strings.

Once I had all the field variables (`site`, `login`, `pwd`, and `note`) loaded from the database, I used the `Csetcontent()` function to write the new value to all the text boxes. Finally, I refreshed the screen with a series of calls to the `Cdraw()` function, to redraw the text boxes with their new values.

IN THE REAL WORLD

Figuring out the correct length of a database field is as much an art as a science. If the field is too small, the user will not be able to get enough information into the database. If the field is too large, there will be a lot of wasted space. Generally, 20 or 30 characters is a good balance for a text field if you don't have too many records. Be careful if you expect to have a large number of records, though. Memory is at a premium in the Palm environment, and people won't keep memory hogs on their PDA for long.

Storing a Record to the Database

The `putRec()` function is much like the `getRec()` function, except the logic is reversed: the function has to copy the values from the text fields to the variables, and then from the variables to the database.

```
putRec(){
  //get information from controls

  site = Cgetcontent(txtSite);
  login = Cgetcontent(txtLogin);
  pwd = Cgetcontent(txtPwd);
  note = Cgetcontent(txtNote);

  //write info to database
```

```
  dbrec(recNum);
  dbwritex(&site, "s30");
  dbwritex(&login, "s30");
  dbwritex(&pwd, "s30");
  dbwritex(&note, "s30");
} // end putRec
```

I start by getting all the information from the text boxes, and then I use a set of `dbwritex()` functions to write the data to the database. It's important to recognize that I use exactly the same format (string of 30 characters) for reading and writing. The fields do not all have to be the same length, but you must be careful that you read and write exactly the same format for a given field, or the data will be corrupted.

It isn't necessary to refresh the screen, because the data in the text fields hasn't been updated.

Moving to the Next Record

With the `getRec()` and `putRec()` functions in place, it's easy to write a function to move to the next record. The only tricky part is determining what to do when the user wants to move beyond the end of the existing data. I decided to create a new blank record in this situation:

```
next(){
  //go to the next record

  //store current record
  putRec();
  //increment recNum
  recNum++;
  //clear the screen if it's the last record
  if (recNum >= dbnrecs()){
    Csetcontent(txtSite, " ");
    Csetcontent(txtLogin, " ");
    Csetcontent(txtPwd, " ");
    Csetcontent(txtNote, " ");
    Cdraw(txtSite);
    Cdraw(txtLogin);
    Cdraw(txtPwd);
    Cdraw(txtNote);
  } else {
```

```
    getRec();
  } // end if

  //display the record number
  Csetcontent(lblRecnum, recNum);
  Cdraw(lblRecnum);
} // end next
```

This function begins by saving the current record with the `putRec()` function. If you think about most of the database programs you have used, you might recall that they rarely have a Save command. Instead, the data is automatically saved as the user manipulates the data. This program continues that practice. Before moving to a new record, the program will store the current record. It then increments the record number. As usual, any time you increment or decrement a variable, you should think about bounds. In this case, the program checks to see if recNum is larger than the number of records in the database. If so, it sets all the text boxes to empty, and redraws them. If recNum points to a previously available record (all but the last one), that record is loaded up with a call to `getRec()`. Finally the function updates `lblRecNum` so that the current record number is displayed.

Moving to the Previous Record

The function that selects the previous record is much like the `next()` function:

```
prev(){
  //go to the previous record
  putRec();
  recNum-;
  //don't let recNum get smaller than zero
  if (recNum < 0){
    recNum = 0;
  } // end if
  getRec();

  Csetcontent(lblRecnum, recNum);
  Cdraw(lblRecnum);
} // end prev
```

This function stores the current record, and then decrements recNum. It prevents the user from choosing a record smaller than 0 (that is, a hunk of memory before the first record in the file), then gets the selected record. Finally it updates `lblRecNum` so that the current record number is displayed.

Moving to the First and Last Records

I added convenience functions to go directly to the first and last record of the database. These functions are very similar, so I'll show them to you together:

```
goFirst(){
  //go to the first record
  putRec();
  recNum = 0;
  getRec();

  Csetcontent(lblRecnum, recNum);
  Cdraw(lblRecnum);
} // end goFirst

goLast(){
  //go to the last record
  putRec();
  recNum = dbnrecs() -1;
  getRec();

  Csetcontent(lblRecnum, recNum);
  Cdraw(lblRecnum);
} // end goLast
```

Both functions begin by storing the current record via a `putRec()` command. The functions then set the value of recNum. `goFirst()` sets recNum to 0, and `goLast()` sets recNum to the last record. Since the record numbers start at 0, the last record will be `dbnrecs()` minus 1. In both cases, the function then calls `getRec()` to put the new value on the screen and updates the record number in `lblRecNum`.

Clearing the Database

When I was debugging this program, there were a couple of times I wanted to start over with no data. You can use the PocketC menu to do this, but I wanted to add the functionality into the program itself. It's a fairly simple procedure:

```
cleardb(){
  //clear the database
  if (confirm("Delete all data?")){
    dbdelete();
```

```
    initdb();
    Csetcontent(txtSite, " ");
    Csetcontent(txtLogin, " ");
    Csetcontent(txtPwd, " ");
    Csetcontent(txtNote, " ");
    Csetcontent(lblRecnum, "0");

    Cdraw(txtSite);
    Cdraw(txtLogin);
    Cdraw(txtPwd);
    Cdraw(txtNote);

  } // end if
} // end clear
```

All the real action in this function happens in one line:

```
dbdelete();
```

It's customary when you're letting the user do something this destructive to offer a chance to back out. The `confirm()` function pops up a dialog box much like the `alert()` dialog box, but this one has Yes and No buttons on it. If the user clicks Yes, the `confirm()` function returns the value `true`. If the user clicks No, it returns the value `false`.

After deleting the database, I called `dbinit()` to create a new database. The rest of the function simply clears the text boxes and redraws them on the screen.

Checking for the Database Owner

To be even moderately secure, the application needs to have some feature that prevents unauthorized people from viewing the passwords. The easiest way to secure a program is—you guessed it—another password. Here's the code that checks for a password:

```
checkOwner(){
  //ask the user for a password to ensure it's the
  //legit owner

  //change this password to something you prefer
  string pwd = "PocketC";
  string guess = "";
```

```
    graph_off();
    clear();
    title("password keeper");

    guess = gets("Password, please:");
    if (guess != pwd){
      alert("incorrect.");
      exit();
    } // end if

} // end checkOwner
```

This function is remarkably similar to some of the programs illustrated way back in Chapter 2. The function simply asks the user for a password and compares it against a password stored in a variable. If the user guesses correctly, the function ends and the rest of the program proceeds. If the user does not get the password correct, the program ends immediately.

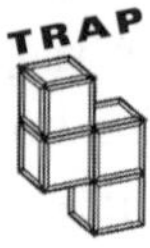

While this is a moderately secure program, it still has some serious holes in it. If you keep the source code on your PDA, anybody who can read C code can learn what your password is by analyzing the code. And it's possible to examine code even after it has been compiled to get things such as passwords. Also, a clever person could read the data files directly without using your program at all. The Password Keeper has enough security to keep a casual snoop out of your password files, but it probably isn't the best place to keep the missile launch codes for NATO.

Don't forget to change the password to something you want to use as a password. A commercial program usually has a routine built in to walk the user through the password change process, but this program is a one-user special. Just change the password as you write the code, and by editing the code if you want to change it again later. Of course, if you want more robust password-changing features, you can write them into the program!

Searching for a Record

Once you have a lot of passwords stored in your program, you will want a convenient way to get to exactly the password you need. The `search` function provides that capability.

```
search(){
  //search for a given site
```

```
  int done = false;
  string lookFor = "";
  int i = 0;
  lookFor = gets("Site name?");
  while (!done){
    //go to record # i
    dbrec(i);
    //pull the value for site into the site variable
    dbreadx(&site, "s");
    //if lookFor is in site, display that record
    if (strstr(site, lookFor,0) != -1){
      putRec();
      recNum = i;
      getRec();
      Csetcontent(lblRecnum, recNum);
      Cdraw(lblRecnum);
      done = true;
    } // end if
    i++;
    if (i > dbnrecs()){
      //if we got here, lookFor isn't there. Tell the user.
      done = true;
      alert (lookFor + " not found.");
    } // end if
  } // end for loop
} // end search
```

This program uses a sequential search to go through all the elements in the database until it finds the one you are looking for. Although there are much more efficient ways to search through data, this one is fine for the Password Keeper program for the following reasons:

- The database is in memory, which is much quicker than a traditional drive.
- Fancier search algorithms usually require the data to be sorted, which would add another step.
- You generally won't have a huge number of records in this database.

The function has three variables. The `done` variable determines if the search is complete or not. The `lookFor` variable contains the text the user is looking for. The `i` variable is an integer that will be used to step through every record of the database. The program gets a value for `lookFor` from the user. It then starts a `while` loop. Inside the loop, the function reads the `site` variable from the first record. It then checks to see if `lookFor` occurs within site. Remember, the `strstr()` function returns a -1 if it cannot find the pattern inside the target string, so if the result of `strstr()` is anything but -1, there has been a match.

If a match occurred, the function stores the current record, sets recNum equal to `i`, and gets the record. The value of `done` is set to `true`, which exits the loop.

If no match occurred, `i` is incremented and the loop continues. If the end of the database is reached without a match, the program indicates that the pattern was not found.

Responding to Menu Actions

The menu actions should be checked when a `mnbMain()` event occurs. The following function occurs whenever any menu action is triggered. It checks all the menu elements to determine which one was clicked, then uses a switch statement to send program control to the appropriate function.

```
checkMenus(){
  string command;
  //checks the menus
  //called from the main event loop

  //check each menu for action
  if(Cgetcursel(mnuProgram)!= -1){
    command = Cgetcontent(mnuProgram);
  } else if (Cgetcursel(mnuRecord) != -1){
    command = Cgetcontent(mnuRecord);
  } // end if

  //direct traffic based on the actions
  switch (command){
    case "About":
      alert("Password Keeper by Andy Harris");
      break;
    case "Clear":
      cleardb();
      break;
    case "Quit":
      putRec();
```

```
      dbclose();
      exit();
      break;
    case "Prev":
      prev();
      break;
    case "Next":
      next();
      break;
    case "First":
      goFirst();
      break;
    case "Last":
      goLast();
      break;
    case "Count":
      alert("You have " + dbnrecs() + " passwords in the database.");
      break;
    case "Search":
      search();
      break;
  } // end switch

} // end checkMenus
```

The main() Function

As usual, the `main` function just ties together the other functions. It also contains an event loop to handle the major events of the program:

```
main(){
  int keepGoing = true;
  int evt;

  checkOwner();
  graph_on();
  clearg();
  title("password keeper");
  createControls();
  createMenus();
  initdb();
```

```
    while(keepGoing){
      evt = event(1);
      //These textbox Cevent calls are necessary so that
      //text will be updated
      if (Cevent(txtSite, evt)){
        // do nothing
      } else if (Cevent(txtLogin, evt)){
        // do nothing
      } else if (Cevent(txtPwd, evt)){
        // do nothing
      } else if (Cevent(txtNote, evt)){
        // do nothing
      } else if (Cevent(mnbMain, evt)){
        checkMenus();
      } else if (Cevent(btnPrev, evt)){
        prev();
      } else if (Cevent(btnNext, evt)){
        next();
      } else if (Cevent(btnOk, evt)){
        keepGoing = false;
        putRec();
        dbclose();
      } // end if
    } // end while loop
  } // end main
```

The main function features the now-familiar `keepGoing` and evt variables.

Before anything else happens, main calls the `checkOwner()` function. If the user does not respond with the correct password, the program will not continue.

The `main` function calls three different initialization functions: `createControls()` generates the visual interface, `createMenus()` generates the menu structure, and `initdb()` initializes the database.

The event loop is standard stuff. It looks for an event, and calls `Cevent()` on each of the relevant controls. Note that it is necessary to run the `Cevent()` function on the text boxes, so the user can edit their contents. It isn't necessary to respond to the text box `Cevents()`, just to call them. All the other `Cevents()` call an appropriate function, except the btnOK event, which terminates the program by setting `keepGoing` to false, storing the current record, and closing the database.

Summary

You covered a fair amount of territory in this chapter—sequential access storage of information in .pdb files, pointers and the way they refer to variables, and writing random access files in PocketC. You also now know how to use Ccontrols to build a menu structure, and you can put all these things together to make a useful and professional application.

CHALLENGES

1. **Add the ability for the user to change the program's password without editing the source code. Hint: You'll probably need to store the password in another database.**
2. **Consider an encryption scheme to make your data more secure. There are a number of interesting schemes freely available on the web, or you can use a simple substitution cypher.**
3. **As the program is currently designed, the user can move to the last record indefinitely, making a huge number of blank records at the end of your database. Figure out a way to prevent the user from doing so. (You might need to store the number of records somewhere)**
4. **Consider storing the password as part of the database, and allowing the user to change the password so it won't be necessary to re-compile the program to change the password.**
5. **Modify the program so it stores some other kind of data in which you're interested.**
6. **Change the user interface so it is better for you. Maybe add a search button, or make the buttons larger.**
7. **Add menu access to one of the programs you wrote earlier in this book.**
8. **Add a Preview feature that displays all the site names in a list box. When the user clicks on a site name, display that site on the screen.**

Using the PToolbox Library: The Animator

The Sketcher program in Chapter 5 is a good start toward basic graphics and event handling in PocketC, but I suspect that you've been wishing you could do more. The section at the end of that chapter challenges you to add some other features to the program, and you've probably thought of a few more that you would have liked to add. Some features you might have imagined (such as drop-down menus for commands) are possible with Ccontrols or other add-on libraries. However, there are a few things that native PocketC code cannot do. Besides its refusal to support color, it's slow to load and save images, and its animations tend to be jerky because it doesn't let you work easily in memory buffers. PocketC also lacks native support for multi-dimensional arrays, or built-in collision detection routines. Joe Stadolnik wrote the library called PToolboxLib that adds all these features to PocketC. In this chapter, you'll apply some of the features of PToolboxLib to a new version of the Sketcher program. Specifically, you will learn the following techniques:

- Using new graphics commands, including polygon, triangle, and plot
- Adding color capabilities to your PocketC programs
- Working with custom fill patterns
- Storing and load images from a .pdb database
- Working with screen buffers
- Storing and load buffer databases.

The Animator

The Animator program is a good way to experiment with the features of PToolboxLib, because most of the functionality in the library is related to graphics.

The Animator program is designed to help the user in constructing animations—that is, images that are shown in succession. The drawing part of the Animator program is loosely based on the same algorithm as the Sketcher from Chapter 5, but the Animator program adds a host of new features that capitalize on your increased skills and show off some of the features of PToolboxLib.

Basic Animator Features

The first thing you'll notice when you look at Figure 11.1 is how spare the screen is. Since this is a drawing program, I tried to reserve as much of the screen as possible for drawing. All the commands are accessible via menus, as shown in Figures 11.2 and 11.3.

FIGURE 11.1

The user interface is extremely simple.

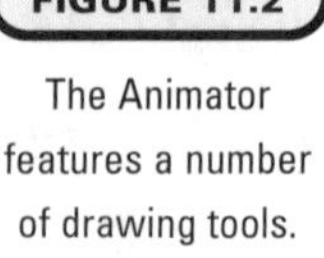

FIGURE 11.2

The Animator features a number of drawing tools.

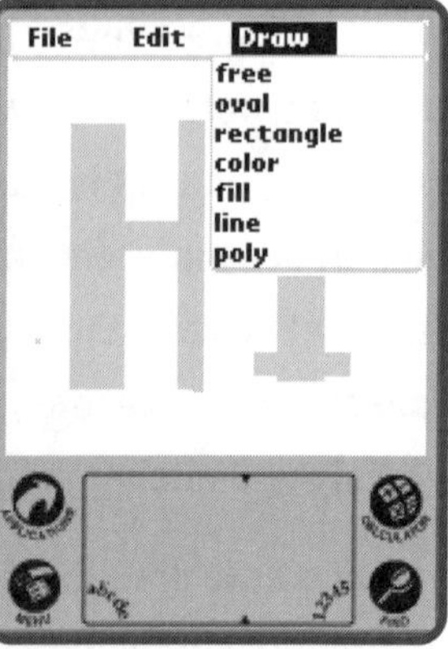

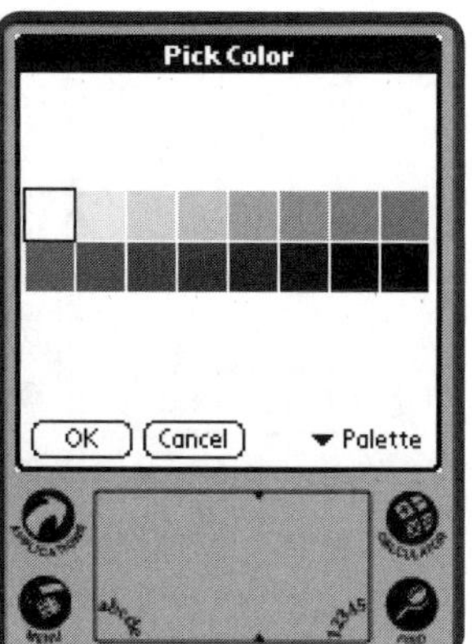

FIGURE 11.3

The program supports several versions of gray, or color if the PDA has color capabilities.

Working with Files and Images

The program allows the user to build a database of related images. Each file can contain several images. Figures 11.4 and 11.5 illustrate the process of getting started with a new file, and Figures 11.6 through 11.8 show an animation in action.

FIGURE 11.4

The animator program features a number of commands for working with files.

FIGURE 11.5

The user can create or open animation files.

FIGURE 11.6

Here's a ball.

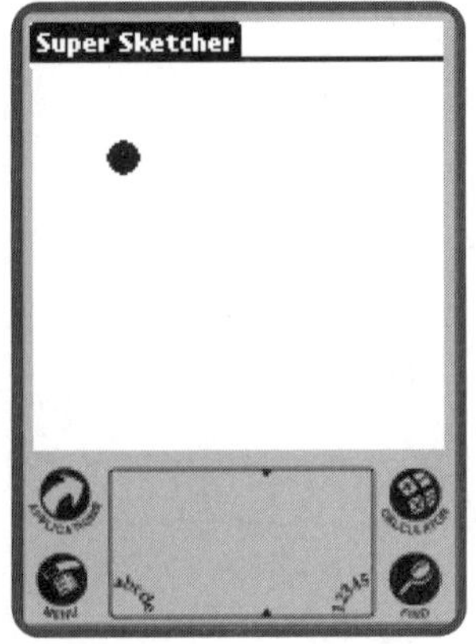

FIGURE 11.7

The user can move forward a screen by pressing the To Do button, or back by pressing the Address Book button. (There are also menu commands for these features.)

FIGURE 11.8

The user can also automate the playback of an animation.

Enhanced Copying and Pasting

Most animation involves repeating images in one way or another. The animation program allows the user to copy and paste images. When you copy an image, you can paste it in a number of different ways. This gives you the ability to rotate and resize parts of your image.

The edit menu illustrates the copy and paste features.

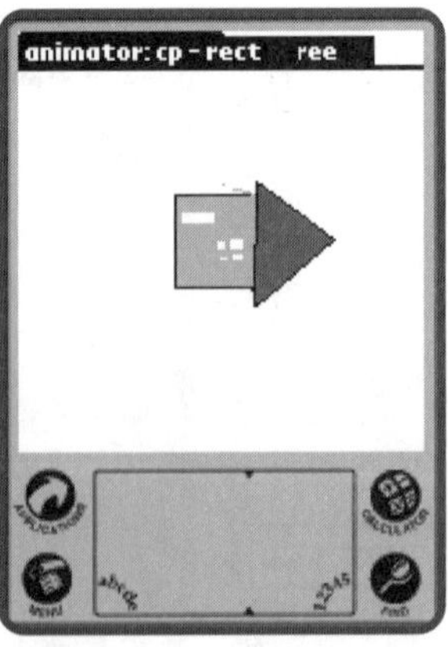

FIGURE 11.10

After copying an image, the user can paste a rotated version.

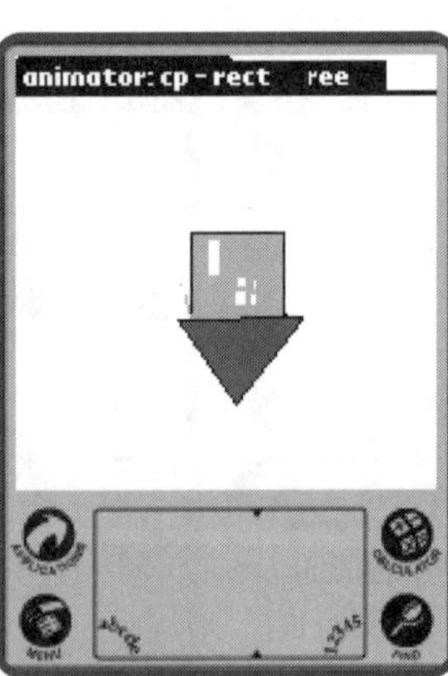

FIGURE 11.11

The user can also flip the copied image vertically or horizontally.

Features of PToolboxLib

PToolboxLib is an example of a *native library*. That is, Joe Stadolnik wrote a series of extensions to PocketC in a more standard form of C (GCC on the Windows environment) and then compiled this entire library to a binary form. A library of this type requires a more extensive set of tools to create than you need to build a traditional include file, and it is more difficult to write and debug. However, it performs much more quickly than similar code written in PocketC. Stadolnik's library is a collection of useful routines that would be inefficient (or perhaps impossible) if written directly in PocketC. Once you include the library into your program, you can use these functions as if they were built into PocketC.

The library also includes a number of modules for working more efficiently with graphics, and for saving and loading a particular image into an image database. You can use another program to design the images, or you can save images you create from within your program.

Working with Colors

PToolboxLib supports the graphics and grayscale features of the modern Palm-based PDAs. If your Palm is using OS 3.5 or later, you can use 16 levels of gray in your programs even if you don't have a color screen. The variations in gray can make your programs much more visually interesting (although there is a cost in memory). If you have a color PDA, you can write programs that support whatever color model your Palm features. Of course, memory issues can come into play: working with many colors will make your programs and their related data files much larger.

The Poly Demo Program

To get a feel for some of the basic features of PToolboxLib, consider the Poly Demo program illustrated in Figure 11.12. This program shows a number of different polygons, all in different shades of gray.

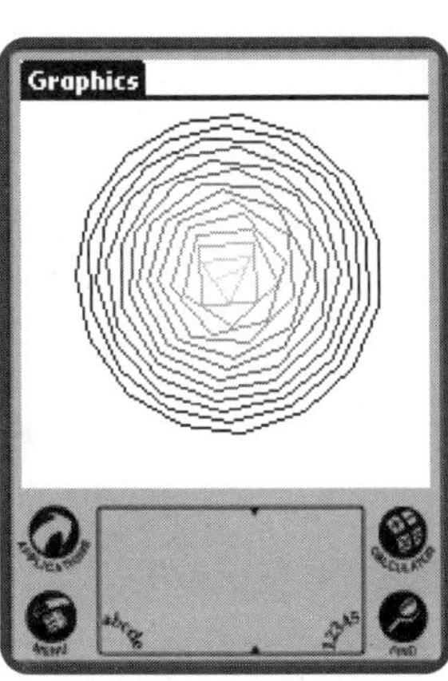

FIGURE 11.12

More than just a doodle! This program puts both shape and color within your control.

Setting a Color Depth

The first new function you encounter when you read the code for the example in Figure 11.12 is `SetDepth()`. This is a PToolboxLib function that allows you to determine the *color depth* of your image. Color depth refers to the number of different colors you can display on the screen. In normal PocketC programming, you could only draw in black and white. With PToolboxLib, PocketC provides a number of other color depth options, as shown in Table 11.1.

In general, color depth is measured by the amount of memory reserved for each dot on the screen. The basic default mode (1-bit, black-and-white) is very efficient, but does not give you much flexibility. The 4-bit models (modes 4 and 5) provide a decent combination of flexibility and memory usage. Modes 8 and 16 work only on devices that support these modes. Even then, the 16-bit mode appears to allow only 256 different colors.

TABLE 11.1 PARAMETERS OF THE SETDEPTH() FUNCTION

Depth ID	Colors	Description
–2	Return color capable	Returns 1 if the PDA supports color, otherwise returns 0
–1	Return color depths	Returns a number indicating the color depths supported by the device
0	Restore device to original state	Restores device to standard (generally black and white) state
1	2-color mode (1-bit)	Black and white
2	4-color mode (2-bit)	Black, white, 2 shades of gray. Supported by OS 3.0+
4	16-grays mode (4-bit)	Black, white, 14 shades of gray. Supported by OS 3.3+
5	16-color mode (4-bit)	16 basic colors. OS 3.5, color-capable PDAs only
8	256-color mode (8-bit)	256 colors. OS 3.5, certain color-capable PDAs only
16	65,536-color mode (16-bit)	Only available on certain devices. Memory intensive.

Once you have chosen a color depth, you can pick a color using the `SetFore()` and `SetBack()` functions. These functions each take one parameter, the color you want to use. In the colorDraw program, I chose not to worry about the background color, but simply set the foreground color. The foreground color is an integer, and the legal values are based on the current color depth. In general, 0 is white, and the largest value allowed in a particular depth is black. In grayscale modes, the other numbers are variations of gray with smaller numbers being lighter shades of gray.

IN THE REAL WORLD

The earliest desktop computers had very similar color systems—memory and display capabilities were equivalent to what is available on the Palm now. Currently, it is common for desktop machines to offer 24-bit color representation, which is over 16 million colors!

Table 11.2 shows the colors in mode 5 (the most commonly-used color mode).

TABLE 11.2 DEFAULT COLORS IN MODE 5

Color number	Color
0	White
1	Dark Gray
2	Dark Red
3	Brown
4	Dark Green
5	Aqua
6	Dark Blue
7	Purple
8	Pink
9	Light Gray
10	Bright Red
11	Yellow
12	Bright Green
13	Light Blue
14	Blue
15	Black

The Color Draw Program

To illustrate some of the ways that PToolboxLib increases your ability to work with colors, take a look at the program shown in Figures 11.13 through 11.16. The colors are currently set to variations of gray, because this book is printed in black and white, and because most Palms still use grayscale. However, you can easily use the techniques in this chapter to work with color if your PDA supports color graphics.

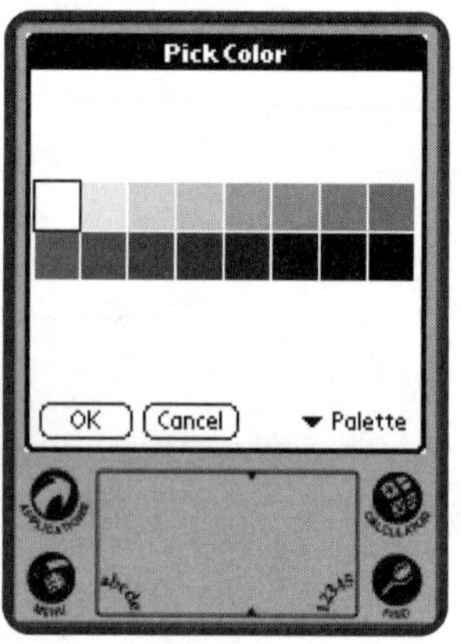

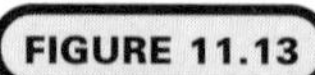

FIGURE 11.13

When the program starts up, it allows you to select from a palate of colors.

FIGURE 11.14

The program draws a normal rectangle.

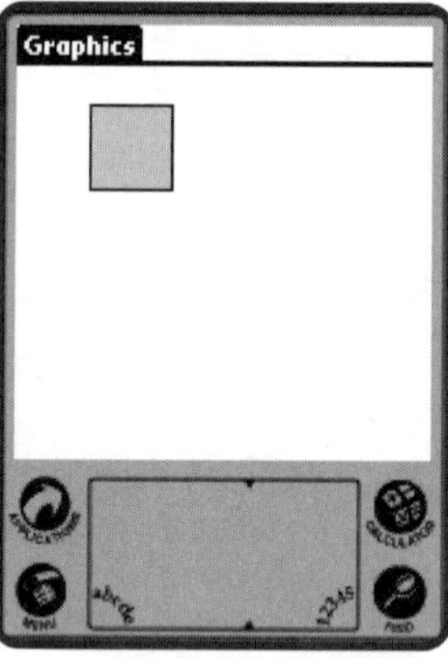

FIGURE 11.15

If you click inside the rectangle, the inside of the rectangle will be filled with the color you specified. If you click outside the rectangle, the outside area will be filled with your color.

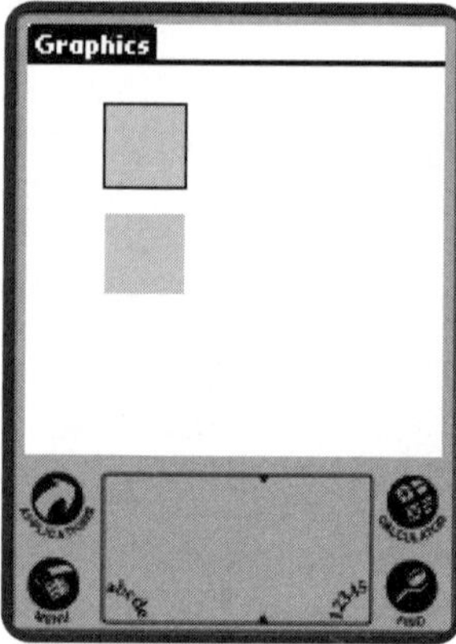

FIGURE 11.16

PToolboxLib has variations of some graphics primitives that can be used to draw in various colors.

The Color Draw program relies heavily on the PToolbox library, as you can see when you look at the source code:

```
//colorDraw
//demonstrates basic PToolbox functionality
// Andy Harris, 5/23/01

library "PToolboxLib"

main(){
  SetDepth(4);                        //grayscale mode
  graph_on();
  clearg();
  frame(1, 30, 30, 60, 60, 0);        //draw an ordinary square
  SetFore(PickColor());               //display color palate
  wait();
  wait();                             //wait for user input
  FloodFill(0, penx(), peny());
  wait();
  //custom fills will be completely in foreground color
  SetPattern("ffffffffffffffff");
  rect(4, 30, 70, 60, 100, 0);  //draw with custom fill (all foreground)
  wait();

} // end main
```

Displaying a Color Dialog Box

Fortunately, it is easy to let the user choose a color. PToolboxLib includes the `PickColor()` function, which pops up a dialog box featuring all the colors available in the current color mode. The easiest way to let the user set the color is to combine the `SetFore()` and `PickColor()` functions, as I did in the Color Draw program:

```
SetFore(PickColor());
```

This line calls the `PickColor()` function, which displays the color (or grayscale in this case) dialog box. When the user clicks on a color, that color is returned as the value of the `PickColor` function, which is then passed to the `SetFore()` function.

After I called the SetFore() function, I called the wait() function so the user would have the opportunity to click on the square. Note that the PickColor() function appears to call an event of its own, so I called wait() twice.

Adding a Flood Fill

The floodFill function lets the user fill in a portion of the screen with a given color. This function has a number of modes, but the easiest one is mode 0, which acts much like the fill command you may be familiar with in painting programs. It fills in an area with the foreground color. Table 11.3 shows the three parameters the function needs.

Table 11.3 Parameters of the floodFill Function

Parameter	Description
mode	Type of fill—0 is fine for most situations. See PToolboxLib documentation for other modes.
x	X coordinate of point inside the shape to fill.
y	Y coordinate of point inside the shape to fill.

Using a Custom Pattern

In addition to flood fills, PToolboxLib modifies some of the normal graphics functions you are used to. For example, the rect() function built into PocketC allows only black and white. (There is a sort of gray, but it is actually just black and white alternated.) If you have PToolboxLib installed, you can use a version of the square function that draws using whatever colors you currently have selected. It would have been great if the new version of the rect() function simply allowed you to put a valid color number in the color field of the rect() function, but it doesn't work that way. Instead, the values 0-3 work just like they always did, but now the rect() function allows color 4, which means to draw with the current *fill pattern.* A fill pattern is a custom pattern based on the current values of the foreground and background colors. To fill in a rectangle completely with the foreground color, you need two lines of code. Here's the first:

```
SetPattern("ffffffffffffffff");
```

This line sets the custom pattern to be entirely based on the foreground color. (There's an explanation of how this works later in the chapter.)

```
rect(4, 30, 70, 60, 100, 0);  //draw with custom fill (all foreground)
```

The call to the `rect()` function uses color mode 4 to tell PocketC that the current pattern will be used as the drawing color.

The pattern scheme is based on a counting system called *hexadecimal notation,* which is base 16 mathematics. You can get along just fine without knowing this, so if the next paragraph or two baffles you, it's okay. Still, you might be interested in how all those "f"s could mean the foreground color. (No, "f" doesn't stand for "foreground"!) The foreground pattern is an 8 by 8 grid of dots that you can use to fill up a flood fill, or in which you can draw a shape. Each dot can be either the foreground color or the background color. If you wanted to represent the dots with a set of numbers, it would require 8 x 8 values, which is 64 numbers. However, Joe Stadolnik took advantage of the fact that many C programmers already know how to use hexadecimal notation as a kind of shorthand for working with this type of number. You can see the patterns in the chart shown in Figure 11.17.

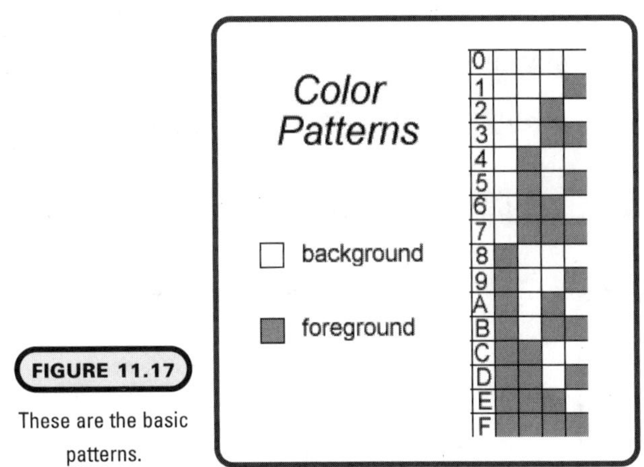

FIGURE 11.17

These are the basic patterns.

Each value from 0 through F represents eight dots. Since each row is eight dots wide, you can use two of the 0–F numbers to represent one row, and 16 of the coded values to represent the entire 8 by 8 pattern.

This strange scheme for representing patterns isn't really new to you. It is similar to the way that PocketC stores bitmap strings. One easy way to make a pattern is to create a 16 x 16 image in Bitmap Studio, copy the resulting string value, and strip off the first two characters. These first two characters describe the size of the bitmap, but a pattern is always 16 x 16, so no size is specified.

If this discussion is making your head spin, don't worry. In the Animator program, I'll only use an all-foreground pattern. Most of the graphics primitives I'm using are the standard PocketC functions. In standard PocketC, there is no such thing as a foreground color. Ptoolbox adds the notion of patterns, but does not re-write every PocketC command to include coverage of the foreground color. To get past this limitation, I'll simply use a dirty little trick. If I can't draw in a foreground color but I can draw in any pattern I want, I'll just make a pattern that consists entirely of the foreground color.

Working with Screen Buffers

PToolboxLib includes the ability to work with multiple graphics buffers. A *graphics buffer* is a chunk of memory that simulates the screen. You can execute drawing commands on the buffer without having the results appear on the screen. You can then copy between various buffers. One common use of buffers is to create a graphics clipboard to support copy and paste.

Figures 11.18 through 11.21 illustrate using screen buffers for copying and pasting portions of an image.

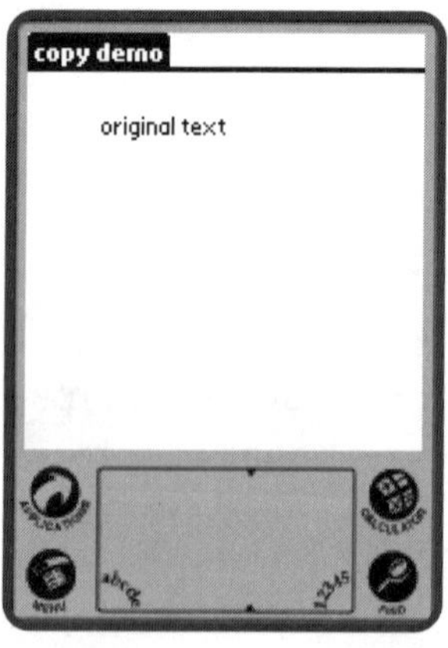

FIGURE 11.18

Here is some text drawn on the screen. Although you can't see it, the program has already written some more text in a screen buffer.

FIGURE 11.19

When the user clicks the screen, the image drawn to the buffer (in this case just some more text) is copied to the screen.

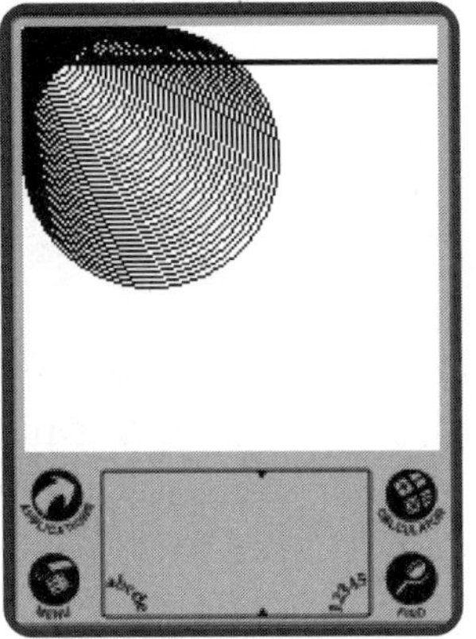

FIGURE 11.20

After the next click, I drew a few circles on the screen so the user would have some graphics to play with. The user will be able to copy and paste this graphic image.

FIGURE 11.21

I clicked on the upper left and lower right corners of the area I wanted to save. That segment was copied to a background buffer, then pasted directly back to the main screen.

To better understand graphics buffers, it's useful to know how computer graphics work. Any commands that are used to draw something to the screen actually modify a piece of the computer's memory, called the *draw buffer* or *screen buffer.* The display hardware (lcd screen for a PDA, but it works the same way in larger computers) reads the screen buffer memory to determine how to display the image. Whenever you do anything that manipulates the screen, you modify this buffer. Since the draw buffer is related to the hardware, there will be some delay between executing changes in the buffer and the actual display of the screen.

However, as the screen buffer is simply a chunk of memory, there's no reason that you must have only one. Programmers frequently use multiple buffers in memory to improve the graphics performance of their programs. There's a number of reasons you might want to do this, but for this chapter, I've chosen to use a buffer as a clipboard for copying and pasting part of a graphics screen. I let the user draw on the screen, which is called buffer 0. When the user wants to copy a piece of the screen, I use pen taps to figure out the part of the screen the user wants to make a copy of, then copy that segment into another buffer. When the user wants to paste, I just copy from the second buffer back to buffer 0. Remember that anything drawn on buffer 0 is displayed to the screen, but operations on any other buffers work behind the scenes.

Here's the code for the Copy Paste program:

```
//copyPaste
//illustrates use of draw buffers for copy and paste
//Andy Harris, 05/25/01
```

```
library "PToolboxLib"

main(){
  int i;
  int x1, y1, clipWidth, clipHeight;

  SetDepth(4);
  graph_on();
  title("copy demo");

  //draw something to the buffer
  //establish an offscreen buffer
  SetDrawBuf(1);
  text(30, 30, "this is in the buffer");

  //draw some stuff on the screen
  SetDrawBuf(0);
  text(30, 30, "original text");
  wait();

  //copy buffer 1 back to display buffer
  CopyBuf(0, 1);

  wait();
  clearg();
  for(i = 1; i < 50; i++){
    ellipse(0, i, i, i, i);
  } // end for loop
  wait();
  x1 = penx();
  y1 = peny();
  wait();
  clipWidth = penx()-x1;
  clipHeight = peny()-y1;

  CopyRect(0, 0, 0, x1, y1, clipWidth, clipHeight, 0, 1, -1);

  //copy buffer 1 back to display buffer
  CopyBuf(0, 1);
```

```
  wait();
} // end main
```

Creating Buffers

When you examine the code for the Copy Paste program, you see a few new functions. One of the most important is `SetDrawBuf()`. This command is used to determine where any drawing commands will work.

If you set the buffer to 0, all subsequent drawing commands happen directly on the screen. Of course, you don't usually have to do this—it's the default behavior. If you want to draw in another graphics buffer, you can set the buffer to some other value. For example, `SetDrawBuf(1)` will create graphics buffer 1 (if it doesn't already exist). All subsequent drawing commands will happen in that buffer, not on the screen.

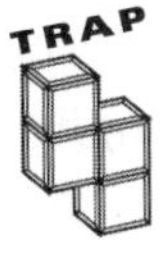

Buffers can take a lot of memory. You should set the color depth before creating any buffers, and you should not create buffers you don't need. Most of the time you will only want one additional buffer. Sometimes when your program involves a lot of screen manipulation and you are very concerned about optimizing the speed of the program, you might consider having two or more off-screen buffers.

At the beginning of the Copy Paste program, I had the following code:

```
//draw something to the buffer
//establish an offscreen buffer
SetDrawBuf(1);
text(30, 30, "this is in the buffer");

//draw some stuff on the screen
SetDrawBuf(0);
text(30, 30, "original text");
wait();
```

First, I set the draw buffer to 1. Since buffer 1 didn't exist yet, it was created in memory. I then used the `text()` function to draw some text. However, since draw buffer 1 is currently active, the text did not go directly to the screen, but to the memory buffer instead. I then set the buffer to 0, which means that any graphics commands will work directly on the screen, just like normal. I wrote "original text" on this buffer.

Copying Buffers

After the user clicks on the screen, I copied buffer 1 to the display screen with this command:

```
//copy buffer 1 to display buffer
  CopyBuf(0, 1);
```

The `copyBuf()` function copies the results of one buffer to another. It's extremely handy because it allows you to very quickly copy the data from a draw buffer to the main display buffer. Working with buffers that don't display is much quicker than drawing directly to the display screen, so you can do complex graphics in an off-screen buffer and then copy the entire buffer over to the screen when the graphics commands are finished. This technique is called *double-buffering,* and it is a staple of arcade game design.

Copying Rectangles

Sometimes copying an entire screen buffer can be overkill. You might want to copy only a select part of the screen into a buffer. For the copy and paste command of the Animator program, you'll generally be working with portions of the screen, rather than the entire buffer. PToolboxLib includes a command that allows you to copy a rectangle from one buffer to another. The rest of the Copy Paste program demonstrates one way to use this function.

```
clearg();
for(i = 1; i < 50; i++){
  ellipse(0, i, i, i, i);
} // end for loop
wait();
x1 = penx();
y1 = peny();
wait();
clipWidth = penx()-x1;
clipHeight = peny()-y1;

CopyRect(0, 0, 0, x1, y1, clipWidth, clipHeight, 0, 1, -1);

//copy buffer 1 back to display buffer
CopyBuf(0, 1);
wait();
```

The program is currently working with the standard buffer, so it draws a series of ellipses on the screen. (The pattern will give you something interesting to copy.) It then waits for a pen tap. The location of the pen tap is stored in the `x1` and `y1` variables. Then the program waits for another pen tap, which will indicate the lower right corner of the rectangle to copy. I used the new `penx()` and `peny()` values to determine the width and height of the rectangle to copy. The `CopyRect()` function has a huge number of parameters, and it works in a couple of different ways. Table 11.4 provides a summary.

Table 11.4 Parameters of the CopyRect() Function

Parameter	Description
int src_buf	Copy from this buffer (usually the destination is buffer 0, but see below for copying to another buffer)
int dest_x	Where in the destination buffer the image should be drawn
int dest_y	""
int src_x	What part of the source buffer to copy
int src_y	""
int width	The size of the rectangle in the source buffer to copy
int height	""
int mode	How the image will be copied (0 for normal copy, see PToolboxLib documentation for other modes)
int zoom (dest_buf)	0,1 = no zoom, 2 = 2x original size, 4 = 4 x original size (can also be used for dest_buf)
int rot	0 = normal copy, 1 = 90 deg, 2 = 180 deg, 3 = 270 deg, 4 = flip horizontally, 5 = flip vertically. -1 = use zoom field for dest_buf

The `CopyRect` function is complex because it is so powerful. The function really should have had 11 parameters, but PocketC does not allow functions to have more than 10, so Stadolnik employed a trick: If you set the value of the rot parameter to −1, you can use the zoom parameter as a destination buffer parameter. The easiest way to understand this is to dissect an actual command, so here's the relevant code from the Copy Paste program:

```
CopyRect(0,         // copy from buffer zero, the drawing buffer
         0, 0,      //  copy to the upper left of the destination buffer
         x1, y1     // copy the value that starts at x1, y1 in the source
buffer
         clipWidth, clipHeight,    //this is the size of the buffer to
copy
         0,         // use the normal copying mode
         1,         // since the rot parameter contains -1,
                    // this value is the destination buffer,
                    //so I'll be copying to buffer 1
         -1);       // this value indicates that the zoom parameter should
                    // refer to the destination buffer
```

Later in the chapter, I show you how to use the zoom and rotation parameters in the normal ways. The main purpose of this demonstration is to prove that you can manipulate buffers and parts of buffers.

Storing and Loading Buffers

PToolboxLib also includes an automated feature for storing multiple buffers into a .pdb database. This is how the save and load feature is implemented in the Super Sketcher program. When you use a buffer database, you are essentially creating a series of buffers that are stored directly in a database file. You can very easily store and load buffers from the file into your main drawing buffer without having to worry about the buffer manipulation commands. The database manipulation is also significantly simpler than the techniques illustrated earlier in the book. Figures 11.22 through 11.24 show a program that illustrates buffers being stored in a database.

The BufDB program has two functions, both called from `main()`.

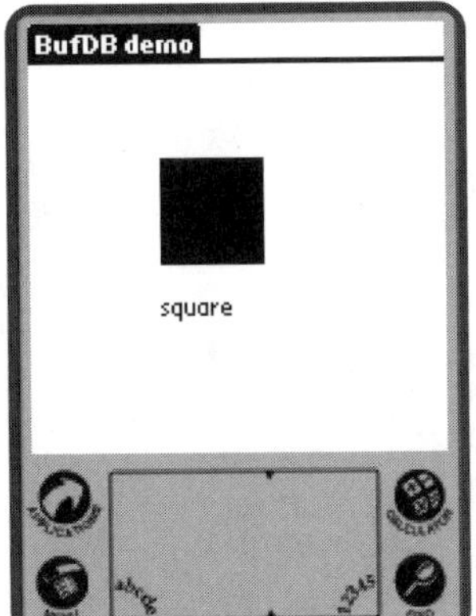

FIGURE 11.22

The first image is a square. This image is stored to the database.

FIGURE 11.23

Then the program generates a circle, which is also stored to the database.

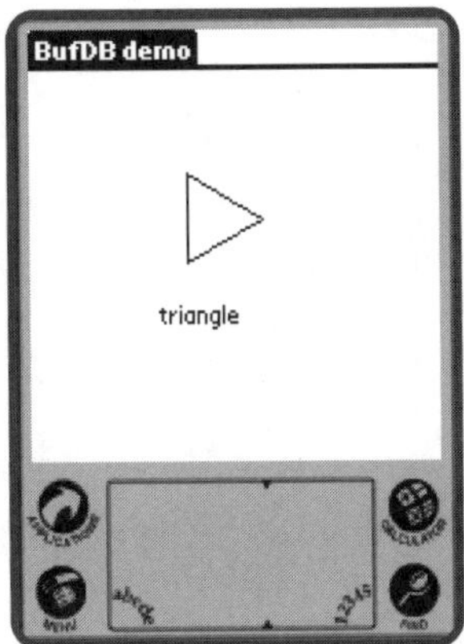

FIGURE 11.24

Finally, the program stores a triangle to the database. Then the program automates these images, creating a flip book–style animation—which is unfortunately beyond the power of the printed page to display.

Creating the Database

The first function creates the database, and it looks like this:

```
createDB(){
   //create buffer database

   SetDepth(4);
   graph_on();
   title("BufDB demo");
```

```
   //Open the buffer database
 OpenBufDb("bdbDemo", 1);

   clearg();
   rect (1, 50, 50, 90, 90, 0);
   text (50, 100, "square");
   SaveBuf(0);
   wait();

   clearg();
   rect (1, 50, 50, 90, 90, 20);
   text (50, 100, "circle");
   SaveBuf(1);
   wait();

   clearg();
   polygon(70, 70, 3, 20, 0);
   text(50, 100, "triangle");
   SaveBuf(2);
   wait();

   CloseBufDb();
} // end createDB
```

The buffer database is created in this line:

```
OpenBufDb("bdbDemo", 1);
```

The `OpenBufDb()` function does pretty much what you might expect. It opens up a database optimized for storing buffers. The database is a .pdb file just like the ones you created in Chapter 10, but it is customized to easily store graphic buffers. The `OpenBufDb()` function expects two parameters. The first is the name of the .pdb file to create, and the second is the backup mode. If you set the second parameter to 0, the database will be created in the ordinary way, and it will not be backed up the next time you synchronize the PDA. If you set the parameter to 1, the database's "backup bit" will be set, telling the Palm OS to make a copy of the database on the desktop during the next hot-synch. If you set the backup parameter to 2, the database will be automatically deleted when you close the program. You would use this option when you are creating a temporary database that doesn't really need to stay in the computer's memory after the program is finished.

The `SaveBuf()` function is used to store the contents of the draw buffer to a record in the buffer database. The single parameter is used to determine which record should be written to in the database. Table 11.5 summarizes the buffer functions.

Once you have created and closed a buffer database, you can use the normal PocketC database routines to manipulate it. For example, if you wanted to count the number of images in a BufDb database, you could open it up with the normal `dbopen()` function, then use `dbnrecs()` to get the number of records and `dbclose()` to close it.

When you look back at the createDB code, you'll see that it simply generates an image, stores it to the database, and repeats until all three images are stored.

TABLE 11.5 BUFFER DB FUNCTIONS IN PTOOLBOXLIB

Function	Description	Example
int OpenBufDb(string *dbName*, int *mode*)	Open (or create) a new .pdb file named *dbName*. Mode = 0: no backup, mode = 1: backup at next synch., mode = 2: delete when program ends. Returns 1 if successful, 0 if failure.	OpenBufDb(myDB, 1);
CloseBufDb()	Close the currently open buffer db.	CloseBufDb();
int SaveBuf(int record);	Save the current draw buffer to the db at the indicated record number. Returns 0 on failure.	SaveBuf(1);
int RestoreBuf(int record);	Read the indicated record from the buffer db and copy it to the drawing buffer. Returns 0 on failure.	RestoreBuf(1);

Animating the Database

If you have a number of images stored in a database, it's reasonably simple to animate them at any speed you wish. Here's how I animated the images in the BufDb program:

```
animate(){
  //show the images in succession
  int keepGoing = true;
```

```
    int evt;
    int recNum = 0;

    OpenBufDb("bdbDemo", 1);
    while(keepGoing){
      evt = event(50);
      RestoreBuf(recNum);
      recNum++;
      if (recNum > 2){
        recNum = 0;
      } // end if
      if (evt == EVT_PEN_DN){
        keepGoing = false;
      } // end if
    } // end while
    CloseBufDb();
} // end animate
```

At first glance, this function looks like a routine event loop, which basically it is. However, there are some subtle differences. Essentially, I begin by opening up the buffer db that was created in the `createDB()` function. I then pause for half a second with the `event()` function. You might recall that the parameter of the `event` function can be used to pause for *n* 100ths of a second if *n* is greater than 1. So, the line

```
evt = event(50)
```

pauses for half a second, and then runs an ordinary event handler. In this program, I'm actually more interested in the pausing behavior than the event trap, although the program will look for a pen tap.

Each time through the loop, the program restores an image from the database, then increments the record counter. As usual, whenever you increment a variable, it's good to check for bounds, so I trapped to ensure `recNum` does not get too large.

I then checked to see if the user tapped the pen. If so, the `keepGoing` variable is set to false, so the program can exit. At the end of the loop, I close the buffer db.

The Buffer DB main() Function

The `main` function of the Buffer DB program is extremely simple:

```
main(){
  createDB();
  animate();
} // end main
```

Once you have defined functions well, your `main` function can be very easy to write.

The Animator Program

You already know most of what you need to write the full-blown Animator program. There are a few more details to learn, but most of the program is simply reorganizing the things you have seen earlier in this (and other) chapters.

Global Stuff

Since this program is a bit involved, there are a number of housekeeping details to handle in the global area of the program:

```
//Animator
//illustrates features of PToolbox
//Andy Harris, 5/25/01

library "PToolboxLib"
#include "Ccontrols.c"
#include "events.h"

//function protos
loadPic();
savePic();

//start with menus
Chandle mnbMain;
Chandle mnuFile, mnuEdit, mnuDraw;
```

```
//global variables
int oldx, oldy;                  //used in drawing commands
string mode = "free";            //what command is user requesting
int recNum = 0;                  //which record in the database is showing
int numRecs = 1;                 //how many records in the current database
string fileName = "SSketch";//determines the name of the current database
int keepGoing = true;            //main looping variable for program
int clipWidth, clipHeight;       //used for clipboard functions
```

Animator uses PToolboxLib, so I need to include it. I've also chosen to use menus from Ccontrols, and my event-handling constants from events.h. It isn't uncommon at all for a program to involve numerous libraries and include files.

For the most part, the function definitions flowed in an order that was easy to determine. However, `loadPic()` and `savePic()` each needed to be defined before the other would work, so I created function prototypes for these two functions.

I created several Chandles for the various menu elements. There are no other Ccontrol objects in the program.

A number of other global variables show up in the program. The `oldx` and `oldy` variables are used in those drawing commands that require two points (such as the `circle`, `polygon`, and `rectangle` commands). `Mode` is an important variable used to determine the current drawing mode. The program will have to act differently in the various drawing modes, so there must be some type of variable indicating what the current mode is. The `recNum` and `numRecs` variables are used in database access. The former shows which image is currently being displayed (or edited), while the latter holds the number of records available in the database. The `fileName` string holds the name of the database to open or save.

The `keepGoing` variable is used in its normal way: it will be `true` whenever the program is intended to continue, and `false` when the user is ready to leave the program. I defined `keepGoing` as a global variable because its value can be changed by two different functions.

The `clipHeight` and `clipWidth` variables are used in copying and pasting. They store the size of the current clipboard image.

Counting the Number of Records

The `numRecs` variable is especially important in this program. It is critical to know how many records are in the database during animation, or the program may attempt to display an image that was never stored. PToolboxLib does not supply a function for returning the number of records in a buffer database, so I wrote one:

```
countRecs(){
  //get number of records (use 'traditional' db access)

  if(dbopen(fileName)){;
    numRecs = dbnrecs();
    dbclose();
  } else {
    numRecs = 0;
  } // end if
} // end countRecs
```

The `countRecs()` function first tries to open the file. Notice that this function uses the normal PocketC database routines. If the file exists, I use `dbnrecs()` to determine the number of records in the file, then close the file. If `dbopen()` was not successful, the database doesn't exist yet, and `numRecs` should be set to 0.

Initializing the Program

As with most programs of any substance, there is some initialization necessary in Animator. I'll need to do a bit of work to set up the color depth, the buffer for the clipboard, and the menus.

```
init(){

  //grayscale mode. Set depth to 5 for color Palms
  SetDepth(4);
  graph_on();
  clearg();
  title("animator: " + fileName + "-" + mode + "         ");

  //set up default color and pattern
  SetFore(3);
  SetPattern("ffffffffffffffff");  //solid fill of foreground color

  //create clipboard buffer
  SetDrawBuf(1);  //clipboard buffer
  SetDrawBuf(0);  //move back to normal buffer

  //set up menu bars
```

```
mnbMain = Cmenubar();

//file menu
mnuFile = Cmenu(5, 80, 40);
Csettopic(mnuFile, "File");
Cadditem(mnuFile, "new frame");
Cadditem(mnuFile, "clear");
Cadditem(mnuFile, "open");
Cadditem(mnuFile, "prev");
Cadditem(mnuFile, "next");
Cadditem(mnuFile, "save");
Cadditem(mnuFile, "view anim");
Cadditem(mnuFile, "exit");
Caddmenu(mnbMain, mnuFile);

//edit menu
mnuEdit = Cmenu(45, 80, 40);
Csettopic(mnuEdit, "Edit");
Cadditem(mnuEdit, "copy");
Cadditem(mnuEdit, "paste");
Cadditem(mnuEdit, "paste 90");
Cadditem(mnuEdit, "paste 180");
Cadditem(mnuEdit, "paste -90");
Cadditem(mnuEdit, "paste flip v");
Cadditem(mnuEdit, "paste flip h");
Cadditem(mnuEdit, "paste x2");
Cadditem(mnuEdit, "paste x4");
Caddmenu(mnbMain, mnuEdit);

//draw menu
mnuDraw = Cmenu(85, 80, 40);
Csettopic(mnuDraw, "Draw");
Cadditem(mnuDraw, "free");
Cadditem(mnuDraw, "oval");
Cadditem(mnuDraw, "rectangle");
Cadditem(mnuDraw, "color");
Cadditem(mnuDraw, "fill");
Cadditem(mnuDraw, "line");
Cadditem(mnuDraw, "poly");
Caddmenu(mnbMain, mnuDraw);
```

```
  //load the first record
  recNum = 0;
  countRecs();
  loadPic();
} // end init
```

Setting the Color Depth

The first order of business is to set the color depth. Remember that you must set the color depth before you invoke a `clearg()` function or create any buffers. This program is written for a 16 grayscale device, but by changing the number 4 in the `SetDepth()` command to a 5, you can easily make this program work for color-capable Palms.

I created a buffer for the clipboard by switching to buffer 1 and then immediately back to buffer 0:

```
//create clipboard buffer
SetDrawBuf(1);   //clipboard buffer
SetDrawBuf(0);   //move back to normal buffer
```

This will make sure that buffer 1 is allocated, but force all drawing to happen in the visible drawing buffer.

I also set the current draw color, just to ensure that there will be one, and set the custom fill pattern to draw completely in the foreground color.

Creating the Menus

The user interface for this program consists entirely of menus. I wanted to ensure a clean design without a lot of buttons cluttering up the screen. I used the menus from Ccontrols to create this effect. Although there are a lot of menu items in this program, the technique for creating and using the menus is no different from the one used in Chapter 10.

Loading Up the First Record

When the program starts, I want it to automatically display the first image in the current animation, so the last part of the initialization code makes sure that will happen:

```
//load the first record
recNum = 0;
countRecs();
loadPic();
```

I set `recNum` to 0, called `countRecs()` to figure out what the appropriate value of `numRecs` should be, and loaded the picture with the index of 0 with the `loadPic()` function. (That function's definition is coming up shortly.)

Saving and Loading Images

The program needs the ability to load and store images to the currently selected database. The `savePic()` function saves the current draw buffer's contents to the record indicated by `recNum` in the current database.

```
savePic(){
  //save the picture to the database
  OpenBufDb(fileName, 1);
  SaveBuf(recNum);
  CloseBufDb();
} // end savePic
```

The function opens up whichever database is indicated by `fileName`. It then saves the current draw buffer into the record indicated by `recNum`, then it closes the database.

The `loadPic()` function is very similar:

```
loadPic(){
  //loads a picture from the database
  OpenBufDb(fileName, 1);
  RestoreBuf(recNum);
  CloseBufDb();
} // end loadPic
```

The only difference between `loadPic()` and `savePic()` is that `loadPic()` uses the `RestoreBuf()` function to read an image from the database and load it into the current display buffer.

Moving to Previous and Next Frame

The code for moving to the previous and next frame of an animation is surprisingly similar to the code you used in Chapter 10 to move among records in a database. (Perhaps this isn't so surprising after all, as you're still moving around in a database—it's just a different kind of data.)

```
movePrev(){
  recNum--;
```

```
  if (recNum < 0){
    recNum = 0;
  } // end if
  loadPic();
} // end movePrev

moveNext(){
  recNum++;
  if (recNum >= numRecs){
    recNum = numRecs-1;
  } // end if
  loadPic();
} // end moveNext
```

Both functions begin by changing the `recNum` variable. Then they check the boundaries to ensure that `recNum` still has a legal value. Finally, they each load up the new picture with a call to the `loadPic()` function.

IN THE REAL WORLD

The first time I wrote these functions, I automatically stored the current image before moving to the next image (as in the database in Chapter 10.) However, I soon got frustrated—any random dot on the screen would automatically be saved. I then tried a prompt that would call for a save each time the user moved to another screen, but that was even more annoying. I decided not to have the program store images at all, but to require the user to store each image explicitly. You might be able to think up a better solution, or you could implement some sort of preferences menu that would let the user choose the saving mechanism that seems most useful for a given project.

Drawing a Polygon

Most of the commands in the edit menu can be accomplished without a special function, but the polygon drawing feature seemed best to implement in a function.

```
drawPoly(){
  //draws a polygon
  //start at center, draw to edge
```

```
  int a, b, sides, radius;
  sides = gets("Number of sides?");
  a = oldx-penx();
  b = oldy-peny();
  //good old pythagorean theorom to determine radius
  radius = sqrt(pow(a,2) + pow(b,2));
  polygon(oldx, oldy, sides, radius, 0);
} // end drawPoly
```

The only thing tricky about this routine is the way it determines the radius. You might recall that the polygon function in PToolboxLib requires a number of sides and a radius. I decided that I wanted to let the user click on the middle of the polygon and drag to determine how far each corner was from the center. The `oldx` and `oldy` variables will hold the point where the user first clicks the screen, and `penx()` and `peny()` will hold the point where the user picks up the pen. (See the `main` function for more discussion of this). To get the radius from these two points, I applied the Pythagorean theorem. (And you told your eighth grade math teacher you'd never need it again!)

Viewing the Animation

The routine for viewing the current animation comes almost verbatim from the BufferDB example earlier in the chapter.

```
viewAnim(){
  //view an animation of the file
  //pen tap to exit animation
  int evt;
  int stayInLoop = true;
  int lag = 50;

  lag = getsd("lag between frames?\r(50 = 1/2 sec)", lag);
  while(stayInLoop){
    evt = event(lag);
    recNum++;
    if (recNum >= numRecs){
      recNum = 0;
    } // end if
    loadPic();
    if (evt == EVT_PEN_DN){
```

```
      stayInLoop = false;
    } // end
  } // end loop
} // end viewAnim
```

I added a new looping variable because the program already uses the `keepGoing` variable. The local `evt` variable is unrelated to the one that occurs in the `main` loop, because they are both local variables. The `lag` variable is used to determine how long to pause between frames of the animation. I decided to let the user choose the lag time, because some animations (like a bouncing ball animation, for example) will look better with a very short lag time. Other animations (like a slide show with captions) will need to stay on the screen long enough for the user to read the captions.

Inside the `main` loop, I waited for lag 100ths of a second long, then incremented `recNum`. I then checked to see that `recNum` is still a valid number, then called the `getPic()` function to get the record from the database and display it on the screen. I then checked to see if the user clicked on the screen with the pen. If so, I set `stayInLoop` to `false`, so the loop will exit.

Copying Part of the Frame

The copy command should also look familiar to you, as you have seen most of the code in the Copy Paste demo earlier in this chapter.

```
copy(){
  //copies a part of the screen to the clipboard

  int x, y;
  alert("click upper left, lower right of section to copy");
  wait();
  x = penx();
  y = peny();
  wait();
  clipWidth = penx()-x;
  clipHeight = peny()-y;

  //copy the rectangle to buffer 1
  CopyRect(0, 0, 0, x, y, clipWidth, clipHeight, 0, 1, -1);
} // end copy
```

The function tells the user what to expect, then waits for two pen taps. The x and y coordinates of these pen taps are used to determine the location and size of the clipboard image. I used the `CopyRect()` function to copy the clipboard from the draw buffer to buffer 1 (the destination buffer is the second to last parameter, because the last parameter is −1).

Pasting from the Clipboard

Once an image is stored on the clipboard buffer, there must be a way to retrieve it to a specified part of the current drawing buffer. The `paste` function does this, but it adds more functionality. The `CopyRect()` function supports various kinds of rotation and zooming options. Since I'll be copying a rectangle from buffer 1 to the draw buffer, the last two parameters can be used for zoom and rotation values. Even though there are eight different paste commands on the menu, they all use the same `paste` function.

```
paste(string pMode){
  //returns clipboard image to screen
  //pMode determines what type of paste will occur
  int x, y;

  alert("click upper left of where image is to go");
  wait();
  x = penx();
  y = peny();
  switch (pMode){
    case "normal":
      CopyRect(1, x, y, 0, 0, clipWidth, clipHeight, 0, 1, 0);
      break;
    case "r90":
      CopyRect(1, x, y, 0, 0, clipWidth, clipHeight, 0, 1, 1);
      break;
    case "r180":
      CopyRect(1, x, y, 0, 0, clipWidth, clipHeight, 0, 1, 2);
      break;
    case "r-90":
      CopyRect(1, x, y, 0, 0, clipWidth, clipHeight, 0, 1, 3);
      break;
    case "flipH":
      CopyRect(1, x, y, 0, 0, clipWidth, clipHeight, 0, 1, 4);
```

```
      break;
    case "flipV":
      CopyRect(1, x, y, 0, 0, clipWidth, clipHeight, 0, 1, 5);
      break;
    case "x2":
      CopyRect(1, x, y, 0, 0, clipWidth, clipHeight, 0, 2, 0);
      break;
    case "x4":
      CopyRect(1, x, y, 0, 0, clipWidth, clipHeight, 0, 4, 0);
      break;
  } // end switch

} // end paste
```

To make the `paste` function flexible enough to work with all the different kinds of paste commands, I decided to have it accept a parameter. The string variable `pMode` contains a string that determines which flavor of the paste command the user intends. Once the function begins, it asks the user to click on the screen. The point of this pen tap will become the upper left-hand corner of the clipboard image's position on the screen.

The function then performs a switch operation on the `pMode` command to determine what kind of copy the user wants to execute. The only things that change in the various copying modes are the values of the zoom and rotation parameters. All the other parameters are identical for each of the other copies. As an example, following is a description of the parameters for the "rotate 90" command:

```
CopyRect(1,    //copy from buffer 1 (the clipboard buffer)
               x, y, //copy to the position of the last pen tap
               0, 0, //copy from the upper left corner of the clipboard
               clipWidth, clipHeight, //copy this size rectangle from the
clipboard
               0,    //use the normal copy mode
               1,   // create the normal size
               1);  // rotate the image by 90 degrees
```

Checking for Menu Input

To conserve screen space for drawing, I decided to rely almost exclusively on menus for program control. As you have seen from earlier programs, it is often most convenient to manage menu control in a separate function. This program features a lot of commands that are accessible by menus, but most of them are quite simple. Here is the menu-checking code:

```
checkMenus(string command){
  switch (command){
    //file commands
    case "open":
      fileName = gets("new file name?");
      countRecs();

      //load up the first record
      recNum = 0;
      loadPic();
      break;
    case "new frame":
      recNum = numRecs;
      numRecs++;
      rect(0,0, 15, 159, 159, 0);
      break;
    case "clear":
      rect(0,0, 15, 159, 159, 0);
      break;
    case "prev":
      movePrev();
      break;
    case "next":
      moveNext();
      break;
    case "save":
      savePic();
      break;
    case "view anim":
      viewAnim();
      break;
    case "exit":
      keepGoing = false;
      break;

    //edit commands
    case "copy":
      copy();
```

```
    break;
  case "paste":
    paste("normal");
    break;
  case "paste 90":
    paste("r90");
    break;
  case "paste 180":
    paste("r180");
    break;
  case "paste -90":
    paste("r-90");
    break;
  case "paste flip v":
    paste("flipV");
    break;
  case "paste flip h":
    paste("flipH");
    break;
  case "paste x2":
    paste("x2");
    break;
  case "paste x4":
    paste("x4");
    break;

  //draw commands
  case "free":
    mode = "free";
    break;
  case "oval":
    mode = "oval";
    break;
  case "rectangle":
    mode = "rect";
    break;
  case "color":
    SetFore(PickColor());
    break;
  case "fill":
```

```
      mode = "fill";
      break;
    case "line":
      mode = "line";
      plot(0, penx(), peny(), 0, 0);
      break;
    case "poly":
      mode = "poly";
      break;
    default:
      //shouldn't ever happen. If it does, I probably misspelled a
command name,
      //so tell me what command is.
      alert(command);
  } // end switch
} // end checkMenus
```

The function expects a command name, which will be the text of one of the menu elements. The function is made up of a huge switch statement that simply passes program control around based on the value of the command. In most cases, the function quickly passes control to another function. In a few cases (such as the "new frame" command), the code was very short, so I put it directly into the switch statement. Note that most of the drawing functions don't really do any drawing at all. They simply set the value of the mode variable. The actual drawing commands are all done in response to pen events in the main loop.

> **IN THE REAL WORLD**
>
> **Notice the default structure. The program was designed so that the default clause of the switch statement should never be hit. However, in a program with this many commands, it isn't surprising that I had some errors when I was testing the program. If the switch statement didn't recognize a command, I got an alert statement telling me what command it did receive. This is a very useful code fragment to keep around, especially when you are switching on a string value.**

The Main Event Loop

The `main` function does a little more work than `main` functions usually have to do, but that is because the program has to check for several different kinds of events.

```
main(){
  int evt;
  string command;

  init();
  hookhard(1);   //intercept button presses

  while (keepGoing){
    evt = event(0);
```

The `main` function starts off in a very typical way. Note that I used the `hookhard()` function to tell PocketC to intercept button presses. I want to use the Phone and To Do buttons as an alternate way to step through the frames of the animation. If you forget to call the `hookhard()` function, all button presses will be sent to the operating system rather than being interpreted by your program.

Looking for Button Presses

Once I have started the event loop, I query the `evt` variable to see what type of event occurred:

```
//check button presses
    if (evt == EVT_BTN_ADD){
      movePrev();
    } else if (evt == EVT_BTN_TODO){
      moveNext();
```

If the Address Book button was pressed, call the `movePrev()` function. If the To Do button was pressed, call `moveNext()`. All the details of moving to the next and previous image are encapsulated into these functions.

Looking for Menu Events

The menu events will be handled by checking the `Cevent()` function. I actually have only four Ccontrol objects in this program: the menu bar and the three menu elements. Of these, only one (the main menu bar) responds to a `Cevent()`.

```
//look for menu events
    } else if(Cevent(mnbMain, evt)){
      if(Cgetcursel(mnuFile)!= -1){
        command = Cgetcontent(mnuFile);
      } else if (Cgetcursel(mnuEdit) != -1){
        command = Cgetcontent(mnuEdit);
```

```
    } else if (Cgetcursel(mnuDraw) != -1){
      command = Cgetcontent(mnuDraw);
    } // end if
    checkMenus(command);
```

If the menu bar responds to an event, the program will check to see which menu was selected. (Recall that the `Cgetcursel()` function will return −1 if the menu has not been selected, so if the value of Cgetcursel is *not* −1, that menu was selected by the user.) If a menu has been selected, the program uses the `Cgetcursel()` function on that menu to determine the actual contents of the menu element the user selected. That value is sent to the `checkMenus()` function.

Checking for Pen Down

If the user has placed the pen on the screen, it will trigger a `pen_down` event. Surprisingly little happens when the user puts the pen down.

```
//check for pen down event
   } else if (evt == EVT_PEN_DN){
     oldx = penx();
     oldy = peny();
     if (mode == "fill"){
       FloodFill(0, penx(), peny());
     } // end if
```

Many modes require two points before they can do anything interesting (think of the rectangle mode, circle mode, and polygon mode). For those commands, the point where the pen first hit the screen will be one point, and the other point will be activated when the pen is picked up. Whenever the pen touches the screen, the location of the pen is stored to `oldx` and `oldy`.

If the user is in fill mode, the program will perform a flood fill operation in the current location.

Responding to Pen Movement

Pen movement is actually not critical in most drawing modes. The only time it is necessary to respond to pen motion is in the freehand drawing mode.

```
//check for pen move event
   } else if (evt == EVT_PEN_MV){
       switch(mode){
         case "free":
         rect(4, penx(), peny(), penx() + 2, peny() + 2, 0);
```

```
        break;
      } // end switch
```

I expected more modes to use the pen move event, so I built a switch statement—but never found another use for it. In freehand mode, any motion of the pen draws a rectangle in the current foreground color. Currently there is only one brush size and shape, but that would be easy to fix.

Responding to Pen Up

Most of the drawing commands do their work when the pen is lifted, because they require two points and don't get the second until the pen leaves the screen. Here's the code that handles the pen up behavior:

```
//check for pen up event
    } else if (evt == EVT_PEN_UP){
      switch(mode){
        case "free":
          rect(4, penx(), peny(), penx() + 2, peny() + 2, 0);
          break;
        case "rect":
          rect(4, oldx, oldy, penx(), peny(),0);
          break;
        case "oval":
          ellipse(3, oldx, oldy, (penx()-oldx), (peny()-oldy));
          break;
        case "line":
          plot(1, penx(), peny(), 0, 0);
          break;
        case "poly":
          drawPoly();
          break;
        default:
          //alert(mode);
      } // end switch
      title("animator: " + fileName + "-" + mode + "        ");
    } // end if
  } // end while
} // end main
```

These options simply call different forms of the `rect` or `ellipse` function. The line command calls the `plot()` function from PToolboxLib, which can be used to draw lines between various points. The `poly` command calls the `drawPoly()` function.

Note the `title` function after the end of the switch statement. It's a good idea to give the user some idea what is going on in the program, so I changed the title bar to indicate the current file name and mode. Because this happens outside the switch statement, the title bar is updated any time the menus are activated. This makes sense, because the database name and the mode will only be changed as a result of menu events.

Summary

In this chapter, you learned how to use the PToolbox library to add considerable functionality to your PocketC programs. While there are a lot of functions in the library that don't show up in this chapter, you have had an opportunity to see the power and flexibility of a native library. Specifically, you learned how to add color to your programs. You have learned a little bit about color depth, and how to set the color. You learned how to use a dialog box to let the user set colors. You have experimented with drawing buffers, and learned how to use a buffer to implement a graphical clipboard. You also learned how to use a buffer database to store and load images. Finally, you put all these things together to build an application that allows you to play with animation.

CHALLENGES

1. **Add different drawing brushes to the program.**
2. **Experiment with the more elaborate color schemes (if your PDA supports them).**
3. **Experiment with the bitmap functions of the PToolbox library. Consider using bitmaps as pens in the freehand drawing command.**
4. **Add your own commands. What about a text command, or sound features?**
5. **Add a toolbar or button controls to the Animator.**
6. **Add a database to keep track of all the image databases created by the program, so the user doesn't have to remember the database names.**

Designing Data for Programs: The Pocket Battle Game

This last chapter is intended to help you stretch your programming skills beyond the "absolute beginner" level. You won't face any new syntax here. Instead, you'll concentrate on putting together the skills you have learned throughout this book to create an interesting and challenging program.

In general, more advanced programmers tend to be more concerned about data than about programming commands. In this chapter, you'll get a chance to look very carefully at the *design* of your data. Specifically, you learn:

- How to go from an idea into a workable program
- How to design data for maximum flexibility and power
- How to write a program to use your data
- How relational data systems work
- How data normalization improves your program
- How to use diagnostic functions to improve the testing and debugging of your programs

The Pocket Battle Game

With all this talk about data, you might be surprised that the sample program for this chapter is a game, not a database. The most critical part of many games is the underlying data structure—this one is a perfect example, besides being a lot of fun.

IN THE REAL WORLD

You'll find that the principles of good programming design are easily transferred to any other program. In fact, game developers appropriated some of the concepts you'll learn about in this chapter from more traditional business developers. It works the other way as well—business programmers have often appropriated good ideas from game developers. To sum it up, good programming is just good programming.

The Pocket Battle program is a Palm-scale tactical wargame simulator. The game was designed to be as open-ended as possible, so that it can be customized on two levels. First, it allows users a variety of ways to play the game. They can generate their own maps and choose their own armies. Second, it's set up so as to make it easy for programmers to modify the game by adding new units, terrain, and other features.

How the Game Works

The Pocket Battle program currently uses very standard (but functional) graphics. Figure 12.1 shows the beginning of a battle.

The Pocket Battle game features a variety of units with different strengths and weaknesses. Of course, the more powerful units are more expensive than the less powerful ones. Part of the strategy is choosing the best mix of units. The next step is to choose a map, as shown in Figure 12.2.

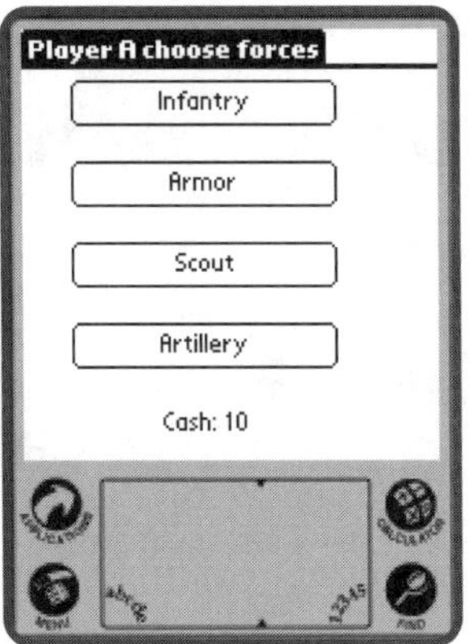

FIGURE 12.1

Player A begins by choosing units.

FIGURE 12.2

If the user does not choose a map, the program generates a blank 10 x 10 grid.

Maps can be generated in the Memo Pad program and loaded into the game. Currently the Pocket Battle program only supports normal terrain and water—shown on the screen as (.) and (~) respectively, as illustrated in Figure 12.3. It would be reasonably easy to add support for other terrain types—you could use (^) for mountains or pine forests, for example.

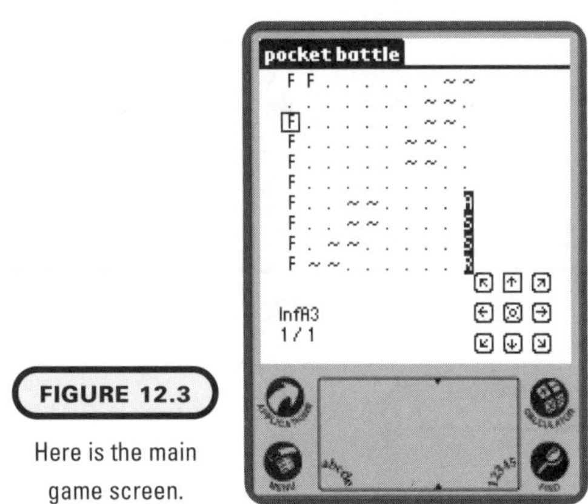

FIGURE 12.3

Here is the main game screen.

This particular game is being played on a map with a river running between the two armies. To simplify programming, all graphics in the game are currently done with ASCII characters, as listed in Table 12.1.

Cities and units belonging to player A are indicated with dark letters on a light background. Cities and units belonging to player B are denoted by inverse video (light letters on a dark background). In the game featured in Figure 12.4, Player A

Table 12.1 Character Representation in the Pocket Battle Game

Character	Name	Description
.	Normal terrain square	Standard terrain on the map
C	Capital city	Each player has a capital. The objective of the game is to take the opponent's capital and protect your own.
~	Water square	No units may enter a water square.
F	Infantry unit	Attack: 1 Defense: 1 Movement: 1 Cost: 1
A	Armor unit (tank)	Attack: 2 Defense: 2 Movement: 2 Cost: 4
S	Scout unit	Attack: 1 Defense: 1 Movement: 3 Cost: 2
R	Artillery unit	Attack: 3 Defense: 1 Movement: 1 Cost: 2

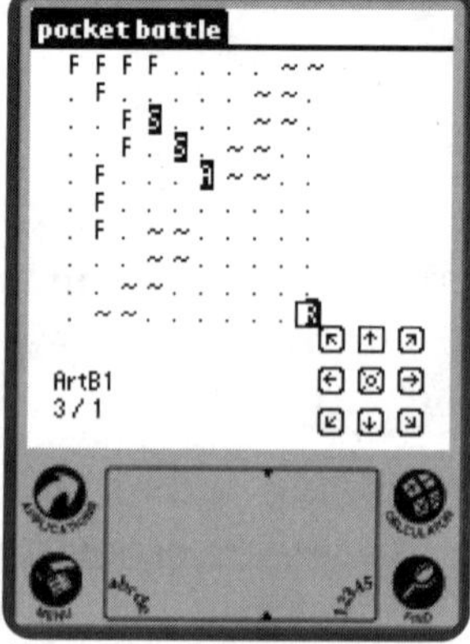

FIGURE 12.4

Here is a game halfway through play.

has chosen a force of many cheap infantry units. Player B opted for a smaller force of more powerful units.

Each player has a capital city. Player A's capital is always in the northwest corner of the map. Player B's capital is always in the southeast corner. At the moment, the capital cities are obscured because they both have units on them.

The arrow buttons in the bottom right of the screen are used for movement. One unit at a time is highlighted with a surrounding rectangle; that unit is the current unit. Clicking on one of the arrow buttons will move the unit in the appropriate direction. The center button tells the current unit to stay in place.

The Pocket Battle program is currently designed to be used by two players on one Palm device. After each turn, the players pass the device back and forth between them.

Player A has chosen a defensive strategy, surrounding the capital with infantry units. The plan is to wear down the opponent's attack. Player B has chosen to attack aggressively, leaving a small but powerful force behind to protect the capital.

Combat is initiated by moving a unit onto a square containing an enemy unit, as shown in Figure 12.5. The success of a combat is based mainly on the relative attack and defense strengths of the units engaged. However, there is also a random factor involved, to simulate the "fog of war."

In Figure 12.6 you can see that player B has managed to battle through player A's defenses. Taking the home base is like taking the king in chess—the game is over.

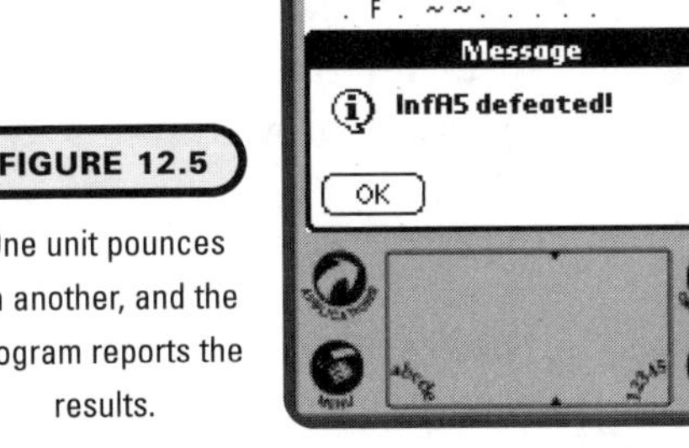

FIGURE 12.5

One unit pounces on another, and the program reports the results.

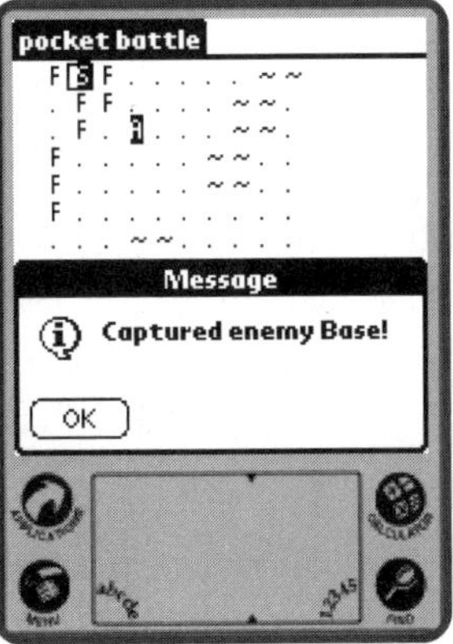

FIGURE 12.6

Player B wins—the attacking unit would move onto player A's city square in the next turn, having taken it this time, but the game won't last that long. As victory is assured to player B, the game is over.

Design Principles

The Pocket Battle program has some flexibility built into its design. First, the program can be changed in some interesting ways by the user. For example, the user can design custom maps and choose a mix of units. The program was built with another level of flexibility in mind, as well: I tried to think carefully about the design so programmers could easily expand the game and add new elements to it. Once you understand the underlying data structures, you should be able to do the following:

- Change the unit names and types to change the era of the game (knights and pikemen, or bombers and fighter planes, for example).
- Add many new types of units.
- Add a unit editor so the user can generate new types of units.
- Generate new terrain types with various effects on movement and combat.
- Allow for generation of new units as the game progresses.
- Add an economic system like the one used in *Empire* or *Civilization*.
- Add naval units and transports.

It may seem crazy to be thinking this much about expansion as you first consider a game, but it really is necessary if you want a durable and enjoyable product. The essence of a computer program is its data. If you design the data well, you will be able to expand the program in all kinds of ways. If you design the data without thinking about what you may want the program to do in the long term, you may find yourself with a program that does not allow you to do what you want it to. It pays to think about the big picture early in the process. And that means data. Data is the key to well-designed programs. If you think about control structures before you understand your data, you may run into big problems.

Data in the Pocket Battle

I began designing this program on paper. (In fact, my kids were coloring at the breakfast table as I began sketching out the data structures for the game. My best programming usually happens far from a computer.) I started by thinking about what kinds of information would be necessary for a game like the one I was imagining.

There clearly were a number of things that would need to be tracked. I first identified two key kinds of information: units and map squares. The game revolves around units moving and interacting on a map. Without some well-defined way to manage these two kinds of information in the computer's memory, the game would never work. A unit has a number of important characteristics that must somehow be stored and manipulated. For example, it will probably have a name, an attack strength, a defensive strength, a movement rate, and so on. Likewise, each square on the map will have a number of very important characteristics, such as terrain type, location, and the names of any units sitting there. My first analysis of the unit data in Pocket Battle produced the list in the next section.

Unit Data

The units are the basic fighting forces in the game. Each unit should have all of the following characteristics:

- Unit name
- Unit type
- Unit owner
- Attack level
- Defense level
- Movement rate
- Class (land, sea, or air)
- Cost (relative expense of the unit)
- Image (what to display on the map for the unit)
- Transport (whether the unit will transport other units)

Note a couple of things: first, I won't use every one of these characteristics right away. (In fact, the class and transport characteristics aren't used at all in the version of Pocket Battle in this book. However, they're the sort of thing a battle simulator wants—and it's much easier to put them in from the beginning than try to superimpose them later.) Also, there's some information that might belong here that you don't see. For example, maybe a unit should have access to its location on the map. As you'll see later, I chose to put this information in a different place, although you could argue that it belongs here.

There's another important charactistic of the list of characteristics shown here. Some of the data (like the name of the unit) is unique for every single unit on the map. However, most of the unit data isn't specific to a particular unit, but belongs to a *class* of units. For example, the attack, defense, and movement rates of all infantry units will be the same. It would be more sensible to organize the data so that each unit would be assigned to a particular class; that way any details that belong to the entire class could be defined only one time.

In the Real World

The process I'm showing you here is called *data normalization.* It is simply a method of making sure your data is well organized. Following are the basic principles of data normalization:

- **Don't repeat data if you can avoid it.**
- **Break data into blocks based on functionality.**
- **Create relationships between the various blocks.**

While the term *data normalization* is usually applied to relational database systems, the principles are equally useful in any application (such as the Pocket Battle program) that uses a large amount of information.

One principle of sound data design is to encode each piece of data in as few places as possible—and preferably in only one place. If, for example, you encode the attack strength of infantry in each infantry unit, you have two problems. First, you have used more memory than you need. On a typical computer, this isn't a major problem, but memory is precious on the Palm OS. The other problem is one of data integrity. If you decide that the infantry units need to be stronger, you would have to go back and change the strength value for each individual unit. This adds complexity to the program, and increases the likelihood of bugs. It would be better to have a block of information about specific units and another block of information about unit classes. These blocks of information are usually called *tables.* Each specific characteristic is called a *field.*

If this talk of tables and fields reminds you of database management, that's because this part of the job *is* managing a database, even though it might not look like one to the user. Just as with any well-designed data application, much of the work happens before you write a single line of code.

Unit Class Data

Unit class data is the information that pertains to a specific class of units. Units of a particular class have many of the same characteristics. For example, all armor units have the same attack and movement values. Table 12.2 shows the class data for Pocket Battle.

Once I had decided what kind of information each unit class should contain, I designed a number of unit classes, shown in Table 12.3. (Note: only the first four unit types are currently implemented in the Pocket Battle program.)

Table 12.2 Unit Class Characteristics

Field	Description	Typical Value
index	Number used to choose a unit. Serves as a key field.	I used constants to simplify choosing a unit type, like INFANTRY and ARMOR.
UTYPE	Unit type. String used to define the type of unit.	"Infantry" or "Armor"
ATT	Attack level. Value used to calculate the relative attack strength of the unit.	Numeric value: 1 is standard, higher number means better attacker.
DEF	Defense level. Used to calculate the defensive strength of the unit.	Numeric value: 1 is standard; higher number means better at defense.
MOVE	Number of moves per turn	Numeric value: higher values will move more often per turn.
CLASS	Movement class of the unit. Could be "land," "sea," or "air."	String value: currently all units are "land."
COST	How expensive the unit is to produce	Numeric value: 1 is standard; higher numbers are more expensive.
IMG	Visual representation of unit	Currently use ASCII characters; could be bitmap strings
TRANS	Whether unit can be used to transport other units	Number of units this unit can carry. Currently no units are transports, so they all have a value of 0.

Table 12.3 Sample Unit Classes

Field	Infantry	Armor	Scout	Artillery	Transport	Destroyer
index	0	1	2	3	4	5
UTYPE	"Infantry"	"Armor"	"Scout"	"Artillery"	"Transport"	"Destroyer"
ATT	1	2	1	3	0	2
DEF	1	2	1	1	1	2
MOVE	1	2	3	1	2	3
CLASS	"land"	"land"	"land"	"land"	"sea"	"sea"
COST	1	4	2	2	2	4
IMG	"F"	"A"	"S"	"R"	"T"	"D"
TRANS	0	0	0	0	4	0

This table illustrates how the various unit class characteristics might be used. The table anticipates a number of types of units, and allows for units with very different characteristics.

Unit Data

As you can see from Table 12.3, much of the information about a unit is not related to the specific unit but to the unit's class. Each unit does have some specific data, however, as shown in Table 12.4.

If you look carefully at the kinds of information in the unit class table and the unit table, you will see that they are organized by *functional dependency.* In other words, the owner of a particular unit is related to that actual unit, but the attack strength of a unit is related to the *class* of the unit. The TYPE field is especially important, because it is used to link a unit to its particular class. Rather than having to store the attack, defense, and movement data for each unit, all I have to do is have a link to which type of unit it is and my program will be able to look up the relevant unit type data whenever it needs to.

Table 12.5 shows what some of the unit data for a typical game might look like.

Unit 0 has a name of "ScoA1" (this name helps immediately identify the unit as Scout unit 1 belonging to player A, but the name could be anything). Player A owns ScoA1, and it is type 2, which is the Scout type. If my program needs to

TABLE 12.4 UNIT DATA CHARACTERISTICS

Field	Description	Typical Value
index	Number used to choose a unit. Serves as a key field.	Each unit will have a unique number.
UNAME	Name of particular unit	String value. User can customize name of each unit, like "InfA1" or "7th Arty."
OWN	Determines owner of unit. If unit is unused or killed, will contain value "dead."	Will be "A," "B," or "dead."
TYPE	Describes type of unit	Numeric value; will be index of the unit class information (0 for infantry, 3 for artillery, and so on).

TABLE 12.5 SAMPLE UNIT DATA

Unit	0	1	2	3	4	5
index	0	1	2	3	4	5
UNAME	"ScoA1"	"ArmA2"	"ArmA3"	"ArtB1"	"ArmB2"	"ArmB3"
OWN	"A"	"A"	"A"	"B"	"B"	"B"
TYPE	2	1	1	3	1	1

know anything else about the unit (such as its movement rate or defense level) it can look up this information in column 2 of the unit class table. There is no need to have a separate table for each player's units, as the program can simply look through this table and extract any units with the OWN value of "A" to get all of player A's units, for example.

Map Data

In addition to unit data, the program needs to be concerned with map information. I chose to use a rectangular map (although many strategic games use hexagons) just to make the data representation a little easier to manage. The map table (illustrated in Table 12.6) will hold information about the various map squares.

Table 12.6 Map Square Data

Field	Description	Typical Value
row	Which row of the map this square is on	0 is top row
col	Which column of the map this square is on	0 is leftmost column
TER	Type of terrain in the square	Currently only . (normal), ~ (water), or C, (city)
PROD	Production value of the square	How much revenue this square is capable of producing. Currently not used.
SOWN	Square's owner	"A" or "B" if a player's city is on the square; otherwise, ""
SUNIT	Which unit is on currently on the square	Index of a unit. For example, if this value is 3, that means that unit 3 (say, "ArtB1") from the unit table is currently in the square. If no unit is in the square, SUNIT is "".

Notice how I related the unit data and the map data. There are two ways to think about this relationship. You could either say that the position of the map belongs to a unit, or a particular unit belongs to a square. How this issue is decided has implications, such as whether multiple units could be in the same square. I chose to store a unit designator in the map square table. This means I can only have one unit per square (of course, there are ways of getting beyond this limitation, but for now, just stay with me on this).

The map data table is different from the other tables in one very important regard. Rather than having one index each square has two indices, the row and the column. I did this just because it seems most natural to refer to a square based on its row and column rather than by a single identifier. However, to refer to a map square you must always have both a row and a column. This means that all references to the map data will be three-dimensional: row, col, and a constant for the specific data. For example, to find out what unit is in the square at row 3 and column 5, you might use this statement:

> **In the Real World**
>
> **In strict data normalization terms, it would be taboo to have two indices for a table, but it is justified in this particular situation because map data is two-dimensional by nature.**

```
alert(map[3][5][SUNIT]);
```

Relating the Different Types of Data

It is critically important to understand the kinds of data a program will need and to define how the various data elements are related. Once you have defined the structure of the data and figured out how to store the information according to this structure, the actual programming is reasonably straightforward. If you try to write a program as complex as Pocket Battle without carefully thinking about your data, you are guaranteed to get lost. Figure 12.7 shows the diagram I kept by my computer as I was writing this game. (My original was done with crayons, so I cleaned this one up a little for you!)

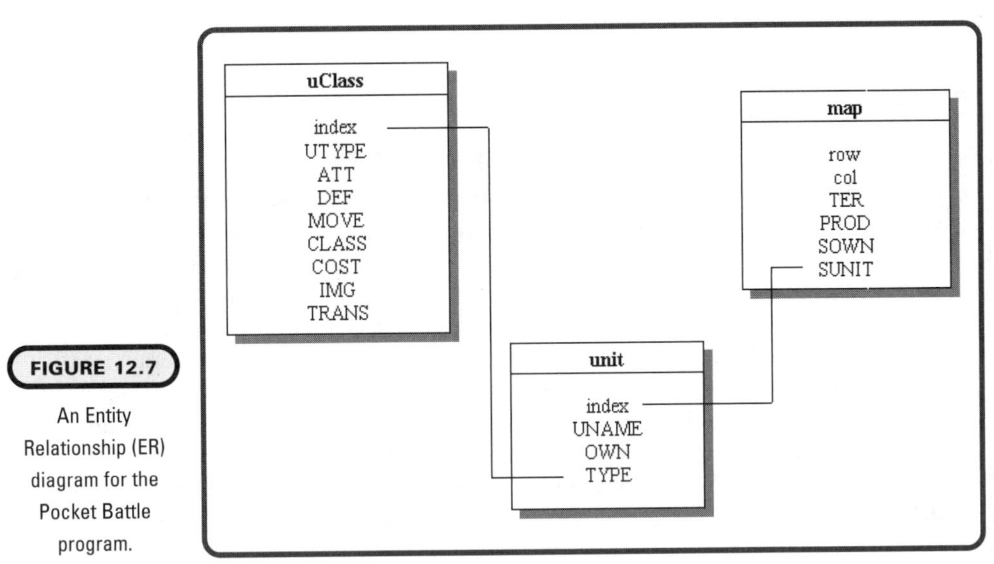

FIGURE 12.7

An Entity Relationship (ER) diagram for the Pocket Battle program.

The type of chart featured in Figure 12.7 is called an *Entity Relationship* diagram. It is useful for looking at the relationships between data elements. Each box in the diagram represents a table, and each row of a box represents a *field*, or specific information in that table. The lines between the boxes represent *joins*, or the relationships between the tables. As you can see, a relationship always involves using the index of one of the tables as a field in another table.

Creating Complex Data Types in PocketC

Once you have decided on a data design, you still have to implement that design. PocketC has relatively limited resources for advanced data design (at least by modern standards), but you can still use multidimensional arrays as a data storage mechanism. I decided to use the multidimensional array tool from PToolboxLib to create a series of arrays for storing the data. The program contains three main arrays, one per table. To simplify reading and manipulating the data, I created a constant for every field listed in the data tables. For example, the uClass array holds unit classes. It is a two-dimensional array. The first index refers to the index of the unit. The second dimension is accessed by a constant representing a field type. If I want to know the Attack level of unit type 2, I can access it as uClass[2][ATT]. The term *uClass* refers to the name of the array. The 2 stands for unit class number 2, and ATT is a constant that refers to the attack strength of the class. All the details appear in the code description. The important thing to understand is that all of the tables described in the first part of this chapter can be translated to arrays.

In the Real World

Unlike many modern programming languages, PocketC doesn't currently allow you to access a relational database management package for working with complex data types. It would be great to be able to create your data design in a high-end package (like Access or Oracle) and then work with the data in PocketC, but you're out of luck. (This may change—it is theoretically possible to attach to any .pdb file on the Palm already, but there just isn't a universal relational data management system there that will let you use it.) Many programming languages also allow you to create custom data types or objects. Sadly, PocketC does not support these features, either. However, the multi-dimensional array approach in this chapter is workable, even if it is a bit less efficient than the more modern approaches to data management.

The Pocket Battle Program

The rest of this chapter is dedicated to describing the Pocket Battle program. This is a longer program than those in the rest of the book, but it involves no new syntax. You have seen all of the concepts before. The only thing that is really new is the heavy emphasis on data. Since the program is so long, I will present it in chunks. See the CD-ROM version for the entire code.

The start of the code is very simple:

```
//pBattle
//basic framework for a strategy wargame
//Andy Harris, 6/5/01
```

```
library "PToolboxLib"
#include "Ccontrols.c"
```

As you can see, the program uses both PToolboxLib and Ccontrols. The only feature of PToolbox that I used is the multidimensional array capability. However, it would make a lot of sense to use some of the other features of this library to optimize and beautify the program. I used the Ccontrols library for the movement buttons and the menu system.

Creating the Constants

Pocket Battle incorporates many constants, which are used in a couple of ways. First, I have a set of constants for the directions. As you may recall from Chapter 6, it can be very useful to have direction constants whenever you are working with motion, because they can make your code easier to read. I also have a constant for every field in the data set. This way, when I'm working on the program, I can just say ATT when I'm looking for the attack strength of a unit, without having to remember which element of the uClass array corresponds to the ATT value. Use of these constants makes debugging this program much easier than it would be otherwise.

I have also created a set of constants that correspond to the various unit types.

```
//pBattle
//basic framework for a strategy wargame
//Andy Harris, 6/5/01

library "PToolboxLib"
#include "Ccontrols.c"

//direction constants
#define NW 0
#define N 1
#define NE 2
#define W 3
#define C 4
#define E 5
#define SW 6
#define S 7
#define SE 8

//unit class constants
```

```
#define UTYPE 0
#define ATT 1
#define DEF 2
#define MOVE 3
#define CLASS 4
#define COST 5
#define IMG 6
#define TRANS 7
#define nUnitClasses 4

//Unit constants
#define UNAME 0
#define OWN 1
#define TYPE 2
#define nUnits 30

//square constants
#define TER 0
#define PROD 1
#define SOWN 2
#define SUNIT 3

//unit types
#define INFANTRY 0
#define ARMOR 1
#define SCOUT 2
#define ARTILLERY 3
```

Constants are never absolutely necessary, but they are sound programming practice because they make it much easier to read, maintain, and modify your code.

Making the Global Variables

The Pocket Battle program also supports a number of variables. You might actually be surprised at how few variables are declared, given the complexity of the program!

```
//arrays
pointer uClass, unit, map;

//image buttons
```

```
Chandle imgDir[9];

//menus
Chandle mnbMain, mnuProgram;

//movement variables
int dx, dy;

//size of map
int ROWS = 10;                //number of rows
int COLS = 10;                //number of columns
int rowWidth, colWidth;       //height and width of a cell
int rowOff = 15;              //row offset - used to give top margin
int colOff = 15;              //col offset - used to give left margin

//main loop control
int keepGoing = true;
```

The program doesn't have a huge number of variables, but many of the variables are arrays, so I can still track a *lot* of data. (The Pocket Battle program probably handles about as much information in memory as all the other programs in this book combined.)

I created pointers for the three critical tables: uClass, unit, and map. Later on, I make arrays based on these pointers. Most of the data for the program will be stored in these arrays.

I made an array of Chandle objects for the direction buttons, a Chandle for the menu bar, and one more for the menu. There are actually a few other Chandle objects floating around in the program, but they are created locally inside functions (especially the `purchase unit` function).

The `dx` and `dy` variables are used to calculate changes in position, just like in the animation programs in Chapter 6.

Several variables are used to handle various features of the map. If you change the value of ROWS or COLS, the values of many of the other map-related variables will be affected. You can adjust the positioning of the map by changing the `rowOff` and `colOff` values.

The `keepGoing` variable is used in the same way I have used it throughout this book. It controls the main loop's behavior.

Creating the Menu

I decided to put all the commands that don't directly relate to game play into the menu system. This maximizes the space on the screen for game elements. Of course, it is necessary to create all the various menu items. The procedure for doing this is quite straightforward:

```
createMenus(){
  //set up menu bars
  mnbMain = Cmenubar();

  //Program menu
  mnuProgram = Cmenu(5, 60, 40);
  Csettopic(mnuProgram, "Program");
  Cadditem(mnuProgram, "About");
  Cadditem(mnuProgram, "Help");
  Cadditem(mnuProgram, "New Game");
  Cadditem(mnuProgram, "Exit");
  Caddmenu(mnbMain, mnuProgram);

} // end createMenus
```

Of course, if you want to add new commands to the program, you can simply add them to the existing menus. If you add a *lot* of new commands, you may want to consider adding another menu to the program.

Creating the Direction Buttons

The direction buttons are reasonably straightforward Ccontrol image objects. I made images rather than buttons so I could have graphics on them. Each image is a 10 x 10 bitmap, created with Bitmap Studio. I added a border around each

In the Real World

Images might be better than traditional buttons when you want to use graphics in a button. Graphics are useful because they can transcend language barriers (if they are clear). They also can be more direct than text (for example, a left arrow may be even more immediately recognizable than the word *left*). For this application, the main advantage of images was space. I could put recognizable arrows on buttons that are much tinier than text would have allowed. Image buttons can also add a GUI feel to a game that makes it seem more customized.

image, so it looks like a button. Since I have added a Cevent check to each image object, it will flash and respond to user input just like a normal button. I decided to store the image objects in an array based on the direction constants.

Here is the direction button generation code:

```
createButtons(){
  //create the direction buttons
  int dir;
  string picNW, picN, picNE, picE, picSE, picS, picSW, picW, picNW, picC;

  //dir buttons
  picNW="0a7f8c0c8049e4984944924804c0c7f8";
  picN="0affc8048849c4aa48848848048O4ffc";
  picNE="0a7f8c0c8049e48648a4924804c0c7f8";
  picE= "0a7f8c0c844824bf4824844804c0c7f8";
  picSE="0a7f8c0c8049248a48649e4804c0c7f8";
  picS="0a7f8c0c804884884aa49c4884c0c7f8";
  picSW="0a7f8c0c8049249449849e4804c0c7f8";
  picW="0a7f8c0c884904be4904884804c0c7f8";
  picNW="0a7f8c0c8049e4984944924804c0c7f8";
  picC="0a7f8c0ca148c49249248c4a14c0c7f8";

  imgDir[NW] = Cimage(110, 115, 10, 10);
  imgDir[N] =  Cimage(125, 115, 10, 10);
  imgDir[NE] = Cimage(140, 115, 10, 10);
  imgDir[W] =  Cimage(110, 130, 10, 10);
  imgDir[C] =  Cimage(125, 130, 10, 10);
  imgDir[E] =  Cimage(140, 130, 10, 10);
  imgDir[SW] = Cimage(110, 145, 10, 10);
  imgDir[S] =  Cimage(125, 145, 10, 10);
  imgDir[SE] = Cimage(140, 145, 10, 10);

  Csetcontent(imgDir[NW], picNW);
  Csetcontent(imgDir[N], picN);
  Csetcontent(imgDir[NE], picNE);
  Csetcontent(imgDir[W], picW);
  Csetcontent(imgDir[C], picC);
  Csetcontent(imgDir[E], picE);
  Csetcontent(imgDir[SW], picSW);
  Csetcontent(imgDir[S], picS);
```

```
    Csetcontent(imgDir[SE], picSE);

    //show all the buttons
    for (dir = NW; dir <= SE; dir++){
      Cdraw(imgDir[dir]);
    } // end for loop

} //end createButtons
```

For design purposes, I found it easiest to create a series of string variables to hold all the images. I then used these images in the `Csetcontent` function to apply the various bitmaps to the image controls.

When you assign a bitmap to an image object, be sure that the bitmap is the same size as the image object, or you will get strange results.

The last part of this function illustrates why I used an array for storing the image buttons. Because the elements are in an array, I could use one Cdraw function inside a loop to draw all the images at once. This is much more efficient than having nine different Cdraw commands. There are a number of other places in the code where having the direction controls stored as an array saves effort.

As a general rule, if you are likely to think of a bunch of entities as one unit, it probably makes sense to make those elements an array. I'm almost always working with all the buttons within a loop, so an array makes a lot of sense here.

Initializing the Unit Class Data

One thing you should do early on is generate the various unit types. I wrote a function to populate the unit class array with a number of units. The procedure is actually very simple: it creates the uClass array and adds items to it.

```
initUClass(){
  //create the unit classes
  //modify this function to add more unit classes
  uClass = Array("s, " + nUnitClasses + ", 8");

  //define infantry
  uClass[INFANTRY][UTYPE] = "Infantry";
  uClass[INFANTRY][ATT] = "1";
  uClass[INFANTRY][DEF] = "1";
```

```
  uClass[INFANTRY][MOVE] = "1";
  uClass[INFANTRY][CLASS] = "Lnd";
  uClass[INFANTRY][COST] = "1";
  uClass[INFANTRY][IMG] = "F";
  uClass[INFANTRY][TRANS] = "0";

  //define armor
  uClass[ARMOR][UTYPE] = "Armor";
  uClass[ARMOR][ATT] = "2";
  uClass[ARMOR][DEF] = "2";
  uClass[ARMOR][MOVE] = "2";
  uClass[ARMOR][CLASS] = "Lnd";
  uClass[ARMOR][COST] = "4";
  uClass[ARMOR][IMG] = "A";
  uClass[ARMOR][TRANS] = "0";

  //define scout
  uClass[SCOUT][UTYPE] = "Scout";
  uClass[SCOUT][ATT] = "1";
  uClass[SCOUT][DEF] = "1";
  uClass[SCOUT][MOVE] = "3";
  uClass[SCOUT][CLASS] = "Lnd";
  uClass[SCOUT][COST] = "2";
  uClass[SCOUT][IMG] = "S";
  uClass[SCOUT][TRANS] = "0";

  //define artillery
  uClass[ARTILLERY][UTYPE] = "Artillery";
  uClass[ARTILLERY][ATT] = "3";
  uClass[ARTILLERY][DEF] = "1";
  uClass[ARTILLERY][MOVE] = "1";
  uClass[ARTILLERY][CLASS] = "Lnd";
  uClass[ARTILLERY][COST] = "2";
  uClass[ARTILLERY][IMG] = "R";
  uClass[ARTILLERY][TRANS] = "0";

} // end unitUClass
```

I created the array with the `Array()` function from the PToolbox library. Recall that this function takes one string parameter, which contains a data type and then numbers for the array dimensions. I created a two-dimensional array of strings, with `nUnits` by 8 values. The first dimension refers to the number of unit types available (which is stored in the variable `nUnits`). The second dimension refers to the number of fields per unit type, which is eight. Since `nUnits` is currently set to 4, the `Array()` function reserves space in memory for a 4 x 8 table of data. I decided to use string data for convenience, because any type of information can be saved in a string value, and PocketC's loose type casting makes it very easy to use the string values as any other type of data.

The rest of the function describes the various unit types. As you can see, having the constants makes it much more clear what data I am trying to store.

If you want to add new units, simply change the value of `nUnits`, create a new unit constant, and create a new block of code to initialize the units.

A unit editor would be a terrific addition to this program. Perhaps you could store all unit types in a database and load them into arrays when the program starts. When the user wants to create a new unit type, the new unit is added to the database so it will be available for future purchase.

IN THE REAL WORLD

During most of the testing for this program, I had only two unit types (armor and infantry). I knew that if I designed the data properly, the code would work the same no matter how many unit types I had. I added the last two units after most of the program was functioning properly.

Buying the Units

In addition to creating the unit types, there must be some way to populate the unit table. This table is also a two-dimensional array. The first dimension is the total number of units allowed, and the second dimension is the number of fields per unit, which is three.

The code in this section isn't what I wrote first—I took a detour that was actually a shortcut and hard-coded in a set of units, much like the `initUnitClass()` function. This let me focus on other parts of the game. Once the main game engine was working, I added the unit purchase screen. I figured a unit purchase system was irrelevant if the movement and combat systems didn't work, so I decided on a simple way to populate the unit data until those other parts of the program were working. This is a common strategy among programmers—if there's an easy alternative, use it. Even if it's not as good as what you eventually want to have, it'll clear the air until you've settled the bits of the program that don't have shortcut approximations available. The hard-coding for the units shows up later in the chapter.

I wanted to give the players some ability to choose their starting forces. I also wanted them to have different but roughly equal forces. I decided to use a unit purchase system to achieve this effect. Each player has a given number of resource points to spend on units—the more capable units are more expensive. One part of the game is figuring out the most cost-effective unit mix for a particular player's strategy and a particular situation.

Setting Up the Unit Purchase Screen

To make the unit purchase system work well, I had to leave the primary screen and generate a new screen. In fact, the unit purchase system feels a lot like a completely separate program. It has its own set of variables, its own controls, and its own event handlers. To make it easier to describe what's going on, I'll break this long function into a few parts. Here's the code that sets up the stage for unit purchases:

```
buyUnits(){
  //allow players to purchase units

  int uNum;           //unit number
  int i;                     //generic counting variable
  int aCash;          //player a's cash allowance
  int bCash;          //player b's cash allowance
  int evt;                   //event handler
  int unitCounter;    //unit counter (separate value for a and b)
  string defName;     //default unit name

  //create array of buttons - one for each class
  Chandle btnUtype[nUnitClasses];
  Chandle lblCash;

  //starting money related to grid size
  //Makes placement algorithm simpler
  aCash = ROWS;
  bCash = ROWS;

  //create the unit array
  unit = Array("s, " + nUnits + ", 3");
  lblCash = Clabel( 20, 140, 100, 0, 0, 1);

  //clear out all units
```

```
for (uNum = 0; uNum < nUnits; uNum++){
  unit[uNum][UNAME] = "";
  unit[uNum][OWN] = "dead";
  unit[uNum][TYPE] = "";
} // end for loop

//build selection screen
saveg();
graph_on();
clearg();

//create buttons for the unit types
for(i = 0; i < nUnitClasses; i++){
  btnUtype[i] = Cbutton( 20, (i * 30) + 20, 100, 15, 1, 3);
  Csetcontent(btnUtype[i], uClass[i][UTYPE]);
  Cdraw(btnUtype[i]);
} // end for loop
```

This function sets up a reasonably large number of variables. It creates a unit counter that helps keep track of which unit in the `unit()` array is being created. I also have a unit counter that is used to count units in each player's inventory. This second unit counter is used to determine the default unit name.

The function also creates "bank accounts" for the two players. After some experimentation, I decided to relate the amount of money each player is given to the size of the map. This has two effects: It limits the number of units on the board to a reasonable number, and it guarantees that there will not be more units per side than the number of rows on the map. This is important for initial unit placement on the map.

I created a number of Chandles for Ccontrols. I felt that the easiest way for the user to choose units was to tap buttons on the screen. To keep things dynamic, I had the function create buttons based on the uClass table. Basically, the program generates an array of Cbutton objects—one per element in the unit class table. Each button is labeled with the name of the corresponding unit type. I also created a label object to hold the current player's bank balance.

The entire unit array will be read by the program, even if not all the units are used, so I started by loading legal starting values into every element in the array. But I didn't want unpurchased units to be able to do anything, so all elements of the unit array start out with the owner listed as "dead." If a unit is listed as dead, it will not move or fight. (Seems obvious, I guess, but nothing's obvious to a computer.)

I built the purchase screen by saving the current screen with the `saveg()` function, then clearing the screen and adding a new title.

The function then steps through the various unit types, building a button for each type of unit. The line

```
Csetcontent(btnUtype[i], uClass[i][UTYPE]);
```

can be read as "set the content of the number *i* button to the unit type of the *i* member of the uClass array."

Purchasing the Units

Once the screen has been set up, the `buyUnits()` function creates a pair of event loops to let the users select their units.

```
uNum = 0;
//Player A purchase
title("Player A choose forces");
unitCounter = 1;
while(aCash > 0){
  Csetcontent(lblCash, "Cash: " + aCash);
  Cdraw(lblCash);
  evt = event(1);
  for(i = 0; i < nUnitClasses; i++){
    //check each unit type button to see if it's been clicked
    if(Cevent(btnUtype[i], evt)){

      aCash = aCash - (int)uClass[i][COST];
      if(aCash < 0){
        alert("you can't afford that!");
        aCash = aCash + (int)uClass[i][COST];
      } else {
        //default name is first three characters of unit name
        //followed by owner and unit number
        defName = substr(uClass[i][UTYPE], 0, 3);
        defName = defName + "A";
        defName = defName + unitCounter;
        unitCounter++;

        //create the unit
        unit[uNum][UNAME] = getsd("Name of this unit?", defName);
        unit[uNum][OWN] = "A";
```

```
          unit[uNum][TYPE] = i;
          uNum++;
        } // end 'can you afford it' if
      } // end 'did this button get clicked' if
    } // end for loop
  } // end while loop

  //Player B purchase
  title("Player B choose forces");
  unitCounter = 1;
  while(bCash > 0){
    Csetcontent(lblCash, "Cash: " + bCash);
    Cdraw(lblCash);
    evt = event(1);
    for(i = 0; i < nUnitClasses; i++){
      if(Cevent(btnUtype[i], evt)){
        bCash = bCash - (int)uClass[i][COST];
        if(bCash < 0){
          alert("you can't afford that!");
          bCash = bCash + (int)uClass[i][COST];
        } else {
          //default name is first three characters of unit name
          //followed by owner and unit number
          defName = substr(uClass[i][UTYPE], 0, 3);
          defName = defName + "B";
          defName = defName + unitCounter;
          unitCounter++;

          unit[uNum][UNAME] = getsd("Name of this unit?", defName);
          unit[uNum][OWN] = "B";
          unit[uNum][TYPE] = i;
          uNum++;
        } // end 'can you afford it' if
      } // end 'did this button get clicked' if
    } // end for loop
  } // end while loop

  restoreg();

} // end buyUnits
```

This part of the function lets the users select their units from the screen. First player A selects forces, and then it is player B's turn. The code will actually be very similar for the two players, so I'll just describe the player A code in depth.

The `uNum` variable starts out at 0. This number will determine the location of a particular unit in the units array. The `unitCounter` variable starts out at 1. It is used to create default unit names. This way, if player B has two infantry units, they won't have the same name. This isn't a critical part of the program, but it is nice.

Unit purchases happen inside a large `while` loop that continues as long as the player has cash on hand. As soon as the player runs out of money, the loop will exit.

The `lblCash` label is updated to contain the amount of cash the player currently has available. The program then pauses for an event, storing the result in `evt`.

Next the program must check all the unit class buttons to see which one was clicked (if any). Since the buttons are arranged in an array, it is convenient to use a `for` loop to check each button. If a button has been clicked, that means the user is interested in creating a unit of that type.

When a player attempts to purchase a unit, the first thing the function does is subtract the appropriate amount (COST from the uClass table) from the player's cash. If the player cannot afford the unit, the money is put back in the account and the player can try again. Otherwise, a new unit is created by setting the appropriate values in the unit array.

Most of the work involves creating a default unit name. I decided to implement this feature so that units would have recognizable names. A player who wants to change the names of the various units (for example, to play out some historical scenario) is welcome to do so. The default name is reasonably descriptive without taking too much space. I took the first three letters of the unit type, followed by the owner value, and the unit number for the player. For example, if the third unit player A chooses is an infantry unit, the default name of that unit will be "infA3."

It is necessary to store the owner and unit type in the unit table, so I added lines to perform these tasks. I then incremented `uNum` so the next unit could be created.

I repeated largely the same sequence of steps for player B. Once both players have finished selecting units, the appropriate number of entries in the unit table will be non-dead. All the units for player A will occur earlier in the array than the units for player B.

Initializing the Unit Data

Below is the original unit creation function I used. It is very simple, but it does the job of setting up a number of units. I used it extensively for the early testing when I was concerned with the movement and combat portions of the game. Later, after I had finished the `buyUnit()` function, I took out any calls to the `createUnits()` function but I kept it in the code so that I can reuse it later when I want to test some more. (For example, if I make extensive changes to the combat system I may need to test the program many times. It would be tedious to purchase units each time, so I decided to just keep this function around to have a set of units ready to go. This is another example of what programmers call an "Easter egg.")

```
createUnits(){
  //used for testing, so I could check with a pre-defined set of units
  //no longer necessary
  unit = Array("s, " + nUnits + ", 3");

  unit[0][UNAME] = "InfA1";
  unit[0][OWN] = "A";
  unit[0][TYPE] = INFANTRY;

  unit[1][UNAME] = "InfA2";
  unit[1][OWN] = "A";
  unit[1][TYPE] = INFANTRY;

  unit[2][UNAME] = "InfA3";
  unit[2][OWN] = "A";
  unit[2][TYPE] = INFANTRY;

  unit[3][UNAME] = "InfA4";
  unit[3][OWN] = "A";
  unit[3][TYPE] = INFANTRY;

  unit[4][UNAME] = "ArmA1";
  unit[4][OWN] = "A";
  unit[4][TYPE] = ARMOR;

  unit[5][UNAME] = "InfB1";
  unit[5][OWN] = "B";
  unit[5][TYPE] = INFANTRY;
```

```
    unit[6][UNAME] = "InfB2";
    unit[6][OWN] = "B";
    unit[6][TYPE] = INFANTRY;

    unit[7][UNAME] = "InfB3";
    unit[7][OWN] = "B";
    unit[7][TYPE] = INFANTRY;

    unit[8][UNAME] = "InfB4";
    unit[8][OWN] = "B";
    unit[8][TYPE] = INFANTRY;

    unit[9][UNAME] = "ArmB1";
    unit[9][OWN] = "B";
    unit[9][TYPE] = ARMOR;

} // end createUnits
```

The code for `createUnits()` is exceptionally straightforward. I created the array of units and populated it. Note that when I was using this routine, I had no other unit types available besides infantry and armor. It would make sense for testing purposes to have armies consisting of all the unit types that are available, so you can check for bugs or inconsistencies in the behavior of a particular unit type.

Initializing the Map Data

In addition to the units and unit types, map data is central to the Pocket Battle program. I have a couple of functions designed to help work with map information. The first simply initializes a blank map, ensuring that every element of the map array begins with legal values. It creates a simple map with no water squares, and with cities in the northwest and southeast corners.

```
createMap(){
  //create the default blank map
  int row, col;

  //generate the map array
  map = Array("s, " + ROWS + ", " + COLS + ", 4");
  for (row = 0; row < ROWS; row++){
    for (col = 0; col < COLS; col++){
      map[row][col][TER] = ".";
      map[row][col][PROD] = "";
```

```
      map[row][col][SOWN] = "";
      map[row][col][SUNIT] = "";
    } // end col loop
  } // end row loop

  //add cities

  //A capital at northwest corner;
  map[0][0][TER] = "C";
  map[0][0][SOWN] = "A";

  //B capital at southeast corner;
  map[ROWS -1][COLS -1][TER] = "C";
  map[ROWS -1][COLS -1][SOWN] = "B";

} // end createMap
```

The first task is to generate the map array. Remember that map information has two indices, row and col, so my map array is a three-dimensional array. Each element in the map can have four pieces of information (besides its indices).

Once the array was created, I needed to initialize it so that each map square would start out with legal values. The easiest way to do this is with a pair of nested `for` loops. First, I step through each row with a `for` loop. Inside that loop, I have another `for` loop that steps through each column. Inside *that* loop will be code that happens once per square in the map. The value map[row][col] can be thought of as the current square. Inside the second `for` loop, I'll set default values for each square. The TER (terrain) should be normal terrain, noted by a period (.) character. The PROD (production) value will be "", which means no production occurs in that square. This version of Pocket Battle doesn't implement production, but perhaps you will want to add it to the program yourself. The SOWN (square owner) value is set to "", because no player owns any of the squares (except the cities, which I'll set up later). The SUNIT (square unit) value also starts out blank ("") because the unit placement will occur in a different function.

Once all the squares have default values, I add the two cities. Adding a city is a simple matter of changing the SOWN and TER values for a particular square. I start by setting the default value of every square on the map with the nested loops. Then, I deal with the two exceptional squares—the players' home cities. The following lines:

```
//add cities
```

```
//A capital at northwest corner;
map[0][0][TER] = "C";
map[0][0][SOWN] = "A";

//B capital at southeast corner;
map[ROWS -1][COLS -1][TER] = "C";
map[ROWS -1][COLS -1][SOWN] = "B";
```

modify the two city squares by assigning the city terrain and owner values.

Drawing the Map

Once the map data has been generated, it needs to be displayed to the user. Actually, this will happen many times because the map data will change when the units move, and the map will be redrawn after every move.

```
displayMap(){
  //show the current map screen
  int row, col;
  int dir;

  colWidth = 100/COLS;
  rowWidth = 100/ROWS;

  graph_on();
  clearg();
  title("pocket battle");
  for (row = 0; row < ROWS; row++){
    for (col = 0; col < COLS; col++){
      //invert cities owned by B
      if (map[row][col][SOWN] == "B"){
        textattr(0, 2, 0);
      } else {
        textattr(0, 1, 0);
      } // end if

      //draw the terrain of the current square
      text( (col * colWidth) + colOff,
            (row * rowWidth) + rowOff,
            map[row][col][TER]);

    } // end col loop
```

```
    } // end row loop

    //display direction buttons
    for (dir = NW; dir <= SE; dir++){
      Cdraw(imgDir[dir]);
    } // end for loop

} // end displayMap
```

Each time this function occurs, it redraws the map data from the map array. It should not surprise you that the function is based on a pair of nested loops.

At each square, it checks to see if that square is owned by player B. (As the program stands now, only the city in the southeast corner will have this property.) If so, I used the `textattr()` function to set inverse video so that the "C" for city will show up on a black background. I then drew the terrain associated with the square at the appropriate space on the map. To draw on the screen, I used a technique similar to the one used in the Life program in Chapter 9. I calculated a width and height for each cell by dividing the screen size (100 x 100 pixels) by the number of rows and columns in the map. I also added an offset to the row and column values so the map would not be directly on the top and left-hand borders of the screen.

In the Real World

It is no coincidence that this technique is directly borrowed from a completely different program. It is very common for programmers to keep an entire toolbox of handy routines that they dust off for new use. As you gain more experience as a programmer, you'll have more and more of these routines available, and you'll get more adept at recognizing when you can recycle an algorithm. The fact that a code fragment might be useful again in a completely different program should also encourage you to design your functions to be as reusable as possible. In general, this means you should avoid using literal values (like 10) and use a variable or constant (like rowOff) instead.

Once the terrain was drawn I redrew the direction buttons, because the screen was cleared at the beginning of the function. Since the buttons are housed in an array, it's a simple matter to redraw them all with a loop.

Printing the Units

As I was working on the unit purchasing system, I wanted an easy way to check the current contents of the unit table. I wrote a quick function that will print out the entire contents of the unit array and display the values to a text screen.

```
printUnits(){
  //print out the units - debugging tool
  //no longer used
  //Could easily be modified to save units to a memo

  int uNum;

  saveg();
  graph_off();
  clear();
  puts("# \tname \town \ttype \n");
  for(uNum = 0; uNum < nUnits; uNum++){
    puts(uNum + "\t");
    puts(unit[uNum][UNAME] + "\t");
    puts(unit[uNum][OWN] + "\t");
    puts(unit[uNum][TYPE] + "\n");
  } // end for loop

  wait();
  graph_on();
  restoreg();

} // end printUnits
```

This function is fairly simple, but it was a big help. It quickly told me what was in the unit array. This was handy because one of my earliest attempts was not filling the array correctly. I used this routine much like an electrician might use an electrical probe, to see the values of my array during the operation.

The function simply steps through all the units in the unit array, and prints out the three fields of each unit. Like the `createUnits()` function, this function is not called in the working version of the program, but I kept it in the code for two reasons: I know that I will continue working on this program, so it will be nice to have this function around as a debugging tool. Also, I've been imagining a feature that would allow the players to save and load a set of units. It would be easy to modify this routine (with an `mmfind()` and a few `mmputs()` functions) so that it saves all unit data to a memo. Then all I would need to write would be the function to load the units from the memo.

Placing the Units

The `placeUnits()` function is used to generate an initial position for each unit. This routine was a little tricky because of the way I set up my data. Originally I had planned for all units to start in the player's city, but since each square can hold only one unit at a time, that would not be possible. I considered changing the data design, but then came up with another solution I liked just as well. I decided to write a routine that would place all the units along the sides of the map. The first unit for player A will be placed in the northwest corner of the map. The next unit will be placed in the next row to the south, but still along the west edge of the map. Player B's units are placed along the eastern edge of the map, but the first unit is placed at the southeast corner, and subsequent units are placed farther to the north. If a player had more units than there are rows, the algorithm would run into problems, but I avoided this by giving the players limited cash. Since the amount of money the players earn is related to the number of rows in the map, the largest number of units each player can own is equal to the number of rows. For example, a player who purchases all infantry units (at a price of 1) could purchase 10 units, which is the same as the number of rows. It will not be possible to purchase more units than there are rows in the map.

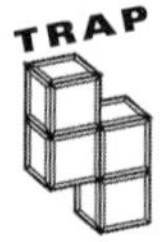

The unit allocation problem illustrates one of the reasons you should plan your data carefully. You might not expect that the amount of cash you give the players to start could cause a bug in unit placement, or that deciding to store units in the map data rather than position in the unit data could have so many consequences. If you plan the data well, your chances of spotting these dependencies are much better.

The code for the `placeUnits()` function is not difficult to understand once you know what it is supposed to do:

```
placeUnits(){
  //initial placement of units on map
  //put all A units on left hand side from top
  //put all B units on right hand side from bottom
```

```
//first unit created goes closest to base

int row, col, uNum;
int numAs = 0;
int numBs = 0;

for(uNum = 0; uNum < nUnits; uNum++){
  switch (unit[uNum][OWN]){
    case "A":
      col = 0;
      row = numAs;
      numAs++;
      map[row][col][SUNIT] = uNum;
      break;
    case "B":
      col = COLS - 1;
      row = ROWS - 1 - numBs;
      numBs++;
      map[row][col][SUNIT] = uNum;
      break;
    case "dead":
      //do nothing, because this unit is unused
  } // end switch
} // end for loop

/*
//old algorithm for placing static units
//used for debugging, but no longer necessary
map[0][0][SUNIT] = 0;
map[1][0][SUNIT] = 1;
map[2][0][SUNIT] = 2;
map[3][0][SUNIT] = 3;
map[4][0][SUNIT] = 4;

map[5][9][SUNIT] = 5;
map[6][9][SUNIT] = 6;
map[7][9][SUNIT] = 7;
```

```
  map[8][9][SUNIT] = 8;
  map[9][9][SUNIT] = 9;
  */
} // end placeUnits
```

I started by setting two counters to determine how many A units had been placed (numAs) and how many B units had been positioned (numBs). I then stepped through every unit in the unit array.

I checked the unit's owner to see who owns the unit. If player A owns the unit, it should always be placed in column 0 (the western column). The row is determined by `numAs`, so if `numAs` is 0, it should be placed in the zero row (which is the top one). The `numAs` variable is incremented each time an A unit is placed.

If the unit is owned by player B, the algorithm is similar. The column will always be COLS −1.

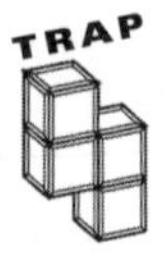

Remember that the last element will be COLS -1, because the counting starts with 0, not 1. Even experienced programming authors forget this sometimes and end up with error messages that can keep them up all night. When I made a mistake in this function, the Palm claimed to be out of memory. It wasn't really out of memory. (I found this out after I deleted everything I could from the device.) Instead, it kept trying to access memory values that occurred after the end of my array.

If the unit's owner is listed as "dead" it is unnecessary to process this unit.

Note that I have an alternate unit placement scheme commented out at the bottom of the function. I used this before I had the more elaborate unit positioning algorithm in place. I also found the direct positioning version of the algorithm more useful when I was testing the combat system, because I could begin the program with the units right next to each other. This allowed much quicker testing because I didn't have to move the units across the map to see if my combat system was working correctly. (It wasn't, at first, but I got it with enough testing.)

Drawing the Units

Once all the units have been positioned and the map has been drawn, it is necessary to draw the units on the map. I chose to draw the entire map first and then draw the units on top of the terrain data. This approach seems to work pretty well. It is not a difficult function:

```
drawUnits(){
  //draw units on map in correct squares
  string uid, uclassname, uimage;
  int row, col;
  for (row = 0; row < ROWS; row++){
    for (col = 0; col < ROWS; col++){
      if (map[row][col][SUNIT] != ""){
        uid = map[row][col][SUNIT];
        uclassname = unit[uid][TYPE];
        uimage = uClass[uclassname][IMG];
        //highlight player B's units
        if (unit[uid][OWN] == "A"){
          textattr(0, 1, 0);
        } else {
          textattr(0, 2, 0);
        } // end if
        //draw the unit at the appropriate spot
        text( (col * colWidth) + colOff,
              (row * rowWidth) + rowOff,
              uimage);
        textattr(0, 1, 0);
      } // end if
    } // end col loop
  } // end row loop
} // end drawUnits
```

Since the unit position is stored in the map data, I used a pair of nested `for` loops to step through every square in the map. I checked the SUNIT value of each square to determine if a unit is present in that square. If the SUNIT value of a square is "", the square contains no units. If it has any other value, the function will need to do some work. I extracted the unit's key field from the map table and stored it in the variable `uid`. I used this value to get the unit's class, and stored the class in uClassName. I used this value to find the text associated with the unit.

In the Real World

Using the map array to get a value related to the unit array, and then using this unit value to find information from the unit class array, may seem like a very convoluted way to get things done. Though it is awkward on the surface to have all these related tables, the effort is worthwhile, because all the information is available if you know how to find it, and none of the data is repeated. When you are working with relational data such as the tables in this program, it is critical that you have an ER diagram or something similar available so that you can see how all the data elements are related. Once you get used to the cross-referencing, you will find it far easier than it appears at first glance. The main skill is to determine the following:

- What information do I know right now (say, the unit number from map data)?
- What information do I need (what character to print for this unit)?
- What is the path to the data? (The unit ID connects the map data to the unit data, and the unit's CLASS field connects the unit table to the uClass table.)

It takes a little practice to get used to this type of thinking, but doing so will pay off in the long run with programs that can be easily extended.

Once I determined the character to draw, I viewed the unit's owner to see if the unit should be highlighted. I then drew the unit on the screen using the algorithm described in the `drawUnits()` function. Finally, I reset the text attributes so that any subsequent drawing would be done in the normal color scheme.

Displaying the Online Help

This program is a bit complicated to play. (At least it is more so than most of the other examples in this book.) It makes sense to give the user some kind of online help system, since PDA users are notorious for *never* reading manuals. The online help system I employed here is borrowed from the graphics program in Chapter 5, with some minor modifications.

```
showHelp(){
  //simple but functional online help system
  saveg();
  graph_off();
  clear();
```

```
title("Overview");
puts("Pocket Battle is a simple two player tactical wargame. ");
puts("The purpose of the game is to storm the enemy's capital ");
puts("city while protecting your own city. You can customize  ");
puts("the battle by choosing your own forces and designing your ");
puts("own maps. ");
puts("\n\n(click for more)");
wait();
clear();

title("Purchasing Units");
puts("When the game begins, player A will be able to purchase  ");
puts("his units. Each player will start out with 10 credits. ");
puts("Player A can choose from the available unit types by  ");
puts("clicking on the appropriate buttons. The more powerful  ");
puts("cost more, so choose wisely. After player A has chosen ");
puts("his units, player B will get a turn. ");
puts("\n\n(click for more)");
wait();
clear();

title("Loading a Map");
puts("Once the units have been purchased, You will be given the  ");
puts("opportunity to load a map for your combat. If you have not ");
puts("created a map (or wish to fight on a plain map) simply click ");
puts("OK without typing a map name, and you will begin the battle. ");
puts("\n\n(click for more)");
wait();
clear();

title("Creating a Map");
puts("You can create custom maps for Pocket Battle with memo pad ");
puts("or any other text editor that can create memo documents.  ");
puts("The first line should be the name of your map. The rest  ");
puts("of the file should have ten lines of ten characters each. ");
puts("Use . (period) for normal terrain and ~ (tilde) for water  ");
puts("terrain.  ");
puts("\n\n(click for more)");
wait();
clear();
```

```
  title("Moving your Units");
  puts("One unit at a time will be highlighted. To move this unit, ");
  puts("click on one of the small buttons in the lower right corner ");
  puts("of the screen. The center button tells the unit to stay in ");
  puts("place. Some units can move more than one time in a turn. ");
  puts("\n\n(click for more)");
  wait();
  clear();

  title("Combat");
  puts("To fight with an enemy unit, simply move onto the square  ");
  puts("containing that unit. Pocket Battle will analyze the ");
  puts("likelihood that your attack will be successful based on the ");
  puts("attack strength of your unit and the defensive rating of the ");
  puts("defender. Some units can attack more than once per turn. ");
  puts("\n\n(click for more)");
  wait();
  clear();

  title("Winning the Game");
  puts("The game is won by moving one of your units onto the opponent's
");
  puts("capital city. Try to balance your forces to lead an effective  ");
  puts("attack while retaining an adequate defensive force. ");
  puts("\n\n(click for more)");
  wait();
  clear();

  title("About Pocket Battle");
  puts("Pocket Battle was written by Andy Harris as an example for the ");
  puts("book 'Palm Programming for the Absolute Beginner'. Please see ");
  puts("that book for complete source code in PocketC as well as some  ");
  puts("hints on how to improve and customize the game. ");
  puts("(click to return)");
  wait();

  graph_on();
  restoreg();
} // end showHelp
```

The function begins by storing the current screen and switching to text mode. It then prints out a screen full of information and waits for a response. When the user taps on the screen, a new screen appears. This process continues until all the screens have been displayed.

There are other ways of presenting online help, but this approach is simple and straightforward.

Saving the Map

Once I got the basic functionality of the program working, I wanted at least one more terrain type, to allow for more interesting tactical situations. I decided to add water terrain that would be impassable by all units. If you have variable terrain, you must have some way to manipulate the terrain. I first thought of building a map editor, but quickly realized that it would be much easier to let the user create the map as a text file in Memo Pad and import that file. As a starting point, I wrote functions to save and load a map in memory. As the program neared completion, it became apparent that the `save map` function would not be necessary, but I kept it in the code because I will need it later if I do choose to create my own map editor. (Perhaps I'll build one based on the new memo editor in PToolbox!) The code for the `saveMap()` routine simply translates the terrain data of the map array to a text file.

```
saveMap(){
  //saves a map to a text file for editing
  //used for debugging. No longer needed, but
  //could be useful if you add a map editor to the program.
  string fileName;
  int row, col;

  fileName = gets("Name of map?");

  mmnew();
  mmputs(fileName + "\n");
  for (row = 0; row < ROWS; row++){
    for (col = 0; col < COLS; col++){
      mmputs(map[row][col][TER]);
    } // end col for
    mmputs("\n");
```

```
    } // end row for
    mmclose();
} // end saveMap
```

The first thing the function does is ask the user for a map name. Once the user enters a name, the program creates a new memo and places the name at the top line.

The function then steps through a pair of nested loops looking at each cell. The terrain for each cell is written to the memo. The function adds a Newline character to the end of every row.

This function does not save the entire map, just the terrain. To save the entire map including unit data, you'd need to go through this loop four times, once for each field in the memo table.

Loading the Map

The `loadMap()` procedure is used to load a map from a Memo Pad database. Maps are expected to start with the map name then consist of ROWS lines of COLS characters each. Each character should be a terrain value (at the moment, legal values are '.', 'C', and '~').

```
loadMap(){
    //loads a map from memo pad
    //this function will crash if the map is too small!

    string fileName;
    int row, col;
    string nextLine;
    string currentChar;

    //create a default map first, so the array exists.
    createMap();
    fileName = gets("Name of map to open?");
    if (mmfind(fileName)){
        //grab and toss title line
        mmgetl();
        for(row = 0; row < ROWS; row++){
            nextLine = mmgetl();
            for(col = 0; col < COLS; col++){
```

```
        currentChar = substr(nextLine, col, 1);
        map[row][col][TER] = currentChar;
      } // end col loop
    } // end row loop
  } else {
    //if you can't find the file (or it's blank) keep with the default map
    alert("sorry, " + fileName + " not found");
    alert("using blank map");
  } // end if
} // end loadMap
```

The function begins by calling createMap. The `createMap()` function actually creates the map array and ensures there are legal values in each square. It also creates the default map, which is all normal terrain except the cities in the two corners.

The `loadMap()` function then asks the user for a map name. The `mmfind()` function opens up a memo file, but it also returns the value `false` if it cannot find the file. If the user enters no file name, or a file name that PocketC cannot find, the function simply tells the user that the file was not found and begins play on the default map. If the file has been found, the bulk of the `loadMap()` function is dedicated to reading the map file and using this data to update the map array.

I used the `mmgetl()` function to grab the first line of the memo, which will be the title. I don't really need the title, but the program needs to get to the next line of the memo, which is where all the real action begins.

I used the now-familiar pair of nested loops to step through rows and columns. For each row, I retrieved a line from the memo pad. I then used the `substr()` function to extract a particular character. The character is then stored to the TER field of the appropriate map square.

Checking the Menus

The menu system is the user's main way of communicating anything but movement and unit purchasing to the program. The Pocket Battle menus are very simple, but they do provide a useful interface to all the various utility functions of the program without taking up too much space on that tiny little screen. As usual, I have chosen to write a function to delegate control based on a command.

```
checkMenus(){
  //standard menu checking routine
```

```
  string command;
  //checks the menus for an input
  if(Cgetcursel(mnuProgram)!= -1){
    command = Cgetcontent(mnuProgram);
  } // end if
  switch(command){
    case "About":
      alert("Pocket Battle by Andy Harris");
      break;
    case "Help":
      showHelp();
      break;
    case "New Game":
      newGame();
      break;
    case "Exit":
      exit();
    default:
      alert(command);
  } // end switch
} // end checkMenus
```

If the user clicks on the menu bar, the function extracts the command from the only menu available. Of course, if you add another menu you'll need to add the code to extract a command from that menu. Most of the commands simply call upon functions you have already seen in action. Note that the `newGame()` function has not yet been defined, but once there's a function prototype for that function, the program will still compile—all it needs to do is find the function anywhere in the code listing.

Notice that I alerted out the command name if it is not a command that is expected. This is a handy debugging tool that the user should never need to know about.

Setting the dx and dy Variables

The pocket battle game has two very distinct phases: setup and play. Most of the functions you have seen so far are primarily used to set up the game. They all revolve around the various data elements. The next few functions are used more while the game is in progress. Once the game is started, the logic of the program is reasonably straightforward: Each unit that is still alive gets to keep moving until one city or the other is captured. If a unit tries to move onto a square occupied by an enemy unit, combat will ensue.

Simple as this seems, there is a lot of code needed to get the movement working correctly. I broke the movement algorithm into a number of functions so that it would be easier to manage. The first of these functions is used to set `dx` and `dy` values. You may recall these variables from Chapter 6, where I used them for animation. `dx` and `dy` are used to indicate the difference in X and Y. This function will be called with one argument, which will be a direction. The function simply analyzes the direction variable and sets the values of `dx` and `dy` appropriately.

```
getDir(int moveDir){
  //calculate dx and dy from moveDir
  switch(moveDir){
    case NW:
      dx = -1;
      dy = -1;
      break;
    case N:
      dx = 0;
      dy = -1;
      break;
    case NE:
      dx = 1;
      dy = -1;
      break;
    case W:
      dx = -1;
      dy = 0;
      break;
    case C:
      dx = 0;
      dy = 0;
      break;
    case E:
      dx = 1;
      dy = 0;
      break;
    case SW:
      dx = -1;
      dy = 1;
      break;
```

```
        case S:
          dx = 0;
          dy = 1;
          break;
        case SE:
          dx = 1;
          dy = 1;
          break;
      } // end switch
    } // end getDir
```

You have probably figured out that X is another term for col, and Y is another term for row.

Getting a Move Direction from the User

Of course, if you understand the code from the `getDir()` function, you are probably wondering where the `moveDir` variable came from. It is generated by this function that reads the direction buttons to see which one (if any) were clicked.

```
getMove(int uid){
  //highlight a unit and respond to a button click

  int dir;
  int evt;
  int moveDir;

  int row, col;

  //highlight the current unit
  for (row = 0; row < ROWS ; row++){
    for (col = 0; col < COLS; col++){

      if (map[row][col][SUNIT] == uid){
        frame(1,
              (col * colWidth) + colOff - 3,
              (row * rowWidth) + rowOff + 2,
              ((col + 1) * colWidth) + colOff - 5,
              ((row + 1) * rowWidth) + rowOff , 0);
      } // end if
```

```
    } // end col loop
  } // end row loop

  //wait for an input
  evt = event(1);
  if (Cevent(mnbMain, evt)){
    checkMenus();
  } // end if
  for (dir = NW; dir <= SE; dir++){
    if (Cevent(imgDir[dir], evt)){
      moveDir = dir;
    } //end if
  } // end for loop
```

This function expects a unit ID. It then highlights that unit, and waits for an event to occur from the direction buttons.

I used a pair of nested `for` loops to check each square in the map until I found the one that contains the unit in question. I then highlighted that square by drawing a frame around it. (I started by deriving the perimeter of the frame from `row`, `col`, `rowWidth`, and `colWidth`. Then I played around with the size and position of the frame until the rectangle around the current unit looked about right.

It is important to highlight the current unit so the players know which unit will be receiving the next movement input. This also tells the players when it's time to hand over the PDA, because the highlighted unit is the other player's color.

It is easy to extract `moveDir`, because the direction buttons are an array. Whichever button was clicked will have the index that should be passed to `moveDir`.

Calculating Combat

At some point, you would expect hostile units to come into contact. When this occurs, combat will ensue. I devised a very simple combat formula for the Pocket battle game. Each unit type has an attack strength and a defensive strength. Whenever a unit moves onto a square occupied by an opposing unit, the computer determines whether the defender is eliminated by using the following formula:

((attacker's attack strength)/(defender's defensive strength))/4

The likelihood of a successful attack in various situations is described in Table 12.7.

Table 12.7 Calculating the Hit Possibility

Attack	Defense	To Hit Percentage
4	1	100
2	1	50
1	1	25
1	2	12.5

I created this formula at that same breakfast table by looking at the results for a number of formulas. This model seemed to be about the right balance for my needs, because it favors the more powerful units but still allows for some surprises. A weaker unit can sometimes beat a more powerful unit.

The code for combat is centered around applying this formula to the data structures of the game:

```
combat(int currentRow, int currentCol, int newRow, int newCol, int uid){
  //manage combat between two units

  //calculate attack and defense
  string attacker, defender;  //units involved in the combat
  int attack, defense;      //attack and defense levels of the units
  float toHit;       //likelihood attack succeeds

  //moving unit is attacker, other is defender
  attacker = map[currentRow][currentCol][SUNIT];
  defender = map[newRow][newCol][SUNIT];

  //are they on same side?
  if (unit[attacker][OWN] == unit[defender][OWN]){
    //do nothing. turn is lost
  } else {

    //get strength levels
    attack = uClass[unit[attacker][TYPE]][ATT];
    defense = uClass[unit[defender][TYPE]][ATT];
```

```
    //calculate hit level -
    //dividing by smaller number makes battles more deadly
    toHit = ((float)attack/(float)defense)/4.0;

    if (rand() < toHit){

      alert(unit[defender][UNAME] + " defeated!");
      unit[defender][OWN] = "dead";

      //clear attacker's old square
      map[currentRow][currentCol][SUNIT] = "";

      //move attacker to new square
      map[newRow][newCol][SUNIT] = uid;

      //check to see if it's the enemy base
      if(map[newRow][newCol][TER] == "C"){
        if (map[newRow][newCol][SOWN] != unit[uid][OWN]){
          alert("Captured enemy Base!");
          keepGoing = false;
          exit();
        } // end opponent's city if
      } // end 'is it a city' if

    } // end 'who wins combat' if

  } // end 'friend or enemy in square' if
} // end combat
```

The combat function takes a number of parameters. It needs to know the current location of the attacker (the unit that is currently moving). It also needs to know the intended location of the attack. (These values will be generated in another function.) It also needs to know which unit is currently moving. All these values are passed into the function as parameters.

The function queries the map table to determine the identities of the attacking and defending units. The indices of these two units are stored in the `attacker` and `defender` variables.

If the attacker and defender are on the same side, nothing happens, except the move is lost. If the attacker and defender belong to opposing forces, it is time to calculate the likelihood of success for the attack. I used a bit of a shortcut to determine the attack and defense ratings of the units. The line

```
attack = uClass[unit[attacker][TYPE]][ATT];
```

could also be written in this way:

```
uType = unit[attacker][TYPE];
attack = uClass[uType][ATT];
```

However, I chose to simply substitute the expression for uType into the second line, creating one longer line of code.

The `toHit` variable was calculated by using the formula explained earlier in this section. It is worth noting that I had to explicitly cast the values of attack and defense into floats for the expression to yield a floating point result.

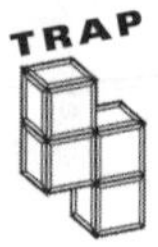

The loose variable type casting of PocketC can make you lax. Be sure to check the results of your expressions. If they don't turn out the way you expected, see if you need to explicitly type cast some of your variables. The automatic type conversion does not always work as you expect it to.

Next I generated a random floating point value with the `rand()` function. The `rand()` value will be less than `toHit` the percentage of time specified by the `toHit` variable. (Recall the discussion of this phenomenon from Chapter 3.)

If the attack succeeds, the function informs the players of the outcome, then resets the defeated unit's owner to "dead." The program then clears out the attacker's square and moves the attacking unit to the square previously occupied by the defender.

Finally, the function checks to see if the unit has entered the opponent's capital city. If so, the game is over, and the function informs the users of this fact.

Calculating the Move for One Unit

You have seen several functions for controlling movement, but you still haven't seen them all. Another function is used to oversee the progress of one unit. It calls many of the other movement functions.

```
calcMove(int uid){
  //checks to see what will happen in move
```

```
//could be impossible move, could be combat
int row, col, currentRow, currentCol, newRow, newCol;

//figure out where unit is
for (row = 0; row < ROWS ; row++){
  for (col = 0; col < COLS; col++){

    if (map[row][col][SUNIT] == uid){
      currentRow = row;
      currentCol = col;
    } // end if

  } // end col loop
} // end row loop

//calculate newRow, newCol;
newRow = currentRow + dy;
if (newRow < 0){
  newRow = 0;
} // end if

if (newRow >= ROWS){
  newRow = ROWS -1;
} // end if

newCol = currentCol + dx;
if (newCol < 0){
  newCol = 0;
} // end if

if (newCol >= COLS){
  newCol = COLS -1;
} // end if

//check to see if another unit is in the square
if (map[newRow][newCol][SUNIT] != ""){
  //calculate combat or friendly fire
  combat(currentRow, currentCol, newRow, newCol, uid);
} else if (map[newRow][newCol][TER] == "~"){
```

```
      //do nothing. You can't move on water
    } else {
      // the target square is empty - move there

      //clear old square
      map[currentRow][currentCol][SUNIT] = "";

      //move unit to new square
      map[newRow][newCol][SUNIT] = uid;

      //check to see if it's the enemy base
      if(map[newRow][newCol][TER] == "C"){
        if (map[newRow][newCol][SOWN] != unit[uid][OWN]){
          alert("Captured enemy Base!");
          keepGoing = false;
          exit();
        } // end opponent's city if
      } // end 'is it a city' if
    } // end 'anything in target square' if
    displayMap();
    drawUnits();
  } // end calcMove
```

The first thing the `calcMove()` function does is figure out the `currentRow` and `currentCol` values of the current unit. It does this by checking each square of the map until it finds one containing the unit ID in its SUNIT field. The `calcMove()` function then uses the `dx` and `dy` variables calculated in `getDir()` to determine the new row and column values. The function checks to make sure that the new position is still on the board.

The program checks to see if there is a unit in the new square. If so, it calls the combat function to handle the combat. If not, the unit can move into the new square. This is done by resetting the current square's SUNIT to nothing, and setting the SUNIT of the target square to the unit's ID.

Finally, the function checks to see if the unit has encroached upon the enemy capital. If so, the game is over, because the current player has won.

Managing All of the Unit Movement

Unit movement is a complicated phenomenon in this game. Ultimately it is controlled by one function that controls a large loop:

```
moveUnits(){
  //master function for handling all unit movement

  int uid;
  int numMoves;
  int move;

  for (uid=0; uid < nUnits; uid++){
    //describe the current unit
    text(10, 130, "                    ");
    text(10, 130, unit[uid][UNAME]);
    text(10, 140, uClass[unit[uid][TYPE]][ATT] +
         " / "  + uClass[unit[uid][TYPE]][DEF]);
    //don't do anything if this unit is dead//
    if (unit[uid][OWN] != "dead"){
      //figure out how many moves this unit gets per turn
      numMoves = uClass[unit[uid][TYPE]][MOVE];
      for(move = 0; move < numMoves; move++){
        //determine what move the user wants
        getMove(uid);
        calcMove(uid);
      } // end for loop
    } // end if
  } // end for loop
} // end moveUnits
```

This function loops through all the units in the unit table. It prints the relevant information about the unit (its name, attack, and defense strength) in the lower left portion of the screen. If the unit is not dead, the function determines how many moves this unit gets. It creates a `for` loop that repeats that many times. Each time through the loop, it invokes the `getMove()` and `calcMove()` functions, which handle the movement and potential combat of the unit.

Starting a New Game

The `newgame` function is automatically called at the beginning of the program's execution, and also whenever the `newGame` function is requested from the menu system. It calls all the functions that initialize the various data elements:

```
newGame(){
  //start up the game
  clear();
  initUClass();
  buyUnits();
  loadMap();
  displayMap();
  placeUnits();
  drawUnits();
  while(keepGoing){
    moveUnits();
  } // end while

} // end newGame
```

The `newGame()` function is easy to read, because it consists almost entirely of calls to functions that have been defined earlier in the program. The end of the function involves repeating the `moveUnits()` function until the user sets `keepGoing` variable to `false` and thus indicates that play is over.

The main() Function

By now you are probably used to seeing a reasonably simple `main()` function in complex programs. In this one—the most involved program of the book—the `main()` function is as terse as any you have ever seen:

```
main(){
  createMenus();
  createButtons();
  newGame();

} // end main
```

The two functions that create the various Ccontrols are invoked here in the main menu. All other functionality properly belongs to the `newGame()` function.

Summary

While there's little new syntax to learn in this chapter, it does give you a chance to look at a more involved program while exploring the importance of data structures. You learned a little about data normalization and relational data design, and had a chance to see examples of several diagnostic routines used to aid in the debugging of a large program. The chapter also demonstrated how a program can make use of data well.

CHALLENGES

I've suggested many improvements to this program in the text of this chapter. Following are some of those challenges, and a few more:

1. **Add combat modifiers to terrain. For example, maybe a unit inside a city should get enhanced defensive strength.**
2. **Add new terrain features, such as roads (to speed movement), forest (improve defensive strength), and hills (improve attack strength of unit attacking from a hill).**
3. **Incorporate a terrain table into the data structure of the game, to better handle the various terrain capacities.**
4. **Add the ability to generate income from cities on the fly, so that new units can be produced during the game.**
5. **Add naval units like destroyers and transports. These will add a profound new strategic element to the game.**
6. **Introduce neutral cities that can be held for increased economic strength.**
7. **Include a unit type editor that allows players to devise new types of units. Store the unit type information in a .pdb file so it will be available for future games.**
8. **Investigate the IR connection features in PToolboxLib. Modify the game so it can be played by two players on two different devices, beaming their moves to each other.**
9. **Add the ability to load and save entire scenarios.**
10. **Improve the game's graphics with bitmaps for the units and terrain types.**
11. **Devise an entirely new game based on all you have learned.**

A Final Word

Congratulations on completing this book! You might have started out wondering if you could do any real programming on your PDA. Now you know that all kinds of programming can be done on these intriguing little devices.

Now it gets *really* fun! It's time for you to apply your skills, your imagination, and your talent to producing unique software that only you could devise. I can't wait to see what you create!

Index

D

E

F

G

O

P

R

S

T

U

V

W

License Agreement/Notice of Limited Warranty

By opening the sealed disc container in this book, you agree to the following terms and conditions. If, upon reading the following license agreement and notice of limited warranty, you cannot agree to the terms and conditions set forth, return the unused book with unopened disc to the place where you purchased it for a refund.

License:
The enclosed software is copyrighted by the copyright holder(s) indicated on the software disc. You are licensed to copy the software onto a single computer for use by a single user and to a backup disk. You may not reproduce, make copies, or distribute copies or rent or lease the software in whole or in part, except with written permission of the copyright holder(s). You may transfer the enclosed disc only together with this license, and only if you destroy all other copies of the software and the transferee agrees to the terms of the license. You may not decompile, reverse assemble, or reverse engineer the software.

Notice of Limited Warranty:
The enclosed disc is warranted by Prima Publishing to be free of physical defects in materials and workmanship for a period of sixty (60) days from end user's purchase of the book/disc combination. During the sixty-day term of the limited warranty, Prima will provide a replacement disc upon the return of a defective disc.

Limited Liability:
THE SOLE REMEDY FOR BREACH OF THIS LIMITED WARRANTY SHALL CONSIST ENTIRELY OF REPLACEMENT OF THE DEFECTIVE DISC. IN NO EVENT SHALL PRIMA OR THE AUTHORS BE LIABLE FOR ANY OTHER DAMAGES, INCLUDING LOSS OR CORRUPTION OF DATA, CHANGES IN THE FUNCTIONAL CHARACTERISTICS OF THE HARDWARE OR OPERATING SYSTEM, DELETERIOUS INTERACTION WITH OTHER SOFTWARE, OR ANY OTHER SPECIAL, INCIDENTAL, OR CONSEQUENTIAL DAMAGES THAT MAY ARISE, EVEN IF PRIMA AND/OR THE AUTHOR HAVE PREVIOUSLY BEEN NOTIFIED THAT THE POSSIBILITY OF SUCH DAMAGES EXISTS.

Disclaimer of Warranties:
PRIMA AND THE AUTHORS SPECIFICALLY DISCLAIM ANY AND ALL OTHER WARRANTIES, EITHER EXPRESS OR IMPLIED, INCLUDING WARRANTIES OF MERCHANTABILITY, SUITABILITY TO A PARTICULAR TASK OR PURPOSE, OR FREEDOM FROM ERRORS. SOME STATES DO NOT ALLOW FOR EXCLUSION OF IMPLIED WARRANTIES OR LIMITATION OF INCIDENTAL OR CONSEQUENTIAL DAMAGES, SO THESE LIMITATIONS MAY NOT APPLY TO YOU.

Other:
This Agreement is governed by the laws of the State of California without regard to choice of law principles. The United Convention of Contracts for the International Sale of Goods is specifically disclaimed. This Agreement constitutes the entire agreement between you and Prima Publishing regarding use of the software.